MADE IN BIRMINGHAM

CITY OF BIRMINGHAM
1889 1989
CENTENARY FESTIVAL

MADE IN BIRMINGHAM

Design & Industry 1889 - 1989

Edited by

Barbara Tilson

KA FB

BREWIN BOOKS

First published December 1989
by K.A.F. Brewin Books, Studley, Warwickshire. B80 7LG

ISBN 0 947731 56 3

Typeset in Press Roman 9pt.
and made and printed in Great Britain
by Supaprint (Redditch) Limited.

FOREWORD

The Design History Society has developed into an organisation of international repute since its foundation in 1977. It deserves a lot of encouragement in its efforts to develop the discipline of design history. In recognising and nurturing its links with other related disciplines, design history covers facets of our cultural life which are not necessarily examined in the disciplines of art history, architecture and the applied arts, or in the histories of technology, business and economics.

It is highly appropriate that the Society has chosen to mark the centenary of the City of Birmingham through a publication which highlights the diversity and importance of its industries. Birmingham is a city of the greatest importance to industrial historians. Despite its recent difficulties, it remains a major industrial centre of the UK and the focal point of the West Midlands. *Made in Birmingham* stands as a permanent contribution to posterity of a century of Birmingham achievement.

The Design History Society and those involved here, in particular, are to be applauded for their enthusiasm and initiative in producing *Made in Birmingham*. Likewise, those industries which provided much-needed sponsorship should be commended for their support. I hope that this liaison between industry and the Design History Society (which is a national charity) will strengthen, thus enabling the Society to undertake further important ventures in the future.

Sir Nicholas Goodison.
Chairman, TSB Group plc., and patron of the Design History Society.
February 1989.

The DHS would like to acknowledge the financial contributions received from Cadbury Ltd. The Joseph Lucas Trust, IMI, Best & Lloyd Ltd. and DCA Design Consultants towards costs incurred during preparation of this book.

PREFACE

On the occasion of the City of Birmingham Centenary it is imperative to produce a lasting record of the scope and variety of manufacturing on which the city's prosperity was built. The subject warrants a multi-volume study, being so vast and complex, for which this modest anthology must seem but an appetiser. A larger undertaking, however, would have necessitated greater financial backing than was available currently.

This book could not have been realised without the interest of our publisher, K.A.F. Brewin, nor without outside funding. It might be thought that the Centenary would have stimulated much keen support. In the event, however, the DHS project was considered in competition with city-wide Centenary celebrations of a more overtly prestigious kind. Nonetheless, several companies with close associations with Birmingham generously provided sufficient backing towards our expenses. This finance funded my determined efforts to gain support through advance orders, enabling the project to proceed to fruition.

The bulk of the book comprises a series of essays by individuals with special knowledge of aspects of industry in Birmingham and its environs. Most of the contributors are academics, and a number of others are engaged in in-house or consultancy work for companies. I also undertook several interviews with experts with inside experience of relevant subjects, particularly those which were considered important to include but for which no contributor could be found. Interviewer and interviewees have collaborated in the production of edited transcripts of these. It also seemed appropriate to include something on those sponsor companies which were not the subject of specific articles. In the absence of writers to tackle these at length, I have endeavoured to prepare outlines, largely from existing sources, which will, I hope, at least partly compensate. Both companies are, in any case, of sufficient significance to the history of design and manufacture in Birmingham to warrant their inclusion. The miscellaneous writing styles and methods of presentation which have inevitably ensued in this publication are united by the dual and complementary themes of industry and design.

Although responsibility for the instigation of this book rests with the editor, the conjoining of these dual themes has a recent precedent. The conference "A Hundred Years of Design and Industry in Birmingham, 1880 - 1980" was held at Birmingham Polytechnic in November 1984 and was organised by Dr. Pauline Madge of the School of History of Art and Design (see my review of this in *Design History Society Newsletter*, 23, 1984). Although they have extensively revised their original papers, or taken a fresh angle, Swift, Child, Leake and Skinner gave papers then which relate in general subject matter to their contributions for this current publication.

It would probably be fair, however, to acknowledge Pevsner as the originator of design and industry studies of the Birmingham area, through his pivotal study, *An Enquiry into Industrial Art in England*, of 1937. Furthermore, there are currently numerous eminent individuals from various disciplines and institutions currently engaged in research into Birmingham present and past, not least the University of Birmingham, Centre for Urban and Regional Studies in the School of Public Policy, successor to the department where Pevsner's research for his *Enquiry* was conducted.

The contents herein commence with studies relating to urbanism, specifically two different ways of tackling problems which arose in relation to urban and industrial growth. One solution was to beautify buildings through colour and decoration, the second by vacating the inner city to establish a more ideal environment in a pastoral setting. There follow several studies which link the subjects of education, training for industry and the crafts, which are particularly illuminating, perhaps, in relation to women, education and work. Barbara Smith's paper on the Jewellery Quarter provides the link between these first studies and those concerned with industry. A paper on R.W. Winfield, brass workers, is included to provide a springboard and context for those papers on the industrial arts and engineering in the metal trades which follow. The subject of plastics design and industry follows on (with perhaps only a tenuous link) from Dunlop rubber, and a similarly tenuous link can be found between plastics and Cadbury's advertising. It exists, nonetheless, through the design work undertaken by the Product Design Unit at BIP for Cadbury's. The interview on Contemporary Design relates to several other papers, such as those on PEL, Best & Lloyd, and plastics, and to the ongoing themes of current architectural and urban planning issues which are outlined in the introduction and conclusion. Lastley, 'leading edge' technology is examined in the paper on Apricot Computers.

By covering such a wide disparity of subjects, some at opposite poles, something of a 'hotch-potch' has ensued. Despite this, it serves to illustrate both the character of Birmingham design and industry and that breadth of commercial and industrial activity for which the city became renowned.

Barbara Tilson
October 1989

ACKNOWLEDGEMENTS

Thanks are due firstly to our sponsors, Lucas Industries plc, Cadbury Ltd, IMI, and Best & Lloyd Ltd. Those who helped with publicity (other than the DHS) included the Victorian Society (Birmingham Group). Thanks are due in various ways to Barbara Smith (Univ. of Birmingham), Ray Bushell (Euro-Cast Ltd), Simon Topman (J. Hudson & Co), Mike Mayo (Lloyds Bank), Barbara Richards (Birmingham Technology Ltd), John Yair, Jane Makower and DCA Design Consultants, British Motor Industry Heritage Trust, Robert Sharp (Science Museum) Margit Feil (Anglepoise Lighting Ltd), Roger Newport (Birmingham Polytechnic), R. Snell, (Hostess Furniture Ltd), Sir Adrian Cadbury, Patricia Dunbar and Helen Davies (Cadbury Ltd), Joanne Gwatkin-Williams (Design Council), Tony Collier, Jim Andrew (Science Museum), Elizabeth Betton (Johnson Matthey Ltd), Denise Foers and Dr. Hawkings (Lucas Industries plc), Maria Haddleton, Peter Batchelor (BIP Chemicals Ltd), Jerry Young, Bruce Walker, various individuals at Birmingham City Council, particularly Will Howland, Tony Rogers, Rosemary Williams, Geoff Wright, Julie Broadbridge. Roy Church and Chris Mullen would like to acknowledge R. Trueman and I. Strachan (Rover Group plc). Peter Atkins' thanks go to Constable & Co, B.T. Batsford, Remo Granelli, Philip Henslowe, J. Pickvance, Margaret Gaynor, Terry Jenkins, Chris Panchieri, Donald Whitmore. Graham Leake acknowledges PEL Ltd. Kate Child's thanks go to Best & Lloyd. My own personal thanks go to those who made this book possible - Simon Reynolds, the contributors and Joan Reynolds.

CONTENTS

LIST OF ILLUSTRATIONS

ILLUSTRATIONS: SOURCES AND ACKNOWLEDGEMENTS

1.2-1.4, 1.6, Birmingham City Council. 1.9 Permission of Ordnance Survey. 1.11 courtesy of Peter Hall. 1.12 *Design for To-Day*, July 1934. 1.13 DCA Design Consultants. 1.14 Joceline Burke.
2.5, 2.6 Ironbridge Gorge Museum Trust.
4.1 - 4.8, Birmingham School of Art archive, Birmingham Polytechnic.
5.1, J. Devine; 5.4, A. Bracey; 5.5, 5.6, B. Lucas.
8.1 Permission of Ordnance Survey; 8.2, 8.3, 8.5, 8.7, 8.10, 8.11, B. Tilson.
12.1 Roy Woodward.
13.3, Science Museum; 13.8, *Cycling*, Feb. 1910.
20.14 Tim Davis.
Other illustrations were provided by individual chapter writers/interviewer or from sources as specified in captions.

BIOGRAPHICAL NOTES

BARBARA TILSON Dip. A.D., P.G.C.E., M.A.
became a freelance researcher and writer, specialising in design, architechture and industry, after some years lecturing in design history in the West Midlands. She is also researching part time towards a Ph.D in plastics design and industry in the Centre for Urban and Regional Studies, University of Birmingham.

MICHAEL STRATTON B.A., M.A., Ph.D.
is a lecturer in Industrial Archaeology at the Ironbridge Institute, a joint collaboration between the Ironbridge Gorge Museum and the University of Birmingham. His research interests concentrate on ceramic and architectural history of the nineteenth and twentieth centuries.

PETER ATKINS N.D.D., A.T.D.
is a member of the Bournville Society and the Birmingham Urban Studies Committee. He worked for the Development Department of Birmingham City Council in 1988-9, researching into historic buildings in Birmingham. He has lectured widely in architectural and design history and is currently preparing his work on Bournville Architecture for publication.

JOHN SWIFT N.D.D., A.T.D., M.A., Ph.D., F.R.S.A.
is Director of Studies, Art and Design Education, and Keeper of Archives in Birmingham Polytechnic's Department of Art. He is UK Consultant for *Canadian Review of Art Education Research,* a member of the editorial board of *Journal of Art and Design Education* and Council member of the National Society for Education in Art and Design.

DEREK FONTAINE A.M.A.
was, when he wrote his article on the West Midlands Guild, Head of the Fine Arts Department of Birmingham Central Reference Library. He originally trained at Bournville School of Art as a sculptor and painter and is now a full time glass engraver. He is Company Secretary to the Guild of West Midlands Artists and Craftsmen Ltd.

TERRY HUNT Dip. C.S.A.D.
studied as a jeweller at the Central School, London. After running his own workshop and teaching in the south east, he came to Birmingham in 1971 as lecturer in the School of Jewellery, Vittoria Street, where he is currently Course Director for HND Design (Crafts).

BARBARA SMITH B.Comm.
lectures in the Centre for Urban Studies, University of Birmingham. She has 40 years interest in the history of Birmingham and its industry, on which she has published extensively. She serves on several Wages Councils and Industrial Tribunals and is Chairman of the West Midlands Branch of the Regional Studies Association.

BARRIE ECCLESTON Des.R.C.A., M.A., M.C.S.D.
retired in 1987 as Director of Studies of the Degree and Postgraduate Courses in Industrial Design at Birmingham Polytechnic. He is an honorary senior research fellow researching the School of Industrial Design's records, also a consultant illustrator for English Heritage.

KATE CHILD B.A. (Hons.)
has studied History of Art and Design at Leicester Polytechnic and completed her part-time M.A. thesis on Best & Lloyd at Birmingham Polytechnic. She is currently working as a Training Assistant at the Light House Media Centre in Wolverhampton.

GRAHAM LEAKE N.D.D., M.A.
lectures in design history at Edinburgh College of Art. After qualifying as a furniture designer he worked in local government and then as a school furniture advisor for PEL Ltd. He subsequently obtained his M.A. in History of Art and Design at Birmingham Polytechnic.

ANDREW MILLWARD B.A., M.Sc., P.G.C.E.
gained his Master's degree in the Social Aspects of Science and Technology at Aston University, where he now lectures. He is currently undertaking a research project, on an E.S.R.C. Competition Award, on the Cycle Industry 1870-1939, for a Ph.D. at the University of Birmingham.

ROY CHURCH B.A., Ph.D., F.R.Hist. S.,
was formerly a lecturer at the University of Birmingham. He is currently Professor of Economic and Social History at the University of East Anglia, Norwich, and Editor of *Economic History Review*. Relevant publications include a biography of Herbert Austin and articles and essays on the motor industry.

CHRIS MULLEN B.A., Ph.D.,
is Senior Lecturer in Design at Brighton Polytechnic and was formerly a Senior Lecturer at the Norfolk Institute of Art and Design, Norwich. He serves on committees of the Eastern Arts Association, and is a specialist advisor to the C.N.A.A. His recent exhibition, *Fortune's America*, the visual achievements of *fortune* magazine, was held at the Rochester Institute of Technology.

JOAN SKINNER B.A. (1st class) in History and Philosophy, B.A. (1st class) in History of Art and Design,
was a member of the Dunlop Archive Project, prior to its termination, researching the history and architecture of Dunlop factories. She is now retired, but continues to work towards a Ph.D. at the University of Liverpool on the works and practice of architects Wallis Gilbert & Partners.

JES DORRELL D.M.S., Dip.C.A.M.
is the Corporate Communications Manager of Apricot Computers plc. A former GKN apprentice, he held several posts in management services and gained the Diploma in Management Studies before entering marketing communications consultancy in 1978. He worked with many of the Midlands' major industrial companies before joining Apricot in 1984.

Fig. 1a. 1899 O.S. Map (detail) overlaid with 1838 Birmingham boundary (dotted), 1891 additions (solid), 1909 additions (dash)

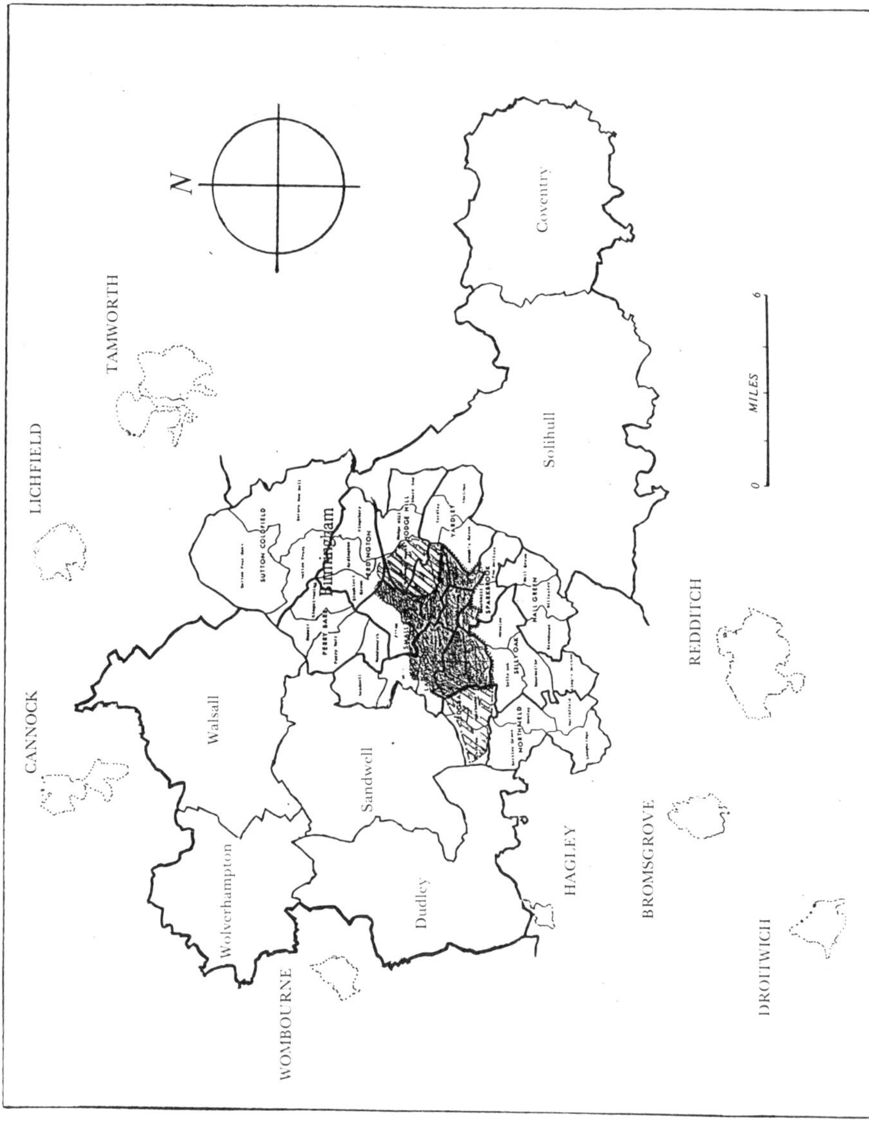

Fig. 1b. West Midlands Map showing 1989 boundaries - Birmingham Ward boundaries 1982, city boundary revised 1974, Metropolitan District boundaries. Also shown - approximate lines of Birmingham boundary 1838 (soft shaded), 1909 revisions (hatched).

CHAPTER 1

INGENUITY AND INDUSTRY: THE BIRMINGHAM EXPERIENCE

An Introduction

Barbara Tilson

Birmingham became prosperous through the ingenuity, toil and endeavour of its people, which ensured its emergence as a great manufacturing centre at the industrial heart of the UK. In the century since 1889, when it achieved city status, Birmingham has mushroomed in size. The population has grown from 515,000 around 1880, doubling to 1,030,000 around 1930, and stood at just under 1 million in 1989.[1] It has expanded its borders by approximately eightfold, from around 8,500 acres to 66,000 acres.[2] The earliest boundary extensions after 1889 occurred in 1891, while the most recent large-scale adjustments to the city boundary took place in 1974, (Figs. 1a, 1b), and minor adjustment within it in 1982. In recent years boundaries have seemed to become more fluid and less exclusive as improved transport and communication networks have shortened travelling times and shrunken distances and consequently 'home to work' impediments have diminished. Birmingham, situated as it is in the West Midlands County, should be seen, in reality, as a part of the Midlands region itself and having close links with other urban areas in this and neighbouring counties. In the same way, at a national level, different regional and national interests are subsumed within a growing 'Europeanization' of political and trading activities, initiated through our entry to the EEC and symbolised currently by the imminent lifting of trading barriers in 1992.

The image of Birmingham citizenship has suffered from the existence of an insulting Brummie stereotype. In reality, Birmingham society comprises a complex mix of classes and races with strong minority groups such as West Indians, Indians, Pakistanis, Chinese and Irish. Inevitably, there exists not one Birmingham culture, but many cultures. This poses interesting possibilities for the future in an era when 'culture' is now linked with 'industry'. The importance of the cultural industries has grown in association with the expansion of the media, information technology, and a 'video society'. 'Communication' in its wider sense has ensured the increasingly crucial role, too, of the graphic designer and advertising executive.

There is a growing appreciation, enhanced by the expanding significance of leisure and tourism, of the ways in which Birmingham's industrial past can be exploited to economic advantage through a celebration of heritage. Inevitably, the balance between retaining the old and providing a fresh 'canvas' for contemporary redevelopments is a sometimes vexed question. The city's industrial history, too, can be viewed against a rise in scope and significance of the service sector, whose growth can be viewed in comparison with problems in the manufacturing sector in the 1970s and 80s. The economic and industrial difficulties of Birmingham and the West Midlands region in recent years has been the subject of much examination, not least in *Crisis in the Industrial Heartland,* 1986.[3] The title itself reflects the agonising experience which the city and region have undergone, re-equipping and rebuilding to compete effectively in a national and global economy.

Urban Regeneration and Architectural Design

The devestation which Birmingham and other parts of the West Midlands suffered through bomb damage in World War 2 has been tackled through policies for regeneration of the urban fabric. However, by 1985 the city still had a massive 75,000 pre-1919 houses in need of renovation and over 10 million sq.ft. of obsolescent vacant industrial land.[4] Earlier, under its Urban Rehabilitation Programme, well over 30,000 houses had already been tackled by 1975, in an ongoing scheme for the regeneration of housing and shopping in inner Birmingham.[5] The current Programme exists as but the latest in a series of town planning schemes and directives throughout the century. The first was the Town Planning Scheme of 1913 (Birmingham being the first English city to put such a Scheme into effect), which followed the passing of the first Town Planning Act in 1909. A City Council Enquiry into housing within the city at the time of the first Scheme found that 50,000 houses were unfit for habitation.[6] The need for regeneration of the building stock therefore is not a problem peculiar to our own era.

An important early post-1945 policy statement was the *West Midlands Plan* of 1948,[7] while another pivotal study, contemporary with this, was *Conurbation,* a work in which the eminent P. Sargant Florence was involved.[8] The expansion of population numbers and the shortage of housing led, in the 1950s and 60s, to an overspill policy with areas such as Tamworth, Telford, Bromsgrove, Droitwich and Redditch being designated as suitable locations.[9] Shortage of land for housing within the city, coupled with the acceptability of Modern Movement high-rise, resulted in the erection of substantial numbers of skyscraper blocks of flats. The obsession with 'travel to work' facility and the pervasiveness of the motor car created a network of roads where transport predominated over the human scale, symbolised by the building of Spaghetti Junction and the Inner Ring Road, with its pedestrian subways. A concern for the appropriate scale and character of urban refurbishment resulted in 1989 in the formation of the organisation Birmingham for People, dedicated to the democratization of urban planning decision-making.[10]

The architecture which survived in the decades after the war in the inner city comprised a wealth of fine buildings, most notably of late Victorian terracotta decoration, but it was also possible to find a crumbling stock of antiquated and increasingly obsolescent building, much of it relating to a bygone industrial tradition, studded with pockets of more recent architectural development. The opportunity to undertake major regeneration of the architectural fabric in the city in the late 1980s consequently provided conditions for a re-think about what existed. The decision to redevelop the Bull Ring area (a £250 million development funded by the London and Edinburgh Trust),[11] can be seen as arising from an awareness that what had already been achieved in recent decades could be bettered and that what might have been considered appropriate in the early post-war years had, perhaps, now become out-of-step with late twentieth century needs and expectations. What Birmingham for People questions, however, is the fundamental ethos of replacing the former with a vast 3-tier shopping mall.

The most significant, but also the most contentious, building programme has been the development in the Broad Street area, focusing on the Convention Centre itself, including conference and concert halls, an indoor arena, hotel accommodation and shopping and leisure resources. (Figs. 1.2 - 1.5) The Convention Centre was designed in 1984 by Renton Howard Wood Levin (RHWL) of London in association with Percy Thomas Partnership, a Birmingham architectural practice, and other specialists. RHWL were previously noted for their design of the Royal Centre, Nottingham, a high-tech Modernist example, upon which *Planning* magazine noted that the Birmingham Convention Centre was to be modelled.[12]

The significance of the building of the Convention Centre (and other related development) to Birmingham and its people is not merely through pride in its capacity to attract international business (estimated business generation was for £300 million per year) [13] the provision of facilities international in scope and standard, and the active participation of Birmingham in international matters, which it represents. Elements such as the pedestrianisation of the concourse around it, the making of a subterranean through-road to enable the formation of a pedestrian link between Centenary Square and the Copthorne Hotel/Central Library area, (see Fig. 1.5) and the refurbishment and conservation of the hitherto neglected adjacent canals, (Figs. 1.6 - 1.8) reflect a desire to 'get things right' in both architectural *and* human terms. Criticisms voiced about its design (most notably by Prince Charles in his condemnation of the kind of modern architecture and planning which he found to be more akin to concrete missile silos) could be considered insensitive or enlightened, depending upon the viewpoint taken. The incoming Arts Council Chairman, Peter Palumbo, renowned for his enthusiasm for Modernist architecture, lent his weight in defence of the City's proposals. [14]

Whatever personal views dictate, the building work undertaken in and around Centenary Square (Fig. 1.3) demonstrates the realisation of prestigious civic architecture and the making of grand public statements. Elsewhere in the inner city, regeneration of the urban fabric is intended to follow a more human scale. Three principal areas are highlighted for regeneration in Bordesley, Bloomsbury/ Nechells and Waterlinks (the area around the Birmingham-Fazeley canal).[15] In the Waterlinks area (enclosing the area between the City Centre and Spaghetti Junction) proposals by Birmingham Heartlands Ltd., in conjunction with City Architect Bill Reed and his team, comprising suggestions and guidelines for developers, include 'nodes' planned in courtyards of the type designed by Will Howland as sheltered accommodation at Belgrave Middleway, which won a RIBA Award in 1987.[16] There is a continuing policy of refurbishing older housing stock, for example by reducing the height of blocks of several storeys to produce maisonette housing. Such results reflect a sensitivity to contemporary currents in urban planning philosophy to which city architects are responsive.

Older industrial sectors, notably the well-publicised Jewellery Quarter (now a Conservation Area) are undergoing substantial restoration, in the same way that older housing stock, such as that in Moseley, Balsall Heath and Sparkhill is being tackled. Indeed, the adaptation to modern demands which industry is making is perhaps reflected in the considerable amount of restoration work which other older industrial areas, too, are undergoing, as at Hockley. Inevitably, conservation is a key question, and a balance must be sought to preserve key examples and areas of significant industrial buildings. It is within this debate that the Birmingham Victorian Society has undertaken an important role over preservation. There is an appreciation that at least the facades of redundant buildings can be retained while the valuable sites and space which they represent can be put to new uses. The reconstruction of Louisa Ryland House in Edmund Street, executed by the City Council and designed by Chris Cronin, is one example of this type, and the plan to transform the Fellows Morton and Clayton warehouse in Fazeley Street is another (see chapter 20 and map, Fig. 1.9). The canal network itself, is envisaged, too, as an amenity with tourism potential and which possesses its own distinctive conservation and development needs.

The expertise of private architectural and interior design consultants, notably those with Birmingham connections, is utilised in the present series of building and refurbishment. However, the Good Design Initiative, led by Graham Shaylor (Director of Development), Prof. Tony Collier (Birmingham Polytechnic) and Councillor Fred Chapman, (Chairman of the Planning Committee) introduced an international context through the architectural competition initiated in January 1988. Younger architects worldwide were invited to submit entries, to be judged in 1989, for 6 inner city sites (see map, Fig. 1.9) with differing functions and

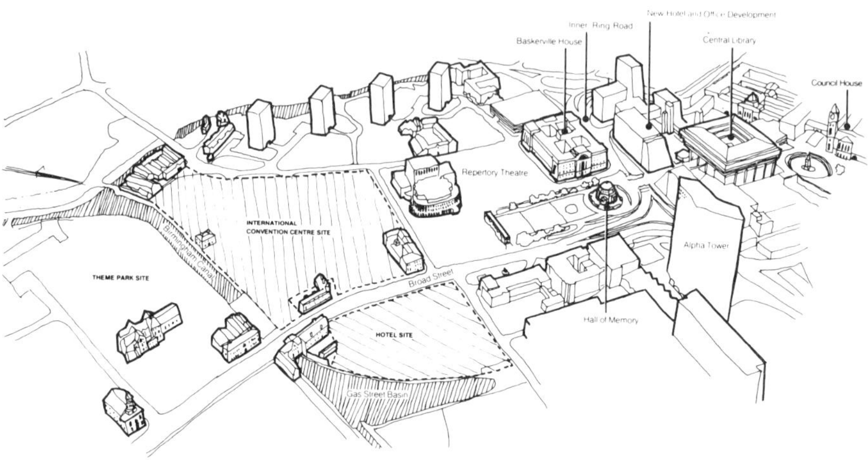

Fig. 1.2 Birmingham Convention Centre: site layout (proposed)

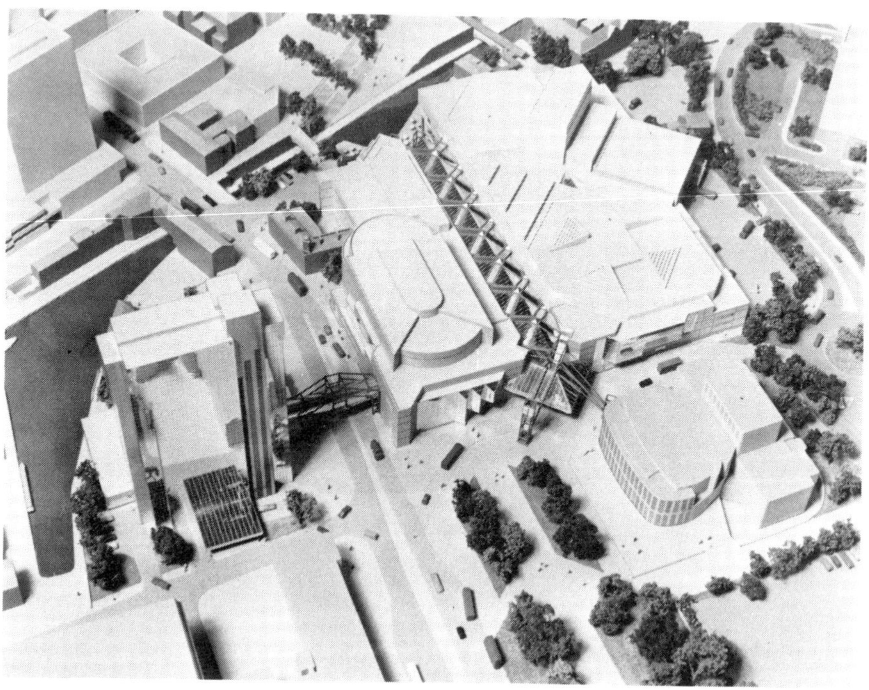

Fig. 1.3 Convention Centre: model, showing Repertory Theatre (bottom right), Convention Centre (top right), Hyatt Hotel (bottom left).

Fig. 1.4 Centenary Square: perspective from Copthorne Hotel towards Convention Centre (top left), Baskerville House (right), Hall of Memory (centre), Rep. (top centre).

Fig. 1.5 Convention Centre under construction February 1989, with Broad Street bridge (far right).

Fig. 1.6 Gas Street Basin c.1987 before clearance of the hotel site, with Broad Street (left), Rep. (top left), site of Convention Centre uncleared (centre left).

Fig. 1.7 Canal at Farmer's Bridge Junction 1984, looking towards Convention Centre site.

Fig. 1.8 Canal at Farmer's Bridge Junction (centre left) looking towards Convention Centre under construction February 1989.

geographical characters, from a proposed leisure attraction in the vicinity of the Convention Centre, to a new primary school in downtown Small Heath.[17] The 6-member jury comprised Geoffrey Darke, Ernest Irwin, Frank McLoughlin, Andreas Brandt (W. Germany), Paola Ceccarelli (Italy), Henri Gaudin (France). The city's centenary year was also to see the staging of a large international conference on architecture(see 'CONCLUSION').A further promotion of design standards through the Good Design Initiative concerned the Good Design Awards which the Initiative offered to renovations and new building projects receiving nomination. Further encouragement to architectural design was also provided by the Centenary City Pride Awards, instituted by the Junior Chamber Birmingham and the first award was given to Prudential Assurance for the £1.4 million refurbishment of 10 Colmore Row by John Madin Design Group.[18]

Industry in Birmingham and its Environs

The emerging dominance of the metals industries in the Birmingham area during, if not prior to, the Industrial Revolution, is a well-documented phenomenon, as is the reliance which arose on industries connected with the manufacture of vehicles. Particularly exhaustive studies undertaken this century of industry in Birmingham and the West Midlands region include those produced by G.C. Allen (1929), P. Sargant Florence (1948) and P. Wood (1976). Through sources such as these it is possible to trace the changing industrial structure of the city and region, from a pre-mid eighteenth century reliance on iron-working to the early mechanisation of the metals trades by the turn of the twentieth century. Indeed, it is clearly evident that when Birmingham became a city in 1889, the foundation for what became, arguably, a twentieth century over-reliance on vehicles, electrical and engineering industries was already established.

Florence noted in his survey of Birmingham trades (undertaken in 1940) that "*the specialization of plants and firms that build up motor cars in the Birmingham area is only part of a specialization of plants and firms in handling metals generally. . . (and that) labour, machines and plant generally are to a great extent adaptable from one metal industry to another*". [19] His findings also lent confirmation to the theory that Birmingham cannot be seen in isolation from the West Midlands region itself, and the urban conurbation in particular, through his assertion that "*the metal industries generally are mainly concentrated in the conurbation formed by Birmingham and the Black Country* ***plus*** *Coventry*" (his emphasis).[20] His table of "The Scope of Larger Metal Industries Localized in Birmingham Telephone District" listed the numbers and types of firms involved in specific metals trades (Fig. 1.10).

Writing nearly 30 years later, Wood noted the continuing density of metal goods and metal manufacturing industries in the West Midlands when he examined the proportion of employment in these in the West Midlands conurbation in comparison with the counties of Warwickshire, Worcestershire and Staffordshire. He found that 58% of engineering, 52% of vehicle manufacturing and 82% of metal goods employment in the wider region was located within the West Midlands conurbation itself. [21] He also noted the way in which vehicle manufacturing occupied a "*crucial culminating position in the sequence of metal and engineering production that dominates the economy of the West Midlands*". [22]

A useful breakdown of 50 major manufacturing firms in Birmingham was undertaken by the City Council's Economic Development Unit in late 1988. This showed that there were only 6 manufacturing employers in Birmingham with over

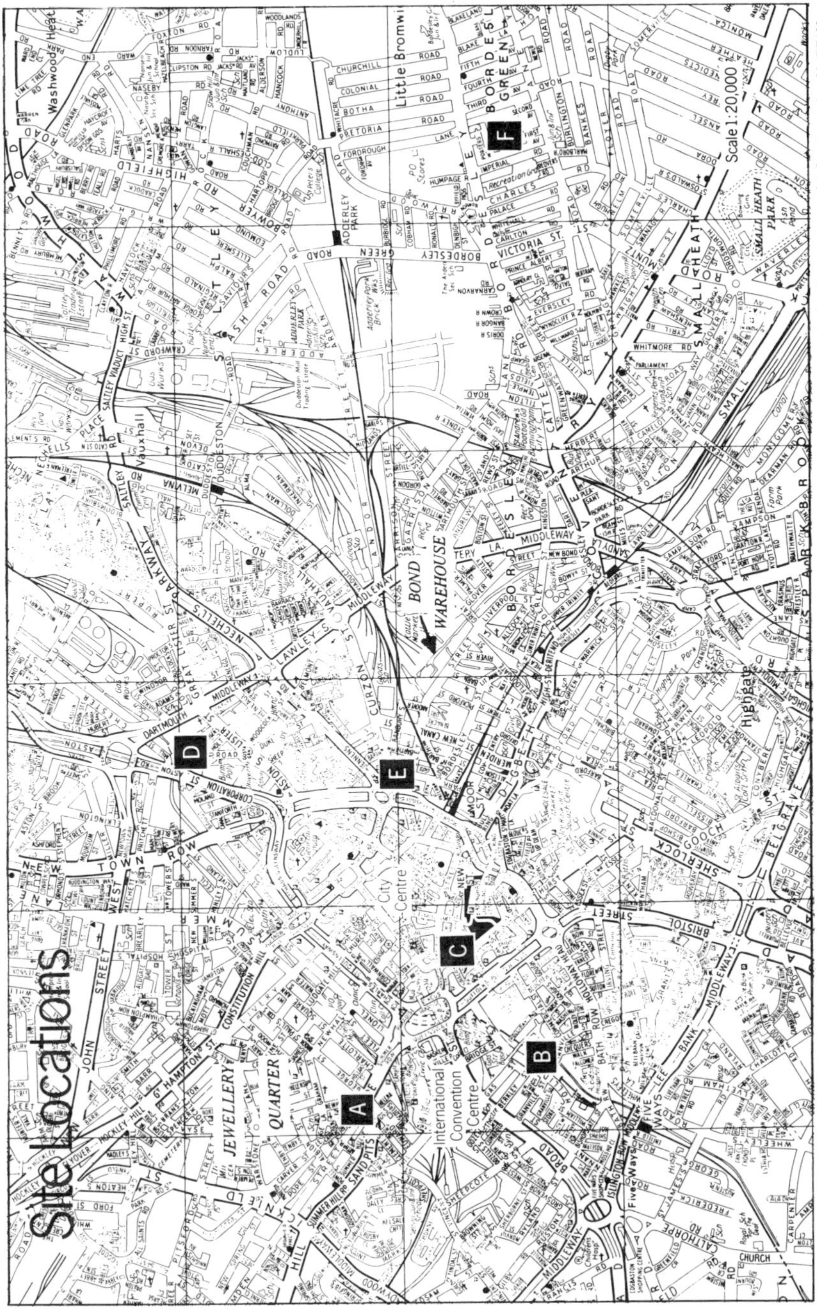

Fig. 1.9 Good Design Architectural Competition, 1988-89. Map of Central Birmingham showing sites (A) Newhall Hill gateway to Jewellery Quarter; (B) Leisure attraction, Holliday Street Depot; (C) Piazza, New Street Station; (D) High-Tech building, Aston Science Park; (E) Masshouse Circus landmark; (F) Primary School, Small Heath. Also shown - Bond Warehouse site (see chapter 20), Jewellery Quarter.

2,000 employees, these being Austin Rover, Cadbury Schweppes, GKN, IMI, Jaguar Cars, Lucas Industries.[23] Of these largest, only Cadbury Schweppes was not connected with the automotive and engineering fields. Of the 50 companies listed, 36 were directly connected with the metals industries and 14 were directly connected with transport and components manufacture. It was precisely in the fields of mechanical engineering and vehicles, metal manufacturing and metal goods, that the greatest national job losses occurred.[24] A comparison of employment in service and manufacturing industries is highly revealing in illustrating the enormous contemporary extent of jobs in the service industries. In 1984 there were 106,535 people employed in metal goods and vehicle industries, 41,734 in other manufacturing industries, 14,624 in extraction and manufacture of minerals and metals, but also that there were 81,761 employed in distribution, hotels/catering and repairs, 25,873 in transport and communication, 54,370 in banking, finance, insurance etc. and a massive 130,884 in other services, out of a total of 479,031 in employment.

In the decades following World War 2, the 1940s and early 1950 can be seen as a time of recovery, followed by a period of prosperity in the later 1950s to mid 1960s. Statistics presented in *Metropolitan Development and Change* indicate that the peak of vehicle manufacture in the region occurred in 1964 and that job losses started to occur from 1966, when there was, for example, a 16% job loss in engineering and metal manufacture (or 138,000 people).[25] In 1966, to take just one example, 5000 workers at British Motor Corporation lost their jobs and the number of unemployed rose to 23,000.[26] With little respite, the decline continued throughout the 1970s and early 1980s. *Crisis in the Industrial Heartland*, a study by what is now the School of Public Policy, Birmingham University, showed that approximately 369,500 job losses occurred from 1965 to 1981, when around 25% of manufacturing jobs were lost in the West Midlands County, and at a higher rate than the national figure.[27] The depth of the recession occurred in the late 1970s to early 1980s with the unemployment peak of 18.2% in Birmingham itself in 1982. By October 1988 the figure had, however, dropped to 10.2%[28] and was accompanied by a feeling of renewed optimism and confidence. This compared with a West Midlands unemployment rate of 8.1%. For much of the period between 1951 to 1966, however, there was an unemployment rate of less than 1% and this rarely rose over 2%.[29]

While the economic turbulence of our contemporary era, naturally, creates the rawest note, there are indications that the recession of the 1970s and 80s was not the first such experience. G.C. Allen, in particular, noted a trough in the 1860s and 70s in Birmingham and the Black Country (roughly the area of much of the West Midlands conurbation) at the end of the age of iron-working. What is perhaps most interesting in relation to our own current experience is that the 1880s saw something of a revival, as industry in the area adopted mechanisation methods of manufacturing, components and processes.[30] At the time that Birmingham became a city, therefore, it was emerging from a decline in its established industrial tradition and was adjusting to different industrial and trading conditions. Much the same could be said of the current situation. Furthermore, the economic and industrial difficulties of the inter-war slump (although, according to Wood,[31] not affecting Birmingham more drastically than the national situation) has given substance to the Kondratieff-Schumpeter theory for cycles of rise, peak and decline in economic prosperity of approximately 55 years. Peter Hall has shown how this theory identified a boom period, followed by an era of product innovations which were greatest during the recession years, subsequently leading to the creation of new industries.[32] The experience of Birmingham in the 1970s and 80s lends further credence to such a theory.

Another feature of industrial evolution which merits attention is the growing investment in West Midlands (and UK) manufacture undertaken by foreign companies, notably Japanese, but also including US, German, Dutch, Italian and

Scope of Larger Metal Industries Localized in Birmingham Telephone District

*Industry and number of Firms** (Telephone Directory) 1940

Processes:	
Smelting and Refining or Forming; or both	Iron and Steel Manufacturers 40, Metal Manufacturers 30, Rolling Mills 40, Steel Manufacturers 50, Wire Manufacturers 30
	Brass Foundries 190, Tube Manufacturers 80, Iron Founders 140, Presswork 100, Drop Forgers 40, Forging and Stamping 30, Malleable Iron Founders 40, Stampers and Piercers 140, Welders 50, Wire Workers and Weavers 40
Machining	Capstan Repetition Work 50, Engineers' Machinists 30, Metal Spinners 30, Sheet-Metal Workers 110
Treating	Electro-Gilders and Platers 40, Enamellers 40, Engravers 40, Galvanizers 30, Planers and Polishers 50

Products:	Stages in Assembling	General Finishing or Fashioning
Components	Bolts and Nuts 70, Nail Makers 30, Screw Makers 50, Spring Makers 70, Washer Manufacturers 40	Chain Makers 80, Electro-Plate Manufacturers 45, Jewellers (Mfg.) 170, Silversmiths (Mfg.) 80, Smallware Manufacturers 30
Sub-Assembly	Cycle Accessories 80, Electric Accessories 30, Electrical Fittings 30, Electrical Supplies 40, Motor Body Builders 30, Motor-Car Accessories 50, Motor-Car Fittings 30, Tubes and Fittings 40	
Assembly	Bedstead Makers 30, Cycle Manufacturers 60, Gun, Rifle and Pistol 30, Hearth Furniture 50, Hollow-ware 40, Lamp 40, Lock Makers 100, Motor-Car Manufacturers 10, Motor Vehicles, Commercial 14	

	Services for Metal Trades:
Constructional Engineers 40, Die Casters and Sinkers 50, Machine-Tool Makers 50, 'Machinery' 40, Pattern Makers 50, Press-Tool Makers 40, Tool Makers and Dealers 120	Tools
Consulting Engineers 30	Advisers
Hardware Merchants 95, Iron and Steel Merchants 90, Iron, Steel and Metal Scrap Merchants 40, Metal Merchants 80, Scrap Merchants 30	Middlemen

* To nearest ten. Firms less than thirty in number omitted except Motor-Car (and Motor Vehicles) Manufacturers.

Fig. 1.10 Table reproduced in P. Sargant Florence *Investment, Location and size of Plant,* 1948.

Taiwanese. The New Town of Telford, a designated area for expansion, was a prime target for foreign investment. Eight Japanese companies had settled there by January 1988.[33] However, Birmingham itself has seen foreign investment of a comparably insidious and profound nature, although it was arguably brought home in January 1985, when Sumitomo Rubber Industries, the third largest Group in Japan, acquired the Dunlop tyre business in Europe from Dunlop Holdings, and (in so doing) became masters of the highly symbolic Fort Dunlop in Birmingham.[34]

The economic situation of Birmingham and the West Midlands showed a more encouraging position, therefore, in the later 1980s. In a 1987 special report the *Guardian* could state that the "city many suspected had gone into terminal decline (was) back in business".[35] The City Council's entrepreneurial determination is symbolised by such ambitious outward and forward-looking projects as the bid to stage the 1992 Olympics, the Superprix and the International Convention Centre. It must be acknowledged, nonetheless, that this strategy has not arisen solely in the years since 1987 and a noteworthy earlier achievement on this scale was the realisation of the National Exhibition Centre (opened 1976).

The High-Technology Industries in and around Birmingham

In examining the changing nature of Birmingham's economic base, it is the city's ability to initiate and develop new growth areas of income-generating activities that will provide economic security. Although it has remained a major centre of manufacturing, another trend, this time towards the creation of new business and high-technology research and development areas, has emerged. Indeed, it was acknowledged that it is in Birmingham's "*wider role as a business city that the future lies*".[36] K.E. Rose was among those who identified the need for industrial diversification (combined with the stimulus of the commercial and tourism sectors) to assist the region's future growth.[37] The establishment of high-technology research centres such as Aston Science Park and Birmingham University's Research Park, the formation of business parks and the identification of new areas on green belt land around Birmingham for the proposed establishment of high-technology industry (at Monkspath (Solihull), Bassetts Pole and Tanworth-in-Arden)[38] are tangible effects of this policy. It demonstrates an appreciation of the revolution in information technology and the growing economic importance of micro-electronics.

The two largest companies in Birmingham in 1988 (and among the 50 largest Birmingham companies) which were involved in information technology and business systems were Kalamazoo and Apricot Computers.[39] Kalamazoo represents a company involved in older IT indudstries which has also evolved into computer systems, while Apricot Computers has arisen expressly in relation to the micro-electronics revolution.

As has been shown by Preston, Hall and Bevan, (Fig. 1.11) more than half all involvement in IT industries has taken place in London and the South East, which still retain the largest share. This arose through the region's acquisition of skills in the older electronics industries, specifically radios and electrical engineering. From the period 1931 to 1981 the West Midlands' share, if anything, decreased slightly from approximately one twelfth to approximately one fourteenth of the national figure.[40] Again, the concentration on traditional areas of manufacture in Birmingham and the West Midlands has given rise to this situation, requiring a determined effort to expand into new activities, which the city and region are indeed demonstrating.

Fig. 1.11 Table reproduced in M. Preston *et al*, *Innovation in Information Technology Industries in Great Britain*, 1985.

Design, Design Training and the Designer for Industry

The term 'design' assumes a number of meanings dependent upon one's background. For the engineer, design would refer to process or product innovations of a technological kind, or to tooling design. Design may refer to the interpretation of a client's brief which is adapted for manufacture. The marketing executive might see styling as one aspect of design, through the updating and adapting of old ideas to suit contemporary taste. Design may concern the flat surface or may communicate ideas and information as in advertising and graphics. In product design, it may not necessarily be the whole item to which the designer's attention is directed, but to the better solution of specific technical features of it. For the architect and interior designer there are other provisions, such as services, to consider, in addition to decisions involving formalist aesthetics.

The emergence of product design as a discipline distinct from engineering or fine art/visual communication is a twentieth century phenomenon which has grown with the expansion in scope and complexity of industrial activity. In the 1930s it was rare to find any firm with a staff product designer. Indeed, when A.H. Woodfull was taken on by Streetly Manufacturing Co. in 1931, (see chapter 18) he was one of the first such designers in any industry, let alone in plastics. As a graduate of the Birmingham School of Art (now Birmingham Polytechnic), Woodfull had studied (as a contemporary of John Barnes) under E. Harvey at one of the two earliest courses in industrial design in the country.[41]

The relationship between the needs of industry and the services of education is obviously crucial to the training of people with the necessary skills to enable not only the city, but the country, to compete industrially and economically. Much has been written about the ways in which the UK has lagged behind, for example, Germany and France in this respect. Nor has this been of recent nature, but has recurred periodically throughout the century. The findings of the Gorell Committee of 1931 were among the more significant studies of the relationship between industry, design and training needs. However, equal emphasis to these subjects was given during the preceding century, centring around South Kensington and the Schools of Design. There was an awareness that training in this country was deficient compared with Continental methods. Writing about Lucas Industries as recently as the 1970s, Nockolds even then lamented the superior technical education which Germans enjoyed.[42] The industry/education link has been a feature of design training, particularly at the Birmingham and Vittoria Street Schools, since the days of B.J. Fletcher, Edward Taylor and R. Catterson Smith in the late nineteenth/early twentieth century. At this time the Arts and Crafts flourished and practical training from the 1890s was in crafts workshops, and aesthetic schooling was largely dictated by a classical tradition of formal drawing.[43]

Much has been written, too, about the need for greater research and development investment in the UK, amidst an appreciation that the country was lagging behind others such as the US and Japan. The existence of large design engineering teams, as at Austin Rover and Lucas Industries, has produced many important advances in product and process innovation. The number of design awards at Lucas Industries, for example, demonstrates the advantages of multi-skilled teams of in-house engineering specialists in the achievement of technological creativity (see Appendix), and the currently expanding use of interactive graphics in design engineering has fostered the further diminishing of the divisions between disciplines. Yet the distinction between industrial designer and design engineer may still exist strongly. It was certainly the subject of much debate when, in November 1958, a conference was staged in Birmingham by the CoID in collaboration with the Birmingham Exchange and Engineering Centre, to address the subject of *Industrial Design and the Engineering Industries*, chaired by Whitney Straight,

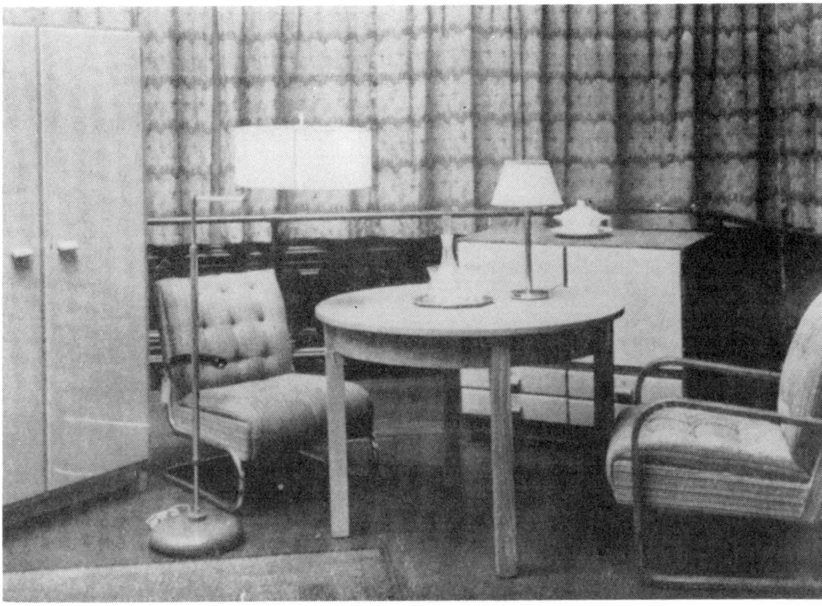

Fig. 1.12. *Midland Industrial Art* Exhibition, 1934. *Design for To-Day*, July 1934.

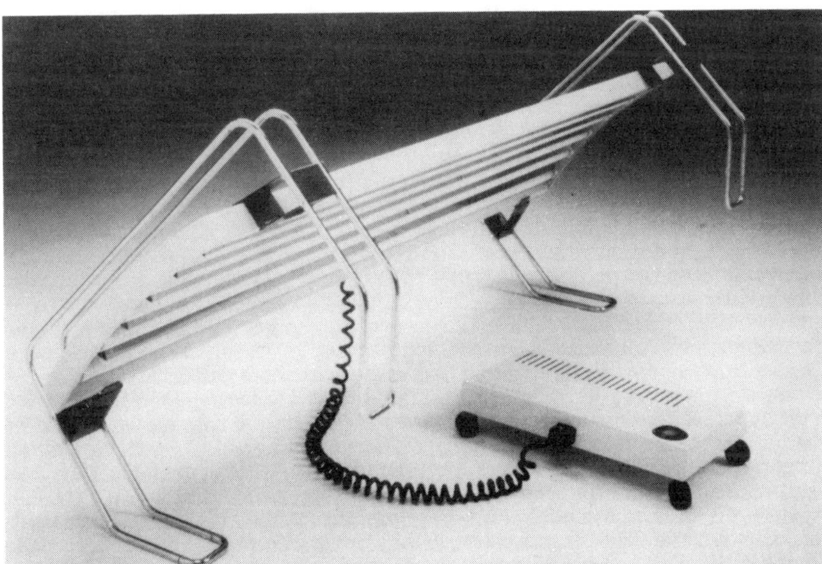

Fig. 1.13 Sunray lamp designed by DCA Design Consultants, manufactured by Horizon Lighting Products, 1985.

Vice-Chairman of Rolls Royce Ltd. Senior Midlands engineering industrialists attended and the conference theme (redolent of evangelical CoID philosophy) was "*to study the role of industrial design in relation to the engineering industries; to discuss what steps should be taken to improve the form and function of engineering products and to consider how best to make use of the service of trained industrial designers; to encourage an appreciation of appearance design among those already employed in the engineering trades, and to examine the problem of training industrial designers for the engineering industries*".[44] In *Design* magazine, the editor commented on matters arising from the conference, finding that there were signs of encouragement, in that certain firms were increasingly more appearance conscious, while others shunned the very mention of the word 'design' in favour of a solely technical approach. Reasons for this were discussed briefly, and included the unflattering conclusion that "*some designers . . . have gone about offering their services and advice in a flat-footed, inept way, thereby confirming and perpetuating preconceived prejudices*".[45]

Few design engineers anywhere have achieved an international eminence as great as Sir Alec Issigonis (1906-1988), who is chiefly recalled for his design of the Morris Minor (launched 1948) and the Mini (launched 1959) for Morris Motors, (see Fig. 12.3) and became a Royal Designer for Industry in 1964. However, Issigonis' fame was found in an era when it was still possible for individual design engineers to undertake supreme responsibility for any single project. This era ended with the Leyland takeover in 1968, when a committee approach was instituted for car design and development, in accordance with modern thinking.[46]

Whereas the emphasis of design in the Birmingham area might be seen as closely linked with the engineering field, the industrial arts, too, have played a significant role. The earliest, most exhaustive, analysis of design and industry in this field was undertaken by Sir Nikolaus Pevsner and was published in 1937.[47] His study had begun as a research project at the University of Birmingham, for which he gained his Ph.D., and examined design and industry in Birmingham and within a radius of 50 miles of the city to take in, for example, furniture manufacture in Banbury.[48] Important and interesting in itself (though frustratingly deficient on clarification of the identity of specific firms), his research findings were arguably made more interesting by the era in which he wrote. Current in his *Enquiry* was the debate about the adoption of Moderne or Modernist principles i.e. the influence of Art Deco and the Paris 1925 *Exposition des Arts Decoratifs* versus the supposed rationalism of the International Style. Leading Birmingham firms which he considered to be embracing Modern Movement principles in their products at the time included Best & Lloyd and PEL Furniture.

The Design and Industries Association (DIA) executed a pivotal role in the encouragement of the practice of design within (and for) industry in Birmingham, in which R.D. Best (of Best & Lloyd) was a major figure. Although the DIA has maintained a presence in the Birmingham area to the present time, the highpoint of the DIA's public profile occurred, nonetheless, in the interwar period, when the exhibition of *Midland Industrial Art* was held at the City Art Gallery and Museum, organised jointly by the Museum and the DIA. (Fig. 1.12) In his review, Hubert George spoke of the "*craft traditions (which) no longer hold good and the new race of machine-designers (which) is not yet in its stride*".[49] Cars were not included in the exhibits, but articles of Midlands manufacture included glass from Stourbridge, pottery from Staffordshire, jewellery, lighting and accessories from Birmingham. A solitary photograph of domestic equipment showed lighting by ? Best & Lloyd and Plan furniture designed by Serge Chermayeff and manufactured for him by PEL Furniture and Henry Stone & Son of Banbury.[50]

Even in 1934 it was evident that it was not possible to separate the practice of design for industry in Birmingham from the Midlands, or indeed the country, as a whole. In the same way that industry looks outwards for its markets, so the free-

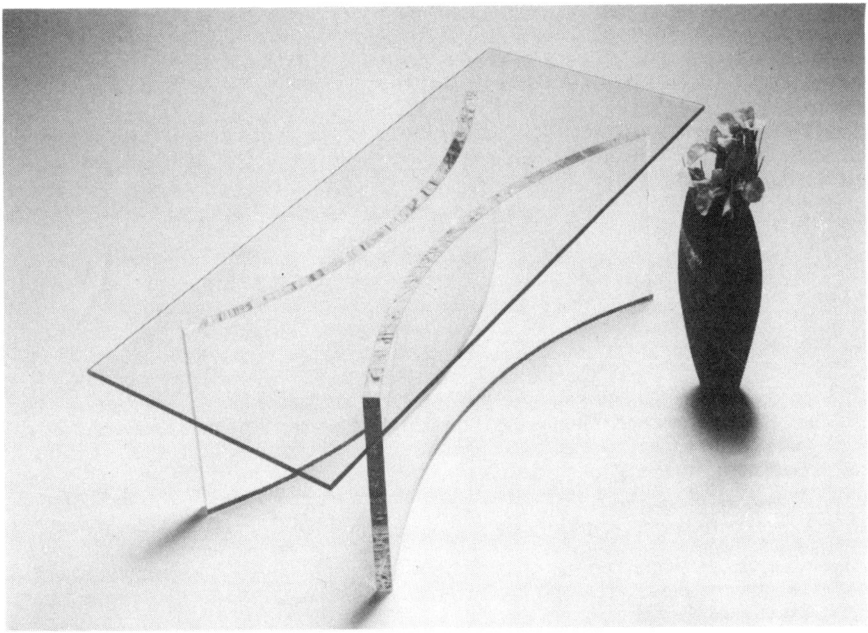

Fig. 1.14 Joceline Burke. Low table, 1987, by sponsorship from ICI and Argo Plastics. Perspex base, printed at edges, made by Argo Plastics, Kidderminster; glass top by UBM Glass, Birmingham.

lance designer has operated within a national, and increasingly, now, an international context. Woodfull's Product Design Unit at BIP, too, which operated from the 1950s to 1970s, provided an outward-looking design service which served industry anywhere.

Freelance design practices in the Birmingham area, such as John Vale's Midland Design Associates, [51] have usually remained small in size i.e. comprising not more than 6 consultants, in contrast with the establishment of a larger number of extended design consultancies in London. An exception to this has been David Carter's DCA Design Consultants, operating from Warwick, (Fig. 1.13) which in 1989 had a staff of around 60, of which approximately 30 were designers,[52] and was the largest practice in the West Midlands. Its location, however, did not presume greater links with industry, or the larger portion of its briefs arriving from within the region. Instead, it has operated, and still does, within a national and international field. The female industrial designer is still a rarity, though will become somewhat less unusual as the profession soaks up the greater number of female industrial designers who are now undergoing training. Furniture designer Joceline Burke, (Fig. 1.14) who exhibited with other female designers in the exhibition *Towards an Image* in March 1989 at Gas Hall, Birmingham (organised by the Ikon Gallery), [53] is in the vanguard of this progression.

A recent trend, which has been stimulated by the growth in retailing outlets and the remodelling of the High Streets, has been the number of architectural and interior design commissions. It may also be that, in Birmingham, the current regeneration and refurbishment of the urban and industrial fabric has provided further stimulus in this design field.

To return full cycle to a point made earlier in this introduction, by way of explanation and emphasis - Birmingham as a city, as a manufacturing base, as a location for designers, as a cultural centre, indeed in every way imaginable, may maintain (in our contemporary era) a degree of understandable self interest in allowing its citizens, its trades and its institutions the benefit of its entrepreneurial endeavours. The city, after all, exists because of and on behalf of, its people. Its future success, however, lies not in inward- but in forward-thinking, and the projects which have been instigated here in the 1980s will reap benefits for the city in the next hundred years of its second century.

REFERENCES

1 Figures obtained from B. Smith, *A Century of Birmingham Industry: A Framework for Comparison,* typescript, Birmingham University, November 1984 and *Financial Times,* 1 December 1988.
2 J.M. Jones, p.61.
3 K. Spencer, A. Taylor, B. Smith, J. Mawson, N. Flynn, R. Batley, 1986.
4 "Dramatic Changes in Birmingham", *The Planner,* July 1985, p.7.
5 Information from City Architect's Department, March 1989.
6 Bournville Village Trust, pp.10 - 11.
7 P. Abercrombie and H. Jackson, 1948.
8 West Midland Group on Post-War Reconstruction and Planning, 1948.
9 P. Wood, pp.221 - 224.
10 The inaugural meeting was held on 25 January 1989. The organisation is fronted by Dr. John Newson, author of the report *What Kind of Birmingham?*, 1989. See *Birmingham Evening Mail,* 26 January 1989.
11 *Financial Times,* op.cit.
12 *Planning,* 2 March 1984, p.5.
13 Information about Broad Street developments from Convention Centre Partnership, *Birmingham International Convention Centre,* Birmingham, March 1985. Development Department, *The International Convention Centre,* information leaflet, Birmingham, n.d. (c.1988).
14 See "Royal Rocket for Centre", *Birmingham Evening Mail,* 27 November 1987. Television condemnation October 1988, discussed in "Convention 'Disaster' Praised", ibid., 3 November 1988.
15 Information from William Howland, City Architect's Department, in interview of 12 January 1989. Further documentation provided by Development Department e.g. *Draft Waterlinks Development Framework,* Birmingham, n.d. (c.1988); East Birmingham Urban Development Agency, *Adoption of Revised Bordesley Development Framework,* n.d. (c.1988).
16 One of 47 awards (DoE Civic Trust, RIBA *et al*) won by the Department for housing etc. since 1960. See City Architect's Department, *Awards and Commendations for Departmental Projects,* typescript, Birmingham, n.d.
17 *Birmingham Good Design Initiative* information pack, Birmingham, October 1987.
18 See *Birmingham Evening Mail,* 26 January 1989.
19 P. Sargant Florence, p.59.
20 Ibid., p.66.
21 P. Wood, p.138.
22 Ibid., pp.155 - 6.
23 Development Department, *Birmingham - The Business City,* typescript, Birmingham, n.d. (c.1988).
24 West Midlands Forum of County Councils, *West Midlands Region, Economy and Employment: Indicators of Change,* October 1984.
25 D. Crompton and L. Penkreth, "Industrial and Employment Change" in F. Joyce (ed.), p.114ff.

26 Ibid., p.123.
27 K. Spencer *et al*, p.56.
28 *Birmingham - The Business City,* op.cit.
29 D. Crompton and L. Penkreth, p.123.
30 G.C. Allen, p.348ff.
31 P. Wood, p.34.
32 P. Hall, "The People: Where Will They Go?" *The Planner,* April 1985, p.4.
33 "Another Japanese Firm Moving In", *Birmingham Evening Mail,* 7 January 1988.
34 "Sun Rises on Fort Dunlop", *Birmingham Post,* 3 January 1985. Fort Dunlop was sold in 1989 to the consortium Tarmac Richardson Developments and was partly destined for re-development as a hotel and shopping complex. See *Birmingham Choice,* 18 August 1989.
35 Special Report on Birmingham, 23 March 1987.
36 Ibid.
37 K.E. Rose, "Changing Financial Resource Base" in F. Joyce, p.107.
38 *Birmingham Evening Mail,* 22 February 1989.
39 *Birmingham - The Business City,* op.cit.
40 M. Preston, P. Hall, N. Bevan, pp.43 - 4.
41 Information from A.H. Woodfull in interviews of 1986.
42 H. Nockolds, p.398.
43 For views on this subject see J. Swift article here on "Birmingham Art School: Its Branch Schools and Female Students 1880 - 1900". See also B. Tilson, "Masterly Art: Birmingham Municipal School of Art 1884 - 1920", review of exhibition held at Birmingham Museum and Art Gallery 25 January 1987, in *Design History Society Newsletter,* 33, March 1987, pp.33 - 7.
44 See *Design*, 118, 1958, p.65.
45 *Design,* 119, 1958, p.73.
46 Obituary of Sir Alec Issigonis in *The Independent,* 5 October 1988.
47 N. Pevsner, 1937. For a study of this book, see P. Madge, "An Enquiry into Pevsner's *Enquiry", Journal of Design History,* vol. 1 no. 2, 1988, pp.113 - 26.
48 See B. Tilson, "Stones of Banbury 1870 - 1978: A Casualty of the Recession", *Furniture History,* 1987, pp.98-107. This will be discussed further in a *Journal of Design History,* article, to be published in vol.3. PEL tubular steel and Stones' upholstery combined to produce Chermayeff's Plan furniture.
49 "Beauty in the Black Country: The Exhibition of Midland Industrial Art", *Design for To-Day,* July 1934, p.267.
50 Plan Ltd was a retailing company located at the Pantheon, Oxford Street, which was formed in late 1932 to retail interior furnishings of international modern style.
51 Information from J. Vale in interview January 1989.
52 In March 1989 the consultancy had 23 senior design associates and around 7 other designers. Senior associates and industrial designers were male, while graphics staff included some female designers. Information DCA Design Consultants, 1989.
53 See "Triple Image of Talent", *The Birmingham Post,* 11 March 1989.

BIBLIOGRAPHY

P. Abercrombie and H. Jackson, *West Midlands Plan,* London, 1948.
G.C. Allen, *The Industrial Development of Birmingham and the Black Country 1860 - 1927,* London, 1929
Bournville Village Trust, *When We Build Again,* London, 1941.
P. Sargant Florence, *Investment, Location and Size of Plant: A Realistic Inquiry into the Structure of British and American Cities,* Cambridge, 1948.
J.M. Jones, *Maps of Birmingham,* Birmingham, 1975.
F. Joyce (ed.), *Metropolitan Development and Change: The West Midlands Region: A Policy Review,* Birmingham, 1977.
H. Nockolds, *Lucas: The First 100 Years. vol. 2: The Successors,* Newton Abbot; London, 1978.
N. Pevsner, *An Enquiry into Industrial Art in England,* London, 1937.
M. Preston, P. Hall, N. Bevan, *Innovation in Information Technology Industries in Great Britain*, University of Reading Geographical Paper 89, 1985.

K. Spencer, A. Taylor, B. Smith, J. Mawson, N. Flynn, R. Batley, *Crisis in the Industrial Heartland,* Oxford, 1986.

West Midland Group on Post-War Reconstruction and Planning, *Conurbation: A Survey of Birmingham and the Black Country,* London, 1948.

P. Wood, *Industrial Britain: The West Midlands,* Newton Abbot; London, 1976.

CHAPTER 2

ARCHITECTURAL TERRACOTTA IN BIRMINGHAM

Michael Stratton

The terracotta architecture of Birmingham presents a concerted effort by the Victorians to create a distinctive public architecture out of the exploitation of an essentially new decorative building material. Terracotta became the architectural symbol of the Civic Gospel developed by Joseph Chamberlain and contemporary political figure-heads of the late Victorian period. The reason for the use of decoratively moulded blocks of clay for Board Schools, libraries and a series of major public buildings lies partly in clear-cut practicalities but also in terms of Birmingham's aspiration vis-a-vis other cities and especially London.[1]

An underlining commitment behind the adoption of terracotta came from a determination to make "*the town cleaner, sweeter and brighter*".[2] Concern over living conditions in Birmingham deepened in the mid-1860s and contrasted markedly with the hard *laissez-faire* attitudes of preceding decades. The city fathers became concerned and ashamed at the high incidence of diarrhoea and diphtheria. Such zymotic diseases were blamed on "*polluted air, impure water and unclean habits*".[3] The Victorians were dilatory in tackling the cause of smoke pollution. Most reports saw the problem in restricted terms, blaming specific factories and the over-stoking of boilers. Responding to strengthened terms of the 1872 Health Act, a smoke inspector was appointed for Birmingham Corporation in 1875, but he spent most of his time taking action against firms with chimneys emitting noxious smoke rather than attacking the broader problems of fumes emitted by domestic hearths. The quality of the air in many cities continued to deteriorate into the Edwardian period, real legislative progress only being made during the inter-war period.

The destruction caused by soot produced desperation amongst architects and many politicians. Layers of grime seemed to nullify all their efforts to create a more attractive city. Amidst such despondency terracotta, and its glazed counterpart, faience, offered bright colours that could be appreciated through smog, and a durability against corrosive soot. Architecture was believed to have a conditioning effect on the population as illustrated in a rather unfair comparison of Birmingham and Italy. In Italy "*the Art-Faculty (was) nourished in this congenial atmosphere*" while in Birmingham "*the air laden with poisonous smoke-clouds, buildings for the most part black, grimy and ugly*" was accompanied by "*dress dull and hideous*".[4]

There were a variety of rather more nebulous factors that served to promote the late Victorian interest in terracotta. Decorative ceramics could contribute towards the development of an architecture with 'meaning' that would reflect both the commercial prosperity and the public aspirations of the new industrial age. A factory-made ornament, combining art with repetition and mass production, could help create a new aesthetic appropriate to provincial cities. Such materials offered a path towards a 'style for the age' that would incorporate recognised historic forms but, through the discipline of repetition and bright colours, could achieve a contemporary originality. The incorporation of figure sculpture, decorative friezes and lettering meant that architecture could have a broad interest.

The Victorian public were clearly fascinated by the changing fabric of their cities and 'read' building facades. They might be attracted to enter libraries by images of knowledge and learning, or into improved public houses by their opulent decoration.

Historians have striven to emphasise the cheapness of terracotta. Victorian clayworkers tended to promote their product on its properties rather than its pricing. The cheapest local stone could usually be obtained for lower cost than terracotta in the nineteenth century and artificial stone consistently undercut faience in price in the inter-war period. Nevertheless, in the Midlands, terracotta was often cheaper than a good quality durable stone once it had been carved. and especially if intricate detailing was repeated across cornices, string courses or other features.

The adoption of terracotta in Birmingham was preceded by the use of decorative brickwork on commercial buildings and middle-class housing, and by the widespread adoption of decorative tiles, initially for floors in churches. St Mary's College, Oscott and St Chad's Roman Catholic Cathedral in the City Centre contain early tiled pavements by Minton dating to around 1840. The most important tile manufacturers in Britain were located within a fifty mile radius of Birmingham, and competed to supply the contracts on offer. The pioneering firm of the tile revival, Minton, was based at Stoke-on-Trent, Maw had a massive factory at Jackfield, near to the plant of their prestigious local competitor, Craven Dunnill. Godwin, a firm that specialised in making medieval style encaustics, had their factory at Lugwardine near Hereford. Only one decorative tile manufacturer was based in the West Midlands - Gibbons, Hinton & Company of Brierly Hill. Established in 1883, this firm supplied tiles for many of the houses built around Wolverhampton.

Fig. 2.1. Pressing Shop c.1982 showing moulds filled with clay at the works of Hathernware Ceramics, formerly the Hathern Station Brick & Terracotta Company, near Loughborough, Leicestershire.

In the same vein, most of the terracotta used in Birmingham was not made within the immediate vicinity, but came from firms located in other Midland towns. Since the middle of the nineteenth century, terracotta garden ornaments and architectural details had been made in brick, pipe and pottery works widely scattered across England. Gibbs & Canning of Tamworth was the first firm to be able to undertake large contracts for public buildings.[5] Terracotta production became established in the Midlands where the coal-measures contained both suitable clays and coal for firing the kilns. Notable firms include Stanley & Company of Nuneaton,[6] George King at Stourbridge[7] and George Woolliscroft & Sons at Hanley in the Potteries.[8] Doulton started making terracotta at their pipe-works in Rowley Regis in 1889, which supplemented their main works at Lambeth in London.[9] The market for terracotta in Birmingham during the twentieth century was dominated by the Hathern Station Brick & Terracotta Company, a firm that only came to manufacture terracotta on a large scale from 1897[10] (Fig. 2.1).

Many of the most distinctive bright red facades to be found in Birmingham were manufactured at Ruabon in North Wales. The main firms were Clark & Rea, Dennis Ruabon, The Ruabon Brick & Terracotta Company and J.C. Edwards, the last emerging as the largest producer of terracotta in the world, the Pen-y-Bont Works having over forty kilns by the turn of the century.[11]

During the 1870s terracotta became closely associated with Birmingham's Civic Gospel, a concerted movement to improve the political administration and fabric of the city. Schools were designed as a corporate expression of the ideals of the Board and the city's councillors. The first Board School coincided in date with the commencement of Joseph Chamberlain's highly productive mayoralty from 1873. He acted as Chairman of the Board until 1876. One firm of architects, Martin & Chamberlain, designed forty-one Board Schools up to 1898 and were therefore able to create a relatively consistent architectural image.[12] The buildings needed to stand out from the meanness of surrounding houses and, by being progressive and economical in their design and use of materials, they could convey a message of educational enlightenment. The style of the schools was consistently Gothic, but it became more refined in later designs. Initially moulded brick, tiling and stone contributed to the exterior decoration, which could include naturalistic carving, as in Oozells Street Schools of 1878. Seven years later, in Stratford Road School, plant and flower patterns were executed in a series of terracotta panels.[13] Terracotta dressings were usually concentrated on the main doorways, windows, gables and the ventilation towers. The bright red blocks of several schools were supplied by Clark & Rea of Ruabon, from their evocatively named Wilderness Works.[14] Despite some resistance to the near monopoly that the practice achieved in winning commissions for Board Schools, Martin & Chamberlain also designed most of the Free Libraries built in the city and a number of public baths, asylums and pumping stations.[15]

Aesthetic interest in brick and terracotta was reinforced by practical considerations. In January 1879 the Central Library was burnt out during attempts to thaw a frozen pipe.[16] Martin & Chamberlain designed the replacement building to be fireproof. Terracotta and tiling were widely used in parts of the interior such as the main entrance, and on the new facade facing Edmund Street. This frontage, completed in 1882, showed Martin & Chamberlain adopting an idiosyncratic interpretation of the Lombardic Renaissance style that had been adopted for the quadrangle of the Victoria & Albert Museum in South Kensington.

The School Board had close ties with the School of Arts Committee and Joseph Chamberlain supported the provision of art training for the great variety of trades found in the city. Politicians and architects were determined that Birmingham should not be dismissed as being second rate in terms of its arts and manufactures.

John Robinson, the Training Master for the Department of Science & Art and the Curator of the South Kensington (later the Victoria & Albert) Museum, recognised this aspiration. He justified the collection of terracotta busts and Della Robbias that he had purchased in Italy on behalf of the Birmingham Corporation by insisting that culture in the provinces should not be "*pitched at a lower level than in London, or that nowadays nothing should be deemed 'caviare' to the multitude*".[17]

While the City Art Gallery was built in stone to blend with the adjoining Council Offices, the School of Art in Margaret Street fully expressed the status of ceramics within the city's emerging architectural style, and in the teaching curricula followed there. The main facade marks the culmination of John Henry Chamberlain's use of terracotta, tiling and mosaic. Dating to 1884-5 it forms a late example of the juxtaposition of several contrasting materials, as recommended in the writing of Ruskin. Terracotta was used in the eaves' cornice, moulded into matrualistic foliage, and for a large blank rose window. This twelve feet diameter panel was designed by Chamberlain, modelled by S. Barfield of Leicester and made and supplied by Messrs King & Co of Stourbridge. The overlaying of a lattice grid by a sweeping lily form symbolised the contrast between regularity and naturalism at the heart of Birmingham's terracotta architecture.

Corporation Street became the most dramatic manifestation of Joseph Chamberlain's Civic Gospel. Construction commenced in 1878 and much of the southern section was lined by offices built with terracotta, though the majority of these buildings have been lost with redevelopment in the 1960s. The upper end of Corporation Street, towards Aston, displays one of the most strking groups of terracotta buildings in the country, rivalling the museums of South Kensington or the arcades of Leeds. The Victoria Law Courts, designed by Aston Webb and Ingress Bell and built 1887-1891, is a high point in the terracotta revival, equalled only by the Natural History Museum in its inventive use of architectural ceramics. More than any work by Alfred Waterhouse, it bridges the gap of Gothic and Renaissance historicism to suggest a way in which terracotta could form the basis of a contemporary decorative architecture.

Waterhouse was the assessor of the competition to find the best possible design for Birmingham's new Law Courts. Webb & Bell showed great cunning in making merit out of the fact that the designs were submitted anonymously. They had titled their entry 'Terracotta' to catch the eye of the assessor who was clearly a strong proponent of the material. Waterhouse commented in his final report that terracotta and brick were the best building materials for Birmingham. He was a strong believer in a graduated use of decoration, from a high degree of richness at the focal point of a composition to simpler forms on side and rear elevations, and the use of moulded terracotta contributed strongly to such principles. Webb and Bell's design was praised in terms of its picturesque composition and its sophisticated detailing.[18]

The Law Courts was the first major public building in Britain to have a frontage faced entirely with red terracotta, to the exclusion of brickwork, and with the material worked into a rich composition (Fig. 2.2). Webb & Bell drew inspiration from the early Tudor style of Hampton Court and sixteenth century Flemish architecture, which supplied a stock of motifs such as scrolls, dolphins, and cable and egg and dart mouldings, to be used for decorating cornices, turrets or arcades.[19] The decoration was designed not so much as part of the structure of the facade, but to flow out of it in curves breaking away from the line of the walls. The outline of most of the decoration was also curved, contrasting with the highly angular outline of the building. Such forms became characteristic features of terracotta decoration. They accorded with the plastic nature of the raw material and the concept of decoration growing naturally out of the structure of the building. Such curving sections could easily be moulded in terracotta but would have been difficult and expensive to carve in stone.

Fig. 2.2. Assize Court, Corporation Street, Birmingham by A. Webb & I. Bell, 1887-91 (J.C. Edwards).

The sculptural detailing was modelled by William Aumonier and his workmen. This firm of modellers had collaborated on several schemes with Gibbs & Canning, who supplied the terracotta for the interior of the Law Courts. Webb & Bell's design left spaces for sculptural work, which was designed and modelled by independent artists. Aumonier was responsible for the figures representing Art and the Crafts, set into the gable wings. W.S. Frith undertook the figure of Justice on the central gable and the cherubs supporting the cornices. He also modelled the figures of Truth, Patience and Plenty in the spandrels of the porch, to designs by Walter Crane. Harry Bates (like Frith, a sculptor from London) designed and modelled the figure of Queen Victoria in the entrance gable. She was strongly overshadowed by an ornate canopy with a moulded coping that curved up to form a finial (Fig. 2.3). The Assize Courts were the product of a complex collaboration between architects and decorative artists. The strong consistency in sculptural style showed how far the new ideas of modesty in scale and natural expression, bound up in the New Sculpture Movement, had diffused by the 1880s. Aumonier went to great lengths to judge the effect of his work *in situ*. The figures were modelled at Ruabon, on a gallery erected above the clay pit at J. C. Edwards' Works so that he could study the appearance from a position sixty to seventy feet below, at the equivalent of street level. [20]

The deep red terracotta on the exterior was supplied by J.C. Edwards, but a more local firm, Gibbs & Canning of Tamworth, gained the contract for the buff lining to the interior. The great hall was lined up to the roof with terracotta, but the finest details were on a pair of archways, with the royal coat of arms being flanked by a lion and unicorn and with cherubs supporting niches. The main corridors and courts were also lined partly with terracotta, worked into panels, arcades and vaulting.

In the Assize Courts, the terracotta decoration virtually took on a life of its own, certainly beyond what the Victorians could justify as a direct expression of the structure of the building. Webb & Bell's design was well received, widely emulated and, in Birmingham, almost directly copied. Some critics were apprehensive. *The Builder* commented on the "*waxy-looking texture*" and the "*hard and cast-iron effect of the ornaments*" and were suspicious that "*the plastic character has betrayed the architect into a somewhat exuberant form of ornamentation in some places*". [21]

The construction of the Law Courts prompted an acrimonious debate concerning the relative merits of architectural ceramics in industrial cities, with discussions in the Birmingham Trades Council defending the quality of stonework on the city's major buildings and with a deputation from the Trade Society of Birmingham Stonemasons lobbying the mayor. It was claimed that the use of terracotta on the Law Courts would deprive the city of £30,000, the estimated cost of equivalent masonry work. The city's stonemasons briefly went on strike following the decision to use ceramics rather than stone. [22]

The Assize Courts is surrounded by other terracotta buildings, the most innovative being the General Hospital, built 1892-97. Again, the design was chosen through a competition assessed by Alfred Waterhouse. Henman had proved to be an advocate of terracotta largely through his concern with hygiene. He had come to specialise in hospitals after undertaking a series of Board Schools in the North East of England, the Midlands and South Wales. There may have been some personal or professional link with Waterhouse since, by the time of the competition for the General Hospital, Henman had taken into partnership Thomas Cooper who had "*held a leading position*" in Waterhouse's office. [23]

The General Hospital was symmetrical round a large forecourt. The forms of elliptical and round arches, projecting cornices and pilasters could have been drawn from Webb and Bell's work on the Assize Courts immediately opposite. They were

Fig. 2.3. Statue of Queen Victoria, by H. Bates, over the entrance of the Assize Court, 1887-91 (J.C. Edwards).

repeated, with little variation, from the gateway to the entrance portico, the balconies and the main towers. The entrance to the administrative block was decorated with large female figures representing the practices of medicine, surgery and philanthropy. Patients passed by figures symbolising the more abstract concepts of Air, Purity and Light.

Much of the terracotta decoration was worked into curving and interlacing motifs, while columns were grooved with diagonal lines. Such forms provided a loosely Romanesque or Celtic identity but also served to obscure any irregularity in the form of the blocks. Problems with warpage may have arisen as a result of Henman's decision to use dark red terracotta made by Doulton at Rowley Regis. The firing conditions for this plum-coloured and slightly vitrified material were reported as being particularly critical.

Such eccentricities were avoided in Ewan and James Harper's design for the Methodist Hall in Corporation Street, built 1899-1903.[24] They chose a complete facing of terracotta and the use of arcades of elliptically headed windows, probably to complement the Assize Courts on the other side of Corporation Street. The composition, however, was far simpler with a tall tower dividing the great hall from the smaller windowed offices to the north. The tracery with tear-drop shaped lights, the Art Nouveau-style decoration round the doorway, and the run of small columns, shell motifs and arcades forming the cornice, were modelled with a combination of rounded forms and crisply defined edges and intersections.[25]

During the 1890s several architectural practices were to develop what was virtually a Birmingham terracotta style. Frederick Martin (of the practice of Martin & Chamberlain) achieved a graduation of ornament in matching red brick and red terracotta from Ruabon, the materials being worked into dramatically original architectural forms. The library in Green Lane, Small Heath, built in 1893, was dominated by a rocket-like tower. A smaller library, at Spring Hill, dating to the same year, was also given a large tower but considerable variety was introduced into the elevations by different forms of traceried windows. The entrance archway was surmounted by the arms of the city and a datestone, while an outer surround ran up from winged beasts perched on corbels. The image was of slightly grotesque fantasy, as if to reflect the richness of knowledge and imagination awaiting the reader inside.

This free Gothic use of terracotta achieved a true originality in the Bell Edison Company Building built on the corner of Newhall Street in 1896. Within the tall arcades that articulated the elevations of the building, Martin created a graduation in decorative effects from simple moulded sections on the arches to swirling acanthus leaves in the spandrels above the gable arches. Leopard-like animals projected as keystones or wrapped themselves over balustrades (Fig. 2.4).

The Bell Edison Building marks the swan song of Martin & Chamberlain's efforts to develop a distinctive terracotta architecture for the city. By the turn of the century such a free combination of motifs and materials was regarded as the height of bad taste. Architectural fashion shifted in favour of grey stone and Neo-Classical decoration. A series of buildings were given elevations of buff terracotta modelled in a loosely Renaissance style, a major example being the Technical School designed by Essex, Nicol and Goodman, and opened in 1895.[26] The frontage of this building (now demolished), showed some reference to the Law Courts, for instance in its wide elliptical arches, but the gables and fenestration allied more with the architecture of the Low Countries.

Later work by Essex, Nicol and Goodman is even more mainstream in character, one large development being Newton Chambers in New Street. Newton & Cheatle designed in a comparable idiom, their work being seen at its most inventive in the City Arcades, dating to 1899, which incorporated figures probably modelled by

Fig. 2.4. Entrance gable, Bell, Edison Company Building, Newhall Street, Birmingham, by E. Martin, 1896 (J.C. Edwards).

W.J. Neatby of Doulton. Some turn-of-the-century buildings were given narrative decoration, the most notable example being County Buildings in Corporation Street, designed by Crouch & Butler and built 1897-9. Panels illustrating carpenters sawing and diners eating reflected the occupancy of the block by a furnishing firm and a restaurant.

The increasingly prosaic use of terracotta in Birmingham was accompanied by the rise of new manufacturers. Relatively newly established firms, such as the Hathern Station Brick & Terracotta Company, offered a highly efficient service for the hard-pushed commercial architect, allowing him to delegate some of the responsibility for the decorative detailing of his designs. Hathern gained a series of contracts to supply terracotta for public houses built around 1900. A spate of pub building and rebuilding in Birmingham involved an extensive use of ceramics, primarily to create an aura of respectability that would counter complaints from teetotallers. Birmingham's pubs traded on the architectural identity given to buildings associated with the city's Civic Gospel. As magistrates restricted the number of licences for the selling of beer, so the value of the larger pubs rose, justifying major programmes of investment. Breweries and their architects adopted richly decorated terracotta for their new facades to appease local officials who influenced the form of rebuilt or newly erected pubs through building by-laws and the need to apply to licensing justices.[27]

Most of Birmingham's terracotta-fronted pubs were designed by one firm of architects and supplied by one manufacturer. Between 1889 and 1914, twenty-six pubs built to designs by James and Lister Lea were faced with terracotta from Hathern. Architects and manufacturers developed a collaboration that bordered on system building. The principal architects were probably too busy to have qualms about delegating the detailing of their designs to draughtsmen and modellers at Hathern. The terracotta draughtsmen worked up small-scale drawings supplied from Lea's office, and developed the details of such features as scrolls and pediments, subject to large-scale drawings being forwarded to Birmingham for approval.

By the end of the century Lea had a carefully worked out formula for the composition of one of their terracotta pubs. It was adapted to each site and varied in detail to provide a semblance of individuality. If located at a road junction, a tower, terminating in a cupola or spire, might be set over the corner entrance. Oversized and steeply sided gables created a vigorous skyline that would stand out above the shallow pitched roofs and dirty chimneypots of surrounding terraces and workshops. Motifs popularised by the Queen Anne style were mingled with those derived from Northern Europe.

Birmingham's terracotta pubs perfectly reflect their date, bridging two centuries. They mark the ultimate debasement of Victorian eclecticism. Different strands of Renaissance architecture were plundered for commercial gain rather than in pursuit of any aesthetic ideal. On the other hand the use of ceramics to clad structural iron and steelwork, permitting large areas of glass and encouraging the delegation of detailed design to specialist manufacturers, heralded some of the most significant features of twentieth century construction.

Hathern charged around £300 for a small facade and up to £600 for a miniaturised Renaissance palace. At a cost of £353 the Salutation in Snow Hill, dating to 1902, was decorated with dolphins and festoons redolent of early Tudor architecture, while the £548 paid to Hathern in the same year for the Red Lion in Soho Road in Handsworth bought more imposing caryatids and 'lions sejants'.[28] Similar decorative details recur from one pub to the next but always in a slightly different size or shape. Hathern were not re-using sets of plaster mould but were respecting the ethics of high architecture by producing a unique series of details for each contract.

In contrast, the tiles and moulded faience installed inside pubs were typically stock designs. Architects perused catalogues published by the major tile firms such as Maw or Minton, and worked with company representatives to develop patterns of floor and wall tiling. The most impressive ceramics to be found inside Birmingham's pubs are the bar fronts made by Craven Dunnill. The fronts were made up of repeated sections, permitting a bar to be fabricated to any desired length and of straight or curved plan. A particularly vibrant colour contrast was achieved in their floral designs as installed in the Red Lion, Erdington, which was glazed in a combination of pink, mustard, soft grey and two shades of green (Fig. 2.5).

Fig. 2.5. Faience bar front, the Red Lion, Erdington, c.1900 (Craven Dunnill).

The colourful qualities of glazed tiling and faience were brought out into the open with a number of pub frontages. Craven Dunnill used a combination of tile, faience and mosaic for the ground floor frontage of the Dog & Duck in Aston. The riser under the central window was set with mosaic portraying a spaniel retrieving game. The upper part of this elevation was executed in Hathern's terracotta, ordered in 1900, to a simple design sketched by Matthew J. Butcher (Fig. 2.6).

The terracotta revival had been downgraded from its loftier ideals. During the latter years of the Edwardian period the material was spurned by the elite of architects and critics who rejected the idea of meaning and narrative decoration in architecture. Their attacks on terracotta could be vitriolic. A letter from P.J.

Konody, printed in the *Daily Mail* in 1908, attacked terracotta under the heading of "*The Bane of Modern Birmingham*". Konody described Webb & Bell's Assize Courts as a "*mess of ineffective ornament*" and the Municipal Technical School by Essex, Nicol & Goodman as "*an absurd jumble of incompatible styles*".[29]

Such bigotry contrasts with the integrity shown by architects such as Henman or Webb & Bell. The commitment of William Henman to a broadly comprehensible architecture is presented by his explanation of the design for the General Hospital. It serves to summarise the significance of Birmingham's terracotta in developing a decorative architecture appropriate to the industrial and urbanised age. Henman stated that "*my approach has been to adopt the spirit and the letter of ancient work, to make the buildings a living monument of the time in which we live, using the materials determined upon in a sensible and legitimate manner without despising modern methods of construction. (My) plan has been to first determine what seems most appropriate to the requirement of the institution, and then to cause ornamental features to grow naturally out of the construction, or so to place them as to emphasise particular parts while preserving the general unity of the scheme*".[30]

Fig. 2.6. The faience, tile and mosaic bar front of the Dog & Duck, Aston by M. Butcher, 1900 (Craven Dunnill and Hathern).

REFERENCES

1 This text draws upon a paper and tour notes presented at a day course titled "Ceramic City: The Use of Terracotta in Birmingham" held at the University of Birmingham on Saturday 7 March 1987, organised jointly by the University and the Victorian Society.
2 R.A. Armstrong, *Henry William Crosskey,* Birmingham, Cornish Brothers, 1895, p.245.
3 J.T. Bunce, p.107.
4 *Birmingham Weekly Post,* 9 April 1881.
5 L. Jewitt, pp.244-5.
6 *British Clayworker,* 11, 1902, p.10.
7 *British Clayworker,* 1, 1892, p.189; 14, 1905, p.56.
8 *Art Journal,* 4, 1852, p.254; *Brick and Pottery Trades Journal,* 4, 1902, pp.66-7.
9 E. Gosse, p.158.
10 Hathernware, *Hathernware 1874-1974,* 1974. A Centenary Booklet that provided a brief history of the firm.
11 For further information on the regional distribution of the terracotta industry see Michael Stratton, 1986.
12 R. Dixon and S. Muthesius, p.239.
13 The Victorian Society (West Midlands Group), "The Best Buildings in the Neighbourhood?" *Martin & Chamberlain and the Birmingham Board Schools,* May 1968, unpaged (in Birmingham Central Reference Library, Local Studies).
14 Advertisement, *Academy Architecture,* 9, 1896, unpaged.
15 Resentment centred on the high 5% commission that Martin & Chamberlain received, though most of the Board appreciated that they were paying for architects of some distinction. *Daily Gazette,* 5 April 1878.
16 A. Briggs, p.111.
17 *Birmingham Weekly Post,* 10 November 1883.
18 *Builder,* 50, 1886, p.301, 51, 1886, pp.151-3, 5, p.649.
19 *Builder,* 51, 1886, p.151-3.
20 Most reports on the Assize Courts provide details on the delegation of sculptural design work to decorative artists. For example see *Builder,* 57, 1889, p.442.
21 *Builder,* 59, 1890, pp.338-9.
22 *Building News,* 51, 1886, pp.401-2, 479-10.
23 *British Clayworker,* 10, 1901, p.LXVI.
24 Ewan Harper was architect to a large number of Wesleyan Trusts. Obituary, *Birmingham Weekly Post,* 7 February 1920.
25 The source of this fine modelling is not clear. Gibbs & Canning had been credited with supplying the terracotta. However, there are contract drawings for windows, the cornice and the tower in the archive of Ketley Brickworks, Brierley Hill. Ref. 771-3-7, Staffordshire Record Office.
26 *Builder,* 69, 1895, p.467.
27 A. Crawford, M. Dunn, R. Thorne, pp.5-8, 10, 36.
28 Hathern Order Book, 1902 (Held in the archives of the Ironbridge Gorge Museum).
29 Letter originally published in *Daily Mail,* 3 November 1908. Reprinted in *British Clayworker,* 17, 1908, pp.260-1.
30 *Birmingham Daily Post,* 18 July 1897, p.7.

BIBLIOGRAPHY

A. Briggs, *History of Birmingham,* vol.2, Oxford University Press, 1952.
J.T. Bunce, *History of the Corporation,* vol.2, Corporation of Birmingham, 1885.
A. Crawford, M. Dunn, R. Thorne, *Birmingham Pubs 1880-1939,* Alan Sutton, 1986.
R. Dixon and S. Muthesius, *Victorian Architecture,* Thames & Hudson, 1978.

E. Gosse (ed. D. Eyles), *Sir Henry Doulton,* Hutchinson, 1970.
L. Jewitt, *The Ceramic Art of Great Britain,* P.P.B. Minet, Chicheley Revised Edition, 1971.
M. Stratton, "The Terracotta Industry: Its Distribution, Manufacturing Processes and Products", *Industrial Archaeology Review,* vol.8 no.2, 1986, pp.194-214.

FURTHER READING

W. Furnival, *Leadless Decorative Tiles and Mosaic,* Stone, 1904.
J. Hawkins, *The Poole Potteries,* Barrie & Jenkins, 1980.

CHAPTER 3

THE ARCHITECTURE OF BOURNVILLE 1879 – 1914

Peter Atkins

Bournville, which rightly occupies a position of major importance in the history of the model housing estate in Britain, providing as it did, an exemplar on which Garden Cities and even some Council Estates were later based, came into existence when George Cadbury and his brother Richard moved their Chocolate and Cocoa Manufactory out into the country, from Birmingham, in 1879. The site had been acquired when the land of Bournbrook Hall, four miles to the south-west of Birmingham, was sold in the summer of 1878, and lay west of the small village of Stirchley along what was then called Oak Lane, now Bournville Lane. To the north it was bounded by a small stream, the Bourn. From that direction the Hall was approached by a tree-lined avenue, The Drive. (Fig.3.1).

Fellow industrialists considered Cadbury's move financially risky,[1] yet it was, after all, similar to that made by Salt when he moved his workers from Bradford to Saltaire in the 1850s. Furthermore, the land at Bournbrook had the advantage of two lines of communication at its eastern edge, i.e. the Worcester-Birmingham Canal and the Birmingham West Suburban Railway. The canal proved useful immediately, for materials for the factory were brought along it.

The first housing on the site was for the foremen of the factory, and was begun in the autumn of 1879. The "Manager's residence and fourteen cottages"[2] of this first phase were sound but unremarkable late Victorian houses by the architect George Gadd, and the last of them survived, embedded among the factory buildings, until 1983.

This small estate was at first to be called Bournbrook, but by the October of 1879 the name Bournville had been decided upon. The brothers liked its French overtones, and as "*French chocolate was then looked upon as the best,*"[3] found this a commercially right name for advertising their wares.

Between 1880 and 1895 George Cadbury further pursued his interest in housing and buildings of social use. Both the brothers were devoted members of the Society of Friends and George especially became concerned with the provision of decent housing for working men, which he considered should be in the country.

The influence of the Society in furthering this aim cannot be underestimated. Cadbury acquired land both in Stirchley and at Northfield (about two miles south west of Bournville) and at both places Institutes which contained Friends' Meeting Houses were built alongside groups of cottages. At Stirchley the cottages came first, a substantial row being erected on Hazelwell Street and the Pershore Road in 1885, possibly by the Birmingham firm of Martin & Chamberlain, the Institute following in 1891. That same year saw both the Institute and six cottages built in Church Road, Northfield. These Institutes provided places for both adult and child education, harmless social amusements (there was a skittle alley at Northfield), and the strict provision against the sale of alcohol promoted the Quaker ideal of temperance. The cottages at Northfield are of fundamental importance for what was to follow. Their architecture reflects the discovery of regional vernacular style and they are, in fact, typical country estate cottages of the period such as could be found in Worcestershire and Warwickshire.[4] The architect of both Institute and cottages was William Doubleday.

1891 seems to have marked the date when Cadbury came not only to develop his especial architectural preference for vernacular style, but also to realise his ideal of placing houses in rural surroundings. His later chosen architect, W.A. Harvey, wrote that Cadbury placed great value upon "*the cultivation of the soil (which) is certainly the best antidote to the sedentary occupations of those working in large towns*".[5]

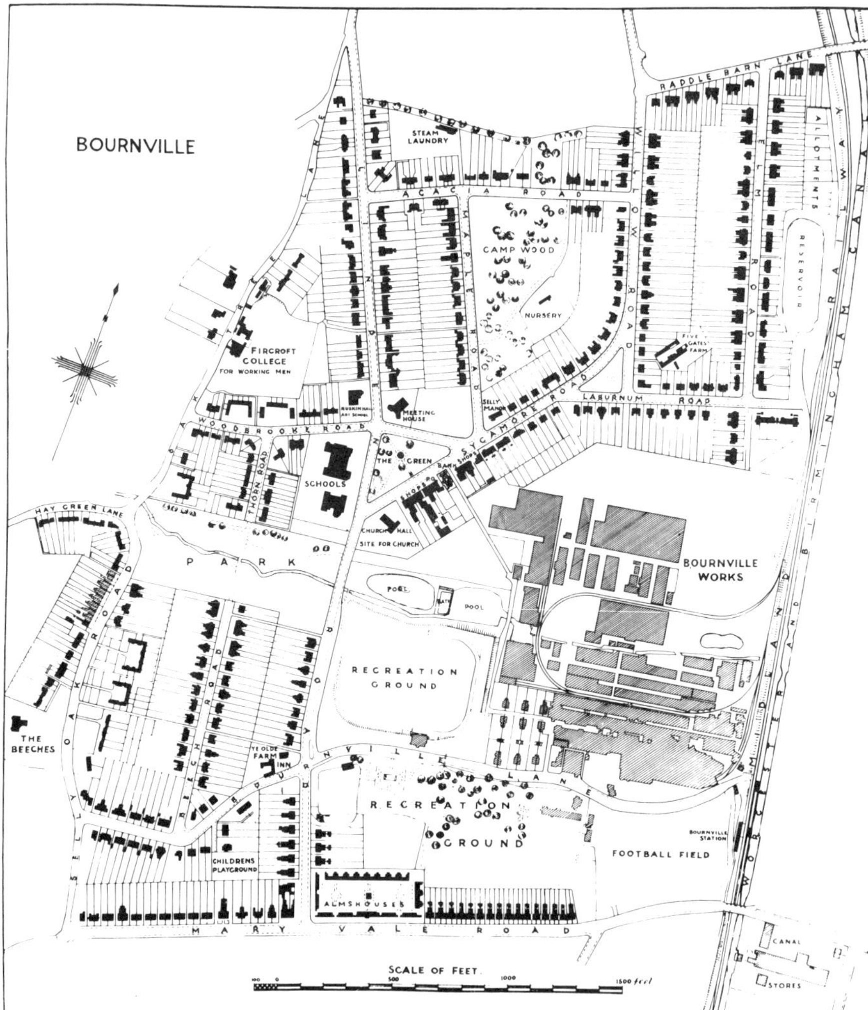

Fig. 3.1. Map of Bournville Development by 1914. Reproduced from P. Henslowe, *Ninety Years on: An Account of the Bournville Village Trust,* 1984, by kind permission of the author and the Bournville Village Trust.

The earliest Bournville houses had large gardens. By 1892 the Northfield cottages were set in an eighth of an acre each and were built in widely-spaced, semi-detached pairs. Even today the area has an atmosphere of countryside about it. (Fig.3.2) These cottages pre-dated by four years what George Cadbury was to create at Bournville proper, the land for which he began to purchase only in 1893.

Fig. 3.2. Church Road, Northfield. The cottages of 1891. Nos. 3-4. William Doubleday, architect.

The building of Bournville village began in 1895, and the first houses arose on the north side of Maryvale Road, which lay along the ridge south of Bournbrook Hall. The new houses lay between Linden Road (which continued the line of The Drive), and Selly Oak Road, or Row Heath Lane as it was then named.

George Cadbury employed as architect Alfred P. Walker, who designed three blocks, designated (in ascending size order) 'A', 'B' and 'C'. They are average for the period, 'B' having some vernacular overtones, but 'C' being floridly decorated. Whether Walker planned any further designs is unknown. A drawing for a large, semi-detached house on The Drive shows him looking back to the style of George Gadd, though his Estate Office in Bournville Lane is a pleasing, robust little building of Tudor style. Walker designed no further buildings in Bournville after 1895, though continuing to work as a surveyor on the Estate.

His place as principal house designer was taken by a much younger man, William Alexander Harvey (1875-1951), who was just twenty. Harvey came from an artistic background, his father and brother Ernest being stained glass painters.[6] The family had travelled in Europe and he had been educated in France, Germany and Italy. By 1894 they had settled at 45 George Street West, on the north side of Birmingham. His main architectural training was with the Birmingham Arts and Crafts architect, W.H. Bidlake.[7] In May 1895 Harvey designed a small block of shops and houses in Stirchley, by the September was working for George Cadbury (he witnessed the agreement to build Walker's houses), and by the December had designed an impressive block of four three-storey houses for Bournville Lane (Fig.3.3). This was commissioned by George Cadbury, received UDC approval on December 15th and then was shortly afterwards cancelled. The reasons remain obscure. However, the design is already confident and the drawing itself pleasing to the eye. Already too, we can see typical features such as the roof being brought down low over the bedroom windows, while some of the detailing reappeared in houses designed for Maryvale Road in January 1896.[8]

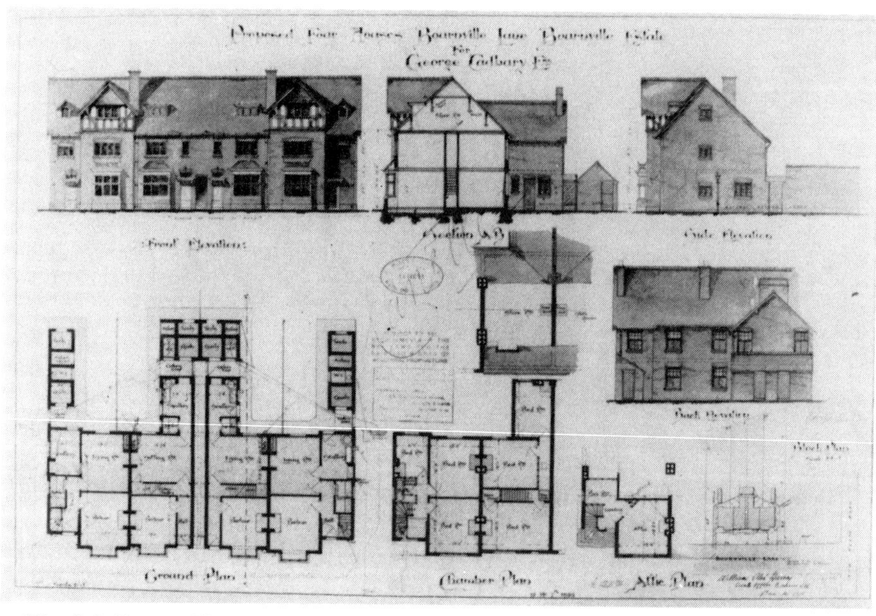

Fig. 3.3. Bournville Lane, Bournville. Unbuilt design, Dec. 1895. W.A. Harvey architect. Reproduced with the permission of P. Henslowe/Bournville Village Trust.

Harvey worked in Bournville, eventually appointed Estate Architect, until the spring of 1904 when he resigned to devote himself to his private practice. He lived in Bournville until 1919 but after that was often called upon to design new buildings or to advise on repairs or additions so that, by 1935 (the date of the arcade at St. Francis' Church) he had been an influence on Bournville for nearly forty years.

In 1896 building (Fig.3.4) was progressing along Maryvale Road, in Bournville Lane, Selly Oak Road and the west side of the southern part of Linden Road. Harvey designed the majority of the houses but clients were not obliged to employ him so that, in all of these roads, there is more than one house by other architects. In accordance with the guidelines laid down by George Cadbury when founding the Estate, all plans had to be approved by the architect of the Estate, so that presumably Harvey (though not officially designated as such yet) oversaw all these plans. These other architects were generally local men, though George Punshon, architect of a Bournville Lane house, lived near Hinckley. The designs are typical of the time, ranging from the straightforward to the flamboyant, as with Francis Andrews' four houses, also in Bournville Lane.

Fig. 3.4. Maryvale Road, Bournville. Nos. 250-252. March 1896.
W.A. Harvey, architect.

George Cadbury's name rarely appears as the applicant for these early houses. It was his lessees and subsequent householders who commissioned the architects, and the surviving documents tell us something of the people who were moving into the new village. With a few exceptions they came from within Birmingham and would all have been described as thrifty working men, who could afford to take out a mortgage (2½% if they put down a 50% deposit), the sort of resident Cadbury hoped to attract. It was not necessary to work for Cadbury to buy or rent a house in Bournville, in which respect it differed from any manufacturer's estate that had gone before.

Of the houses by Harvey in Maryvale Road in 1896, all but one pair, commissioned by George Cadbury, were for private clients. The first were Nos. 238-240 designed in January 1896 and on these appear bay windows and porched doors with fanlights over, fairly certainly derived from the unbuilt Bournville Lane block. The building time for these houses was generally between five to seven months.

George Cadbury's first large commission to Harvey was for a group of sixteen houses in Selly Oak Road, while another was for washing baths in the small right-of-way (now Laurel Grove) off Bournville Lane (Fig.3.5). This was a means by which the absence of a bathroom in some houses was remedied. Some of these early Bournville houses had bathrooms from the start, therefore their presence or absence must reflect what the individual client was willing to pay.

Fig. 3.5. Laurel Grove, Bournville. Lodge and Washing Baths. July 1896. W.A. Harvey, architect.

Building now continued apace. All of Beech Road but two blocks was designed in September 1897, building continued in Bournville Lane and houses were begun on the north east side of the village in Elm and Laburnum Roads. The first shops, the half-timbered block (apparently derived from a typical market house) were built on the Linden Road/Maryvale Road corner site, while the same day in January 1897 saw the application made to build the Almshouses across the road. This was Richard Cadbury's particular interest, though George Cadbury was the applicant. The architect was Ewen Harper. The pace of building was maintained during 1898 with numbers of houses ranging from two to fifty under construction in ten separate areas. Raddlebarn Road, where houses occupy only the south side, was completely built in this period. In the village as a whole, apart from a couple of unascribed houses, all these buildings were by Harvey, in addition to which he added the elegant little post-office to Northfield Institute. The rate of new building slowed in the next two years, although important things were realised. In particular, further shops in Maryvale Road were built and the ten very decorative houses in Holly Drive (now Grove) near the railway, which were apparently intended to arouse interest in Bournville among passing travellers.

As the nineteenth century ended and Bournville began to take shape, it is interesting to look at Harvey's development. He was only twenty five at this time. Beginning with a simple brick vernacular he moved rapidly on to formulate a style that was assimilated from a genuine interest in, especially, English architecture of the 16-17th centuries and the influence of contemporaries such as Crouch and Butler[9] and, of course, Bidlake, from whom he learned much, I feel, about sensitivity to materials.

By the late 1890's Harvey's style was both picturesque yet practical (Fig. 3.6). His own house near the brow of the hill in the northern half of Linden Road is typical in this respect with its roofs sweeping low over the eaves and becoming of shallow pitch towards them, rafter ends exposed and visible behind the sinuous iron curlicues holding up the guttering, purlins likewise exposed and the gable ends themselves on brackets, in addition to which it has a half-timbered boxroom built over the entrance porch in the angle of the facade. Two features are purely decorative - the half-timbering in the gables and the brick angle buttresses. The house, furthermore, demonstrates his ability to make semi-detached houses into a repeating unit, suggestive rather of one house with a courtyard in front. The low roof line shelters the upstairs windows and saves the expense of extra brickwork, its change of angle lessens the impact of rain and the half-timber porch and room would not have the problems that arise when timbering is only decorative. Above all, whatever the cost or style of the house, Harvey aimed to provide a sound structure of good materials, adequately provided with means of heating, water supplies, drainage and storage space.

Fig. 3.6. Linden Road, Bournville. Nos.24-26. March 1898. W.A. Harvey, architect, 24 being his own house.

Half-timbering became less frequent in Harvey's work, although used convincingly as late as 1909 and, in a paper of 1904, *Cottage Homes*[10] (delivered to the Birmingham Architectural Association), he spoke against it. It is noticeable that his later use of the material developed what we have seen in 1898, isolating it from the brick structure as a stair tower or bay windows.

At the end of the 1890's, his most obvious influences were Shaw and Voysey.[11] It is not necessary to pre-suppose a personal acquaintance. He may have known them but, in any case, the occasional publication of their work in *'The Studio'* would have provided a good pictorial source of inspiration. The Shaw-Voysey influence is at its strongest in the Holly Grove houses and in the later shops and houses in Maryvale Road.

Fig. 3.7. Linden Road, Bournville. Nos. 8-14. March 1904.
W.A. Harvey, architect.

After 1903, all these influences subsumed into a plainer, but relaxed mature style, the best example of which is the group of eight houses along the west side of Linden Road, south of its Oak Tree Lane junction. (Fig. 3.7) These were designed in March 1904 and seem to be the last houses by Harvey as Estate Architect, before leaving to run his private practice. They show an assured mixing of forms that he had identified as his, including hipped roofs, contrasting forms of tiling, white roughcast contrasted with brick, segmental window arches, and (on the central pair of houses) a three-part window with Palladian echoes. All these elements, plus others of eighteenth century origin, had already appeared in his houses in Maple and Acacia Roads and continued to be part of his style until World War I.

At the same time he could still design the simplest brick cottage (Fig. 3.8) with as much quiet elegance as he gave to large private houses; witness the ten cottages (in three blocks) on the west side of Selly Oak Road, designed in late 1902, but which assumed the simplicity of two of his earliest (opposite) of June 1896.

Fig. 3.8. Selly Oak Road, Bournville. Nos. 48-50. December 1902.
W.A. Harvey, architect.

By the time of Harvey's departure as Estate Architect, Bournville had been for nearly three and a half years run by its own Village Trust (set up in late 1900) and having its own Deed of Foundation. The formation of the Trust effectively marked the transformation of Bournville from a Building Estate into a Garden Village, and Bournville was the appropriate venue for the first Garden City Association Conference in 1901. Just after this date the village began to acquire its first large public buildings, Ruskin Hall (which became the Art School), designed by Harvey in 1902, and the school, the drawings for which were made in November 1903 (but the application to build only in August 1904) along with the Friends' Meeting House.

The style of all remained faithful to elements of Gothic, Tudor and early 17th century English architecture. Ruskin Hall adhered most closely to a period style whereas the other two were more inventive. A relationship of the design of the Meeting House facade to that of Edgar Wood's Church of Christ Scientist at Droylesdon has been pointed out, but a comparison shows that it is one of external outline rather than anything else.[12] Wood's composition is reversed and his almost expressionist accentuation of form removed by Harvey. The building appears rather rooted in the English past, or should we say pasts? - the large west window is of Tudor, the main door of Romanesque inspiration, yet the two co-exist quite well together.

The design of the school even better illustrates what Remo Granelli, in speaking of Harvey's houses, has characterized as *"details and features of different periods brought together. . . . .in contentedly unresolved confusion".* [13] For example, the classrooms have large, functional windows of slightly Georgian appearance,[14] other windows being of Tudor inspiration and all the major doors Gothic arches with ornamental rustication.

Fig. 3.9. Thorn Road, Bournville. Nos. 20-22-24. January 1909.
H.B. Tylor, architect.

It was the largest building Harvey had yet designed and its plan followed that generally used for schools at this time, the classrooms opening from the main hall. The boys and male teachers had their cloakrooms and toilets grouped on the north-west corner, the corresponding rooms for the girls and female staff being at the south-east corner, and the teachers' staff rooms also followed this arrangement, as did the placing of the entrances for the two sexes. The building was given a dramatic visual accent by the large tower which rose castle keep-like at the south-east angle but which had a practical function, containing the library, the laboratory, and having on its flat roof a topograph from which the children would learn their local geography. The north-west corner of the school repeated a suggestion of the bulk of the tower, but at a lower level.

From 1904-14 Bournville housing continued under the direction of Harvey's assistant and successor, Henry Bedford Tylor. His houses are plainer than those of

Harvey, but still attain an individual style, features of which are exposed rafter ends and roofs brought low over upstairs windows, long segmental arch mouldings across whole facades, gables of curved form, and deep porches and verandahs on timber posts (Fig.3.9). Like Harvey, he also introduced windows of Palladian form on occasion. Elm Road was completed by him and he built housing in

Fig. 3.10. Woodlands Park Road, Bournville. (Bournville Tenants Estate) Nos. 12-14. December 1906. H.B. Tylor, architect.

Linden, Thorn and the new Woodbrooke Roads, also in the Bournville Tenants Estate, which began about a mile to the south west in 1906, and where he built four houses in Woodlands Park Road (Fig.3.10). Apart from four by David Glass, the rest in Northfield, Kingsley and Hawthorne Roads are by Harvey, who had now entered a new phase much indebted to English houses of the 17th century and later, using roofs of steep pitch, tall chimneys sometimes turned diagonally to the house and sometimes linked by arches into a monumental form astride the roof ridge. Exposed rafter ends give place to neat rows of brick dentils immediately below the gutter line, and similar treatment is found in gables, while flat barge-boarding also appears on some of these houses. Half-timbering, as noted before, is used only for complete units such as stair towers. A definite language of form exists throughout these years and up to 1914, similar forms emerged in buildings of dissimilar use. The domestic style becomes a paradigm, house-like features appear in public buildings and features from a large structure such as the Infants School (Fig. 3.11), designed in 1909, echo the contemporary houses of Hawthorne Road (Fig. 3.12). They are linked too by the use of brindled Staffordshire brick,[15] which gave Harvey variety of colour and also produced walls of

Fig. 3.11. Linden Road, Bournville. The Infants' School. September 1909. W.A. Harvey, architect.

Fig. 3.12. Hawthorne Road, Bournville. (Bournville Tenants Estate) Nos. 1-3-5. March 1909. W.A. Harvey, architect.

strong, weather-resistant quality. He used them for the lower courses of walls in Estate houses, but for the entire walls in his private commissions, such as the house for Mr. Archibald in Oak Tree Lane of 1907 (Fig. 3.13).

During these years Harvey was also responsible for the dismantling, bringing to Bournville and reconstruction there of the largely mediaeval Selly Manor, which stood about a mile away; an exercise in restoration which he carefully documented in photographs.[16] Harvey, in addition, created one building based on a definite prototype - the Rest House on the Village Green, modelled on the late mediaeval market house at Dunster in Somerset and a Silver Wedding gift by the Village to George and Elizabeth Cadbury. This was completed by the May of 1914.

The historic centre of Bournville was now nearly complete and photographs of the 1900s show that it already had its familiar well-tree'd appearance.[17] Tylor's last houses were private commissions in Woodlands Park Road. He died early in 1915, his death depriving Bournville of its second estate architect. Harvey was largely occupied with work for the Ministry of Defence. It comes as a surprise when we look back to realise that, by the autumn of 1914, only thirty five years had gone by since the first houses were begun, that nineteen years had seen the development of the village and that the greater part had been the work of two architects.

Fig. 3.13. Oak Tree Lane, Bournville. No. 172. House for George H. Archibald. June 1907. W.A. Harvey, architect.

REFERENCES

1 This is mentioned in A.G. Gardiner, p.35. No specific people are cited. The same is echoed in I. Williams, p.56. It was considered risky because Cadbury was moving away from his main source of labour and from the easy supply of raw materials.
2 Borough Surveyor's Records, Kings Norton UDC Building Register, Plan 403, Oct. 16, 1879.
3 I.A. Williams, p.58.
4 A.G. Gardiner suggests, op.cit., that George Cadbury's interest in the rural cottage as the best form of working class housing may have been aroused by his staying occasionally in the 1860s at a cottage near Bittel Reservoir.
5 W.A. Harvey, p.5.
6 Ernest Harvey was involved with the firm of Ashby & Harvey. John Harvey, father, was recorded in *Hulley's Directory* of 1876-7 as working on his own as a glass painter at 24 Icknield Street East.
7 It may have been at evening classes given by Bidlake. No certain evidence to substantiate this theory can be found.
8 For example, porches and their iron curlicue supports, the fanlights over porches and the style of some of the bay windows which, were square bays with three lights and mullions over, as illustrated in Figs. 3.3, 3.4.
9 Mention by R. Granelli, ibid. They were evidently a general influence as they were the chief architects practising in Arts and Crafts style in Birmingham (although incorporating traces of earlier English motifs such as half timbering), along with Bidlake, when Harvey began. Harvey later worked on a housing estate (executed) at Oldham in collaboration with Joseph Crouch. This was one of seven post-Bournville estates in which Harvey had a part. The others were at West Bromwich, Kettering, Newburn-on-Tyne, Widnes, Bromsgrove, and part of the Calthorpe Estate, Edgbaston. These are listed in an obituary notice in *RIBA Journal,* vol.58, April 1951, pp.247-248.
10 In typescript in Birmingham Architectural Association papers 1902-4 (Birmingham and Five Counties Architectural Association Library, Margaret Street, Birmingham).
11 There is no documentary evidence to link these architects with Harvey, although stylistic comparisons can be drawn. For example, from Shaw, half timbering, the use of rough cast and windows with small leaded panes. From Voysey, similar features, the use of brackets to support guttering, the white painting of rough cast and corner butresses. Voysey's style showed beautifully in Harvey's drawings for the shops of 1899 in Maryvale Road, which are held in Bournville Village Trust archives.
12 R. Granelli mentions this comparison in *By Hammer and Hand,* p.57.
13 R. Granelli, ibid.
14 A drawing of the school in *The Model Village* (Fig. 7) shows the classroom windows with their centre lights under pointed arches. The architect's original drawings for the elevations of this building do not appear to survive.
15 Mentioned by Harvey in *Cottage Homes,* p.17.
16 These photographs are preserved in albums kept at Minworth Greaves Hall, Bournville.
17 In addition to the preservation of existing trees on the site, as at Camp Wood, the roads were bordered with trees and eight apple and pear trees were usually planted in the back garden of each house. See *The Model Village,* p.24.

BIBLIOGRAPHY

Borough Surveyor's Records. Building Registers, Kings Norton UDC/Kings Norton and Northfield UDC/Birmingham, 1879-1914.

A.G. Gardiner, *The Life of George Cadbury,* Cassell & Co. 1923.

R. Granelli in A. Crawford (ed.) *By Hammer and Hand: The Arts and Crafts Movement in Birmingham,* Birmingham Museums and Art Gallery, 1984.

W.A. Harvey, *Cottage Homes,* Birmingham Architectural Association papers, 1902-4 (unpublished).

W.A. Harvey, *The Model Village and its Cottages: Bournville,* Batsford, 1906.

P. Henslowe, *Ninety Years On: An Account of the Bournville Village Trust,* Bournville Village Trust, 1984.

I. Williams, *The Firm of Cadbury 1831-1931,* Contable & Co. 1931.

CHAPTER 4

BIRMINGHAM ART SCHOOL: ITS BRANCH SCHOOLS AND FEMALE STUDENTS 1880–1900

John Swift

This study addresses a period of rapid growth in art school education and training. In common with many art schools, Birmingham had to satisfy apparently conflicting requirements - the local manufacturers' needs for more artistic workpeople and more proficient designers, the initial and further qualification of art teachers, the teaching of drawing to all local elementary Board Schools, and the personal fulfilment of middle class students pursuing studies for their intrinsic value.

Between 1880 and 1900 Birmingham Art School changed its location and size, its financial status, and its theoretical and practical education. The constants were the majority of the Management Committee, its headteacher, Edward R. Taylor, and the ubiquitous National Syllabus of the Department of Science and Art (DSA). The growth of the School was rapid. Within twenty years one Central School, temporarily housed in the Birmingham Midland Institute, and six Branch Schools,[1] had developed into a new purpose-built and extended building with fifteen Branch Schools.[2] Student numbers grew from c.1,320 in 1880 to 4,268 in 1900, with over 1,300 attending the Central School.[3] In 1880 the combined staff of the schools numbered 23, of whom most were part-time and by 1900, 87 staff were in post, over 50 being part-time. The representation of female staff had increased from 4% of 23 to 9% of 87, with 9 further women teaching the female art-pupil teachers classes.[4] Throughout the period, Birmingham was the largest art school in Britain.

The status of the School changed from one typically supported by grants from the Government's DSA, subscriptions, and student fees, to that of a municipal art school. The changed responsibility towards the new 'owners' - the ratepayers of Birmingham, with the DSA having an examining and quality control role, led to an increase in independence. This was marked by more local entry scholarships, further liaison with local industries, a tendency to challenge the DSA over appropriate art and design education, and the development of the Arts and Crafts Movement into an educational practice. The latter had a significant effect on the role and success of female students in the Art School.

The Arts and Crafts Movement could be described as distancing itself from established authorities and their manifestations, questioning the equation between economic success and industrial mechanisation, and being ambiguously linked with social reform. It might be considered odd that Birmingham Art School embraced such a policy whilst being set in a multiplicity of manufacturing industries. The explanation lies in the fact that many influential 'art industrialists', and some politicians and philanthropists were followers of Ruskin, and collectors of Pre-Raphaelite and Arts and Crafts work.[5] Many of the above had aligned themselves with the 'Civic Gospel', and were members of the various committees that amongst other things approved and directed policy for the Art School.

To develop artists as craftspeople and vice versa, a change in art educational methods was effected by Edward Taylor and his supportive committee. The change was both attitudinal and practical - the latter involving executing designs in the materials for which they were intended. The 'hands-on' argument for design was not new. It had been attempted in the early Schools of Design, but now it was a widespread movement with powerful and articulate proponents. Whilst too much designing in art schools was non-specific - designing in the abstract - with no precise outcome or materials in mind, this had begun to change before 1880. It was common to find students drawing, painting, designing for specified materials on paper,[6] and modelling[7] in most large art schools, but to find no evidence of crafting in materials, or any real understanding of design's technical consequences. Birmingham was the innovative Art School in introducing executed design.

The Growth of Executed Design at Birmingham Art School, with Specific Reference to Female Students.

From a small beginning when students were designing in the Central Art School and making the object at their work-place in the 1880s,[8] a steady (if small) increase is discernible, mostly in *repoussé* work until the 1890s. Although a number of local manufacturers (some of whom were School of Art Management Sub-Committee members) offered prizes, initially these were rarely for applied or executed design. Most were for drawing or for two-dimensional designs where technical understanding was less important.[9] In 1883, plans for the new Art School contained no practical workshops; each space was designated on traditional lines.[10]

When the new building opened in 1885 as the first municipal Art School in the country, it appointed a new modelling master who happened to be a *repoussé* expert, attracted prizes for modelling for *repoussé*, and a year later proposed actual technical instruction in the area,[11] which by 1887-1888 had been recognised as a prize category.[12]

1889 was an important year in that it saw Walter Crane's *Examiners Report* on the School, the Technical Instruction Act, proposals for a technical teaching class in Birmingham's Jewellery Quarter, and further moves to extend the new Art School building. Crane's *Report* praised the School's work, in that it considered design in relationship to materials and usage, and not surprisingly suggested that the School should extend its established *"workshops...where students might familiarise themselves with methods and materials, and practise some of the simpler forms of handicraft".*[13] Crane's suggestions both confirmed and encouraged the Birmingham School's ambitions.

The Technical Instruction Act affected the more elementary level of the science and art classes, prohibiting the teaching of a trade or industry in the guise of manual instruction, but making modelling obligatory at elementary art levels i.e. in all Branch Schools.[14]

The success of the Birmingham Jewellers and Silversmiths Association (BJSA) joint-class at Ellen Street Branch School led to a larger and more appropriate property in the Jewellery Quarter on Vittoria Street, where space was requested *"for teaching processes".*[15] The BJSA's willingness to fund a practice already close to the committee's heart, resulted in a classroom for teaching the processes of, *"engraving, enamelling, chasing, embossing in high relief, die-sinking, applied wire ornamentation, carving, lapidary work, damascening..... "*[16]

The intention to extend the new building was taken not only in terms of increasing student numbers,[17] but also to realise the implications of Crane's *Report*, to build on the practical tuition of jewellery students, and to extend the success of executed design work in outside competitions.[18] With the opening of the Vittoria Street Branch School and the extension of the Central School a few years later, a burst of activity was occasioned.[19] In March 1891, Taylor had made more radical proposals, specifically, "*proper facilities....to carry out....designs in (i) Repoussé and kindred subjects e.g. niello, chasing, etching and engraving on metal, damascening and filigree (ii) Enamelling: Cloisonné, Champlevé and Limoges, and (iii) Wood-carving, wood-engraving, needlework, terracotta, encaustic painting, the making of decorative cartoons, and working in fresco, tempera and sgraffito etc.*" [20]

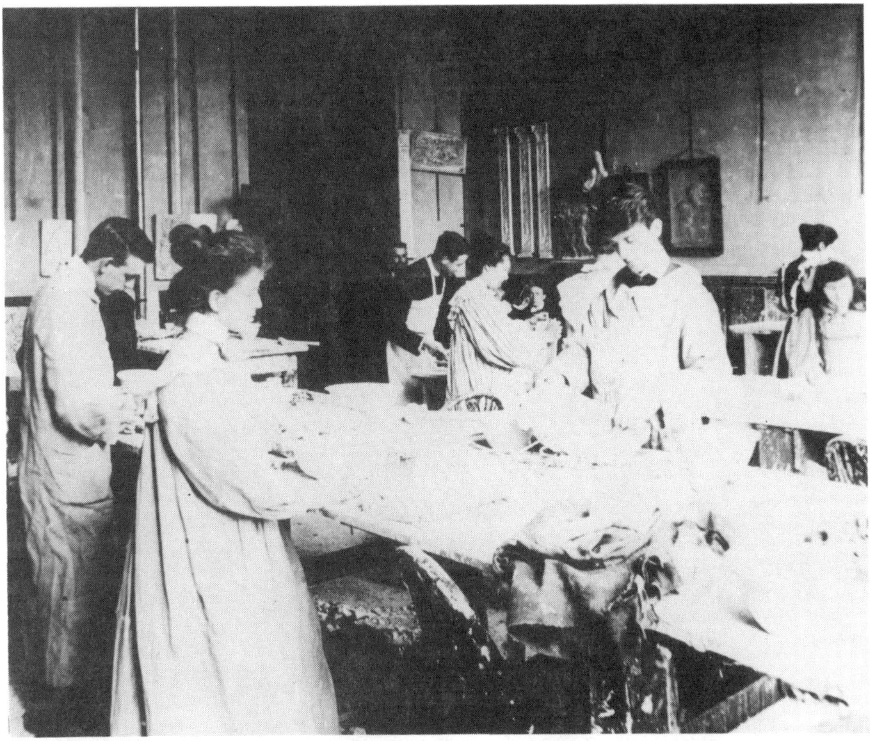

Fig. 4.1. The modelling and casting room c.1900. Linked with the Art Laboratories these were upgraded to allow students to cast, mould and complete their work in the Art School.

Rough plans accompanied the proposals with space allotted for two Art Laboratories (workshops) in the basement linked with the modelling and casting rooms (Fig. 4.1), and a cartoon and fresco room (Fig. 4.2) on the first floor.[21] The extension opened in September 1893, by which time appointments for embroidery/ needlework, wood-engraving, and enamelling had been made, and equipment ordered for a wide variety of crafts. [22]

Most of this activity was initially linked with the local metal trades, but some was not. Many crafts were introduced as a result of Arts and Crafts enthusiasm and predeliction e.g. the stained glass, mural work and book illustration. This flavour was acceptable to many clients and the large number of illustrated books, the commissions for interior decoration and fittings including murals, glass and many other crafts, are testimony to the taste of the new, wealthy middle class patron, especially around the Birmingham area. However, when the same style and work ethic was transposed into small or large commercial workplaces, especially in the metal trades, the result was different. We know from a few existing records and on stylistic grounds that only four or five local metal manufacturers actively welcomed the Birmingham School's approach to commercial needs, and this is hardly surprising if the students took with them the typical Arts and Crafts aversion to machine manufacture.[23]

The effect of the increase in executed design work through craft practice, and the stylistic and philosophical influence on students was varied. Elementary level students i.e. apprentices, free admission and scholarship pupils at Branch Schools, would have little experience in executing designs (apart from at Vittoria Street where practical working was customary) and would not necessarily have absorbed an Arts and Crafts ethos. Vittoria Street Branch School had a narrower and direct relationship with the surrounding metal trades, and arguably was less Arts and Crafts in style or ethos initially. Advanced classes at the Central School (i.e. more experienced artisans and designers) might have had more difficulty as they would have been taught by staff with beliefs unlikely to find sympathy with the majority of local metal industries.[24]

Fig. 4.2. The cartoon and figure design studio c.1900, where fresco, tempera, oil painting and other techniques were studied, involving actual commissions wherever possible.

Fig. 4.3. Florence Camm. Still-life study, watercolour, 1897. One of a series of still-life studies probably made for examination for either Stage 14 or 15, both of which allowed for colour study of still-life groups.

Fig. 4.4. Florence Camm. Portrait, watercolour, 1899. One of a series of paintings from life, it was successfully submitted for examination for Stage 17b (The human figure or animals in colour from nature) at South Kensington.

Fig. 4.5. Metal workshop, c.1900: part of the Art Laboratories.

The mixture of class attendance, personal and professional needs, and the novelty of the Arts and Crafts emphasis affected student number, background and purpose. Typical earlier patterns of art school students reveal a large number of subsidised or free elementary level pupils and evening-only artisans, with a much smaller number of advanced students, of which a large section were trainee teachers, teachers taking further qualifications, and people studying for pleasure. Art schools had taken care to increase their advanced level student number, for reasons of esteem and finance.[25] Many of the advanced students studying at the Central School were women. Most of these would have been from middle class backgrounds and some were the daughters of local 'art industrialists'. As such they probably had a superior (or at least a broader) education than the typical artisan or ex-Branch or Board School scholar. Female students at the Branch Schools were in the minority, and generally trade-related or working class. The 'pleasure classes' could be relatively free from the DSA's regulations. It was common to find their names appearing on registers over long periods of time as their interests changed and their skills developed.[26]

What is slightly unexpected is the degree of enthusiasm and success with which they embraced executed design. Whereas predictably many still-life, (Fig. 4.3) flower, and portrait works (Fig. 4.4), especially in watercolour, were won by female students, it would not follow that working manually, with what could be described as trade materials, would similarly engage their interest. Whilst partly confirming Callen's findings, that Arts and Crafts women generally worked in 'feminine' crafts, the students at Birmingham worked across a wider range, thus appearing to partly counter the socially-determined and conflicting roles of 'woman' and 'artist', and 'lady' and 'work'. [27] (See Appendices 1 & 2).

There is a discernible growth in the success of female students for local prizes in art, and in designing on paper. Until the extension opened, many female students were prize-winners in the traditional areas of drawing, painting and modelling, with design skills slowly evolving.[28] After 1894, new prizes were introduced for outstanding advanced art and design work and, whilst the average percentage for female art work fluctuated between 40% and 60%, with a peak of 74% in 1899-1900, the prizes for paper designing were consistently in the mid 60 percentile.[29]

The growth of local prizes for executed designs from 1890 onwards, is even more surprising. Ranging from 40% to 100%, the prizes won by female students between 1890 and 1900 numbered 74% of the 157 listed awards. Outside bodies' awards repeated the tendency e.g. the Armourers and Braziers Awards from 1890 to 1893 showed female students winning 47% of the executed design prizes; the Arts and Crafts Exhibition of 1893, 58% of all executed designs; and the Paris Exhibition of 1901, 77% of all executed designs.[30]

Given this successful female student competitiveness, what crafts did they succeed in, and how far do the crafts confirm or deny Callen's thesis of feminine activities?

The c.307 listings for executed design undertaken by female students reveal that 54% was combined metalwork and enamelling, specifically 40% for a variety of metal crafts (Fig. 4.5) and 14% for the three main types of enamelling (Fig.4.6); 28% was needlework and embroidery; 7% was gesso; 5% was book illustration and prints (Fig. 4.7). The remaining 6% was spread fairly evenly over vase decoration, fan painting, *grisaille* (glass painting) (Fig.4.8), leather work, and carving (usually plaster, but also wood and ivory).

There were many other activities and, that female students were not mentioned specifically, does not necessarily indicate that they did not undertake them. Some areas, although practised, were rarely undertaken by Birmingham students during this period e.g. mosaic, terracotta, ceramic murals, stained glass, poster designs, bookbinding, and metal casting. Some were normally practised at an elementary level e.g. chipped metal and die-sinking, leaving a few areas where perhaps male-dominated trades inhibited female acceptance e.g. cabinet and furniture making, iron foundry work, stone carving, and house painting (male only class).

Finally, what effect did Birmingham's female successes have on the School and its branches, and its Arts and Crafts emphasis have in general?

Fig. 4.6. Enamelling workshop c.1900: part of the Art Laboratories.
Louis Joseph - enamelling master.

Fig. 4.7. Florence Camm. Book Illustration, 1898. Probably illustrating a detail from the Arthurian legends, the study was successfully entered for examination for Stage 23d (Advanced Design).

Whilst the School was proud of its local, national and even international success due to its innovatory teaching of design through execution, much of it due to its middle class female student population, it had made no attempt to rectify its staffing imbalance.[31] In 1899, 9% of the Central School staff were women, and the same percentage was found in the 15 Branch Schools. Only in the Branch School for female trainee teachers was it different where 9 female assistant teachers outnumbered the 1 male master-in-charge.[32]

The success of female students had disturbed two of the external examiners. Both W.J. Wainwright's and W.R. Lethaby's comments from 1897 to 1900 reflected an unease at so many 'amateurs' winning so many prizes. Wainwright commented on the preponderance of personal ornament in gold, silver and jewellery work.[33] Whilst such items were not exceptional, one suspects that it was the gender of the maker that most disturbed him, a point picked up the following year by the new examiner, W.R. Lethaby. He was concerned by the number of amateur 'prize-gainers'[34] winning awards planned for artisans.[35] His solution was to make every class trade-related i.e. specifically directed towards occupation. This would have had the effect of removing almost all of the female students from most of the

Fig. 4.8. Florence Camm. Design for Stained Glass window, 1899. The cartoon depicts Francis of Assisi. This work was entered for the National Competition in 1899, gaining an Honourable Mention.

executed design classes. Lethaby used the terms 'ladies' and 'amateur' in a way which leaves one with little doubt that "*special classes should not be for a floating population of amateurs....but....should....be for those in the trade....and other serious students*". [36] Despite the pointed suggestion, Birmingham neither responded nor reacted. I doubt whether this was the result of enlightenment, I suspect it was due to the fear of losing prestige, fees, and the support of the 'art industrialists' whose daughters were part of this group, and remained so for several decades following.

The Birmingham School of Art's overall success was important in several ways. It helped to redirect the national system of examining and teaching design. [37] In September 1894, the DSA's Directory had been modified to allow a wide range of craft activities from 1895, but with a curious proviso: "*the Department would accept for examination....designs carried out in various materials....as long as the work was submitted to fully illustrate or explain the original drawn, painted or modelled design*". [38] Thus, whether they wished or not, art schools were obliged to continue the presentation paper or clay designs, with the executed designs in their actual materials serving as illustrations or explanations. The first DSA award for executed design was given one year earlier than regulated for, to two female Birmingham students.[39]

Locally the School had developed 15 branches, 2 of which were unusual. Moseley Road was purpose-built, opening in 1899, and Vittoria Street had particular links with the local metal and jewellery trades. The other 13 were in rooms rented from the City's Board School Committee. Nationally, Birmingham became a model for other art schools, initially Leicester and London, and internationally its reputation grew.[40] The School was the Midlands centre and focus of a strong and virile Arts and Crafts Movement,[41] where a policy of collaborative Arts and Crafts ventures between staff and students was generated and continued during the first two decades of the following century.

Tension over the DSA's central control had grown with the municipalisation of the Art School. Financial autonomy had not been matched by educational independence. However, although the School was to fight for and gather an increasing and untypical independence in its teaching style, content and method, it remained typical in its approach to its female students and staff. Although the School's national fame arose in part from the success of its middle class female students working within an Arts and Crafts practice, the majority of its students were elementary level rather than advanced, and consisted of school-aged children, apprentices, trade-released designers, and teachers, most of the above being classed as 'artisans' by the School. [42] The advanced sector and its middle class element was both a minority and a largely female minority. The School was happy to maintain their number and activity, but their untypicality clashed with an increasing pressure to meet trade requirements. The pattern remained for approximately another twenty years, by which time designing more closely allied to industrial expectation and mechanisation had begun to replace the 'pure' Arts and Crafts belief.

An uneasy tension was maintained between the opposing beliefs by the inheritor of Taylor's empire, Robert Catterson-Smith, his firm Arts and Crafts tendencies becoming increasingly modified by the need to meet local industries needs. As the needs were met, so the Arts and Crafts' manual emphasis diminished, and so did the number of successes of middle class female students in executed design work.

APPENDIX 1. BEGINNING AND GROWTH OF EXECUTED DESIGN AREAS

EXECUTED AREA	80–85	85–90	90–92	92–94	94–96	96–98	98–1900
3D METAL							
Repousse	M	M	MF	MF	MF	MF	MF
Embossed			M				MF
Engraved	M		MF		MF	MF	MF
Etched			MF	MF		MF	MF
Carved							MF
Pierced				MF			MF
Chased			M		MF	MF	MF
Foundry Work					M		M
Casting						M	M
3D OTHER							
Vase Decoration			F				
Carving (Wood)				M	MF	MF	MF
Carving (Stone)						M	
Terra Cotta					MF	MF	
Cabinet/Furniture					M		M
Die Sinking						M	
Iron Work					M		M
Bookbinding					MF	MF	
COMBINED							
Caskets						MF	MF
Jewellery					MF	MF	MF
Ornam. Books							MF
2D TEXTILES							
Needlework			F	F	F	F	F
Embroidery				F	F	F	F
Linen				F		F	F
Silk				F		F	F
Lace							F
Stencil/Print				F	F	F	F
2D PRINT							
Book Illustration				MF		MF	MF
Wood Cuts				MF	MF		
Wood Engraving					MF	MF	MF
Etching				F			
Lithography					MF		
Poster Design						MF	MF
2D OTHER							
Gesso				MF	MF	MF	MF
Painted Panels			F	F		MF	
Oil Painting						MF	
Mural Painting				MF	MF	MF	MF
Decorative Cartoons			MF	MF	MF	MF	MF
Fan Painting				F			
House Painting						M	M
Enamelling				MF	MF	MF	MF
Ceramic Murals						MF	MF
Stained Glass					MF	MF	MF
Leatherwork				MF	MF	MF	MF

*M = Male; F = Female. Information extracted from Minute Books 1880-1900. The non continuation of certain crafts may not be accurate. Craft examples, usually via Prizes, Awards or Examiners' Reports had to be mentioned to be included, therefore their absence does not necessarily indicate their termination.

APPENDIX 2. PRIZES AND AWARDS TO FEMALE STUDENTS

	FEMALE LOCAL PRIZES					FEMALE NATIONAL PRIZES					
YEAR	ART AND DESIGN		PAPER DES	EXEC DES		MEDALS, A & DES		NBPs of DSA* DES		OTHER EXEC DESIGNS	
	%	NOS	%	%	NOS	%	NOS	%	NOS	%	NOS
1880-81	16	36	0	–	–	18	16	0	16	0	2
1881-82	14	29	0	–	–	26	19	0	19	–	–
1882-83	24	38	0	–	–	19	21	0	21	–	–
1883-84	32	41	2	–	–	35	31	0	31	–	–
1884-85											
1885-86											
1886-87	26	31	9	–	–						
1887-88	32	47	13	0	2						
1888-89	30	39	10	0	1	–	30	–	–	–	–
1889-90											
1890-91	24	67	10	40	5					47	21
1891-92	43	23	26	95	20	42	47	48	35	–	–
1892-93	27	26	27	87	15	35	52	63	27	58	31
1893-94	45	42	–	86	7	44	81	64	39	–	–
1894-95	47	15	67	70	10	22	76	33	30	–	–
1895-96	63	19	62	57	7						
1896-97	41	34	93	40	15						
1897-98	49	39	65	100	19						
1898-99	38	52	–	74	19	–	76	–	–	–	–
1899-00	74	23	–	81	37	–	90	–	–	77	13
				74	157					55	67

*NBPs of DSA: National Book Prizes of the Department of Science and Art.

REFERENCES

1 'Central' referred to the more advanced teaching, 'branch' to the more elementary - thus the branch schools fed the central school. In 1880 all the branch schools consisted of rented rooms in Birmingham's School Board elementary schools.

2 Two were untypical in that one was jointly run by trade and another purpose built. Vittoria Street School for Jewellers and Silversmiths opened in 1890, and Moseley Road Branch School opened in 1899.

3 Some of the 1,300 were elementary students having gained admission by competitive scholarships offered by the School and various legacies.

4 *Birmingham Society of Arts and School of Art Minutes (BSASA)* Volume 14, 1881-1884, p.9; and *Birmingham Municipal School of Art Management Sub-Committee Minutes (BMSAMSC)*, vol. 22, 1897-1900, appended 273-274 & 94, pp.7-8.

5 J. Swift, p.14.

6 The *"designs for specified materials"* included *"certificates, wallpaper, fans and stained glass, to jewellery, silverware"*, utensils, and rooms containing the above. Such prizes for *"designs for"* continue throughout the twenty years under scrutiny and form an increasingly specific and numerous feature of Birmingham's prize lists.

7 "Modelling" involved the manipulation of clay and other materials in figurative or ornamental work. Whilst the students handled the materials, they did not understand anything of the firing, casting or mould-making necessary. The model would be sent to specialists and returned completed. Equally, the modelled designs could be intended for a wide variety of different materials with different characteristics, but nothing apart from lectures on technical matters informed students' awareness of the implications of this.

8 *BSASA*, vol. 14, 1881-1884, p.58.

9 Ibid., pp.100-101. The committee noted that *"the nature of the designs asked for no special knowledge of the difficulties of construction..."* (adding) *"to the weight of proof that the ill success of art students in ordinary design, as applied to manufactures, is due in large measure to their want of technical knowledge....the student must be brought by some means or other into close proximity with the workshop."*

10 *BMSAMSC*, vol.20, 1890-1893, appended 69-71. The plan of the proposed extension

shows the usage in 1891, demonstrating the traditional titling of space. The new building was designed by John Henry Chamberlain, a long-time friend, supporter, and committee member of the art school, to personify a Ruskinian view of nature and naturalness as the source of artwork. Thus the stone carvings, terracotta decorations, glazed tiles and mosaic work were intended to reveal a sensorial and primary exploration of Nature, as opposed to the historicised and conventionalised sources advised by the Government's regulatory body.

11 *BMSAMSC,* vol.18, 1885-1888, p.111. The first master specialist in *repoussé* work was Thomas Spall, a designer for Elkington & Co.

12 Ibid., p.268. The prize list for 1887-1888 offered a J.H. Chamberlain Memorial Medal for *"two designs for a door plate modelled or executed in repoussé."*

13 *BMSAMSC,* vol.19, 1888-1890, appended 215, p.28 & *BMSAMSC* vol.20, op.cit., appended 111, p.7.

14 *BMSAMSC,* vol.19, ibid., appended 223, pp.4-5. Technical instruction *"shall not include the teaching of any trade or industry or employment.... the expression 'manual instruction' shall mean instruction in the use of tools, processes of agriculture, and modelling in clay, wood and other materials."*

15 Ibid., pp.237-240.

16 *BMSAMSC,* vol.20, op.cit., pp.7-12.

17 From 5 branch schools in 1884, the number had risen to 11 by 1891. The consequent pressure for places at the Central School demanded more space.

18 *BMSAMSC,* vol.20, op.cit., p.6. In the Armourers and Braziers Exhibition of May, 1890, Birmingham students won 8 prizes for executed design, three by female students, in *repoussé*, engraved, etched, chased, and embossed metalwork and brasswork.

19 *Ibid,* appended 15, pp.5, 8-9. The *Report* describes increases in numbers, Board School drawing supervision and teaching, the growing number of Branch Schools, the proposed opening of Vittoria Street School for Jewellers and Silversmiths, and the increase in free admissions and types of students attending as reasons for the new extension.

20 Ibid., appended 69.

21 Ibid., appended 70 (3 sheets).

22 *BMSAMSC,* vol.21, 1893-1897, pp.208, 233, 267, also appended 255-256. Mary Newill, Bernard Sleigh and Louis Joseph had been appointed to teach emboridery, wood engraving and enamelling respectively. New equipment had been ordered for enamelling, annealing, etching, lithography, wrought and beaten ironwork, terracotta, glazing and stained glass work, and carpentry.

23 See A. Crawford (ed.), pp.33-4, 110-118.

24 It is difficult to be precise. Records linking students to workplaces are rare and one would still need evidence of any short or long-term effect.

25 Many art schools earlier in the 19th century had been in danger of bankruptcy; the lesson would have been learned.

26 One such long-attender was Florence Camm who, with her brothers and sisters, were students at the art school. A daughter of the local stained glass firm of T.W. Camm & Co. Florence undertook an enormous variety of art and craft activities, eventually specialising more in painted/stained glass. She was registered as a student from 1892, almost continually until 1912.

27 A. Callen, pp.218-221.

28 Until 1884 a maximum of 2% of female students had won design prizes, although their success in pictorial art had grown from 16% to 32% in four years. Whilst the percentage of overall prizes increased from c.30% to over 40% by 1893-1894, the design prize percentage had increased to 27%.

29 Birmingham awards from the DSA, although not completely documented, show a parallel growth, from 18% to 35% to 44% in 1880, 1883, and 1893 respectively. The female prizewinners in design rose from zero for the first two years to 64% in 1893.

30 *BMSAMSC,* vols.14, 18, 19, 20, 21 and 22 - figures extracted from details of Prize Lists, Awards and other documents.

31 There had been a national financial inducement to employ young students to teach at elementary level, and/or in branch schools, but the proportion of young female students so appointed remained disproportionately low.

32 *BMSAMSC,* vol.22, 1897-1900, appended 94, pp.7-8.

33 Ibid., appended 140, pp.6-8.

34 Ibid., p.7.

35 Ibid., p.6.
36 Ibid., p.12.
37 *BMSAMSC,* vol.21, op.cit., appended 276, pp.9-10.
38 Ibid., appended 52.
39 Ibid., appended 84, pp.14-24. Local executed design categories were ironwork, engraving on metal, *repoussé,* woodcarving, woodcuts, stencilling, needlework, leatherwork, gesso, and enamelling; 70% of which were won by female students. The DSA awards totalled 76, of which 30 were for design, 14 being won by female students. The two executed design awards were for a gesso design and *'an etching from nature'.* The latter term is rather confusing - it could refer to an etching on metal, i.e. metalwork or to a print, e.g. in A. Crawford, op.cit., pp.157-160, it is stated that by 1895 illustrated works had been published by Birmingham artists, one book being directed by A.J. Gaskin and comprising of fellow staff and student work. Quite apart from the Kelmscott links, by 1890 over 70 books had been illustrated by Birmingham's Arts and Crafts workers, most of whom were staff or students at the art school.
40 *BMSAMSC,* vol.22, op.cit., pp.255, 289-291. Executed design work was requested for the 1901 Paris International Exhibition. 13 were selected of which 10 were by women, in crafts as diverse as wood carving, chased copper, *champlevé* enamel, gesso, silver *repoussé,* steelwork, lace, needlework, and embroidery. Glasgow requested works accompanied by preparatory studies and designs, "*and any other such work... (which will)...illustrate the course or courses of study pursued*".
41 See A. Crawford, op.cit. For example pp.27-30, 37-39, 43, 62-65 ff, 85-86, 90-93, 103 ff, 120-128.
42 *BMSAMSC,* vol.20, op.cit., appended 15, pp.5, 8-9. "*All the students at the Branch Schools are artisans, and the great majority of them directly apply to their trade the knowledge which they acquire in the classes. Most of the students of the Central School also are artisans... (including)...architects, builders, designers for all local manufacturers, artists in stained glass, brassworkers, die sinkers, modellers, lithographers, draughtsmen, machinists, persons in training to become art teachers, etc.....at Ellen Street...a special class...(of 155 students)... for the Jewellers and Silversmiths Association... (and)...over 300 female Pupil and Candidate Pupil Teachers at Bristol Street Board School*".

BIBLIOGRAPHY

A.Callen, *Angels in the Studio,* Astragal, 1979.
A. Crawford (ed.), *By Hammer and Hand: The Arts and Crafts Movement in Birmingham,* Birmingham Museums and Art Gallery, 1984.
School of Art Archive, Birmingham Polytechnic.
J. Swift, "Birmingham and its Art School: Changing Views 1800-1921", *Journal of Art and Design Education,* vol.7, no.1, 1988.

FURTHER READING

(Birmingham)

The Art Student, 1886-1887, Birmingham Art School staff/student magazine.
Birmingham Museums and Art Gallery catalogues.
J. Muirhead (ed.), *Birmingham Institutions,* Cornish Brothers, 1911.
E.R. Taylor, *Drawing and Design,* MacMillan, 1893.
E.R. Taylor, *Elementary Art Teaching,* Chapman & Hall, 1890.

(General)

Centenary publications of Coventry, Hornsey, Manchester and Sheffield Art Schools.
R. Carline, *Draw They Must,* Arnold, 1968.
S. MacDonald, *The History and Philosophy of Art Education,* University of London Press, 1970.
G. Sutton, *Artisan or Artist?* Pergamon, 1967.
J. Swift, *The Birmingham School of Art Archives 1880-1900,* exhibition catalogue, Birmingham Polytechnic, 1989.
J. Swift, *The Role of Drawing and Memory Drawing in English Art Education 1800-1980,* unpublished Ph.D thesis, Birmingham Polytechnic, 1983.

CHAPTER 5

CONTEMPORARY CRAFTS AND THE GUILD OF WEST MIDLANDS ARTISTS AND CRAFTSMEN LTD.

Derek Fontaine

Mention 'crafts' to the average person and s/he immediately forms a picture of smock-clad craftworkers, serenely working at a slow pace in a country workshop, with a background of idyllic countryside and the clucking of free-range hens around the back door.

While this may be reality for the fortunate few, the majority of today's craft-workers are where they have been since the Middle Ages or before: in small towns and cities, in work-shops in their homes or backyards, or in small light industrial work-shops. Nothing much has changed in a continuous cycle, waxing and waning in time with the cycles of prosperity in each successive century, each generation of craftworkers believing they can succeed where others have failed.

Mediaeval Guilds represented the common interests of masters and skilled workers within individual trades, being both trades unions and marketing bodies. In time, more ambitious masters became entrepreneurs and merchants, less concerned with the craft and more concerned with turnover and profit. As the merchants' interests expanded, the corporate strength of the Guilds weakened, eventually leading to the collapse of the craftsman-led workshop system and its replacement by the factory system and the industrialisation of the late seventeenth century.[1] Only a few Guilds still retained a corporate strength, like the Gold-smith's Company.

The Victorian revival of craft Guilds grew out of the ideas of Ruskin and William Morris mixed with the Pre-Raphaelite Group's preoccupation with the romance of the Middle Ages. Their consequent revival of the Mediaeval studio tradition was a reaction against the factory system, coupled with a wish to practise a benign form of paternalistic Socialism. This led to the birth of the Arts and Craft Movement, bringing skilled craftsmen and enthusiastic amateurs together in the celebration of a respect for Mediaeval craft traditions, coupled with imaginative self-expression, leading to an increased public awareness of the designer-craftsman relationship.

The Art Workers' Guild founded an annual exhibition in which each exhibit carried the names of both the craftsman and the designer, meeting with the enthus-iastic approval of critics and public as demonstrating the new 'artistic Socialism'. Throughout the country many philanthropic bodies ran Arts and Crafts classes and workshops for amateurs in both city and country areas. Some of these turned into small workshops producing goods for sale, leading to accusations that to include 'Guild' in the title of a shop gave an unfair commercial advantage in terms of free publicity in local newspapers.[2] The modern equivalent is the gift shop which calls itself a 'Craft Gallery' but sells cheap souvenirs made and imported from the Far East.

The most famous of the Arts and Crafts workshops, like De Morgan's Art Pottery and Ashbee's Guild of Handicraft, disappeared in insolvency, because they were run on romantic artistic and social experimental lines, rather than with sound business sense. The Birmingham Guild of Handicrafts fared better as it was administered by volunteers from the local business community. It was run as a self-supporting Co-operative Workshop, becoming a limited company in 1895.[3] The aim of the Guild was *"to supply hand-made articles superior in beauty and design and soundness of workmanship to those made by machinery; and to make only such as will give pleasure both to the craftsman and to the buyer of them."*[4] The Guild produced a diversity of crafts, furniture, printing and publishing, the latter mainly for members of the Birmingham Group, Gaskin *et al.* The Group followed in the footsteps of Burne-Jones and the Pre-Raphaelite tradition of King Arthur and the Quest for the Holy Grail.

In 1906 the Guild amalgamated with Gittens Craftsmen Ltd, a firm producing light fittings and door furniture designed in the Arts and Crafts style. Between 1906 and the 1920s, the Guild turned to cast metalwork, gates, railings and other architectural metalwork. This represents the remorseless progression from artist-craftsman to production worker, which has so often proved necessary for a firm's survival.[5] It finally became a successful firm making metal window frames. A similar history is attached to The Allied Arts & Crafts Guild, a combination of designers and craftsmen, artists, sculptors, masons and plasterers which was based in Charlotte Street, Birmingham. It had a large half-page advertisement in the *Studio Yearbook of Decorative Art* in 1924.

The 'Mediaeval Mystery' that attracted the Victorian artist/craftworker led to the romantic idea of a 'religious order of artists' founded on christian ideals to be reflected in the honest workmanship of its members. This kind of christian-artistic community is typified by The Guild of St. Joseph and St. Dominic at Ditchley in Sussex, which was made famous (some might say notorious) by its association with Eric Gill, who was one of its main springs until he quarrelled over money and left for Capel-y-ffin in the Brecon Beacons. The Ditchley community and others such as the Guildhouse at Stanton and Blackberry Hill, still survive today as a cross between a rural craft work-shop and a religious retreat, the latter an establishment run by a Quaker family on the philosophy that a reflective peace leads to the quiet contemplation that helps creativity. This connection between crafts and inner peace gained strength once again after World War 2 and received yet more converts during the mid seventies, when the disillusionment caused by the collapse of the world economy, together with the growing anti-war movement, led many to follow the ideals of an alternative economic life style, seeking once more that Golden Age that never really existed.[6]

Crafts and the Craftsperson

According to the 1983 Crafts Council report *Working in Crafts,*[7] no-one really knew exactly how many people were practising a craft or in exactly what proportion these practitioners would consider themselves as professionals, as so many had to rely on alternative forms of income. This lack of information was to a certain extent remedied by the Crafts Council survey. Their researchers made a brave attempt to obtain the facts, arriving at an estimated total of 20,000 craft-workers throughout England and Wales, excluding employees in craft businesses. Out of these 20,000, 6.8% (or 1,360) craftworkers were estimated to be serving the 10.5% of the nation's population represented by the West Midlands' population of 5.136 millions. This was, I believe, an under-estimation of the true number. The report painstakingly defines various categories of craftworkers, relatively few of which could make a comfortable full-time living from their craft alone, *"since prices for work cannot often be commensurate with the labour involved."*

Selling their work is the most difficult problem facing craftworkers, probably up to 50% will start through craft fairs and exhibitions, which are the main sales outlets for many part-time workers. The late seventies saw a phenomenal growth of craft fairs, supplementing the annual exhibitions long organised by established craft guilds, and the network of shops selling crafts ranging from tourist souvenir shops to craft galleries. All of these began to attract a wider cross-section of the public. Some fairs were organised by alternative communities to fund their new life-styles, others by professional organisers, who saw a way of making a living by serving the needs of enthusiastic, but often hopelessly unbusinesslike, new converts to crafts as a career. These craft fairs offer a way for the craftworker to meet the public and by doing so generate new commissions. However, appearing at a craft fair can be a limiting factor as some craftworkers discover they may be forced economically to limit their designs to an attractive but fairly safe, traditional product. This will sell at a low price and will ensure enough sales to both cover the day's expenses and provide a living. Craft fair fees are considerably more, *pro rata*, than the conventional markets with which they are often identified.

Fig. 5.1. Jill Devine, glassmaker. 'Angel' Perfume Bottles, 1980s, cased colour, freeblown with 'pinched' decoration, sandblasted and acid-polished.

A look at the readers' letters in *The Craftsman* shows that craftworkers are keenly aware that they must respond to the pressures of the market-place and that they do not wish to rely on state aid for support. In 1983 the participants in the Crafts Council survey were asked how they felt about their own attitudes to craft work and the public's perception of crafts. Opinion was equally divided between craftworkers who felt that work was only worth producing if it was readily saleable and those who felt work should be done for its own sake, despite the fact that it may never be sold. There was a genuine concern that traditional skills were being lost because they were deemed no longer viable by the cost accountant.

It is a sobering thought that many of the intricate pieces of Victorian glass made at Stourbridge and now admired in museums all over the world, were too expensive to be saleable at the time they were made. Much of the skill that went into their making has been lost in the streamlined production of the modern glass-house. Some of these skills are now being rediscovered by the studio glassmaker, who in turn is being invited to share this knowledge with the trade. By 1983, even the most optimistic craftworker felt their public image was dismally low, a complex mixture of being regarded as an anachronism in a modern age and 'if you enjoy your work, it must be a hobby so you shouldn't expect to get paid'. This image can still be projected onto the craftworker as "*the little man down the street from whom you can get something cheaper.*"[8]

Since this report reflecting the situation in 1983, the situation has got marginally better. The status of the 'artist-craftworker' is more widely recognised, thanks largely to more informed coverage in the quality press and to the proliferation of craft fairs and festivals of the better sort, such as Crafts in Action at Waterperry House, near Oxford, where the public can watch working demonstrations of craft skills. This doesn't mean that earning a living by craftwork has become any easier, but commissions can now be expected from a much wider cross-section of the public. Architects and public bodies are more likely nowadays to commission works to embellish their building. Although the American idea of allocating 1% of the budget of a new building for artworks has yet to be adopted widely here, it is reported that a sum of this nature has been allocated to the decoration of the new Birmingham Convention Centre. Britain and Europe are following the American trends in raising the status of the artist-craftworker above that of the more traditional craftworker. The end result is more likely to be a decorative art-object than a decorative but potentially useful product.

There are many more sales outlets in the West Midlands now than in 1983, varying from new craft centres, where the public may see the craftworker in action, such as the Jinney-Ring at Hartlebury, the Ridware Arts Centre, Hatton Craft Centre, Winyates Craft Centre and the Museum at Bewdley, to new craft galleries like the Stafford Art Gallery, Centre Crafts at Coventry and Ombersley Gallery near Worcester. Some attempts to bring crafts to Birmingham failed, like the Birmingham Craft Centre in the Old Square. Others moved away to greener pastures, like the Collection Gallery at Ledbury, which started life at Quinton, but some have stayed on to succeed like the Jewellery Workshop in the Great Western Arcade, which was first started as a co-operative sales venture by Diane and Bob Cross in Harborne. It then transferred to the re-furbished Great Western Arcade, where they have been joined by Glassmark, which sells studio glass, something that would not have been viable in 1983, as this area of the market has only developed in the last few years. Exhibitions of internationally known artists organised by the Midlands Arts Centre at Cannon Hill plus these galleries and craft-centres, and others too numerous to mention, have helped the West Midlands craftworkers through difficult times by marketing the more unusual, expensive work. As a measure of the growing confidence in the arts in the West Midlands, one might point to the growing number of interior design practices which have started up over the last few years, which are uniquely placed to help the craft-worker by commissioning work.

During this century many guilds have been formed by craftworkers determined to help themselves by forming co-operative marketing groups. During the thirties there were guilds formed in East Sussex in 1931, Somerset and Gloucestershire in 1933, and Welwyn Craftworkers Guild during the post-war revival in 1945, although many crafts were encouraged during the war e.g. basket-makers turning out cycle baskets for the home market and parachute baskets for dropping supplies

Fig. 5.2. Derek Fontaine, glass engraver. Crystal Vase, 1985, engraved using diamond drills and wheels, commissioned by Austin Rover and presented to the Standard Motor Company of India to commemorate the launch of the Stampro car displayed on the Madras Golf Course.

to the Resistance. Worcestershire Guild of Artist-Craftsmen started in the fifties together with similar guilds in Norfolk, Devon, the Lake District and Herefordshire.[9] Many more came in the sixties and seventies, including extra societies in Gloucestershire and Herefordshire. The degree of sophistication in the financing and administration of any one craft guild is less important than the fact that they all, large or small, focus interest in craftwork and keep alive the traditions and creative drive.[10]

The Guild of West Midlands Artists and Craftsmen

The Guild of West Midlands Artists and Craftsmen Ltd is one of the latest on the crafts scene. It was first formed in 1978 to serve the needs of those craftworkers unable to join neighbouring county guilds as they were outside their catchment area. The widest interpretation of 'West Midlands' was allowed, firstly, in order to bring together the best talents which could be found without having too much duplication of crafts and to ensure a good social mix and, secondly, because the Guild's events cover a wide area between Lichfield, Leamington Spa and Malvern, due to the scarcity of suitable venues.

The ratio of female to male members is roughly 2 to 1. There are 5 jewellers, 6 potters, 11 working in textiles (although in many different forms), 6 toymakers, 6 painters, 5 glassworkers (each in a different way), 2 leatherworkers, 6 woodworkers and other assorted craftworkers. The membership is generally limited to 5 in any one category to avoid over-duplication. As it is rare for all members to attend the same craft fair, any spare space is offered to guest craftworkers who are on the waiting list for membership. The aims are strikingly similar to those of the original Birmingham Guild of Handicrafts - i.e. to form a showcase for its members' work, to help correct the popular view that skills, handed down through the years, are disappearing for ever and to demonstrate that a considerable number of skills still survive in our society.

The Guild became a non-profit-making Limited Company in 1987, employing a manager to organise its craft fairs on a profit-sharing basis. The Guild's share is used for the members' benefit, being spent on corporate packaging, publicity and the finance of exhibitions such as the *Annual Summer Exhibition* at Dinham House Craft Gallery in the historic town of Ludlow. This is timed to coincide with the influx of visitors for the Festival. The 60-odd members also play their part in the furtherance of craft education by arranging demonstrations and 'hands-on' experience (where appropriate) to children in schools. Some of these events have lasted up to one full week, as did the 1989 visit to Blackwood Middle School, Streetly. Here, Guild members demonstrated, gave talks on their crafts to the children during the week and laid on the exhibition for the parents at the weekend.

In the world of modern crafts, the Guild members' work leans as much towards our traditional heritage as to the avant garde, although many members have a foot in both worlds. Silversmith Ken Palmer B.Ed., F.R.P.S. is a prime example. He has produced a range of stylish silver trophies for organisations such as the Minolta Camera Company and the Midland Counties Photographic Federation, and yet he can also produce traditional 1/12 scale silver artefacts for collectors of dolls house miniatures which are eagerly sought after in Germany and other countries.

Peter Cosentino is well-known in the ceramics world. While teaching at schools and evening classes, he set up his own home studio. He later launched a full-time studio in Birmingham incorporating his own gallery. In 1981 he was appointed Lecturer in Ceramics at Milton Keynes College. He has since written two extremely successful books on the techniques of pottery[11] and his work is shown in a wide number of galleries. His work is quite distinctive, some pieces being

Fig. 5.3. Derek Fontaine engraving glassware with a flexible drive dental drill, 1980s.

sculptured with incised lines separating overlapping areas of pastel colour. Others are organic in shape, often inspired by naturalistic forms like fungi and plant seeds, these may be glazed on oxides, or smoke-fired to produce rich patinas and vari-coloured surfaces.

Jill Devine is one of the breed of studio glassmakers, producing exciting work of her own design in the Glass Foundry at Royal Brierley Crystal at Brierley Hill, where she demonstrates the art of glassmaking to visitors. Her glass is free-blown crystal, (Fig. 5.1) worked hot straight from the furnace using traditional methods and tools, but the result is not to any set repetitive pattern. Each item evolves into delicate, curvilinear shapes, some cased with colour, others with splashes of colour worked in the transparent glass. Some of her glasswork is bought by visitors to the Foundry, while other pieces are snapped up by glass collectors, who believe they are collecting the antiques of the future.

Glass engraving is a traditional skill practised by the writer, who is also a Guild member, and is inspired by the example of Lawrence Whistler (Figs. 5.2, 5.3). A flexible drive dental drill is used, holding diamond-coated drills and stones to put in the broader detail. Further work may be done using tungsten steel and diamond tipped scribers for the finer detail. Textures are closely modelled on wood engraving (Figs. 5.2, 5.3).

Fig. 5.4. Anne Bracey, designer jeweller, soldering earrings in her Vyse Street workshop, c.1984.

Anne Bracey makes gold and silver jewellery, much of it to commission, in her workshop in Vyse Street in the Jewellery Quarter. (Fig. 5.4 and see chapter 6). Nearby, in Hockley, Gavin Weston, an accomplished leatherworker, runs a successful workshop-cum-craft gallery, producing beautifully finished wallets, writing cases and other functional leather ware, and at the same time selling the work of other Guild members. You can't get more traditional than a rocking horse restorer, yet Peter Watts has almost more work than he can cope with. Another woodworker, Bill Lucas, has found a market for elaborate bas-relief carvings in exotic woods, such as his mirror frame in cherry using an Ancient Egyptian motif (Figs. 5.5, 5.6).

Fig. 5.5. Bill Lucas, wood carver. Mirror Surround c.1986 in cherry wood using an Ancient Egyptian motif of a pharaoh and his queen.

The Guild has a constantly changing register of members as some craftworkers find they have acquired as much work as they can handle and drop out of the Guild to run an established business. Other members cease through their inability to make a reasonable living from their skills alone. The Crafts Council report recognised that the market has been depressed in the West Midlands due to the slow revival of the economy. In the past this has led to a migration of West Midlands' talents to London, such as Sally Greaves-Lord, (a daughter of Anthony Greaves-Lord, one of the Guild's fondly-remembered early members). Recently the Guild has been approached by some extremely talented young designers in both the graphics field and in furniture making, which augurs well for the Guild's future.

By means of its grants the Crafts Council encourages craftworkers to take risks, and produce experimental work, but no-one can depend on these grants being continued as the Council's funds are squeezed, so it may be that the more down-to-earth market-orientated approach forced on the West Midlands' craftworker is in fact the trend-setter for the future. After all, it may be significant that a much larger proportion of the art world makes a full-time living from crafts than from art. That there is a new sense of confidence in British craftwork is borne out by the introduction of contemporary crafts into the London auction rooms. Much of that work has been done in the last 20 years by craftworkers who are still working, such as the freely-handled figurative sculptured bowls by David Prytherch, the superb glass artist, now living at Stourbridge. All we need is for that confidence to be reflected by an upturn in the market-place here in the West Midlands.

Fig. 5.6. Bill Lucas. Mirror Surround in cherry wood (detail).

REFERENCES

1 G.M. Trevelyn, pp.88-91.
2 A. Crawford, p.22.
3 Ibid., p.31.
4 Ibid.
5 Ibid., pp.100-1
6 J. Lewis, p.67.
7 A. Bruce and P. Filmer, 1983.
8 Ibid., p.146.
9 J. Lewis, op.cit, chapter 6.
10 Ibid.
11 P. Cosentino, 1985; 1987.

BIBLIOGRAPHY

A. Crawford (ed.), *By Hammer and Hand: The Arts and Crafts Movement in Birmingham,* Birmingham Museums and Art Gallery, 1984.
A. Bruce and P. Filmer, *Working in Crafts: An Independent Socio-Economic Study of Craftsmen and Women in England and Wales,* London, Crafts Council, 1983.
P. Cosentino, *Creative Pottery,* London, Ebury Press, 1985.
P. Cosentino, *Potter's Project Book,* London, Windward, 1987.
J. Lewis, *Handbook of English Crafts and Craftsmen,* London, Robert Hale, 1978.
G.M. Trevelyn, *Illustrated English Social History,* vol.1, Harmondsworth, Pelican, 1964.

FURTHER READING

J. Houston (ed.), *Craft Classics Since the 1940s: An Anthology of Belief and Comment,* London, Crafts Council, 1988.
E. Lucie-Smith, *The Story of Craft: The Craftsman's Role in Society,* Oxford, Phaidon, 1981.
E. Lucie-Smith, *World of the Makers: Today's Master Craftsmen and Craftswomen,* London, Paddington Press, 1975.

CHAPTER 6

CRAFTS JEWELLERY-MAKING IN THE JEWELLERY QUARTER

Barbara Tilson interviews Anne Bracey, designer jeweller, at 81 Vyse Street.

Tilson: **Can you tell me when you trained at the Vittoria Street School, which is part of the Polytechnic now?**
Bracey: It was part of the Polytechnic when I was there but it was still known as the annexe to the Polytechnic, which we called Vitt Street - the School of Jewellery and Silversmithing. (Fig. 6.1). I trained from 1972 to 1975.
Tilson: **Was it a Degree course?**
Bracey: It was a three year City and Guilds course. It's been improved because it's a four year course now with one year out in the trade, which they didn't do in my day. It's very useful experience and something I would have liked to have done.
Tilson: **Did the School still have its own separate character at that time?**
Bracey: Yes, very much so. I think that, being so far away from the main Polytechnic, it was able to keep its own identity. Gerald Whiles became headmaster in my second year. He came from the Polytechnic, I think, and so he very much began to knit the two together, whereas Mr. Baxendale was of the 'old school' and I think he'd been headmaster for so long, prior to it ever being a Polytechnic, that he was very much for keeping it with its own identity.
Tilson: **Was there any visible, tangible evidence of the jewellery and silversmithing tradition stretching right back, in items made, the drawings, or whatever?**
Bracey: The benches that we used to work at were probably there from when the School was first built. I couldn't absolutely verify that, but I assume they wouldn't have been replaced. There wouldn't have been any need to replace them. There were some rolling mills that we rolled the metal on to make it thinner and I think they had been there right from the year dot. A lot of the equipment was, and probably still is, being used because it's just things that are not going to be replaced, but are good for the next generation as well. That's not to say that new technology was not introduced when it became available. We had the use of one of the first micro-welds on the market, for example.
Tilson: **Were people expected to train for crafts workshops or were they expected to go into industry proper?**
Bracey: On the City and Guilds course it was intended that you went into the trade afterwards. The course that I went on divided into four sections after the first year and you specialised in engraving, silversmithing, fine or costume jewellery. Of the group that I was with during the first year, there were a couple who went to engraving and a couple who went to silversmithing and the majority went to jewellery. There were about 100 or 12 in the first year group and the second and third years were combined, so it was 16 to 20.
Tilson: **Was it men and women?**
Bracey: Mostly men. Women were very much a minority.
Tilson: **Why was that? I'm quite surprised at that.**
Bracey: These days I think it's more acceptable for women to do that sort of thing but I think it was only just becoming more customary to accept women on

Fig. 6.1. School of Jewellery and Silversmithing, Vittoria Street, Frederick Street frontage, Jewellery Quarter, 1989.

that course. However, on the Diploma in Art and Design course, which was much more art and design based, rather than skill based, the majority were women. So, I think if you were more 'arty' and had the qualifications you tended to go on to that course. But I didn't have the qualifications. It was the City and Guilds or nothing.

Tilson: I don't suppose there was a lot of difference in the kinds of skills that you obtained.

Bracey: The City and Guilds was a very good grounding, but we weren't really taught design and I find that a disability now, whereas the Diploma students were, although they probably couldn't make a cluster ring as I can. So it was very much the choice of the two avenues that you could have gone down. Whether some people went on after that to learn more skills and vice versa I couldn't say. But by that time you'd been at college for three years you had to start and make a living.

Tilson: What about the Arts and Crafts approach? You recall Birmingham's tradition in the nineteenth century and early twentieth century? Was there any trace of that at all?

Bracey: Of the Gaskins and people like that? Not directly no. I think we were very much being taught to go out and make a living at jewellery by working in an established company, not as a craftsperson in the Arts and Crafts sense. I was very aware of the history of the School, although I don't know if some of the men were. At the time you were enclosed in your own little world learning your trade.

Tilson: Can you name a few teachers that you had and the kinds of backgrounds that they came from?
Bracey: My tutor in the second and third year, Frank Russell, had actually been in the trade and then he taught full-time at the college as well. He was the tutor I had for the fine jewellery.
Tilson: What do you mean by 'fine' jewellery?
Bracey: Another name would be traditional jewellery - cluster rings, big spray brooches and things like that, in precious metals and stones such as diamonds and emeralds. Once you can make that sort of thing you can go on and make the basic simple silver twist ring, whereas a person who was just taught how to make a simple twist ring wouldn't know the mechanics of making a cluster ring or a spray brooch. Costume jewellery is very much the fashion side of it - a big stone with a fancy surround or suchlike. But with the fine jewellery that I did I stayed with the tradition of using lots of diamonds, mass *pavé* settings, but designed in a more modern way (Fig. 6.2). Rather than doing a spray brooch with flowers and leaves I'd do my own abstract design, using triangles and so forth, and it worked reasonably well. Steve Fisher was in charge of costume jewellery, I believe.
Tilson: Was it an all-male teaching staff at the School?
Bracey: I had one female teacher, Jenny Griffiths, who taught my group on Friday mornings, to get us away from thinking traditionally all the time and to think slightly more modern. Frank Russell had an assistant called Tony Thurman, because it was such a big group that it needed two tutors. In the first year I had Steve Fisher and I also had Sik Perkins, who taught engraving, which we did in the first and second years.

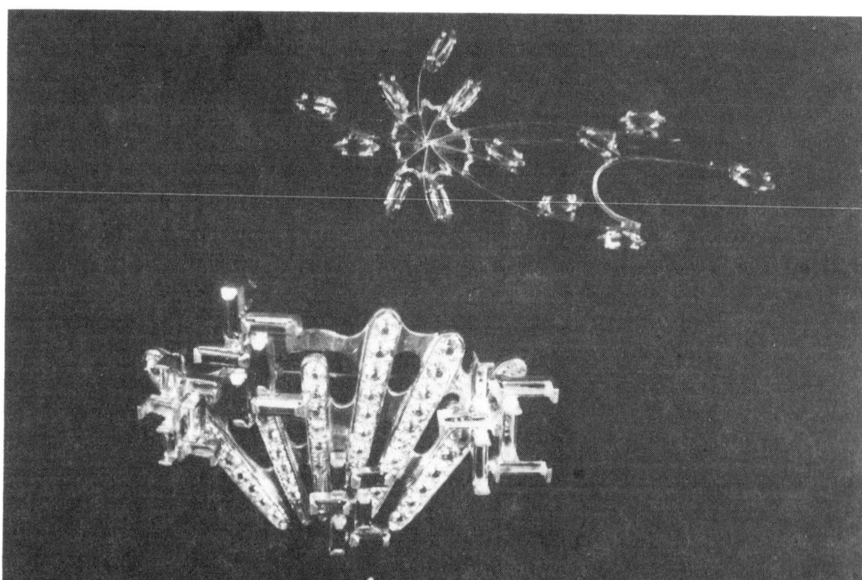

Fig. 6.2. Student pieces by Anne Bracey, School of Jewellery and Silversmithing, c.1974. Top: Spray brooch in 9ct gold, set with navette shaped amethysts. Below: Silver brooch set with synthetic white and red spinels to represent diamonds and rubies.

Fig. 6.3. Johnson Matthey Ltd. Working liquid gold in stages prior to casting. Photo reproduced from a colour original courtesy of the company.

Tilson: Did you learn enamelling?
Bracey: Yes. Mrs. Baxendale, Mr. Baxendale's wife, used to teach us that. Mr. Cook taught enamelling but he retired not long after I started, and then Mrs. Baxendale took over. Mr. Moody taught silversmithing. Mr. Baxendale lectured on the theory part of the course and taught us about heraldry and things like that in the first year.
Tilson: Did you actually go out into the Jewellery Quarter to visit firms or did people who worked in the Jewellery Quarter come in to talk to you at all?
Bracey: Not so much for talks, but we used to have extra teachers who came in for evening classes. We used to have design in the evening and of course it wasn't compulsory so a lot of students used to skip off that. We also had a couple of people from the trade who came in. Also, John Russell, Frank Russell's son, used to teach setting. I went back after I'd finished the course and did an evening class in setting for a couple of terms, just to build up my skills on that.
Tilson: Where did they get the materials from?

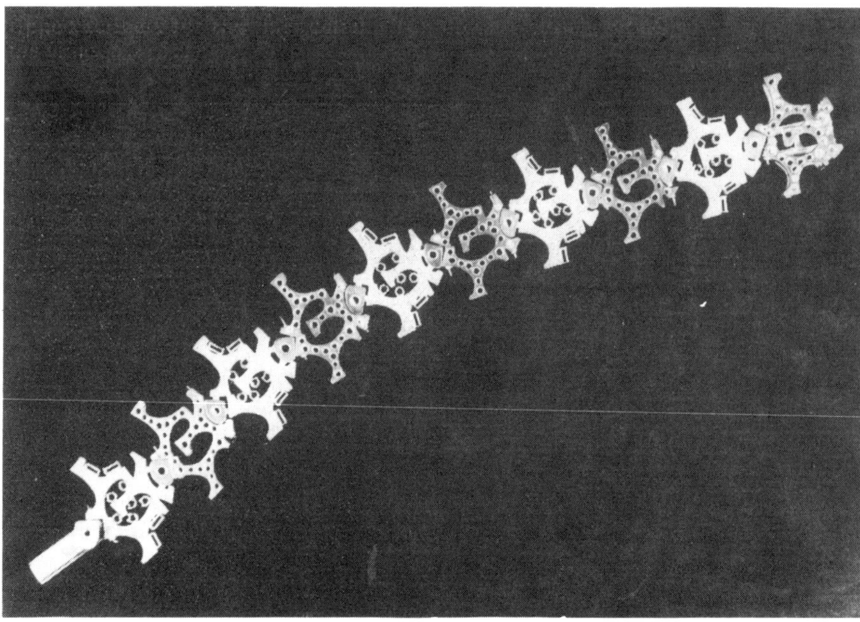

Fig. 6.4. Student piece by Anne Bracey, School of Jewellery and Silversmithing, c.1974. Silver bracelet, unfinished, intended to be set with synthetic spinels.

Bracey: We used to buy gold and silver from the bullion dealers. I think they had some sort of contract originally with someone like Johnson Matthey Ltd (Fig. 6.3) for the students to go over and buy the materials, as a gold licence was needed at that time. I applied for a licence on my own behalf when I left college. We worked in copper and gilding metal in the first year, and then we moved on to silver and finally to gold. But on a grant you were a bit limited as to what you could afford. We had to buy the gold, silver and gemstones ourselves. In the first year we had to learn the use of the tools and the techniques in handling metals.

One of the first things I made was a range of large tubes which were turned up from flat sheet, soldered then decorated in various ways i.e. acid etching, drilling holes, applied decoration and so on. That taught me so many things in one exercise. From there I moved on to actual pieces of jewellery I had designed and was shown various ways the drawing could be interpreted in metal. In the second and third years I moved on to more complicated work, getting more intricate in the designs and the mechanics of the piece (Fig. 6.4), such as making the fastener on a bracelet I had designed so that it had a totally integrated look. This training taught me confidence to tackle most jobs.

Tilson: Were there competitions and suchlike?

Bracey: We had a form of assessment for work done throughout the year. There were college awards with prizes sponsored by firms in the trade. There were also special awards such as the H. Samuel Travelling Scholarships. The college awards were categorised into jewellery mounting, setting, engraving, drawing and design etc.

Tilson: Were the students encouraged to take part in national competitions?

Bracey: Not on our course. I think it was more of a Diploma course activity.

Tilson: Can we go on to talk about when you became freelance, or whatever it was that you went on to next?

Bracey: What happened was that I couldn't get a job. Nobody wanted to employ me, and this relates to what we were saying about women working in the jewellery trade. In the trade itself, working at the bench was not recognised as a woman's job. Women were either in the offices doing the paperwork or sorting stones. There was a very great prejudice - from the men in the workshops - against taking on a woman because they felt they would be inhibited with a woman sitting there. With the two jobs I applied for with two of the better companies in the trade, I met that both times. I was offered a job stone sorting and I was offered a job in an office, but, of course, having been at college I didn't want to end up doing that. I could have gone straight from school to do that. Then Tony Thurman, my tutor, happened to know of Sue Vedadi, with whom I share a workshop now. She was sharing with another woman at the time and they wanted a third person to share costs of the workshop we had in Spencer Street, so I joined them there. I worked there part-time and worked in a shop in Sutton Coldfield part-time as well to bring some money in while I was getting myself established.

Tilson: How long did you spend trying to get into one of the firms?

Bracey: Not very long. There weren't many vacancies at that time. It was 1974/1975, just at the time of the oil crisis. The jewellery trade was going through a recession at that time. When I first went for the college entrance interview and started college, employers used to come and pick the students. Over the three years that I was there that changed completely, and we had to go out and look for jobs. Some of the male students were employed, but there was this female thing.

Tilson: How overt was it? Did they make excuses for not giving you employment?

Bracey: One firm, particularly, said the workmen felt as though they wouldn't be able to swear if there was a woman in the workshop, and that's really stuck in my mind. But the other ones were just rejection letters, not even getting as far as an interview.

Tilson: Do you think it's any better now, or is it difficult for you to say?

Bracey: I don't know. I don't know how many women there are wanting to go on to the bench now. I think the trade's changed quite a bit in the last few years, as well. It's now more mechanised than it was. It was still very, and there still is, a lot of hand-made work being made around here, but it's very much on the production line basis. So I don't know what opportunities there are for women with skills equal to men's. In theory you should get the job whether you are male or female.

Fig. 6.5. Anne Bracey, designer jeweller, in her former workshop (+ traditional bench) at 98 Spencer Street. Photo courtesy of the designer.

Tilson: Did the men on your course specialise in any different kinds of skills from you?

Bracey: No. We were all learning the trade and we were all, hopefully, going into it. I know one chap who went to work for one of the companies and they really started him from scratch to learn things the trade way. Whereas we had been able to spend two to three months making one ring, of course you had to get things out much quicker in the trade. There are various short cuts in doing that. But at least you'd learnt to handle the tools by being at college. You'd served a basic apprenticeship. I can't remember the proportions of people who went into the trade. People went off in various directions, jobwise. There was quite a wide spread of people from different parts of the country and they obviously went back to where they started from and probably worked locally.

Tilson: Do you know what happened to some of the other women on the course?

Bracey: One friend of mine, who is now married, worked in the trade for a while, while her husband was training to be an architect. She did get a job at the bench, but she had left a year prior to me, and I think it was in that last twelve months that the job market changed. One of the other women went to work for one of the jewellery companies, but in the office. I don't know what happened to the women on the Diploma course.

Tilson: You mentioned that several of the men got jobs. What firms did they work for?

Bracey: One chap, in particular, worked for Alabaster & Wilson, a company which makes very high quality goods. I think they're still in the trade, in Legge Lane. I don't know directly whether they do work for Aspreys and those sorts of firms, but it was that calibre of work. That was one of the companies I applied to. I've seen various people around the trade, but I couldn't tell you what companies they went to work for. People obviously wanted to try and work for the best, having been at college.

Tilson: In my own mind, I see the Vittoria Street School as having an almost unique character about it, as far as not just Birmingham, but the country, is concerned.

Bracey: Certainly, there's no training school in Hatton Garden, which is what people think of automatically when they think of jewellery. Many people who work in Hatton Garden must go directly as apprentices into the companies there. There are Art Schools in London, obviously, which have specialist jewellery courses, such as (I believe) the John Cass College.

Tilson: Can we discuss what sort of work you did when you joined with the other two people?

Bracey: I joined with Susan Vedadi and Kathy McHugh. We had a workshop at 98 Spencer Street on the top floor (Fig. 6.5). They had their own private customers in the same way that we have now, making to commission. Sue had been at the Polytechnic at Gosta Green and Kathy had been at Vitt Street, but she'd been doing the Diploma course. There are two of us now as Kathy left a few years ago and Sue and I moved here, to Vyse Street, because we needed more room.

Tilson: Do you sell to the market, or are you commissioned by clients?

Bracey: Both. I sell stock pieces direct to the customer at craft fairs and clients commission pieces, too. Also, pieces advertise themselves.

Tilson: What sort of thing was in vogue at the time you started out?

Bracey: Very large scale work. Sue's work is very much her own style, being large and highly decorated with tiny gold beads (Fig. 6.6). My work tends to have cleaner lines and is less decorated, which extends back to my training, whereas she's more art based. Though, when I first started I just did whatever anybody wanted. I could adapt to do engagement rings for people, wedding rings or just a little silver chain if somebody wanted it, and that's very much how I work now (Fig. 6.7).

Tilson: Do you tend to carry through a piece right from start to finish?

Bracey: Yes, although I get things like engraving and stone setting done in the trade. Certain settings I'll do myself, but cluster rings and things like that are very specialised and it's best to give them to somebody who's working on them every day. If I really had to, I could probably sit down and set them myself, but the time I'd spend doing that I could be making something else.

Tilson: There are particular people who specialise in doing what might be called 'outwork'?

Bracey: You could say it was outwork. We're very reliant on polishers, engravers and setters etc. Although I do a little of the finishing and final polishing myself, a lot of the polishing goes out to be done, and then it goes to be engraved.

Tilson: When I went through an alley next door there were a couple of men in there who seemed to be doing some finishing.

Bracey: That's right. They were polishing. They would be working for somebody else. They're not making the goods themselves and then polishing them. They take the polishing in from other companies. The trade is very inter-related like that.

Tilson: Do you share customers?

Bracey: Not if we can possibly help it.

Tilson: How unique do you think you are? I had the feeling that you weren't that typical of what's going on.

Bracey: No, there's not that many of us.

Tilson: What do you mean by 'us'? Would you call yourself a craftswoman?

Fig. 6.6. Susan Vedadi, designer jeweller. Pendant necklace in textured silver sheet with applied gold beads, set with a large nautilus pearl and freshwater pearls. For a private client, c.1985. Photo courtesy of the designer.

Bracey: I would say we are designer jewellers. As more people go through the college system as it is now, and probably want to and are more able to set up on their own, there's going to be more people able to do this. But five or six years ago, there weren't many of us.
Tilson: Did you find it difficult to get going because of that or was it easier because you were opening up a fresh market?
Bracey: As any small business person will know, it is always a struggle with money going out as quickly as it comes in, but the most important thing has been to keep overheads down as much as possible. That way you can be competitive on cost. I feel I do provide a much-needed service. Fortunately, not everyone wants to shop in the usual High Street jewellery shops and, strangely, it hasn't been a problem for clients to accept their work being carried out by a woman.

Fig. 6.7. Anne Bracey, designer jeweller. Left: Pied Piper brooch, 1989, silver base, saw pierced, overlaid with layers in textured red and yellow gold. Right: Dragonfly brooch, 1988, silver base inlaid with hand-cut mother-of-pearl. Both for private clients.

Tilson: What do you think about this new idea of giving crafts in the Jewellery Quarter a higher profile?
Bracey: I don't mind that if the public appreciate what they're looking at, but very often they don't. There are people who are certainly trying to make it into a tourist area.
Tilson: What signs are there of that sort of thing?
Bracey: A lot of publicity is in the *Hockley Flyer* about the Council's ideas for the area, but there's very little action. Take, for example, the building next door but one, which is a factory that closed.[1] Suddenly they decided to close, every-

body went out, the doors were locked and it's just left as it was. That was ten or fifteen years ago. There was talk of opening it as a musem, but then of course they've got to have facilities for pulling up coaches and things like that, so there's a lot of planning to do. There's lots of talk of renovating buildings as museums allied to the jewellery trade but I don't know whether it will ever get under way.

Tilson: I expect all that would benefit you indirectly.

Bracey: It would be a nuisance, to be perfectly honest, to have people walking around. It is a working area and if you're trying to get up the road to a bullion dealers and you're having to fight your way through people who are asking the way to 'Eric's the wholesalers' or something like that, you just wouldn't want to know. I'd like to see the area preserved and it's nice to have some visitors, but it's also a working place, so there are pluses and minuses.

Tilson: Do you sell through the Art Gallery and Museum shops in Chamberlain Square?

Bracey: No, but Sue does. I've got my work in Diane Cross's Jewellery Workshop in the Great Western Arcade which is a retail shop specialising in selling the work of designer jewellers. I also do some of their special orders.

Tilson: What other outlets do you have?

Bracey: I do craft fairs which bring in the private customers, which I like because I can really go to town on them on the art side. Last year, too, I did a trade show in Harrogate and I've now got a shop in Windsor that I deal with, and one in Cambridge, and there's another one in Hampstead in London. I've booked to do Harrogate again this year as I'm trying to get more in the way of shops to buy from me as well. You've got to do anything and everything. You can't rely just on private customers.

Tilson: Do you have an agent?

Bracey: No, and I've never taken my work around the shops either. Everyone's come to me, either by word of mouth or seeing the work somewhere or on someone.

Tilson: Harrogate is the main exhibition venue for jewellery, isn't it?

Bracey: Yes, it's called the British Trade and Craft Fair, though it's not just for jewellery, but for anything that is hand crafted. A lot of people who are 'one man bands' exhibit there. I went last year and shared the stand with someone else to keep costs down. It was our first trade show and we were pleased with the results.

Tilson: Do you do craft fairs with the West Midlands Guild?

Bracey: Yes, and they are also multi crafts, not just jewellery. We organise the craft fairs which average out about one a month throughout the year, all over the West Midlands. Malvern and Leamington Spa are the furthest south that we go. We don't hold them in Birmingham because there are not suitable venues.

Tilson: Would you say that the Guild is the most useful organisation you could belong to?

Bracey: Locally, yes. There are other craft fair organisers, but they don't have the back-up. They're out to make the money themselves, whereas we're a non profit-making organisation.

Tilson: Do you have any links with the Jewellery and Giftware Federation?

Bracey: No. I think that organisation is more for the larger manufacturers.

Tilson: Do you find the *Hockley Flyer* a useful local magazine?

Bracey: I like to read it to see what's going on locally and obviously the adverts are useful. However, the *Watchmaker, Jeweller and Silversmith* is a trade magazine which is quite useful for keeping up with designs and regulations which are being brought in that affect the jewellery trade.

Tilson: Getting on to that, have there been any specific developments which have affected you in that respect?

Bracey: The Hallmarking Act is one example. You always had the option of getting things hallmarked, but I think it was in 1975 that hallmarking was made compulsory, i.e. that gold over one gram and silver over seven grams had to be hallmarked. That was something which, from a consumer's viewpoint, was a good thing. There's an Assay Office in Birmingham. That is the only regulation which affects me directly, but they're now trying to bring in a code of conduct for valuations, to prevent inflated insurance claims. That affects the retail side more.

Tilson: Do you find you are called on for certain things rather than others, whether rings, chains or whatever?

Bracey: At the moment brooches are very popular but it depends on the occasion. If someone's getting married obviously it's going to be rings and if it's a birthday present it might be a bracelet or a brooch.

Tilson: Usually in precious materials?

Bracey: I only work in gold and silver now, but using any types of stones - gem stones or agates, for example.

Fig. 6.8. Loading the casting machine with gold pieces at Euro-Cast Ltd, 1989. Photo by permission of the company.

Tilson: Do you buy all your materials locally?

Bracey: No. Some of the stones come up from London. All the metals I buy locally.

Tilson: Do you buy the stones from Hatton Garden?

Bracey: No. One company, a stone dealer, is in North West 3, London. They supply certain goods that I can't get around here. You can be more flexible about the stones because obviously you've got various qualities to choose from, so if no-one can satisfy your needs around here you can go elsewhere. We also have an Indian chap who comes round. He actually goes back to India and buys and he

Fig. 6.9. Casting trees in wax awaiting casting in gold (mould canisters behind) at Euro-Cast Ltd, 48 Carver Street, Jewellery Quarter, 1989. Photo by permission of the company.

comes in and sells varous stones. He goes up to Scotland and all over the country selling his goods.

Tilson: Can you give me some idea of major activities that are going on here and major firms?

Bracey: A lot of mass-produced goods are being made - crosses that are stamped out and rings that are cast and then set. One or two companies actually sell to people like Argos and Ratners now, which is a big retail company, and they obviously want mass numbers of the same ring.

Tilson: Are Ratners in the Jewellery Quarter?

Bracey: No, but they've been buying up retail chains like Samuels so they have a vast number of shops to stock. Whoever manufactures for them has to be able to put the same ring in each shop, so there's got to be the mass-produced aspect of it.

Tilson: Are these manufacturing firms with hundreds of workers?

Bracey: I wouldn't have said hundreds, because you can mass-produce a ring by the casting method. You have a casting tree with hundreds of rings on it (Figs.6.8, 6.9). You've still got to have someone to polish and set it, but that doesn't involve hundreds of people. An example of a major firm here is Deakin & Francis. They are a specialised company which deals with the very expensive, fine jewellery end of it. I think they do work for the big shops in London.

Tilson: It's not just a local trade, then, it's serving the country.

Bracey: That's right.

Tilson: There are so many small two or three person enterprises aren't there, it seems, from walking up and down?

Bracey: Yes, and they very often do work for the bigger companies, who haven't necessarily got the skills in their workshop at the time. This is where the outworker comes in. They'll know that 'Joe Bloggs down the road can do part of this job', and the work goes to him. That's how they're kept in business. But it can happen that, if the trade is in a slight recession, these people do feel the pinch. If the companies at the top of the tree are feeling the effect, then further down it's going to be felt again. That is why I'm lucky here in that I don't rely completely on the retail trade. I have my own private customers who, hopefully, will keep coming back for those special occasions.

REFERENCES

1 This is the Smith & Pepper factory which is to be a 'discovery centre'. It is situated within the block bordered by Vyse Street, Hockley Street, Branston Street and Spencer Street, which is due to be renovated as a Jewellery Business Centre through finance provided by the Duchy of Cornwall.
See "Prince's Sparkling Gesture", *Birmingham Post,* 6 October 1989.

CHAPTER 7

THE VITTORIA STREET SCHOOL OF JEWELLERY AND SILVERSMITHING IN 1989

Terry Hunt

If it was possible for Mr. Warwood, Superintendent of the Vittoria Street School in 1890, to visit the School in 1989 he would, no doubt, appreciate a certain continuity evident in several sights and sounds. The tools and materials used in hand crafts are unlikely to have changed over such a relatively short period and he would be able to recognize much of what he saw and heard - the layout of the workshops, the sounds of ringing hammer blows (Fig. 7.1) and scratchy piercing saws.

Equipment such as windlass drawbenches with broad leather belts, still in use, are as effective today as they were then, in addition to being quieter and aesthetically more pleasing than the contemporary steel joist and roller chain version. Hand tools are likely to be exactly the same (though possibly now made in Taiwan or India!) Benches and hearths would be familiar in that their shape, size and material would be identical, but they would no longer be cluttered with foot-operated bellows (compressed air is now piped to each workshop) or by glass magnifying globes filled with water (electric strip or tungsten lights are now above each bench). Electric lights are so effective and taken for granted that one wonders just how much detailed work could possibly have been undertaken on dark winter days before its introduction.

The rear of the building, which used to house live animals such as sheep and goats for drawing studies, is now the student canteen. Observers of today's youth may say that this constitutes little change at all! Changes *have* occurred of course, with some having more prominence than others. The exterior of the Vittoria Street building (see Fig. 6.1) looks very much as it did in 1890, though the sign on the front which now reads 'Birmingham Institute of Art and Design' signifies a most profound change indeed.

The Institute (BIAD) was formed in April 1988 by the merger of Bournville College of Art and Design with the Art and Design Faculty of Birmingham Polytechnic, making it the largest single unit of art and design education in the UK outside London.

The Vittoria Street building itself is now an annexe to the main site of BIAD at Gosta Green, as are also the Margaret Street building and those at Bournville. So, rather than being contained within one building the School of Jewellery and Silversmithing is now a department, with additional studio and workshop facilities at the Gosta Green and Bournville sites. The School is one of six departments that comprises the BIAD, which is itself a constituent faculty of the Polytechnic.

As a department the School has fourteen lecturers, three technicians and a secretary and calls upon the services of at least fourteen specialists as visiting teachers throughout the year[1] (Fig. 7.2). In the 1988/9 academic year there were 116 full-time and 194 part-time students. By attending full-time, students may study the design and manufacture of jewellery, silver, (Figs. 7.3, 7.4) clocks and watches, as well as specialised techniques such as engraving and die-sinking, on

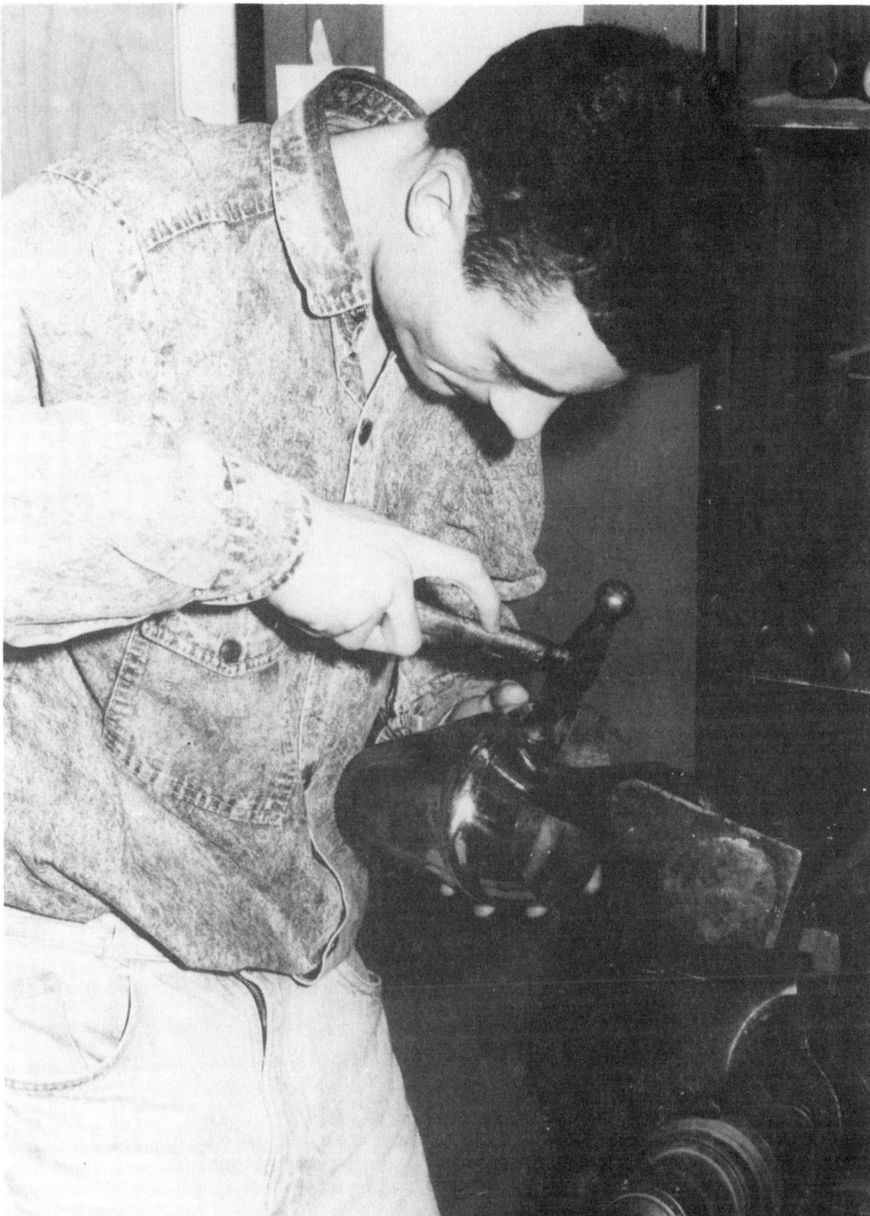

Fig. 7.1. Student at the School of Jewellery and Silversmithing, Vittoria Street, hammering metal hollow ware into shape, 1988.

courses leading to City and Guilds, Higher National Diploma, B.A. (Hons) or M.A. qualifications. These subjects may also be studied on a part-time basis in addition to those of stone-setting, gemmology, diamond grading and jewellery retailing skills.

This uniquely wide provision of courses at Birmingham has always been characterized by a sound concern and commitment to the training and education needs of local industry. A relatively recent example of this is the development of the Youth Training Scheme (YTS) in concert with the British Jewellers Association (BJA), which is the main trade association for the industry. While the BJA have been involved with the School for many years through their annual awards, presented to full-time and part-time students at an event attracting much media coverage, the YTS scheme is seen to be a milestone in the provision of skills training.

Fig. 7.2. The Mace of Birmingham Polytechnic, designed by Terry Hunt and made by staff of the School of Jewellery and Silversmithing in 1987. Largely made of titanium to exploit its optical colour effects. The School researched the decorative effects of this material in the 1960s in conjunction with IMI.

More recent co-operation has arisen from the publication of a report[2] which surveyed the British jewellery industry with particular reference to its management and training needs. One of the report's conclusions was that, the industry, in needing to become more competitive to meet the challenges of 1992, would benefit from more appropriate training schemes, especially those concerned with new technology and business management skills.

Since 1988 the School has been a partner, in collaboration with the City's Economic Development Unit and the BJA, in a Local Collaborative Project (LCP),

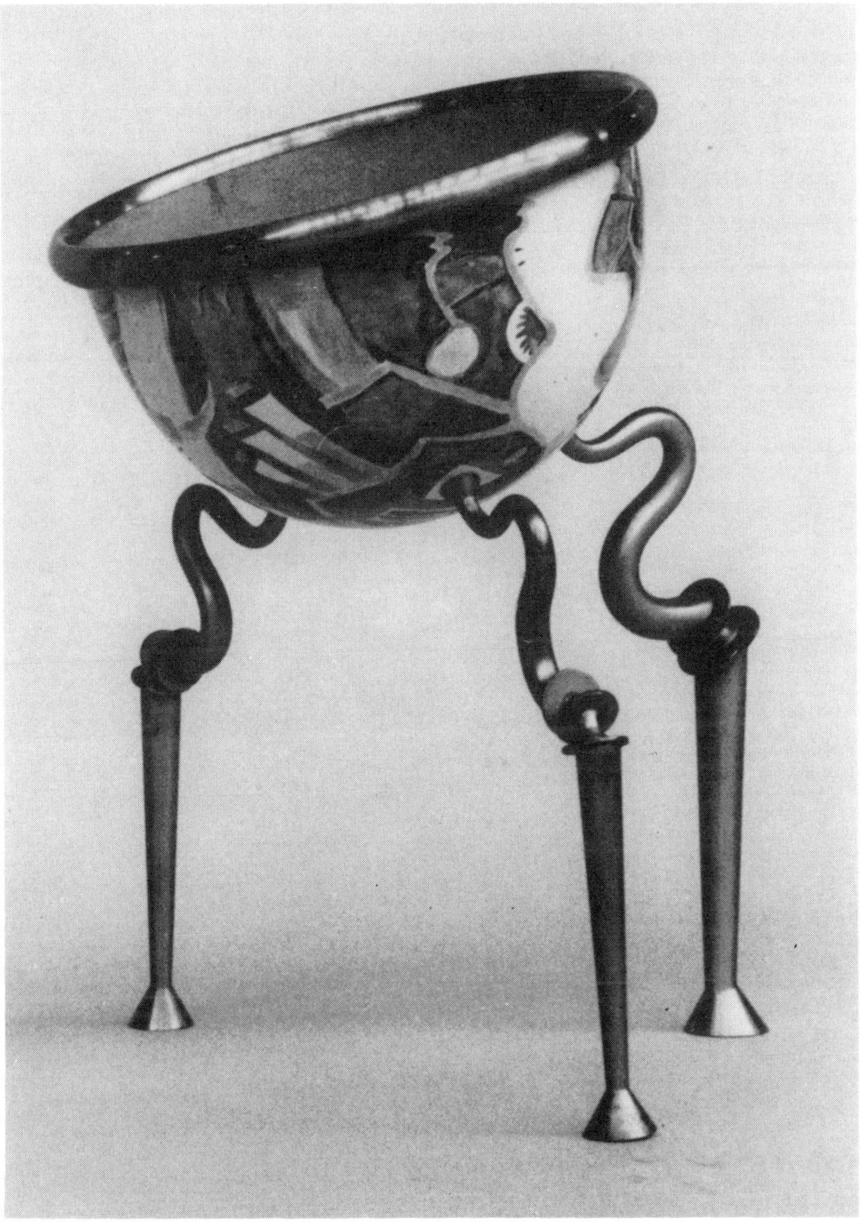

Fig. 7.3. Bowl by B.A. (Hons.) student, Catherine Evans, in copper decorated with painted vitreous enamels, using traditional techniques, 1989. Height: 30cm.

working with the industry, helping to define its specific needs and how to meet them. The LCP aims, through management development and technology up-dating programmes, to make the industry better able to exploit new market areas and thereby expand both production and employment potential.

The School, as a focal point in this project, has already introduced several in-service training courses for managers, supervisors and operatives within the industry. Some of these courses relate to the use of advanced technological equipment which the School has acquired in areas such as CNC machining, casting and electro-forming of metals and the identification of gemstones.

The impetus for the establishment of the School one hundred years ago came from the Birmingham jewellery and metal-working industry, an industry which (though one of the city's oldest and most well known) has declined from employing around 10,000 in 1963 to 4,800 in 1988. It is to be hoped that the current collaborative initiative will go some way to ensuring the industry's future for the *next* hundred years.

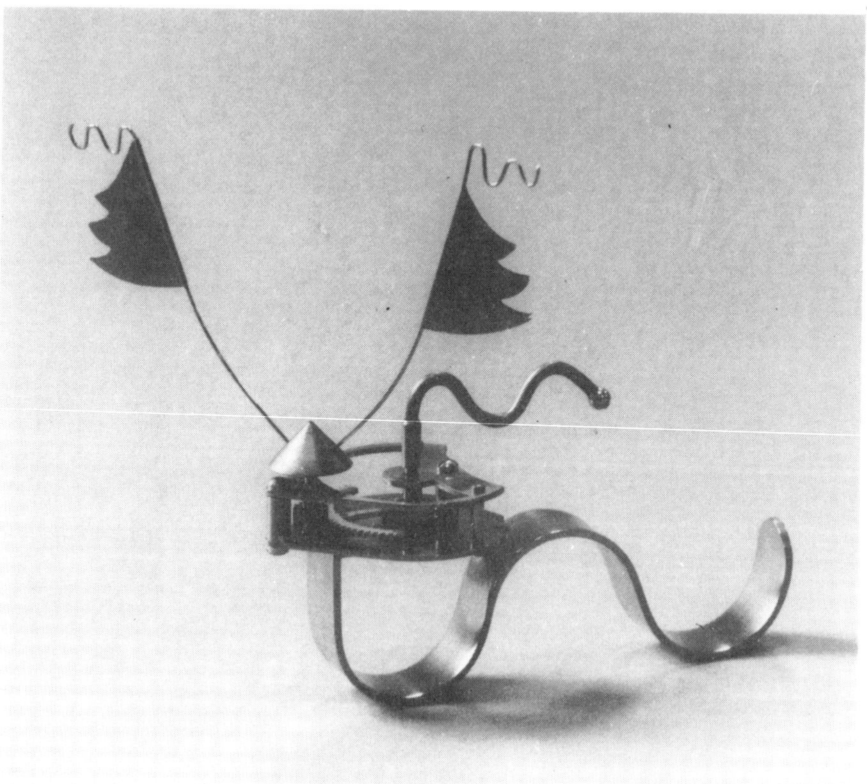

Fig. 7.4. Kinetic finger decoration by B.A. (Hons.) student, Sharon Ulldemolins, assisted by Ian Sadler. It gained equal 1st prize in the international 'Jewellery in Movement' competition open to professionals, organised by Gesellschaft fur Goldsmiedekunst, Hanau, West Germany, 1987.

REFERENCES

1 *Presentation Ceremony 1988,* British Jewellers Association programme.
2 *The Future Education and Training Needs of the Jewellery and Silverware Industries,* The Brtish Jewellers' Association and the Goldsmiths' Company, 1987.

CHAPTER 8

THE BIRMINGHAM JEWELLERY QUARTER, A CIVIC PROBLEM THAT HAS BECOME AN OPPORTUNITY IN THE 1980s.

Barbara M.D. Smith

Adjacent to the city centre in Birmingham lies a fascinating area where the jewellery and precious metals industry has predominated for not a hundred but a hundred and fifty years or more. (Fig. 8.1) A quarter of Britain's jewellery and silverware industry, fragmented into a diversity of specialist industries or trades is located in this square half mile. Present too in useful proximity are the bullion dealers, jewellery box makers, tool suppliers, Assay Office and others providing essential services to the industry. A controversial addition of the last twelve years has been the veritable flood of jewellery retailers, including some selling non-Birmingham made rings and chains at discount prices - and attracting into the Quarter many welcome and some less welcome customers, felons and sharp practices. It is the pull of gold and silver, intricate skills with export potential, and fine and striking buildings and street scenes, as well as an interesting history, all in a small geographical space close to the city centre and International Convention Centre, that has presented to Birmingham and its City Council a unique opportunity. The Council can at one stroke promote a key traditional local industry, provide a new tourist attraction and continue the rehabilitation of an important but deteriorating collection of often remarkable buildings.

The design and implementation of the civic opportunity requires careful planning by the City Council, working often through its Development Department. This needs to harness the policies and financial assistance of the central government's industrial and inner cities initiatives, EEC's regional and social funds and the interests of landowners and developers, both those already in the Quarter and potential inward investors, while also satisfying the jewellery industry.[1]

The Birmingham Jewellery Industry

The jewellery industry had been established in Birmingham nearly a century when Birmingham became a city in 1889. Almost from its start, it has been concentrated in the Jewellery Quarter. Jewellery manufacturing has also always been an industry of small businesses, with 150 employees still almost an upper limit at least in the Quarter with a somewhat larger scale in popular jewellery and electroplating.[2] (Figs. 8.2, 8.3)

It became and remains a densely developed part of the city. In 1948, Johnson found a peak density of 923 works in a single square kilometre in the Quarter.[3] Such crowding has reflected the undergrowth of small firms and outworkers (or jobbers to the trade) occupying small workshops, often single rooms, or 'renting a peg' (or bench and 50 sq.ft.) in a shared room. The low overheads of these small firms have often hidden poor practices, lack of machinery and power, and poor working conditions, which have discouraged recruitment to the industry.[4] Associated with this has been the increasing division of labour between firms with these effectively linked by a human conveyor belt which carried small but valuable articles from workshop to workshop around nearby streets and within factories.

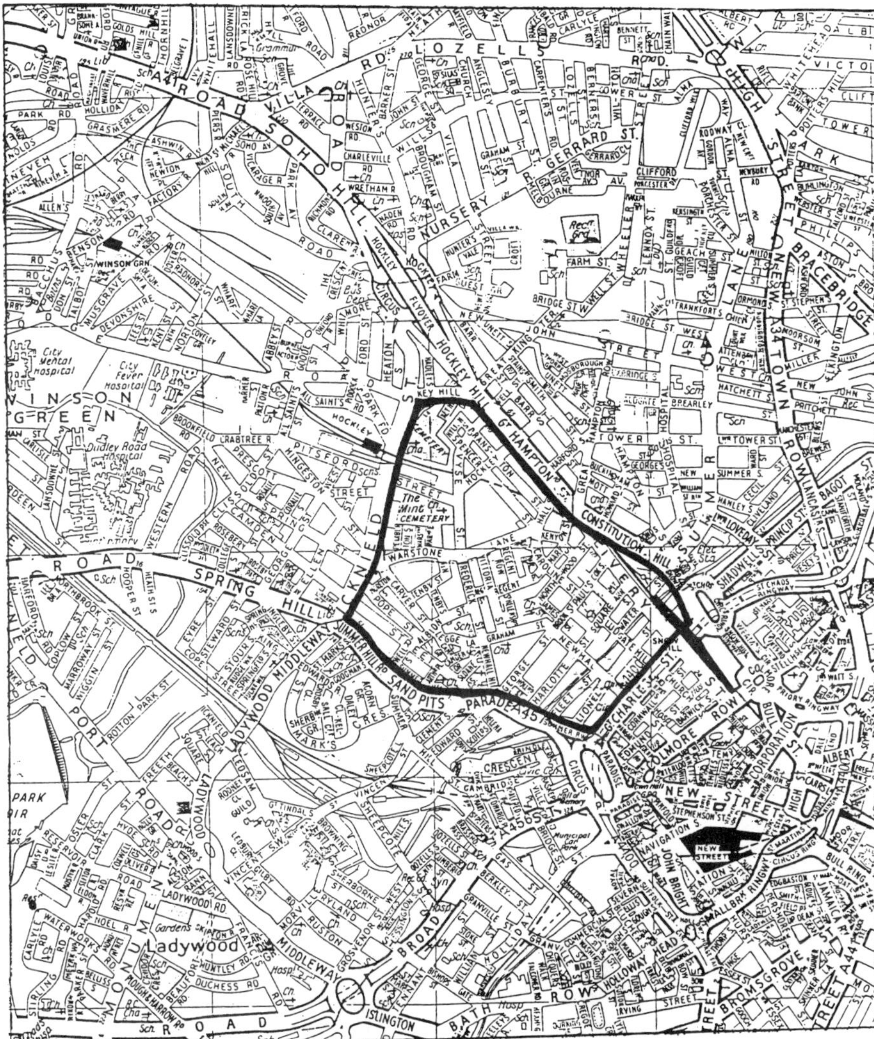

Fig. 8.1. Map of the Jewellery Quarter Industrial Improvement Area.

The exceptional incidence of small firms at all dates has reflected a) the ease of entry to a trade with such minimal plant requirements;[5] b) the large demand at many periods (other than in the 1880s and 1930s), which encouraged craftsmen to set up on their own; c) the availability in the Quarter of small premises for sub-division, though thereby perpetuating the absence of power and machinery and the out worker network which represented useful support as well as compet-

Fig. 8.2. Silver tea sets illustrated in Elkington's last catalogue, February 1965, showing designs by David Mellor and Eric Clements.

ition; d) the hand press, still in use in the 1980s; e) the merchant factors to organise distribution and often supplies, credit and orders too. Some of the latter in the nineteenth century began to co-ordinate outworkers, effectively taking on the role (and often the title) of manufacturers, even if without any factory of their own. While the popular jewellery side became more and more mechanised and in larger units often employing, from the 1880s, women and semi-skilled workers instead of craftsmen, (Fig. 8.4) the supply of small and very small businesses has persisted particularly on the 'process' side, often working on materials and work-in-progress belonging to someone else.[6]

Little had changed by the onset of the 1980s. Gilbert in 1972 commented that "*the present position of the industry seems to be that of a closely-knit group of interdependent trades organised and operated on lines which seem inappropriate for the development of a modern, viable, progressive industry.*"[7] International competition, inadequate investment in design and mechanisation, failure to fit the craftsman, (now often an outworker) into the larger firm and even to perpetuate craft skills by the training of youngsters, poor working conditions in deteriorating buildings and inept management, seem to have been long term problems in the industry and the Quarter though shutdowns during two wars, restrictions on precious metal supplies and the damaging level of purchase tax post-1945 have been external additional impositions. While the product and organisation of the jewellery trade are both distinctive, the uncompetitiveness and its causes have much in common with a lot of British manufacturing in Birmingham and elsewhere, both now and throughout the last hundred years. Like so much British industry, the jewellery industry's best years were 1864-1914, around the depression years of 1876-80 and 1883-6 and, more recently, 1950-66.

A key dilemma, not yet fully resolved, has been that large scale mechanisation (see Figs. 6.8, 6.9) cut costs and opened markets of one kind but hand craftmanship and a smaller scale made for the more exclusive design that raised value added. Another dilemma has been whether to abandon reliance on making only minor changes to well-established and popular reproduction designs that economically made use of existing dies in order to introduce completely new and untested styles and even materials like stainless steel and platinum.[8] New orders have often been met by reproducing old designs using existing dies,[9] while the new styles have tended to be the artistic products of small 'studio' workshops. (see Fig. 6.5-7, 5.4).

The industry in Birmingham, however, has benefitted enormously in volume, if not in profitability, from three evolutionary steps down (rather than up) market. The first of these came between 1815 and 1860, when the price of gold and silver fell as new mines in Australia and California opened up supply; the second in the 1900s and the third in the mid-1970s and especially in the last five years. On each occasion, sales to the less well off opened up new opportunities and called into place cut price, more mechanisation and mass production. Pressure has come, especially in the last fifteen years, from the retail jewellery chains, first Samuels and Walkers[10] and (since 1983) Ratners.

Gerald Ratner, retailer of the year in 1986, "*with a radically different trading strategy*", "*has succeeded in bringing gold jewellery within the range of a young and growing group of consumers.*" [11] With 565 shops at the end of 1987, Ratners now has 24% of the British market. [12]

Ratners is a new force on this scale and with this philosophy. The other new development has been in sales through mail order or catalogues such as Argos, Kaleidoscope and others. Both these have created opportunities for manufacturers[13] capable of meeting price, quality and scale criteria even if (in the process) bringing about a revolution in mechanisation, design, style, and working practices and even if, also, generating less variety, much tedious repeated work and less hand

Fig. 8.3. Silver sweet dishes illustrated in Elkington's last catalogue, February 1965.

skill for the employee and outworker. Given a short-sighted practice of many manufacturers of not putting their names on their products and not advertising, independence from Ratners, even if desired, is difficult to develop. This new retailing has boosted the popular, imitation, fancy, costume jewellery side of the trade that is often short life in quality and fashion (rather than the high quality that can provide an investment). [14] Sales, of course, continue through independent jewellers' shops on the high streets, department stores and exports, often through the few remaining factors and wholesalers. [15] Finally, there are the 80 or so shops selling jewellery in the Jewellery Quarter, some of which retail rings, necklaces, etc. made by craftsmen within sight of customers. [16]

So the new feature of the jewellery industry at the marketing end has been the big orders from these new forces in the retail sector. At the supply end, too, the jewellery manufacturer meets very large and well-resourced gold and diamond suppliers and bullion dealers. (see Fig. 6.3) Thus, jewellery manufacturers, none of whom is large in these terms, tend to be uncomfortably positioned between these two stronger forces, with international competition (from Italy, for example), another mounting pressure. [17]

Employment in the jewellery industry has always been modest with a peak of 28,000 in 1914, 6% of total employment in the city. [18] But, on the other hand, it has persisted for 150 years, even if not expanding with Birmingham's population. The broad figures for employment in Birmingham are these:- [19]

1825	1860	1880	1900	1914	1927	1950	1960	1970	1984
3700	9000	14000	16000	28000	19000	9000	6500	7600	5000

Since 1945, employment has been far lower, only partly accounted for by the omission of the 1,000 local self-employed from the count. Recent estimates suggest 5,000 remain in the industry in the Quarter (20% of the industry nationally). Only a few hundred have worked outside the Quarter within Birmingham and another 1,000 in the rest of the West Midlands region. [20] Women held about half the jobs in Birmingham. [21]

Thus, in 1984, employees in employment in the industry in Birmingham were only half the number that they had been twenty years earlier and two thirds of their number in 1978. Broadly, this rate of job loss was much the same as in Birmingham manufacturing as a whole (so jewellery had not done worse than its peers) and jewellery in Birmingham had a better employment record than its sister industry in Sheffield. Significantly, too, the Jewellery Quarter seems to have held on to its share of the industry. Exceptionally compared to manufacturing as a whole, jewellery employment has not been dispersing from the Quarter or from Birmingham in the 1970s. [22] Nor was control moving as in other industries. [23]

Thus, in several ways, the jewellery industry in the Jewellery Quarter has shown distinctive trends. However, its most remarkable characteristics have been its restless mobility and the high failure rate for firms moving between one and two miles from the Quarter. First, the number of jewellery businesses in Birmingham although down to about 700 from the 1,000 of 1946, [24] seems to be maintaining itself, with births replacing deaths and departures. [25] Second, Gilbert [26] found that, on average, 14.5% of the stock of firms in the West Midlands region moved every year between 1971 and 1946 and this extraordinary mobility was still evident in the 1980s. [27]

Where did the firms move? Virtually all moves were short - or fatal to the firm. Even those moving out of the Quarter only went an average of 991 yards. [28] Most went to places like Handsworth, Solihull, Rubery or Warstock. [29] The longer moves tended to be by makers of popular jewellery who became larger and much more self-sufficient after the move, reducing their links to the Jewellery Quarter.

Fig. 8.4. Women craft workers in the Jewellery Quarer ?around the turn of the century (Compare with Fig. 8.9).

Gilbert's dramatic finding was the high failure rate (77% failing) amongst the 102 firms moving out of the Quarter between 2,000 and 3,600 yards. This was an uneconomic distance apparently, not far enough to save on rent or force the cutting of links but too far for links to outworkers, the Assay Office, etc. to be maintained economically - too far to walk with goods involving time-wasting parking or to share information.[30] The impetus for this seemingly restless movement was to improve competitive position, not to accommodate growth.[31]

Inquiries in the Jewellery Quarter in 1987 confirmed the continued volatility and mobility of businesses within the Quarter and the preference, especially by small process firms, for a location near the clock tower and Vyse Street. Many new start-ups were also found, often one person businesses, some started with the help of an enterprise allowance.[32]

Thus, the Jewellery Quarter has exerted great holding power over jewellery businesses, even in the last decade, in marked contrast to the inner areas around it for manufacturing.

The Birmingham Jewellery Quarter

The Jewellery Quarter has developed in size and location and as the home of the jewellery industry as building has spread northward from Colmore Row.[33] About 1750, the first signs of clustering amongst jewellers occurred on the Newhall

Estate, while the adjacent Colmore Estate, whose leases put no ban on the erection of workshops in tenants' gardens,[34] provided small workshops for craftsmen, including jewellers. Between 1770 and 1800, a second phase began in the neighbourhood of what became St. Paul's Square, where the church was built in 1779.[35] (Fig. 8.5) The Square remains on the southern edge of the Quarter.

Fig. 8.5. Renovated buildings on St. Paul's Square. Photographed 1989.

The 1840s saw jewellery businesses appearing to the north of St. Paul's in the Great Hampton Street-Warstone Lane sector and (soon afterwards) a new clustering to the north-east of Great Hampton Street. In the 1860s the flow came into the Vyse Street-Frederick Street area from the east rather than the south,[36] representing new, additional firms opening in these years of growth in what is now the heart of the modern Quarter, partly on the Howard Vyse Estate north of Warstone Lane. As the Quarter filled up, infilling and extension occurred in the early twentieth century (Fig. 8.6) with larger factory units along the main Birmingham to West Bromwich road into the Soho district and (after 1945) consolidation and recolonisation of the Quarter itself with individual and collective redevelopment and building schemes since 1945.

Three forces pushed the boundaries of the Quarter outwards: property prices and supply, business growth (causing medium sized firms to take over whole houses and, thus, push out existing tenants to find rooms elsewhere) and the need for larger, more modern factories.

Thus, some buildings and businesses in the Jewellery Quarter survive from the eighteenth century before Birmingham became an industrial centre, let alone a city, but the major boost to the industry and the Quarter occurred in the 1840s and 1850s. Expanding jewellers moved into, or developed, their own residential properties or purpose-built workshops, often in the gardens and yards of the existing houses in Frederick Street, Vyse Street and Warstone Lane and elsewhere. These houses ranged from handsome middle class mansions to terraces of small artisan dwellings. (Fig. 8.7.). It is these in their dozens that make up the historic base of the Jewellery Quarter in the 1980's, and it is their deterioration, and the falling in of leases over the last century, that has been the planning problem and potential opportunity of the last forty years.

Fig. 8.6. Congestion of older housing and industrial buildings, as illustrated in *When We Build Again*, 1941.

Redevelopment Proposals for the Quarter

The condition of the Jewellery Quarter attracted attention before and during World War 2. Two of the first interested bodies (Bournville Village Trust and the Birmingham Jewellers Association)[37] were each shocked into dramatic proposals involving both extensive clearance "*of cramped and inconvenient workshops which are dark and inefficient*"[38] and flatted factories, five or six storeys high, to replace them. However, the costs - the Chatterley scheme for the Jewellers Association was priced at £3m and rents equivalent to 19 pence per sq.ft. in 1944 - frightened the jewellers, their existing rents being less than half this. The City of Birmingham, after a survey of 1953, also recognised 23 acres of old workshops as beyond repair but the cost and rent implications remained prohibitive.[39]

Fig. 8.7. Residential buildings in the Jewellery Quarter (? Albion Street) taken over for industrial and workshop uses. Source: *Conurbation,* 1948.

There was deadlock on collective action from 1955-67, except that Birmingham City Council took over the freehold of the Vyse Estate properties in 1963 north of Warstone Lane. However, the discovery that industrial development certificates could be obtained by jewellery firms, because of their special ties to the Quarter, generated a number of individual private proposals from Johnson Matthey, Frank Hawker, Payton Pepper and others, while the City Council provided Hockley House beside the new flyover.

But alternative proposals were agreed between the City Council, Kay-Bevan and Norwich Union Insurance in 1967. [40] These proposals related to 10 acres (plus roads) on which 375 industrial premises (78% used by jewellers; 23% by one person firms) existed in the heart of the Quarter. In their place, there was to be an eight storey flatted factory, some single storey workshops under a car park, an exhibition hall, a new Assay Office, restaurant, bank, etc. The Hockley Centre opened in 1968 with 70 or so units from 235 sq.ft. upwards. Rents were high at 47-77 pence per sq.ft., reducing with increasing size but not totally unacceptable. The workshops below the car park were built by Bryants in 1978 and a shop/workshop precinct along Warstone Lane, opposite which the non-jewellery firm of Tenby Electrical Accessories built its new factory at that time too. (Fig. 8.8)

There have been other new buildings, in Key Hill for example, but far more has happened in the last decade through rehabilitation. An Industrial Improvement Area (IIA) was declared in 1980 (covering the area marked on the map) (Fig. 8.1) and also three conservation areas (St. Paul's Square, 1971; the Jewellery Quarter and Key Hill, both in 1980). (Fig. 8.9) In addition to IIA grants, there has been a specifically Jewellery Quarter Grant Aid Scheme.[41] 314 out of the 560 eligible buildings have been upgraded and 52 refurbished at the cost of £4.5m public and £6m private funds, including two subventions from EEC for Anvic House and a scheme in Constitution Hill,[42] and an Historical Buildings Grant from English Heritage.[43] As well as the City and Edward VI School Foundation, Inner City Enterprises is now committed to work in St. Paul's Square and at Victoria Works in Graham Street. Gillott's old pen works, which had become a multi-storey slum around a huge courtyard, the back view belying the face shown to the world in Graham Street, is in process of being rehabilitated at the cost of £1m.[44] Elsewhere, burnt out or bomb-damaged parking lots have existed beside fashionable restaurants or architectural offices. But much is happening daily with new uses entering the Quarter spilling over from the more expensive central business district to the south - fashion shops, recording studios, video producers, advertising agencies, environmental engineers, and a transport concern. In addition, considerable non-jewellery manufacturing continues to exist in the Quarter and around its edges. (Figs. 8.10, 8.11).

Fig. 8.8. Warstone Lane, 1989, showing Tenby Electrical (left).

JEWELLERY QUARTER - INDUSTRIAL IMPROVEMENT AREA

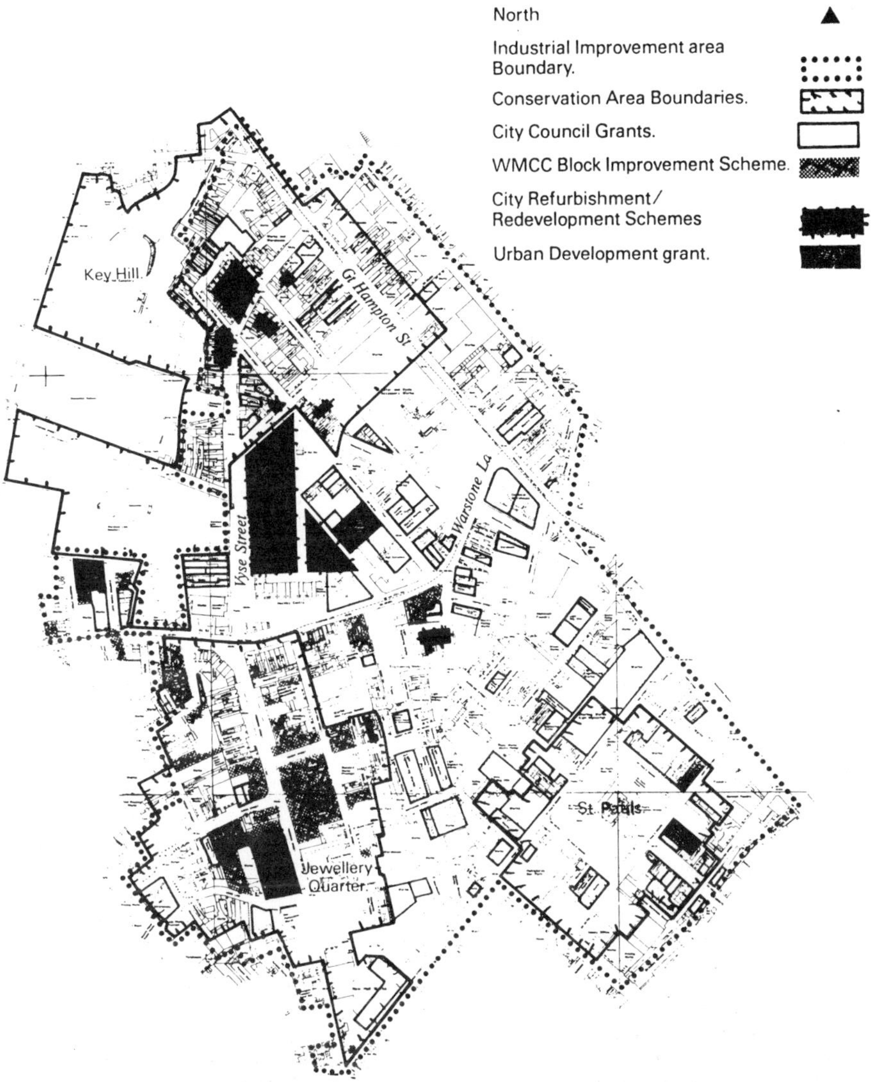

Fig. 8.9. Plan of the Industrial Improvement Area, showing the improvement schemes.

Fig. 8.10. The Argent Works, junction of Legge Lane and Frederick Street, designed by J.G. Bland, built 1863 for W.E. Wiley, gold pen manufacturer. Photographed 1989.

Alternative Jobs

All these ventures help to preserve the buildings and offer alternative jobs to replace those lost by labour saving and depleted markets in the Quarter and elsewhere in Birmingham - and Lucas Industries, Great King Street headquarters is closing just 500 yards away. These jobs have been much needed in the Birmingham of the 1970s and especially of the 1980s. This is so even though, in the last two years, the city's unemployment rate has happily fallen back to about the national average (though remaining three times that average in areas adjacent to the Quarter).

Moving on from the development of offices in the 1970s, Birmingham City Council has recently, like so many others, been pursuing tourism development and jobs. The International Convention Centre with its entourage of attractions lies only 500 yards from the Quarter, cross-country or along the canal. Its business tourists will help the 'latent tourism potential' of the Jewellery Quarter to be realised. Various proposals are in embryo. The whole area may become a heritage park, with three focal points in a discovery centre, a jewellery trade centre and a science centre (at the existing Science Museum in Newhall Street.[45] The £75,000 discovery centre is planned as a 'time capsule' based on Smith & Pepper's 73-year old jewellery works in Vyse Street which has stood untouched since work there stopped five years ago.[46] Next door, an 157-year old building is to be a visitors centre with modern exhibition facilities. Covent Garden rather than Hatton Garden seems to be the inspiration. These, and others, could provide "*pearls on a necklace*"[47] for tourists (and more local residents) to visit perhaps while they follow one of the trails that have been documented for several years.

Fig. 8.11. Finishing operations in progress at J. Hudson & Co, whistle manufacturer, Barr Street, 1989.

The jewellery industry is also being fostered with the 'Made in Birmingham' labels of 1987, the new training proposals[48] (Fig. 8.12) and the jewellery centre and enterprise workshop "*where graduates from an upgraded jewellery school could go into business.*"[49] A local collaborative project for the jewellery industry is funded by the (late) Manpower Services Commission, via Birmingham City Council, and is directed at management skills in the industry, with an eye on 1992 and at promoting wider utilisation of design skills.[50] The collaborators also include the School of Jewellery and Silversmithing and the British Jewellers Association, the Assay Office and half a dozen prominent firms. Individual firms are also exercising new initiatives to seize market opportunities at home and abroad.

Hopefully, these initiatives and plans, and the multi-million scheme unveiled in February 1989,[51] will come to successful fruition in a grand design that will make 1989, and the early 1990s, exciting and prosperous years for the Jewellery Quarter, the jewellery industry and Birmingham City.

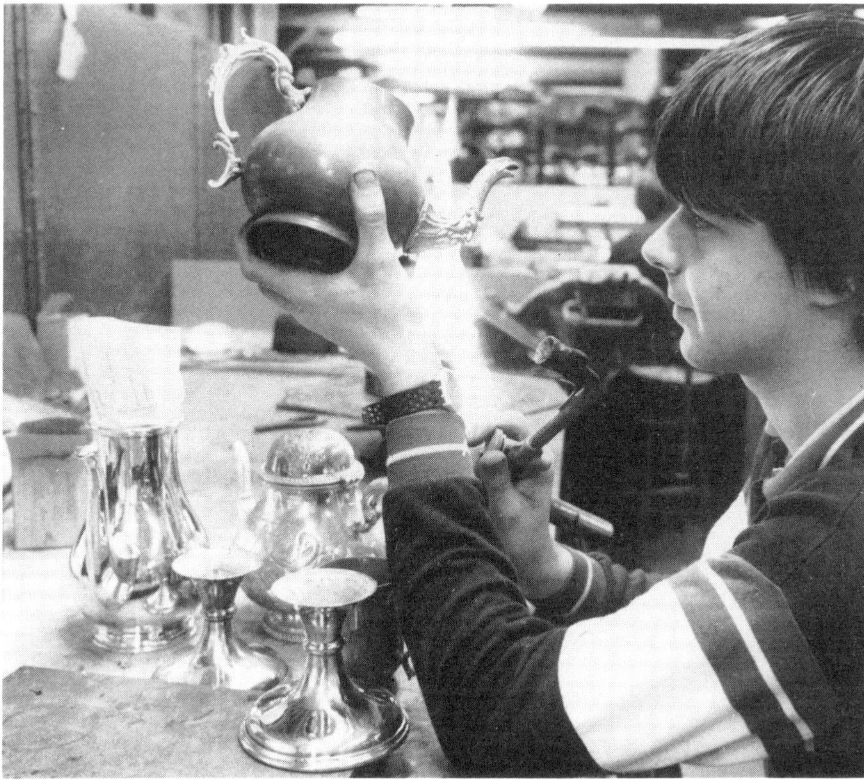

Fig. 8.12. Trainee silversmith, Ian Rickhuss, working on a teapot at Barker Ellis, Hockley, under a £3000 grant from Birmingham City Council. Source: *The Birmingham Post,* 9 March 1989.

REFERENCES

1 Whose views are usually expressed through the British Jewellers' Association (est. 1887), located in the Jewellery Quarter. In 1989 it represented 800 firms or 40% of the national trade.
2 The 'king-pin' firm was Elkington, employing 500 in 1850 and 2,000 in 1887, which moved to Walsall 1953 and failed in the 1960s when a Delta Metal subsidiary. See Victoria County, History, vol. 7, pp.127, 145; G. Hughes, 1967 p.228.
3 B.L.C. Johnson quoted in C. Gilbert, p.4.11.
4 C. Gilbert, p.4.12.
5 See J.S. Wright, 'The Jewellery and Gilt Toy Trades", in S. Timmins (ed.), 1866, in C. Gilbert, p.5.5.
6 B.M.D. Smith, 1987, pp.8-11.
7 C. Gilbert, p.1.6.
8 G. Hughes, pp.87-9, for account of J. & J. Wiggin of Bloxwich, makers of stainless steel tea services etc.

9 C. Gilbert, pp.6.28-29, 32 said 80% of silver ware on offer in 1937 and 1955 and 67% in 1970 was a reproduction of an old design, with designs of handles, spouts etc. switched.
10 C. Gilbert, p.6.30.
11 Ratners Group, *Report and Accounts*, 1987, pp.4,6. In 1989 Ratners owned Samuels (acquired 1986), shutting its manufacturing down) and Walkers et al.
12 *Financial Times*, 12 October 1988; 12 December 1988.
13 Ratners had 110 core suppliers, 1987. Ratners, op.cit, p.12.
14 B.M.D. Smith, 1987, pp.42-4, 72-3 and *Financial Times*, 19 April 1988 refers to 9ct. gold 'throwaway' articles.
15 B.M.D. Smith, 1987, pp.41-2.
16 URBED, 1987, pp.6,21.
17 Segal Quince Wicksteed, June 1987, p.17.
18 G.C. Allen, 1929 and 1959, in C. Gilbert, p.5.17.
19 C. Gilbert, pp.5.4, 5.12-13, 5.20. The Warwickshire figures for 1931, 1921 etc. come from the Census of Population.
20 The peak post-war years were 1974-5 in Birmingham and 1961 and 1977 in Britain, when employment reached 40,000 nationally, with 23,000 nationally in 1984 plus several thousands self-employed. See B.M.D. Smith, p.64.
21 Ibid., p.70. 53% in 1960; 43% in 1981, the latter being close to the national proportion.
22 Ibid., p.65.
23 Pentos has sold Barker Ellis back to its managers. See *Birmingham Post*, 12 June 1987; 12 January 1989.
24 C. Gilbert, pp.2.24-5. 1,000 in 1946 in Birmingham (86% in the Quarter) and 770 in 1971 (83% in the Quarter).
25 B.M.D. Smith, p.4. 534 names were found in the *West Midlands Trade/Business Pages Telephone Directory,* 1986, to which were added 100 firms found in the Quarter.
26 C. Gilbert, p.7.29.
27 B.M.D. Smith, pp.30-5.
28 An exception was Abrahams & Co. (Birmingham), electro-platers, who moved to Newcastle-upon-Tyne in the 1960s through regional development assistance and an advanced factory. See C. Gilbert, p.7.7.
29 Laughton & Son employ 750 in popular jewellery at Warstock. See *Birmingham Evening Mail,* 20 August 1987.
30 C. Gilbert, chapter 7, found that, from 1946-71, 25 firms moved out of the W. Midlands region; 17 moved over 3,600 yards from the Quarter within the region; 331 moved within the Quarter. Those moving in were mainly outworkers opening workshops.
31 C. Gilbert, pp.7.35-7, 7.45.
32 B.M.D. Smith, pp.29-34.
33 Based on M.J. Wise, 1949, pp.68-70.
34 Also true of the Vyse Estate (unlike the Calthorpe). J.C. Roche, 1927, in *The Dial*, 1928, quoted in C. Gilbert, p.4.5n.
35 Victoria County History, vol.7, p.47.
36 C. Gilbert, p.4.6; Victoria County History, p.47.
37 C. Gilbert, pp.7.47-8.
38 Bournville Village Trust, 1941, p.107, and 1943.
39 C. Gilbert, pp.7.50-55, using unpublished proposals found in Birmingham Planning Dept., in 1972, but mentioned by H. Manzoni, *J. of the Town Planning Institute*, March 1955, pp.97-8. A 12-storey factory was proposed in mid 1960s.
40 Gilbert, p.7.60. The 120-year lease was signed in 1969.
41 URBED, pp.3-4,8.
42 Segal Quince Wicksteed, pp.2, 66, 69.
43 *Birmingham Post*, 24 November 1988.
44 Ibid., 27 July 1988, 28 January 1988.
45 URBED, op.cit. This is a new jewellery centre.
46 *Birmingham Post*, 18 December 1987; 28 July 1988.
47 URBED, pp.25, 60.
48 *Birmingham Post,* 13 October 1988.
49 Ibid., 22 June 1987.
50 Ibid., 13 and 14 October 1988.
51 Ibid., 14 February 1989, speaks of 50 businesses, 250 jobs, 100,000 visitors and £4m

private investment being triggered off by action by a combination of Birmingham City Council, the Inner Cities Minister's City Action Team, and the Chamber of Commerce and Industry.

BIBLIOGRAPHY

Bournville Village Trust, *When We Build Again,* George Allen & Unwin, 1941.

Bournville Village Trust, *Our Birmingham,* 1943.

C. Gilbert, *The Evolution of an Urban Craft: The Gold, Silver and Allied Trades of the West Midlands,* unpublished M.Soc.Sc. thesis, University of Birmingham, 1972.

G. Hughes, *Modern Silver,* Studio Vista, 1967.

J.C. Roche, *The History, Development and Organisation of the Birmingham Jewellery and Allied Trades,* University of Birmingham thesis, 1927, published as supplement to *The Dial,* 1928.

Segal Quince Wicksteed, *Jewellery Industry and Jewellery Quarter Development Study. Stage 1 Report: Assessment of the Jewellery Industry: A Report to Birmingham City Council,* Birmingham City Council Economic Development Unit, June 1987.

B.M.D. Smith, *Report of an Interview-Based Survey in the Birmingham Jewellery Quarter Relating to the Jewellery Industry,* University of Birmingham, Centre for Urban and Regional Studies Research Memorandum 107, 1987 (This was part of the Segal Quince Wicksteed and URBED study).

URBED, *Jewellery Industry and Jewellery Quarter Development Study: Developing the Jewellery Quarter's Potential,* Birmingham City Council Economic Development Unit, June 1987.

Victoria County History of the Counties of England, *A History of Warwickshire, Birmingham,* vol. 7 (R.B. Pugh, ed.), 1964.

M.J. Wise, "On the Evolution of the Jewellery and Gun Quarters in Birmingham, *Institute of British Georgaphers' Transactions,* 15, 1949.

FURTHER READING

G.C. Allen, *The Industrial Development of Birmingham and the Black Country 1860-1927,* 1929 and new edition, Cass, 1959.

City of Birmingham Planning Department, *Brum Trail 6. Jewellery Quarter,* (by Clive Gilbert and Birmingham Urban Studies Committee), 1981.

City of Birmingham Planning Department, *St. Paul's Square and the Birmingham Jewellery Quarter Trail,* n.d.

M. Haddleton, *The Jewellery Quarter: History and Guide,* YBA Publications, 1988.

B.L.C. Johnson, "The Distribution of the Factory Population in the West Midlands Conurbation", *Institute of British Geographers' Transactions,* 1958.

B.M.D. Smith, "Industry and Trade, 1880-1960" in R.B. Pugh (ed.), *A History of Warwickshire. vol. VII, Birmingham,* Victoria County History of the Counties of England, 1964, pp.140-208.

J.S. Wright, "The Jewellery and Gilt Toy Trades" in S. Timmins, *Birmingham and the Midland Hardware District,* Hardwick, 1866.

CHAPTER 9

R.W. WINFIELD AND THE BIRMINGHAM BRASS TRADE

Barrie Eccleston

When Birmingham acquired city status in 1889, the firm of R.W. Winfield was on the brink of foundering commercially. The company ceased trading in 1900. The inclusion of an account of Winfield's activities may be justified in the context of this book on the grounds that the firm could stand as a representative of the inventive excellence of the town's nineteenth century industry on which its prosperity and claim to city status was ultimately based.

By the second half of the eighteenth century, Birmingham had become the acknowledged centre of the metal trades. This ascendency was based on four staples:- the buckle and button trade (known as the toy trade); jewellery and silversmithing; the gun trade; and brass foundry. Of these, the brass foundry trade was to become increasingly important. Winfield's design manager wrote in 1866, "*what Manchester is in cotton, Bradford in wool, and Sheffield in steel, Birmingham is in brass.*"[1] R.W. Winfield was a brass founder. The last physical traces of his factory have inevitably been removed by the construction of the new International Convention Centre in Broad Street. At its greatest extent, the company occupied most of the site between Broad Street and Cambridge Street as far as King Alfred's Place. (Fig. 9.1.)

In 1829, before he was twenty one years old, R.W. Winfield set up in business on his own account, his trustees having enough faith in his abilities to advance the necessary capital. His first premises were in a little stuccoed building "*just at the bend which Cambridge Street takes to arrive at the Crescent.*"[2] By the 1880s the work covered some nine acres. "*Pile after pile of extensive blocks of buildings rose, one after another, on grounds adjoining the original manufactory. . . . . . Many of the buildings were five or six storeys high.*"[3]

R.W. Winfield was remembered as one of the great entrepreneurs of his day. Writing in 1892, W.J. Davis who, in 1872, had organised the first trade union in the brass foundry trade in Birmingham, recalled the achievement of R.W. Winfield in these terms: "*Birmingham was a brass founding domain, Robert Walter Winfield was one of its princes. . . . . Winfield was one of those men who not only built up a trade and made it pay, but also won respect of honour for it, carved out fame for it, and made it part and parcel of the nation's eminence.*"[4] Winfield was also remembered as a practical philanthropist. Early in the history of his firm, he leased a room as a night school for the boys in his employ. Attendance was compulsory on three nights per week for every boy under eighteen. Before the Education Act of 1870 established Board Schools, this school was seen as a considerable advantage to Winfield's employees. "*Many parents eagerly sought employment for their children at the works. . . . . and Mr. Winfield soon had the 'pick' of the youths of the town.*"[5] The school attendance grew rapidly, and a new school room was built within the factory at a cost of £2,000. A properly qualified school master was engaged and the average nightly attendance rose to 250 pupils. "*Drawing was made a special feature of the instruction, and successful pupils in this class received government awards.*"[6] Winfield's design manager, W.C. Aitken, understood the importance of drawing, and pointed out that anyone who comes into contact with workmen knows "*how much more useful is he who can draw than he who cannot.*"[7] Winfield's school thus anticipated the kinds of link between art, education, and industry that was intended by the establishment of the Schools of Design.

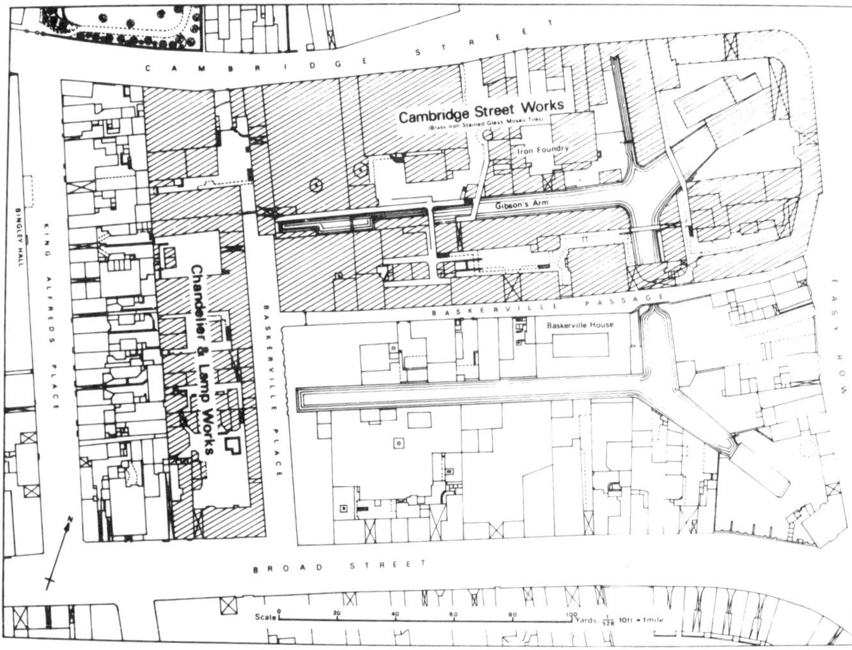

Fig. 9.1. Plan of Cambridge Street Works. Redrawn by B. Eccleston from City Surveyor's maps, c.1886-8, at a scale of 10ft. : 1 mile.

For some forty years, R.W. Winfield was the sole proprietor of his extensive business. He was assisted by his only son, John Fawkener Winfield, who was being groomed to take over from his father, but these plans were cut short by the son's untimely death in 1861. Winfield never recovered from this blow. He became a confirmed invalid and died in December 1869.

In a town where the processes of manufacture were split up and carried out by small firms specialising in one branch of a trade only, Winfield's factory is of a special interest because of its integrated structure and the vast range of its products. "*This firm was as exceptional in the Birmingham brass trade of 1860 as the Soho factory had been three quarters of a century before.*"[8] By mid century, Winfield had become the largest of the Birmingham brass foundry manufacturers employing about 10% of those employed in the industry. By 1866 the workforce numbered 800. Winfield's produced sheet metal, wire and tube in their own rolling mills and castings in their own foundry. The range of their domestic products included gas fittings and chandeliers and (later) electroliers and other electrical fittings and appliances; metallic bedsteads, cots and other furniture; art and ecclesiastical metalwork; wrought iron; stained and painted glass; tiles and mosaics, as well as a thousand and one domestic items in brass needed to satisfy the Victorian taste for elaborate ornamentation.

Winfield's Products at the *Great Exhibition*, 1851

Under the guidance of W.C. Aitken, the firm exhibited its range of products at all the important national and international exhibitions of the 19th century. The reputation of Winfield's firm perhaps stood highest in 1851. It may, however, be of interest here to mention their participation in the *Birmingham Exposition of Arts and Manufactures* held under the auspices of the Royal Society for the Advancement of Science in 1849. Coming as it did only two years before the *Great Exhibition*, the Birmingham Show was a successful curtain-raiser for the London exhibition of 1851. Prince Albert himself was a visitor and it was believed (at least in Birmingham) that the success of the exhibition convinced the Prince of the practicabililty of staging the *Great Exhibition* itself. A special temporary wooden building was erected in the grounds of Bingley House in Broad Street. Winfield's products were prominently featured. Gas fittings, curtain bands, window cornices, chandeliers etc. were shown at the entrance occupying the entire side of the exhibition hall with the metallic bedsteads displayed opposite to them. Prince Albert did not fail to notice the exhibits. "*His Royal Highness paused for a few moments at the stall of Mr. R.W. Winfield and made enquiries as to the mode of tube drawing and the methods employed in giving colour all of which were answered by Mr. Winfield who was in attendance.*"[9] Birmingham had become the centre for mechanised tube manufacture. Technical developments were stimulated by simultaneous demands in the gun trade, gas lighting, and the advent of the newly fashionable metallic bedstead. "*No patent of importance relating to these developments was granted outside the town and its vicinity in the first half of the nineteenth century.*"[10] Winfield's most important technical contribution at this time was the yielding die method of drawing tubes, stemming from Ward and Winfield's patent of 1848, enabling tapered and fluted tubes to be readily produced. In this method, the soldered tube was placed on a tapered mandrel and drawn through a soft metal die. "*The substance of the die gave way as the tube was drawn, but offered sufficient resistance to close the grain and give a bright surface.*"[11] Fluted, twisted and decorated tubes were also available, and with these the 'Brummagem' brass founders were able to give their products (and in particular that quintessential Victorian artefact, the four poster brass bedstead) a splendid ornamental appearance.

At the *Birmingham Exposition* of 1849, the naturalistic style of ornamentation favoured by Winfield was typified by the curtain bands and gas fittings. Opaque glass flowers of remarkable botanical accuracy were combined with stamped brass foliage. Fuchsias and anemones adorned the curtain bands while arum lilies were used for the motif decorating the curtain pole ends (Fig. 9.2).

The reputation of Winfield's firm reached its zenith in 1851. It was awarded a Council Gold Medal for its products and two of the light fittings, incorporating parian ware figurines by Minton, were acquired by Queen Victoria and Prince Albert, a fact that the *Art Journal* considered "*supersedes the necessity for any further reference, and bears ample testimony to the excellence of the work.*"[12] Great interest was shown in such items as the 'Angel' cot. Here the associationist theory comes into play, suggesting the traditional idea that "*in the early stages of our existence, these unseen beings are present to watch over and protect us.*"[13] The great 'Renaissance' bedstead, a show-piece specially prepared for the exhibition, included all the virtuoso metalworking techniques of which Winfield's were

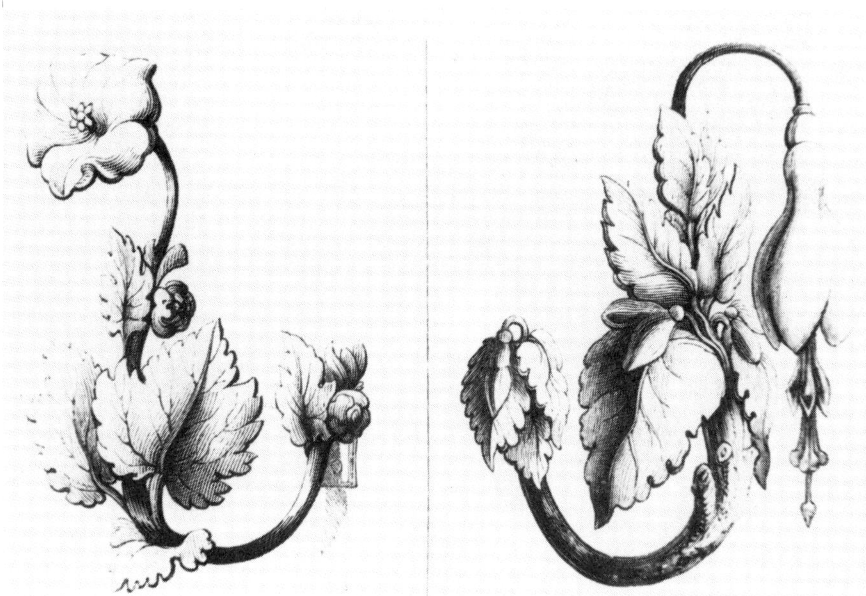

Fig. 9.2. R.W. Winfield. Curtain pole brackets with opaque glass flowers and stamped brass foliage, shown at the Birmingham Exposition of 1849. *The Art Journal,* October 1, 1849.

capable. Figures, foliage and scroll work were introduced at every conceivable point. Although the work shown by Winfield at the *Great Exhibition* received praise in the "*Reports of the Juries,*"[14] there were those who had struck a more critical note. A.W.N. Pugin referred to "*those inexhaustible mines of bad taste, Birmingham and Sheffield,*"[15] and commented that "*gleaming, showy, and meritricious ornament was never so much in vogue as at present.*"[16] Ruskin decried "*all the stamped metals. . . all the short, cheap and easy ways of doing that whose difficulty is its honour.*"[17] It is fair to say, however, that when Winfield executed a design for a bedstead with restraint, a simple and elegant product could result. This may be exemplified by a half-tester bedstead of the 1880s. Plain brass tubing was used throughout. The only decoration occurred in a repeated motif, in flat brass strip, that was reminiscent of the dignity of Ionic volutes (Fig. 9.3). The bedstead carried Winfield's plate - "R.W. Winfield & Co. patentees and manufacturers to the Royal Family."

There was however, one item of furniture exhibited by Winfield in 1851 that, at the time, passed without comment or any apparent interest but which has come to be seen as the firm's most significant contribution to the furniture of the Victorian era. It was listed simply in the catalogue as "*Brass rocking or lounging chair with Morocco furniture.*" It has been said of the chair that "*it showed in its unusual simplicity of design and control of material both a startling contrast to the other exhibits and an approach far ahead of its time. With its carefully balanced curved supports it foreshadowed the metal furniture of Mart Stam, Marcel Breuer and Mies van der Rohe.*"[18] The chairs of these designers have long been available in modern reproduction. A version of the Winfield rocking chair has now

Fig. 9.3. R.W. Winfield & Co. Half-tester brass bedstead, 1880s. Photo courtesy of Royal Pavilion, Art Gallery and Museums, Brighton.

had its importance in the history of modern furniture recognised by joining this elite group in reproduction.[19] It is perhaps worth remembering that this product of Birmingham industry appeared some seventy years before the tubular cantilever chairs of the Bauhaus circle of the 1920s. The version of the chair shown at the *Great Exhibition* was in tubular brass (Fig. 9.4). An example is now in the reserve collection of the Victoria and Albert Museum. Later versions were in strip brass and were shown at the London Exhibition of 1862 (Fig. 9.5). In these chairs, the upholstery of the seat was slung in the frame, and was in no way connected directly to the sides. The weight of the sitter was taken by the top rail and semi-cylindrical member, to the front of which the upholstery was attached. The curved side frames were spaced apart by cross rods. In purely structural terms, therefore, the Winfield rocker had little affinity with the true cantilever chair. Winfield's innovation was in the use of continuous lengths of tube or strip metal to produce an elegant design. In this sense it was clearly a forerunner of modern tubular metal chairs.

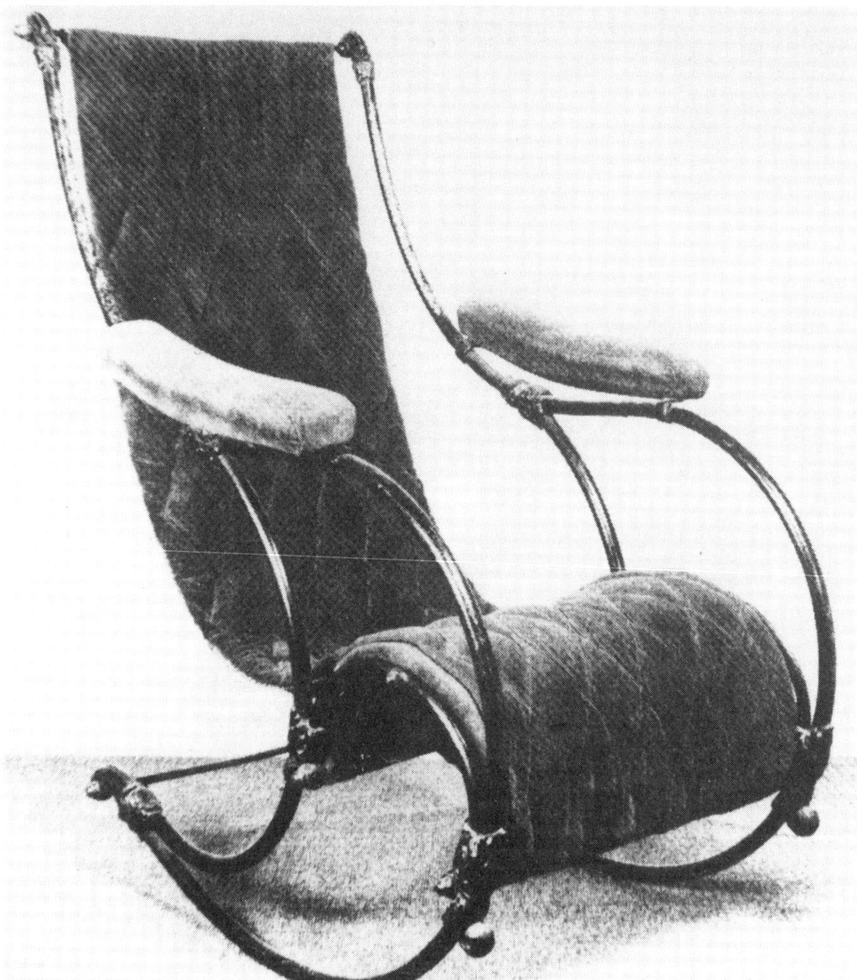

Fig. 9.4. R.W. Winfield. Tubular brass rocking or lounging chair, upholstered in morocco, shown at the *Great Exhibition*, 1851. Photo courtesy of Victoria and Albert Museum.

Fig. 9.5. R.W. Winfield. Rocking or lounging chair in strip brass, upholstered in plush, shown at the London Exhibition, 1862. Photo courtesy of Victoria and Albert Museum.

In both visual and structural terms a closer parallel existed between the Winfield rocking chairs and the Thonet bentwood products of the time. However, rocking chairs did not appear in the range of products shown by Thonet at the *Great Exhibition*. The traditional date for the production of rocking chair No.1 was 1860, and it was first illustrated in Thonet's broadsheet catalogue of 1886. The view of a leading authority on Thonet furniture was that, "*its design...... undoubtedly derives from the brass and iron rockers exhibited at the Crystal Palace in 1851.*"[20] Whereas most nineteenth century rocking chairs were conventional side or arm chairs with curved runners added, both the Winfield and Thonet rockers treated the rocking element as an integral part of the design and exhibited a similar fluidity of line in their use of bent material. As in the Winfield chair, the Thonet rockers had a continuous curved member running from the foot of the rocker to the top of the back and this was braced by one or more internal curved members. The side frames were joined by circular section rails with simple screwed joints. The main side members were, however, pitched lower in the Thonet examples as, in all cases, the separate seat and back units were fixed directly to the side frames (Fig. 9.6).

Fig. 9.6. Thonet bentwood rocking chair no.1, c.1860, first illustrated in Thonet's broadsheet catalogue of 1866. *Architectural Review,* October 1968.

There is little evidence that Thonet was widely travelled and it is likely that the English architect P.H. Desvignes played some part in making Thonet aware of the existence of the Winfield rockers. The two men had been associated since 1842-3 when Desvignes was engaged on the renovation of the Palais Liechtenstein in Vienna. In c.1849 Desvignes returned to England while Thonet remained in Vienna. Desvignes had such faith in the ultimate success of Thonet's bentwood technique that he sent regular payments from England to assist in the new business and was thus in regular contact with Thonet at around the time of the first appearance of the Winfield rockers. The evidence presented above would seem to point to the fact that the Winfield rocking chair, in its original tubular form, preceded the first Thonet rocker by some ten years. It could be, however, that later versions of the Winfield chair were themselves influenced by the Thonet types. Visitors to Harewood House in Yorkshire may see in the Old Library a version of the Winfield rocker. It is of the tubular type but was enamelled brown to resemble wood and there are additional curlicues within the side frames similar to those found in the Thonet rocking chairs.

Fig. 9.7. Dr. Calvert's 'Digestive' chair in strip iron. This type of chair appeared at some time subsequent to the *Great Exhibition*. Photo: United Photographers.

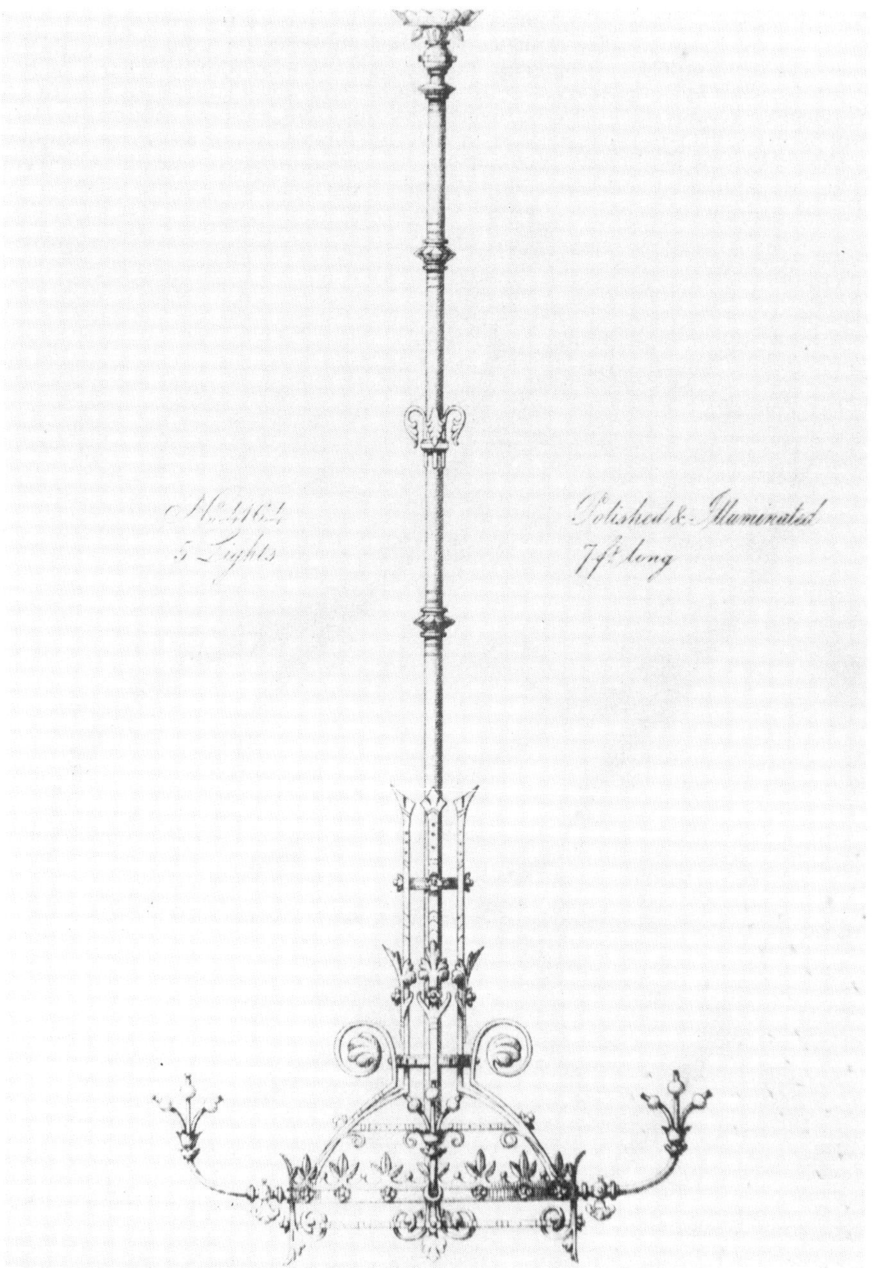

Fig. 9.8. R. W. Winfield & Co. Gothic lighting fitting, c.1877, illustrated in their catalogue of *Mediaeval Metalwork for Ecclesiastical Use.*

Rocking chairs in general were more popular in the United States than in Europe. "*Many Europeans considered rockers suitable only for the sick and invalid.*"[21] This would seem to be borne out by the fact that, at some time subsequent to the *Great Exhibition* of 1851, rocking chairs of almost identical design to the later Winfield types were produced in iron strip, apparently under the direction of a certain Dr. Calvert, whose name became associated with this particular model of chair. Calvert called these pieces 'Digestive' chairs and recommended them for use by ladies and invalids. Chairs of the Dr. Calvert type were exported to the United States and were also made there. An example of one of Dr. Calvert's 'Digestive' chairs, which was repaired by Ernest Race for its owner, Mr. C.F. Colt, "*bears a brass label with the inscription: Dr. Calvert's Digestive Chair.*"[22](Fig. 9.7). It is unclear whether there was any business connection between Winfield and Calvert.

Winfield's Products after 1851

With the departure of W.C. Aitken from his post as Winfield's design manager, the innovative nature of their design policy seems to have slackened. Aitken left Winfield shortly after the death of John Fawkener Winfield, to whom he had been closely attached. He was briefly employed by Messrs Hardman & Co. and then spent a short time as manager of Skidmore's Art Manufacturing Company in Coventry. Winfield's were to take over this firm in c.1878. Aitken returned to Birmingham as manager of Hardman's new works in Newhall Street, a position he held until about 1872. In Winfield's products from the 1860s the historical styles and a variety of oriental influences predominated. A valuable article in the *Cabinet Maker and Art Furnisher* of 1886 described Winfield's London showrooms at 47 Holborne Viaduct and stated "*whatever the style of the bedroom suite may happen to be, whether Early English - so called - Jacobean, Queen Anne, Adam, or even Anglo Japanese, it can be matched up in this eclectic bedroom department.*"[23] The writer of the article went on to say "*it was trying enough for some cabinet makers, years ago, for Birmingham to blot out the wooden bedstead trade, without further attempts at encroachment.*" The *Cabinet Maker* need not have worried. Heals' ultimately successful campaign to re-introduce the wooden bedstead was to turn the tables on the (then) flourishing Birmingham metallic bedstead trade. From the 1880s Winfield's products were dominated by a Puginesque Gothic style (Fig. 9.8). A high percentage of the work, including tiles and stained glass, was for ecclesiastical purposes.

On the management side of the business there were difficulties. Soon after the death of his son, R.W. Winfield took into partnership his relative, Charles Weston, and his confidential clerk, James Aitkins. Both his daughters had married church ministers in 1852. The estate was then divided between the Rev. Snepp and Rev. Browne, the rest of the firm's capital being held by the managers Aitkins and Weston. Capital became short, and new partners, C.W. Torr and H.C. Taylor were brought in with £5,000 each in 1873. On the death of two of these partners, the firm was sold in 1887 to Winfields Limited, a public company, for £143,000. Torr remained as manager until 1890 when he was succeeded by W.R. Lane. Most of the directors were Londoners. Losses were made and liabilities in 1899 exceeded assets. The firm finally ceased trading in 1900.[24]

REFERENCES

1 W.C. Aitken, p.5.
2 E. Edwards, p.118.
3 Ibid., p.119.
4 W.J. Davis, p.35.
5 E. Edwards, p. 121.
6 Ibid.
7 W.C. Aitken, in a letter to William Scholefield, M.P., which was appended to the *Report of the Select Committee on the Schools of Design,* 1849.
8 G.C. Allen, p.125.
9 *The Art Journal,* vol. XI, 1849, p.378.
10 R. Prosser, p.85.
11 Ibid., pp.93-4.
12 *The Art Journal Illustrated Catalogue of the Great Exhibition,* p.242.
13 Ibid., p.243.
14 "Reports of the Juries", *Official Catalogue of the Great Exhibition,* p.497.
15 A.W.N. Pugin, p.24.
16 Ibid., p.30.
17 J. Ruskin, Chapter 5, paragrah 24.
18 E. Joy, pp.203-4.
19 "Design up for Auction", *Observer Magazine,* 5 June 1988, p.35.
20 C. Wilk, p.35.
21 Ibid.
22 *The Architects' Journal,* 1 September 1949, p.218.
23 *Cabinet Maker and Art Furnisher,* 1 March 1866.
24 The financial affairs of R.W. Winfield were reconstructed from surviving records in "R.W. Winfield & Co., Brassfounders, Cambridge Street, 1829-1900," in B.M.D. Smith, p.101.

BIBLIOGRAPHY

W.C. Aitken, *An Early History of Brass and the Brass Manufacturers of Birmingham,* Birmingham, 1866.

G.C. Allen, *The Industrial Development of Birmingham and the Black Country 1860-1927,* London, 1929; 1959.

The Art Journal Illustrated Catalogue of the Great Exhibition, 1851.

W.J. Davis, *A Short History of the Birmingham Brass Trade,* Birmingham, 1892.

E.Edwards, *Personal Recollections of Birmingham and Birmingham Men,* London, 1877.

E. Joy, *English Furniture 1800-1851,* London, 1977.

Official Catalogue of the Great Exhibition, 1851.

R. Prosser, *Birmingham Inventors and Inventions,* Birmingham, 1881; reprinted Wakefield, 1970.

A.W.N. Pugin, *The True Principles of Pointed or Christian Architecture,* London, 1841.

J. Ruskin, *The Seven Lamps of Architecture,* London, 1849.

B.M.D. Smith, *Local Business Records,* typed manuscript, 1964 (in Birmingham Central Reference Library, Local Studies).

C. Wilk, *Thonet: 150 Years of Furniture,* New York, 1980.

CHAPTER 10

BEST & LLOYD LTD. 1868 – 1989

Kate Child

The history of the light fittings firm of Best & Lloyd Ltd. spans the full one hundred years and more of design in Birmingham. A family concern, now in its fourth generation, it is representative of the innumerable traditional, small to medium sized manufacturing businesses in the brass foundry and metal trades which flourished in Birmingham in the nineteenth century.

The firm's origins go back to 1840 when Robert Best (1804-1863) set up as a candle-lamp maker in Ludgate Hill, close to the Jewellery Quarter. The firm expanded and moved to larger premises in nearby Charlotte Street in 1863. The partnership of Best & Lloyd was formed in 1868 between Best's son, Robert Hall Best (1843-1925), and Harry Lloyd, the son of a wealthy industrialist, who found the business new premises next to his red lead mill at the Cambray Works, Wattville Road, Handsworth (now Smethwick). Harry Lloyd retired from the business in 1878 and the firm was made into a limited company in 1898, with Best as Chairman.[1]

By 1889 Best & Lloyd was an established business known for its fine art brasswork, producing quality decorative light fittings for a growing middle class market at home and abroad. R.H. Best was the main influence on the firm until after World War 1. His design policy was aimed at survival, in an increasingly competitive trade, through manufacturing to a high standard of workmanship, by keeping ahead of contemporary fashion (and sometimes leading the way) and by producing fittings based on the practical solution to a problem. An entrepreneurial designer himself, he produced a number of inventions improving the flexibility of the gas chandelier. His 'flagship' design was the 'Surprise' pendant of 1893 which, with its original joint system, permitted the light to be moved both horizontally and vertically. Largely due to the popularity of this innovative fitting, which included a prestigious sale to royalty when it was purchased for King Edward VII's library at Sandringham (Fig. 10.1), sales were increased five-fold between 1893-1914.

To meet the growing demand for the 'Surprise' pendant, capstan lathes were installed from 1894 to make, economically and speedily, the small component parts such as gas cocks and swivels. In so doing, the firm became one of the first manufacturers to use mass-production methods for gas fittings. When the change-over to electricity occurred in the domestic market from the 1890s, Best & Lloyd adapted its production to meet this new demand. In general, electric pendants (or 'electroliers') and brackets followed the same design as those for gas fittings, the body of the design being made of sheet metal, or brass cast from the vast library of patterns in stock. The drawing office at Best & Lloyd c.1913 included staff who had been with the firm since 1868, such as Mr. Cowley, Mr. Osborne and Mr. Hamlyn, who designed elegant lanterns with an eighteenth century appearance. Younger designers included William Morris, chief designer in the 1920s, and Frank Cashmore (b.1893), who joined the firm as an office boy in 1909, attending Birmingham School of Art part-time. He went on to become the firm's only resident designer in the 1930s. R.H. Best also kept his products up-to-date

Fig. 10.1. 'Surprise' Pendant no.S.262 (first marketed in 1897) in King Edward VII's Library, Sandringham. Source: R.D. Best, *Brass Chandelier,* 1940. Photo by permission of Best & Lloyd Ltd.

and fresh by drawing from what he saw on his frequent trips to the Continent. One such successful design was the alabaster bowl pendant, introduced to Best & Lloyd from Italy in 1910.[2]

Following the impact of electrification, the firm underwent a period of updating from 1905 when a new Works Manager, B.B. Blackburn, was appointed. Blackburn rationalised production in the light fittings department and introduced a successful Automotive Products Department. Lathes, previously used to make gas fitting parts and not required for producing electric light fittings, were instead turned to the manufacture of accessories such as petrol caps and tank fillers for the booming local motorcycle and automobile industries. Best & Lloyd supplied Triumph motorcycles and 25 out of 36 other models displayed at the 1913 Paris Motor Show with petrol pumps.[3] During World War I the capstan machines were turned to munitions production in common with most other local firms in the metal trades. When regular production resumed in 1918 the Department expanded and between 1925 and 1929, its sales exceeded those of the Chandelier Department.[4] In 1931 the Automotive Products Department was sold to the Birmingham brassfounders, Benton & Stone.

Fig.10.2. 'Knole' Pendant model no. 26388, c.1925, in cast brass. Photo courtesy of Best & Lloyd Ltd.

R.H. Best was an enlightened manufacturer with an interest in social reform and technical education in particular. Through his annual sales trips to the Continent and his research for two influential pamphlets[5] he concluded that the German industrial training system was far in advance of that in England. He sent his children to the Continent as a preparation for working in the firm.

His son, Robert Dudley Best (1892-1984), was to become the main influence on the firm from the middle 1920s to the 1970s. He was educated first at Bedales, the advanced co-educational boarding school, before spending a year going through the workshops at Best & Lloyd. Thereafter he spent the year of 1911 at the Düsseldorf School of Industrial Art, which was then under the directorship of the Deutsche Werkbund member Wilhelm Kreis. This was followed by a period in Paris at the *atelier* of a designer of interior decoration and furniture,[6] before returning to Best & Lloyd to complete his training in the drawing office. The continental experience opened his eyes to developments in modern design and prepared him for experimentation in the 1920s and '30s.

Design in the Inter-War Period

The majority of the firm's products in the 1920s were rooted in tradition and there remained a large home and export market for period brass light fittings. Designs were produced which closely followed original period fittings, such as the 'Knole' pendant, model no. 26388, of c.1925, (Fig. 10.2) which was a copy of a well-known Carolean candelabra of c.1690 at Knole Park, Kent. There was always tough competition in the lighting trade (Best & Lloyd being one of around 25 electric light fitting firms in the Birmingham area), particularly from cheaper, mass-produced US products, but it appeared that this did not affect the demand for high quality, traditional brass wares. A substantial order from a US client for richly decorated fittings in eclectic styles was secured in 1921, following the firm's display at the *British Industries Fair* in Castle Bromwich. The success of the products in America led to a branch being opened in New York between 1928 and 1937.[7]

First indications of a more adventurous approach to design occurred around 1925, when the young and enthusiastic R.D. Best succeeded his father as Chairman. Throughout the inter-war period he carried out a policy of experimentation in design alongside the traditional products. Following a visit to the 1925 *International Exhibition of Modern Decorative and Industrial Arts,* Paris, Best puchased Guillaume Janneau's catalogue of light fittings, *Le Luminaire et les Moyens d'Éclairages Nouveau* (Paris, 1925), which contained many examples of Lalique's pressed, etched and moulded coloured plate glass, slotted into or clipped together by a minimum of metalwork. This publication provided the Best & Lloyd design studio with its source for a collection of modernistic French-inspired fittings, which were adapted to suit British tastes (by softening edges, for example), and the firm was among the first to work in this idiom in Britain. Moulded glass involved expensive dyes at this time and, with no guarantee of a market in England for modernistic designs, Best opted for reproducing a textured effect. He developed an economical way of producing an orange peel-like surface called 'obscured rimpled' by spraying one side of the glass with cellulose paint. An orange-shading-to-yellow colour range was selected which produced a glowing effect and designs in this range were called 'Firelight'. Commercially successful, 'Firelight' was popular with architects and was used in 1927, for example, in the Architectural Association Members' Room, Bedford Square.[8]

Architectural lighting became practical from this period and the firm adopted an active policy of securing architectural commissions in addition to selling direct to retailers. From c.1926 the new campaign to attract architects included sales lunches, improved sales literature (including the 1929 catalogue *Modern Lighting*) and a new West End showroom. Important contracts which established the firm's reputation as designers and manufacturers for the modern buildings being erected in England were the London School of Hygiene, Gower Street, (by P. Morley Horder and Verner Rees)[9] and the Royal Horticultural Hall (by Easton and

Robertson),[10] both of 1928. The modernistic style was particularly favoured by the picture palace architects and the firm became specialists in theatre and cinema lighting. Its most notable commissions were for the Paramount cinemas in Leeds and Newcastle-upon-Tyne in 1931, for which it produced spectacular electro-gilt and etched glass fittings to the specification of the US designer, Charles Fox (Fig. 10.3).[11]

Fig. 10.3. Lantern Pendants in the auditorium, Paramount Cinema Theatre, Newcastle-upon-Tyne, 1932, showing pilaster wall brackets and centre fixture for 249 lamps, height 12ft., produced in bronze, electro-gilt and aluminium, with obscured and etched glass panels, bent and waved by a special process. Source: *Fittings for Theatre and Cinema Lighting,* 1932. Photo by permission of Best & Lloyd Ltd.

Best & Lloyd is most well known today for its pioneering Modern Movement fittings of the 1930s, particularly inspired by German 'rationalist' designs. The economic depression had a sobering effect on the trade and the luxurious modernistic styles gave way to the machine aesthetic which was first seen here in tubular steel furniture. Through his education, his knowledge of the Bauhaus school of architecture and design (which he had followed since 1926) and his foreign sales trips, Best was quick to recognise the potential of this German rationalist design style. The source for the firm's first (and most famous) design of this type in this period, the 'Bestlite' table lamp of c.1930 (Fig.10.4), was encountered on one of

THE 'BESTLITE'

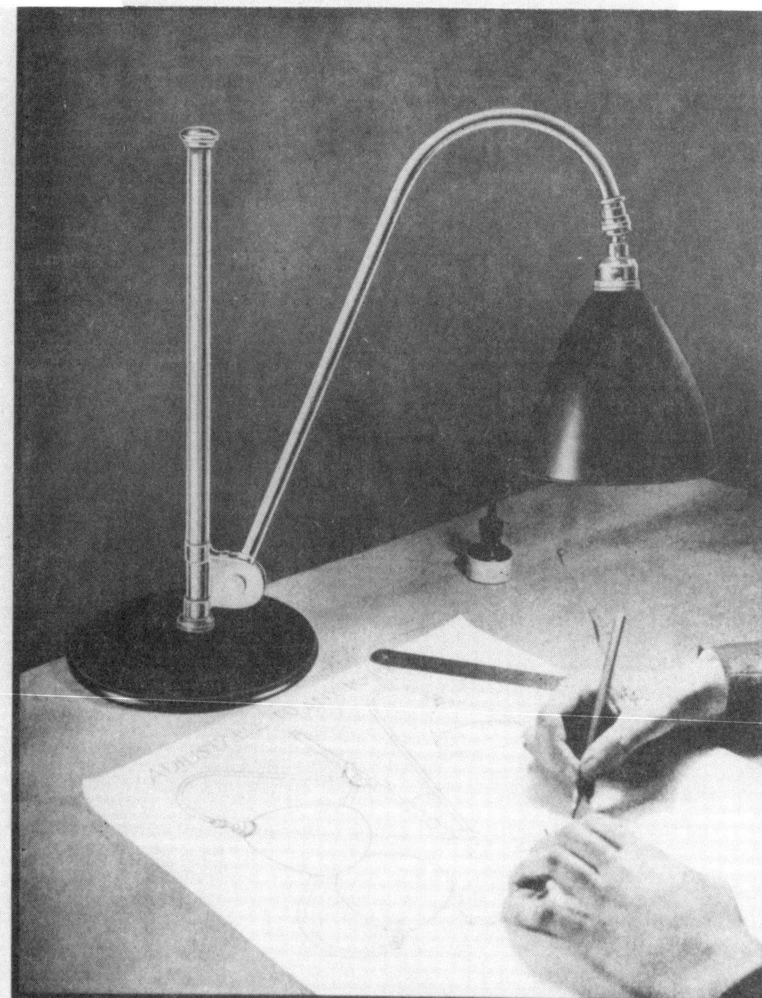

THE 'BESTLITE' ADJUSTABLE DRAWING LAMP

Made for all offices and studios where designing and drawing are done

Fig. 10.4. The 'Bestlite', designed by R.D. Best c.1930. Source: Catalogue no.206 c.1949. Photo by permission of Best & Lloyd Ltd.

these trips, when he first saw an adjustable desk light in chrome and aluminium in Switzerland in 1929.[12] To Best it recalled his father's 'Surprise' pendant which, though of traditional form, was likewise adjustable, but it also bears a close relationship to Christian Dell's 'Rondella' adjustable table lamp (Fig. 10.5), designed at the Bauhaus in the early 1920s and put into production in 1928 by Richard Franke in Frankfurt am Main. A number of variations of the Dell original were produced and one of these was almost certainly seen by him in Zurich. Concerned to appeal to the British market, which he felt would reject the angular outline of the German light, Best 'anglicised' the design by making the spun aluminium shade and lead base of the lamp slightly curved in section. While he retained the pillar clip joint, a new universal ball joint was introduced above the lamp holder, giving adjustability of 360 degrees.

Designs took about 18 months to develop and the 'Bestlite' was launched in May 1931, with features in journals such as *Design for To-Day.* [13] It can be seen as an early manifestation of Bauhaus design in England. *The Architects' Journal* called it in 1931 "*one of the most interesting events of the year in the British electrical industry. It is remarkable that it is a really modern desk lamp, designed for production in large quantities in England at a startlingly low price*" (it retailed at 35 shillings, while Terry's anglepoise lamp of 1934 was £4.00) and continued: "*essentially, mass production design is talked about today but in this country it had seldom been put into being.*" [14]

Within a short time different coloured enamel finishes became available and the 'Bestlite' was produced in a number of related designs from wall lights to ceiling pendants. All used similar component parts except for the larger standard light, which had its own large aluminium shade. Although the 'Bestlite' comprised approximately one sixth of the firm's output in 1933, [15]its manufacture still entailed a considerable amount of hand finishing and its economical price was perhaps the result of using cheaper materials. The design was very successful, being popular with modern architects, both for their own personal use and to enhance the modern image of their buildings. Examples include the Lawn Road Flats by Wells Coates[16] (the light fittings chosen by Pleydell-Bouverie, the associated interior designer) of 1934. Also, Serge Chermayeff designed an adaptation of the 'Bestlite', manufactured under the name 'Bestplan', which he used in his Weekend House at the 1933 *Industrial Art in Relation to the Home* exhibition at Dorland Hall,[17] and in many of his subsequent interior designs. In 1939 the 'Bestlite' was still very popular and its appeal seemed so universal that it was remarked that "*if Best & Lloyd had never done anything but produce the Bestlite lamp, we should still have a good deal to be grateful for. Practically every architect has one in his office. It has probably been the thin end of quite a large wedge for it must have been people's first introduction to rational design in light fittings and it is still one of the best standard models.*"[18] It continued to be a best seller into the 1950s and recently, with the revival of interest in 1930s products, it has become a modern classic, undergoing production once again and retailing from London stores.

Best developed his range of rationalist designs by employing freelance modern designers. For example, in 1932 Christian Barman designed six ceiling fittings, including model 30656[19] (Fig. 10.6) and, in 1937, and ex-Bauhaus *emigré* metalworker, Naum Slutzky, [20] designed another version of the 'Bestlite'.[21] In the 1930s, due to staffing economies, there was only one in-house designer, Frank Cashmore and, alongside the more traditional designs for architectural contracts, he also produced modern designs, adapting original German designs in ceramic for manufacture in brass.[22] Fittings such as the lipless glass sphere, suspended from the ceiling by a chromium plated tube, c.1932 were made which demonstrated economy of form, and were used, for example, in schools, hospitals, town halls, pit-head baths and airports. These fittings were produced under less labour-

Fig. 10.5. 'Rondella' lamp designed by Christian Dell at the Bauhaus in the early 1920s, manufactured in 1928. This version was published in *Die Form*, Book 13, 21 July, 1929.

intensive methods, which arose in part due to the effects of recession felt in the firm in the early 1930s, when a great number of redundancies were made and production was scaled down.

In the early to mid 1930s, Best & Lloyd was in competition with a few other pioneering lighting manufacturers, such as Troughton & Young and Merchant Adventurers. Products of the later 1930s designs were less purist, and more broad-ranging in style, which was evidently (according to Best himself) [23] to accommodate market changes.

Design Reform and the Design and Industries Association (DIA)

The strong influence of the Modern Movement came not only through his education on the Continent, but also from his enthusiasm for the design reform movement in Britain. Best joined the DIA in 1921, became Chairman of the local branch in the 1930s and Vice-Chairman of the national DIA group in the 1940s. He continued as an active supporter of the regional DIA, attending meetings until his 90th birthday in 1982.

Through the DIA he started to work with designers, theorists and educationalists, including B.J. Fletcher, Head of Birmingham School of Art, a founding member of the DIA, and a keen promoter of art school/industry links. Fletcher designed two wall brackets for Best & Lloyd in 1925. [24] Another DIA member and friend, Herbert Simon of the Kynoch Press, became his advisor for catalogues, product design and marketing. [25] Best became more active in the DIA when a regional branch was formed in 1931. This followed a DIA exhibition of *Design in the Home* at Barrow's store in Corporation Street [26] in April that year. The branch was formed because of the city's importance as a main centre of manufacture in Britain, and because it possessed one of the best art schools in the country. E.O. Ransome, Chairman of Barrow's, became the Secretary of this new group and early enthusiasts included Sargant Florence, Professor of Commerce at the University of Birmingham, and Herbert Simon. Best became involved shortly after its foundation, attending the first AGM in 1932, when Herbert Simon discussed the Gorell Report. The branch undertook propagandist activities in keeping with national policy, such as slide talks, exhibitions, show houses and lectures. An activity peculiar to the Birmingham branch was 'quizzing', a type of co-operative design group discussion which involved non-competing firms and interested designers, who helped each other by criticising each other's products. These started at Birmingham University in 1932, but were found to be more successful in the informal atmosphere of members' homes, including Best's. Visiting DIA members such as Noel Carrington also contributed on occasion.[27]

The regional branch showed an independent spirit when it initiated the *Midland Industrial Art* exhibition at the City Art Gallery and Museum in June-July 1934. [28] Its catalyst was the 1933 Dorland Hall exhibition, on tour in 1934. While Birmingham was one of the planned venues, it coincided with the Gallery's 50th Anniversary celebrations which included a programme of exhibitions exclusively on local themes. Best (by then Chairman of the branch), together with the Director of the Gallery, Kaines-Smith, organised a local version of the Dorland Hall exhibition. A reviewer in *Design for To-Day* noted that kitchen ware was the best section, while the weakest sections were the hand crafted jewellery and church furniture.[29] Pevsner (who had recently been made a research assistant at Birmingham University under Sargant Florence) was collecting information for his Ph.D. which provided the basis for his book *An Enquiry into Industrial Art in England* of 1937. He made considerable use of the exhibition to conduct a market research survey and R.D. Best helped him to make initial contact with manufacturers.[30] While Best became friendly with some of the leading designers and theorists, his approach, influenced by his role as a commercial manufacturer was always one of a pragmatic reformer.

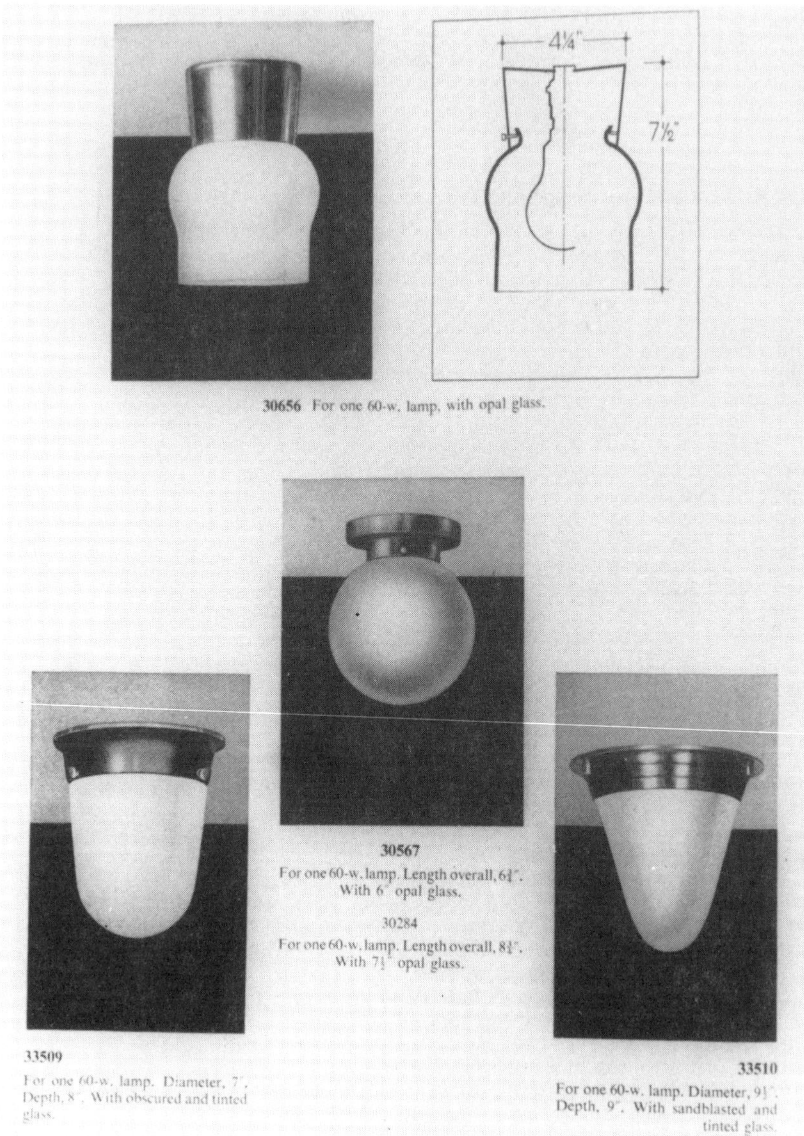

Fig. 10.6. Page of 'rationalist' designs, including model 30656 designed by Christian Barman, 1932, displayed alongside his original outline design. Source: Catalogue, early 1950s. Photo by permission of Best & Lloyd Ltd.

One of Best's most interesting contacts in the 1930s was with Walter Gropius. Best was familiar with Bauhaus theories through published material, but he also met Gropius himself when he was an *émigre* in England, both in London in 1934 and again in 1935, when he was guest of honour at the annual DIA dinner in Birmingham. Best was most concerned with the Bauhaus timetable as he thought it and the laboratory methods might be applied to the teaching at Birmingham School of Art, with which he became officially associated in 1938.[31] From the 1960s, while in contact with the Industrial Design Department, he allowed students to extend their practical training by opening up his design studio and workshops to their use. Unlike Gropius, Best believed that craft and industry would remain separate disciplines. He saw Gropius' main contribution as "*giving a new significance to the idea of economy, the maximum effect with the minimum means*" ('mit geringsten Mitteln grosste Wirkung').[32] He acknowledged Gropius' design philosphy and the Dessau Bauhaus as sources of inspiration, bue he advocated pluralism rather than standardisation of design style.

By the late 1930s, Best was a noted expert in his own design field and was invited to become the Chairman of the committee which prepared the Report on *Design and the Designer in the Light Metal Trades* for the Board of Trade Council of Art and Industry in 1937. This was a survey of manufacture, design and education in the local metal trades which was eventually published in 1944 and became a factual reference document. It was one of the first of many writings undertaken by Best. Others included *Brass Chandelier*, a biography of the firm under his father (published in 1940), and its sequel, *Design and be Damned,* an unpublished typescript of 1957, as well as numerous contributions to journals and publications.

Best & Lloyd Ltd. in the Years Post-World War 2

The production of decorative wares ceased during World War 2 when the firm made pedestal lamps and metal accessories for military use. When peacetime production recommenced, a certain expansion took place and the firm also acted as designers and manufacturers of architectural metalwork. A significant development at Best & Lloyd Ltd. was the introduction of the workers' co-operative system of management, known as the Co-partnership, which ran from 1950 until the early 1970s.[33]

In 1961, R.D. Best's son, J.R.H. Best, returned to the firm, having spent some years working with AEI Lamp and Lighting in London, following an earlier spell of training in the family business. The concern for better design standards, for which R.D. Best became renowned, has continued through his son, who likewise served on the committee of the regional branch of the DIA, acting as Chairman from 1984-7.

Outstanding designs of this period have included the cantilever desk lamp which won a Design Centre Award in 1966 (Fig. 10.7). Designed by Gerald Abramovitz, a South African who had trained at the Royal College of Art, it was an innovative example of the use of small fluorescent lamps and is represented in the permanent collection of the Museum of Modern Art in New York.

The firm continued a policy of trying out new designs and its work with architects led to an acclaimed range of adjustable 'task' lights for office use, developing the original concepts of Arup Associates for the CEGB at Bedminster Down, Bristol.[34] In 1984 it produced a floor-standing uplighter, using the latest technology sodium lamp, which was designed and developed in conjunction with the London consultants Fether & Partners (Fig. 10.8). Despite strong competition from cheap imports (especially from Spain, Japan and Italy), Best & Lloyd maintains its niche in manufacture for the top end of the architectural and domestic market. Fittings are still made in a wide range of reproduction[35] and traditionally inspired designs as well as examples of its modern classics.

Although not a world leader in the lighting field (no British firm was), Best & Lloyd took a leading position in the forefront of British Modernism, particularly in the 1930s. Today, Best & Lloyd Ltd. continues, maintaining its individualism and resisting merger. As a small firm connected with the metal trades it is representative of Birmingham industry's ability to adapt and survive through responding to changing market currents. Its involvement in design innovation and theory has, furthermore, ensured Best & Lloyd's contribution and reputation are not only of regional, but also of national significance.

Fig. 10.7. 'Cantilever' Desk Lamp, deisgned by Gerald Abramovitz, Design Centre Award winner, 1966. Photo from a colour original coutresy of Best & Lloyd Ltd.

REFERENCES

1 For further information about the firm's early history see R.D. Best, 1940.
2 Ibid., p.120. The alabaster bowls were supplied by Robert Bridgeman & Son, Lichfield.
3 R.D. Best, 1969, p.146.
4 In 1926, for example, sales were £59,300 in the AP Department and £44,136 in the Chandelier Department. Figures compiled by R.D. Best, 1974.
5 R.H. Best, W.J. Davis and C. Perks, 1905, and R.H. Best and C.K. Ogden, 1914.
6 M. Boisselier, who had earlier supplied new designs to Best & Lloyd.
7 Notes compiled by R.D. Best, 1974.
8 Ibid., p.115, model no. 26546.
9 Best & Lloyd Ltd. *Architectural Lighting,* no.173, p.3.
10 *Architectural Review*, no.382, September 1928, p.lxvii.
11 Best & Lloyd Ltd. *Fittings for Theatre and Cinema Lighting,* no.185, 1932, pp.8-15. See also M. Battersby, p.51.
12 R.D. Best, 1957, chapter VI.

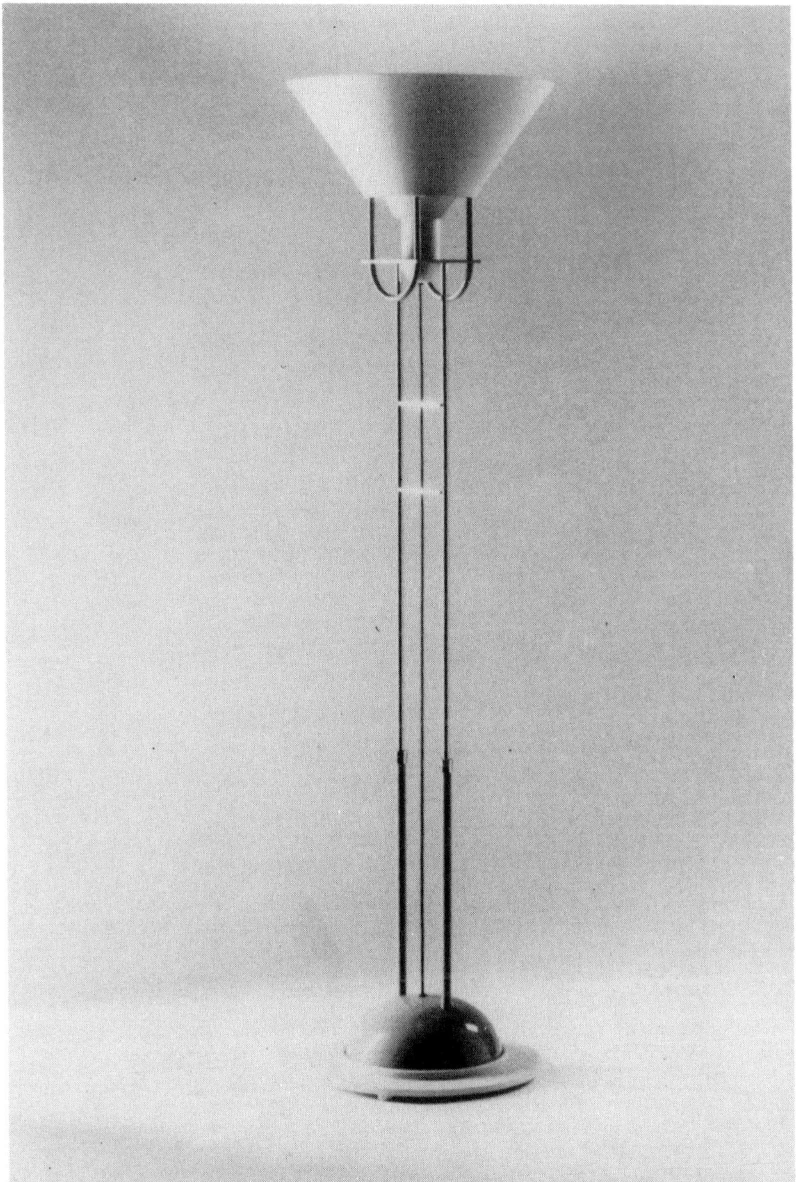

Fig. 10.8. Floor-standing Uplighter (prototype), designed in conjunction with Fether & Partners, 1984. Photo courtesy of Best & Lloyd Ltd.

13 *DIA Quarterly*, no.15, May 1931, p.2.
14 *The Architects' Journal*, no.1897, 27 May 1931, pp.741-2.
15 An advert in the *Midlands Industrial Art* catalogue stated that over 4,000 were sold in 1933, i.e. about one sixth of total sales of £30,467. Notes compiled by R.D. Best, 1974.
16 *Architectural Review*, no.454, September 1934, p.xlvii.
17 Ibid., no.440, July 1933, p.20.
18 *The Architects' Journal*, no.2294, 5 January 1939, p.29.
19 *Design-in-Industry*, no.2, New Series, Autumn 1932, p.19.
20 Slutsky was Head, School of Industrial Design, Birmingham College of Arts & Crafts, 1957-64. See G. Hughes, 1967.
21 *The Architects' Journal*, no.2190, 7 January 1937, p.35.
22 Wilhelm Lotz, *Licht und Beleuchtung*, Berlin, 1928, probably provided another source book, being in the firm's collection.
23 N. Pevsner, 1937, p.28.
24 R.D. Best, Chapter 5, 1957. Illustrated in Best & Lloyd Ltd. catalogue no. 144, p.7 (model 26020), p.8 (model 26049).
25 While he worked at the Kynoch Press, 1921-33, H. Simon produced the firm's catalogues. He then became a fellow director of the Curwen Press. *The Times*, 16 November 1974.
26 *Birmingham Post*, 14 April 1931.
27 See N. Carrington, 1976, p.114.
28 See *Midland Industrial Art* catalogue, 1934; P. Madge, "An Enquiry into Pevsner's Enquiry," *Journal of Design History*, vol. 1, no.2, 1988, p.120.
29 *Design for To-Day*, July 1934, p.267.
30 N. Pevsner, 1937, p.5; R.D. Best, Chapter 10, 1957.
31 Best was a co-opted member of the Birmingham Education Committee from 1938-60 and in the 1960s a Governor of Birmingham School of Art. *Design*, May 1966, p.401.
32 R.D. Best, "Postscript to Pevsner", *DIA Yearbook and Membership List*, 1965-6, p.98.
33 Records of this management system can be found in *B & L News, information facts, figures*, 1949-50.
34 Information supplied by John R.H. Best.
35 E.g. a brass chandelier for Bockleton court, now a Birmingham Education Committee Field Studies Centre, nr. Tenbury Wells, 1986.

BIBLIOGRAPHY

M. Battersby, *The Decorative Thirties*, London, 1971.
R.D. Best, *A Short Life and a Gay One: A Biography of Francis Behrens Best, 1893-1917, 1969*, in Birmingham Central Reference Library.
R.D. Best, *Brass Chandelier: A Biography of R.H. Best of Birmingham*, London, 1940.
R.D. Best, *Design and Be Damned*, unpublished typescript, 1957, coll. Best & Lloyd.
R.D. Best, "Postcript to Pevsner", *DIA Yearbook and Membership List, 1965-66*, London, 1966, pp.96-9.
Best & Lloyd News, Information, Facts, Figures and Discussion (an experiment in industrial relations at Best and Lloyd Ltd.), typescript, vols. starting from 1949-50, Birmingham Central Reference Library.
H.N. Hiley, *Brass Saga*, London, 1957.
G. Hughes, *Modern Silver Throughout the World, 1880-1967*, London, 1967.

FURTHER READING

R.H. Best and C.K. Ogden, *The Problem of the Day Continuation School and its Successful Solution in Germany: A Consecutive Policy*, London, 1914.
R.H. Best, W.J. Davis and C. Perks, *The Brassworkers of Berlin and Birmingham - a Comparison*, London, 1905.
Board of Trade, *Design and the Designer in the Light Metal Trades*, London, 1944.
G. Holme, *Industrial Design and the Future*, London, 1934.

CHAPTER 11

PEL FURNITURE

Graham Leake

In July 1931, a company called Practical Equipment Ltd. was formed within the group of tubular steel manufacturers, Tube Investments (TI). That initial company name could have meant almost anything. The following March the name was changed to the simpler PEL Limited[1] which had the distinct advantage of meaning absolutely nothing! In the subsequent period 'PEL' has come to signify a major manufacturer of furniture based upon tubular steel.

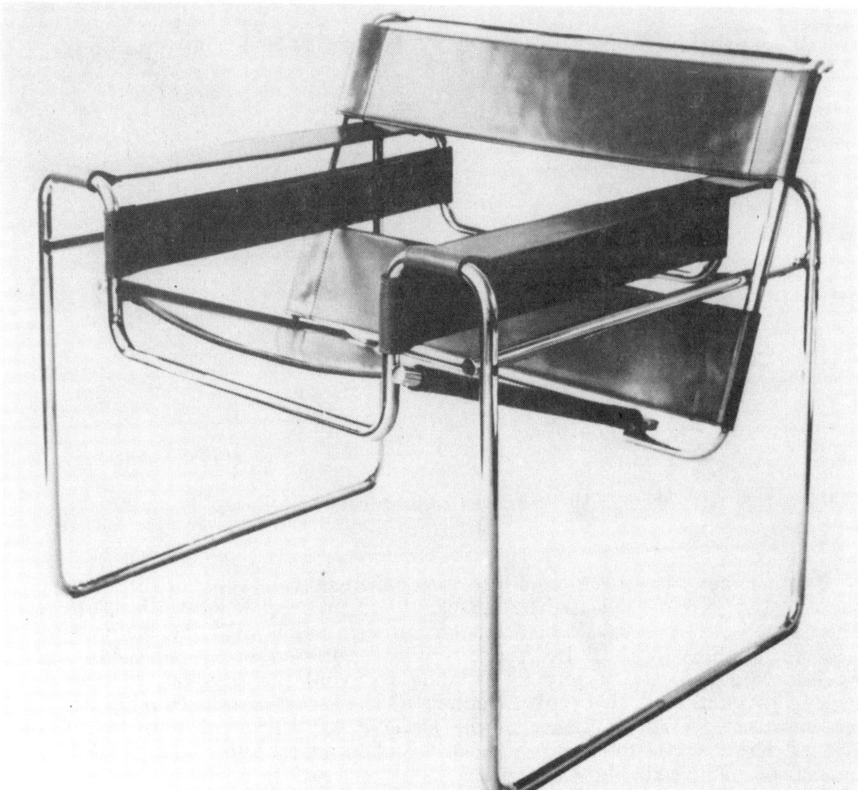

Fig. 11.1. Marcel Breuer. 'Wassily' chair, originally designed 1925. Photo courtesy of the Design Council.

The development of this company was not entirely a pioneering venture. Rather, it was a matter of seizing an opportune moment to exploit ideas which had already been developed and applied commercially elsewhere. The time was opportune because TI was provided with an outlet for its product in the furniture industry at a time of economic depression, and the enterprise appears to have been a considerable success from the outset.

An interest in the possibilities of steel tube for furniture making had developed in Germany in the 1920s. In 1925 Marcel Breuer, a designer closely associated with the Bauhaus, had produced the 'Wassily' chair (Fig. 11.1). It was the first, but perhaps not the most imaginative, of a number of designs using tubular steel (and other metal sections) to be produced by Breuer and some of his associates over the next few years.

Fig. 11.2. SP1 chair, c.1931, and RP2 chair, c.1932. Photo by permission of the Design Council.

Tubular metal had been employed long before in some types of furniture manufacture, but it had been used, rather like wood, in short lengths joined to form a structure.[2] The designs which emerged in the 1920s used the material for its peculiar qualities, and those qualities were expressed in the finished product. Forms were achieved largely by bending to avoid the complicated and costly process of jointing. This took advantage of the fact that tube could be as long as was necessary. The resilience of the material was exploited in flexible frames. Rather than disguise the metal, the finishes chosen were appropriate: paint, stove-enamel and, above all, chromium plate.

In view of the similarity in appearance between bentwood and tubular steel and their potential for mass-production, it is not surprising that the major manufacturer of the classic designs of the 1920s was the long-established bentwood furniture firm Gebrüder Thonet.[3] The first tubular steel furniture to be employed in any quantity in Britain was certainly manufactured by that firm, and it was Thonet furniture, seen by two directors of TI in the Strand Palace Hotel in London, which provided the stimulus for the formation of what was to become PEL.[4]

Accels & Pollock, one of the founding companies of TI, had been making metal furniture frames, some in tubular steel, from 1929.[5] Its offspring, PEL, continued to occupy part of the Accles & Pollock works in Oldbury until after World War 2. It moved to its present site in Rood End Road, Oldbury, in 1956.[6]

PEL and Modernism

In the early period of furniture making, any upholstery was providcd by outside specialists. A good example of this was the most interesting of the early chairs, the SP1[7] (Fig. 11.2). This resembled closely the 1926 'MR' design of Ludwig Mies van der Rohe. Like some versions of its precedent, the seat and back were woven, the frames in this case being sent to the Institute for the Blind in Birmingham for the purpose. This very successful chair continued in production after the formation of PEL. The chair on the right, the RP2 of 1932, was far less novel, being a traditional heavy upholstered chair which happened to have a tubular frame.

There were many instances in the 1920s and early 1930s of 'close resemblances' or even downright plagiarism. For instance the HT9 table[8] of 1931-32 (Fig. 11.3) is very similar to a design by Breuer, and the SP2 chair of 1930-31 beside it resembles a design by Mart Stam, another major pioneer.

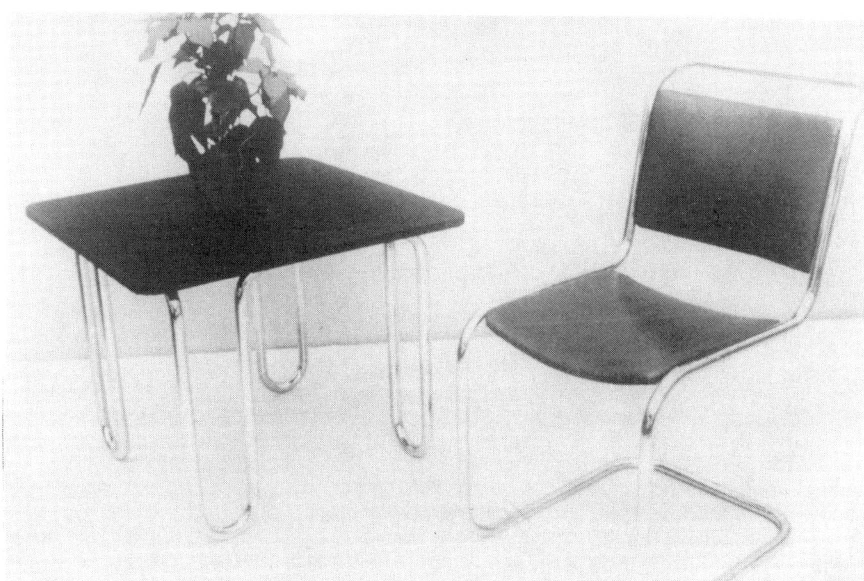

Fig. 11.3. HT9 table, 1931-2 and SP2 chair, 1930-1. Photo by permission of the Design Council.

Fig. 11.4. RP6 nesting chairs in a school hall. *PEL Catalogue,* 1937. Photo by permission of PEL Ltd.

PEL was sued by the British agent of a Polish designer, Bruno Pollak, for using a system for a nesting chair patented by Pollak in 1931.[9] The matter was resolved in 1934 when PEL bought the patent and went on to produce the well-known RP6 chair [10] (Fig. 11.4) in vast quantities for over thirty years.

The typical RP6, although there were several variations, had a canvas seat and back. Apart from the fact that they were cheap, these chairs were the almost universal choice for multi-purpose halls because they nested very closely and could be stored in a very small space. The discomfort, readily remembered by all who have sat through a performance on one of these, earned it the name of the 'Numbum' chair.

Fig. 11.5. HT21 dining table, 1933-4 and SP9B chairs, 1932-4. Photo by permission of the Design Council.

By the mid 1930s PEL had found its own forms. A group, photographed at the time of an exhibition of PEL and other tubular steel furniture at the Architectural Association in London in 1977 (Fig. 11.5), shows an original approach to the design of tubular steel furniture in an idiom very much of its period. The table is the HT21 of 1933-34 and the chair the SP9B of 1932-34.[11] The quality of design by this stage was not acquired by chance.

The Managing Director from the start, and one of the two visitors to the Strand Palace Hotel, was Captain P.G. Carew. Through his membership of the Design and Industries Association he came into contact with some of the foremost designers working in Britain. Oliver Bernard, Raymond McGrath, Serge Chermayeff and Wells Coates all designed for, or specified, PEL for both contract and domestic applications.[12]

Some contract work, such as that for hotels and large department stores,[13] called for PEL's more expensive furniture involving good quality upholstery and chrome-plated frames, but the bulk of the market was for large quantities of the more basic seating, including nesting chairs, and tables in paint finishes. Major contracts included the much publicised new Broadcasting House in London.[14]

In the 1930s, however, tubular steel furniture enjoyed a vogue in the domestic market, in a way which was never to be repeated. PEL, as well as having its own London showroom, sold its products through major shops such as Heal's, Harrods and the Army and Navy Stores,[15] and it was patronised by some royal and aristocratic patrons whose interest was, to the firm's advantage, widely publicised.

Fig. 11.6. Taper tube chair design, c.1955. Photo by permission of the Design Council.

The success of this new material with an entirely new, modern appearance raises an issue of constant interest to the designer and, therefore, the design historian. In the familiar circular relationship between manufacturer, retailer and consumer - a situation in which neither the manufacturer nor the retailer is often willing to take risks that innovative design entails, and the consumer is restricted by the choice available - who can inject an influence to affect design? In a major study of British industrial design published in 1937, Nikolaus Pevsner suggested that the manufacturer could. He wrote that "*such an interest* in tubular steel *could not have arisen nor be kept alive, had producers not decided to push tubular furniture. This is important in a much wider sense. Here is a proof that manufacturers, directly they want to push a certain type of goods, can succeed in creating a fashion or even creating a true change of popular taste, which may be for the better or the worse.*" After qualifying his argument he concluded: "*by the determined attitude of a few producers a type of goods has been made saleable, although of a material and shape never used for such goods before.*" [16]

The fact is that since its application in the 1930s, tubular furniture - of one form or another - has become commonplace, even if it has lost its place in the home.

Towards Diversification in the Post-War Period

The outbreak of war in 1939 brought the production of normal furniture ranges to a stop. The company was engaged on war contracts, especially for the Admiralty. Its expertise in the production of robust furniture found a particularly suitable outlet in equipping warships.[17]

In the immediate post-war period there was a severe shortage of steel, and PEL (like many other furniture producers) used surplus aluminium in the construction of some furniture. However, comparison of the 1937 and 1946 catalogues demonstrates that, when the firm was able to resume production, the range offered was very similar to that of the 1930s. [18] It is clear, though, that the fashion had changed, and fairly quickly PEL had to adapt to new circumstances.

The subsequent history is one of response to changes in the market, developing techniques and utilising new materials. From now on PEL was to concentrate on contract furniture at the inexpensive end of the market - and to diversify. This in no way implies that the firm compromised on quality of materials or ceased to innovate.

Some steps in diversification were the branching into shopfittings in 1948, specialising in fixed booth seating for cafés in the 1950s (both these are still important PEL activities) and, also in the 1950s, the company made transport seating. This last involved a departure from tubular steel construction, but opened the way for major contracts worldwide, particularly with railway undertakings.

New techniques of tube production in the 1950s allowed for the use of 'taper tube' especially for tables and chairs (Fig. 11.6). This form of tube gave an appearance of lightness to the furniture and was discreetly in keeping with current style; the splayed tapered leg was a feature of so-called 'Contemporary' furniture. The illustration clearly shows that, even in this period, welds were kept to a minimum - here only three. The tops of the back legs were sprung to retain the back, and the four fixing points of the seat formed an integral part of the chair' structure.

Early in the 1960s, polypropylene was developed as a tough, resilient material suitable for one-piece moulded chairs requiring only an underframe for support. It superseded laminated plywood (which PEL had used) and glass reinforced plastic (glassfibre) as a suitable material for such a purpose.

Fig. 11.7. Polypropylene chairs, 1964. Photo by permission of PEL Ltd.

PEL was beaten by Hille [19] in the race to launch a polypropylene chair. PEL's chair, the PP1 (Fig. 11.7), which was launched in August 1964, was perhaps less elegant than its Hille counterpart, but it was at least as comfortable, had a price advantage and the fixing of seat to frame was far more satisfactory. This chair, with variations, became the staple contract seat to supersede the RP6.

For the general range of contract furniture in the 1960s, and thereafter, square rather than round tube became the predominant material. This change reflected a move towards crisp, simple shapes and the emphasis on straight lines characteristic of the period (Fig. 11.8). It brought about a break from the long-standing approach to tube furniture because square tube does not bend very satisfactorily. Square tube furniture was constructed from straight lengths of tube with welded joints and, for some time, few new designs really used the material for its resilience.

PEL in the 1960s entered another market, that for fixed stadium and lecture theatre seating. The latter was of a particularly neat and effective design, preferable in many ways to the tip-up seating of PEL's prestigious competitors.

The installation of a new finishing plant in 1968 was a major technical innovation. The plant, possibly the first of its kind in Europe, could be used for stove-enamelling and, far more significantly, for epoxy powder coating of metal surfaces. This process, in which a synthetic resin was electrostatically fused to the metal, rendered all paint finishes obsolete.[20]

School Furniture

A seemingly modest step taken in 1966 was to lead to an unforeseen new venture for PEL three years later. The step was to develop a range of chairs of five different heights for use in schools. These chairs had a separate polypropylene seat and back, which was considered anatomically more suitable for growing children than a single shell. Research for the school chair had shown that the school population was increasing.[21] This must have been very much in mind when PEL tendered (successfully) to the Government for the manufacture and supply of a comprehensive range of school furniture. Production started in 1969. This was to be one of the company's most interesting developments, and the greatest departure from its original purpose as an outlet for tubular steel, because of the high proportion of woodworking this furniture entailed.

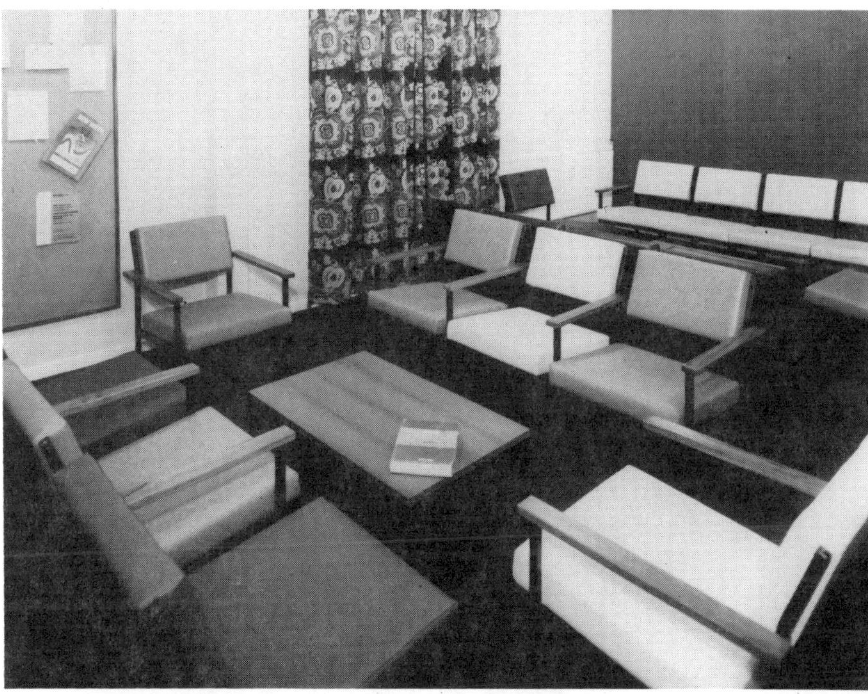

Fig. 11.8. 'Cubis' contract furniture, c.1970. Photo courtesy of PEL Ltd.

The furniture had been designed for the CLASP building consortium by its own designers, designers from the Architects' and Building Branch of the Department of Education and Science (DES), and outside consultants.[22] Many local education authorities were, at the time, moving away from traditional classroom teaching. The design of school buildings, pioneered by the DES, provided more open, flexible space. Furniture became the means of organising work within that space. The old locker desks were replaced by tables (which could be grouped in differing configurations) chairs and individual plastic trays in trolleys. Beyond this basic provision, general storage, too, took the form of trolleys together with large cupboards and units fixed to walls. Mobile furniture of various kinds could divide space in ways which could readily be changed. PEL marketed the range under the name 'Omni-Forme'.

Fig. 11.9. School furniture: teaching space. Multi-forme chairs and stools with polypropylene seats and backs. Photo by permission of PEL Ltd.

The illustrations (Figs. 11.9, 11.10, 11.11) were used in the first full catalogue published in June 1969. It was prepared in conjunction with the DES and the Ministry of Public Building and Works which administered the contract. The first, simulating a general teaching space has three sizes of tables and chairs as though for a rural school with a small number of children of wide age range. The second is of a reading corner in which various trolleys are used to enclose the area. The third, a workshop, includes the worktop system extended by co-ordinating trolleys.

Since the furniture was available in several sizes for different age groups, the number of items available was very large, and understanding how to exploit the choice in the fullest way was not easy. For this reason the DES designers, who worked very closely with the company, suggested that PEL should set up an advisory service to help teachers, education advisors and architects.[23]

The demand for this furniture in a period of exciting developments in education was such that the company found it difficult to keep pace. The high proportion of cabinet work, in particular, presented problems. The solution was another major step, which indicated great confidence in the range and its future. A large factory space on the TI Broadwell site was equipped to provide a woodworking facility that should have enabled the firm to cope with the increasing demand. The factory, which represented a huge investment, started production in January 1974.[24] However, within months, the Budget in April heralded major cuts in public spending. By this period most of PEL's output, perhaps as much as 75-80%, was purchased by local and central government. Projects in hand were, of course, completed but within two years the fall in orders was seriously affecting business. There were attempts to sell school furniture abroad but their success was limited. 'Package deals' for the Middle East, in which PEL took the responsibility for supplying all equipment for a number of school projects, though promising at first, did not fill the gap.

Fig. 11.10. School furniture: reading corner. Forme storage and worktop in *PEL Catalogue*, 1970. Photo by permission of PEL Ltd.

Fig. 11.11. School furniture: workshop. Forme trolleys, storage and worktops in *PEL Catalogue*, 1970. Photo by permission of PEL Ltd.

Recent Developments

In March 1978, after the company had been making consistent and increasing losses with no obvious prospect of a change in fortunes, TI sold PEL to the Uniflex Group of companies for what was described as "*substantially less than the book value of the assets.*" [25] Reputedly, the actual sum was a nominal one pound. Ownership has changed once more since then; the management bought out the company in June 1984. Shortly after Uniflex purchased PEL, the company reduced its production facilities and its workforce. The latter was cut by about one third within a month. The Broadwell works was vacated and once again PEL was contained within the Rood End Road site. Recently, operations have been further compressed within that site.

In the early 1980s it became the policy to employ consultants rather than in-house designers, and at least two ranges were designed and prototyped in this way. Some of the individual pieces made satisfactory use, once more, of the resilience of tube. Others were less successful, mixing wood and tubular steel in rather a self-conscious and confused way. There has been a distinct diversification into the manufacture of domestic furniture so that the company places less reliance on organisations purchasing with public money.

PEL has been in existence for more than half the century marked by this book. During that time it has responded repeatedly to the changing circumstances experienced during the period. It is evident that the most successful phases of PEL's history have been those associated with strong unified product ranges for clearly perceived markets. When there has been this positive sense of direction many of its products have been notable and successful examples of industrial design.

There are two periods, however, of particular importance: the heyday of tubular steel furniture in the 1930s and the involvement in a pioneering educational movement in the early 1970s. These alone earn PEL a significant place as a major Birmingham enterprise.

REFERENCES

1 D. Sharp *et al,* p.21.
2 R.W. Winfield & Co.'s rocking chair of the mid nineteenth century was a notable exception.
3 A useful study of Thonet furniture, with an extensive bibliography, is C. Wilk, 1980.
4 D. Sharp *et al,* pp.20-21.
5 Ibid.
6 Press release, June 1975, issued as a general background to PEL and its products by the public relations consultants, Phillips and Hind Associates.
7 The PEL catalogue number system indicates whether a chair is 'spring pattern' (SP) or 'rigid pattern' (RP), the former type exploiting the resilience of tube.
8 HT signifies 'Harmony table'. The name 'Harmony' was to have been applied to a furniture range, designed by Oliver Bernard, but never produced.
9 A nesting chair is piled on and forward of the chair underneath, as opposed to a stacking chair which stacks vertically.
10 Fig. 11.4 shows RP6 chairs at Burlington School, Hammersmith, as illustrated in the 1937 *PEL Catalogue.*
11 These pieces, and other examples of PEL furniture, are now in the collection of the Victoria and Albert Museum.
12 D. Sharp *et al,* p.25, shows furniture manufactured by PEL in a Lyons Corner House interior designed by Oliver Bernard c.1935.
13 Ibid., p.24 shows PEL furniture in Marshall and Snelgrove and p.27 an interior in the Hotel Metropole, Brighton, both from the 1936 Catalogue.
14 Ibid., p.22, shows PEL furniture in use in Broadcasting House. The previous page shows furniture by Cox & Co. This firm, founded by Rowland Wilton Cox, started to produce tubular steel furniture in 1930 and was to be PEL's principal competitor. Later known as Cox of Watford, the firm was merged with PEL in the 1960s.
15 D. Sharp *et al,* p.23
16 N. Pevsner, p.44
17 D. Sharp *et al,* p.25.
18 PEL published full catalogues at least in the years 1932, 1936, 1937, 1939 and 1946. There is a good deal of overlap between them as the range evolved.
19 The London based firm founded by Salamon Hille, then registered as Hille of London Ltd.
20 "Chair Frames at PEL Treated in £100,000 Plant", *Industrial Finishing,* vol.20 no.237, March 1968. This article, re-printed as a PEL 'hand-out' under the title *How Your Furniture Frames are Finished,* is very detailed in its description of this important development in the furniture industry.
21 Documents in the files of the managing director at that time, the late Eric Hill, show that justification was sought before the development of a new product for a fresh market.
22 CLASP stood for Consortium of Local Authorities Special Programme. The initial purpose was to design a system of pre-fabricated school buildings suitable for areas of mining subsidence.
23 The author was appointed as an advisor, specialising in school furniture, from 1973-8, as a result of this suggestion. Information on school furniture is based upon knowledge of the range and his experience in this period. School furniture was still in production in 1989 although not nearly on the same scale as in the 1970s.
24 TI companies occupy a number of sites in the Birmingham area. Broadwell is one of the main ones, to the north of Birmingham Road, Oldbury.
25 Mr. Brian Kellet, Chairman of Tube Investments, quoted in *The Birmingham Post,* 16 May 1978.

BIBLIOGRAPHY

N. Pevsner, *An Enquiry into Industrial Art in England,* London, Cambridge University Press, 1937.

D. Sharp, T. Benton, B. Campbell-Cole, *PEL and Tubular Steel Furniture of the Thirties,* London, Architectural Association, 1977.

PEL catalogues and leaflets for past years are not readily obtainable. The most informative are those for 1932, 1936, 1937, 1939, 1946.

The first full school furniture catalogue was published in June 1969, followed by a 3-part metric catalogue in August 1971 and January and February 1972. A full metric catalogue was issued in November 1973.

An explanatory brochure was originally issued for the 11th European Educational Fair (DIDACTA) in Hanover, March 1972. This, revised and enlarged, was issued as *School Furniture 74* in 1974 and as *School Furniture* and *PEL International Service to Education* in 1978.

FURTHER READING

B. Archer, "Steel Furniture for New Markets", *Design*, January 1956.

Journal of Design History, volume 3, 1990, devoted to furniture including tubular steel furniture.

J. Myerson, "Partners in Chrome", *Design*, December 1983.

"Pioneering Structure, 30s, 40s, 50s, 60s, 70s", *The Cabinet Maker and Retail Furnisher,* 11 February 1977.

A. von Vegesack, *Deutsche Stahlrohrmöbel: 650 Modelle aus Katalogen von 1927-1958,* Munich, Bangert, 1986.

C. Wilk, *Thonet: 150 Years of Furniture,* New York, Barrons', 1980.

CHAPTER 12

ENGINEERING IN BIRMINGHAM: A PERSONAL VIEW OF A CENTURY OF CHANGE, FOCUSING ON THE HISTORY OF THE WOLSELEY GROUP.

Barbara Tilson interviews Laurie Bidmead, Consultant Group Personnel Advisor,[1] and Roy Woodward, retired Deputy Chairman of Wolseley plc, Droitwich, also Chairman of Avoncroft Museum.

Tilson: How many years have you been with the company?
Bidmead: From 1946 until 1958 I was employed by BSA (the Birmingham Small Arms Company) which made guns, motorcycles and cycles, latterly as Personnel Officer. The BSA Group included the Daimler car, which was later bought up by Jaguar Cars, who still make the Daimler. In February 1958 I joined Wolseley Engineering Ltd., which in May 1958 merged with Geo. H. Hughes Ltd., to form what was known as Wolseley-Hughes Ltd., and is now known as Wolseley plc.
Tilson: Where did you work before you were involved with BSA?
Bidmead: I originally served my apprenticeship at Fisher & Ludlow Ltd., Birmingham, where I commenced in 1936. They became part of British Leyland (Rover Group). I trained as an engineer before I was called up.
Tilson: What were Fisher & Ludlow producing?
Bidmead: They made motor car panels - in other words the body work - for Standard Motor Company and then for Rover Group, Jaguar and others. They were a reasonably large employer, based in Bradford Street, before moving into what was the Castle Bromwich aeroplane factory.
Tilson: Do you think Fisher & Ludlow were a typical engineering company?
Bidmead: Yes, I would say so, in those days.
Tilson: The Bradford Street area was full of small firms, with a lot of metal working and components manufacture?
Bidmead: That's right. They had two sites, each side of Bradford Street, one stretching from Bradford Street to Deritend. They had fairly heavy presses, and a design and drawing office, where I started, designing tools for panel making. They had their own tool room etc.
Tilson: How many of you were there, approximately?
Bidmead: In the drawing office there were about 20 people, so it was reasonably large.
Tilson: When you joined BSA, what was their situation?
Bidmead: It was fairly reasonable, I believe. They were a leading manufacturer of motorcycles (see chapter 14), with a reasonable range of motorcycles and a range of pedal cycles (see chapter 13). Also in that group were BSA Tools, Burton & Griffiths and numerous other companies. Burton & Griffiths, I think, sold a lot of machinery on behalf of BSA Tools.
Tilson: Were they all in Birmingham?
Bidmead: Yes, BSA Tools was in Armoury Road, BSA Cycles was in Waverley Road and Burton & Griffiths and BSA Spares were at Montgomery Street, all in Small Heath. BSA Tools also had a factory at Marston Green and the Daimler Motor Company was at Coventry.

Tilson: Small Heath is still quite an industrial centre.

Bidmead: Yes, and Greet was another industrial centre where, for example, Serck Radiators was sited. Just round the corner was the motorcycle company, Velocette.

Tilson: What would you say about the mechanisation of BSA at the time?

Bidmead: That particular sub group of BSA employed about 7,000 people and it was housed in a typical factory, of those days, which had three floors. Here they did assembly and automatic machining, making most of their parts. They had a rather large press shop, a forge and a drop forge, which made the engine castings for motorcycles.

Woodward: The other well known Birmingham motorcycle manufacturers were Norton, Ariel, Velocette and New Imperial. Triumph was at Coventry and then Allesley and AJS and Matchless were in the London area.

Tilson: Where have you worked?

Woodward: I was Assistant Secretary at Tube Investments (now TI Group plc) from 1947 to 1955, so I knew the TI Group intimately in those days. I then joined Geo. H. Hughes and from 1958 onwards worked for Wolseley plc, where I eventually became Deputy Chairman. Tube Investments Ltd. was even then a very big company, one of the leading groups in Birmingham. But if you look at a list of the subsidiary companies that were in TI in 1947 and at those that are in it today you probably won't find one of them left. They've all been sold off or closed down as the Group has moved into higher technology businesses. Tube Investments was established in 1919 to effect a merger between Tubes Ltd. of Rocky Lane, Aston, and Accles & Pollock at Oldbury. The Chairman at this time was Arthur Chamberlain, a member of the well known Birmingham family.

Tilson: Accles & Pollock were the precursors of PEL Furniture.

Woodward: That's right, it was an outlet for their tubes. Accles & Pollock also did shafts for fishing rods and golf clubs. Most of their output, however, was straightforward engineering seamless steel tube, some of it in stainless.

Bidmead: Didn't Accles & Pollock make a very small tube for the surgical industry?

Woodward: Yes. They claimed to make the smallest tube in the world. You could prove it was a tube by blowing bubbles through it. In the early years after the Second World War the largest and most profitable division of TI was the steel tube division making cold drawn and welded steel tubes (Fig. 12.1). Tubes were also made in various cross sections. Most tube we use today is welded because it's a much cheaper and quicker process than cold drawing, but seamless cold drawn tubing is still used for certain applications. TI also produced hot finished tube and had an aluminium division making aluminium tubes, sections and plates, an electrical division making domestic appliances and a bicycle division, which was very profitable, making roadsters and sports cycles of various specifications. In 1946 they bought the Hercules Cycle Company which was in Aston but they were in the cycle trade from almost the time they were formed in July 1919. They also acquired J.A. Phillips in Smethwick in 1919, soon after TI was formed in July 1919. They also owned a number of companies that were unrelated, too, for example, a company called Gowshall that made traffic and illuminated signs and a fairly small paint company called Drynamels. Now probably none of those businesses are in the TI Group.

Tilson: Is that because the industry has moved on to other things?

Woodward: Lack of demand for particular products such as locomotive and marine boiler tubes, and the moves towards higher technology products.

Tilson: The former were inappropriate products for our contemporary era, perhaps?

Woodward: That's right. Later on, TI bought Raleigh cycles. The cycle trade has declined in later years. Now, because of the interest in sporting cycles in particular, it's staged a partial recovery in recent years.

Bidmead: Raleigh of Nottingham in turn bought BSA Cycles.

Woodward: A number of large companies in Birmingham contributed to its development, and a number of small ones, too. There has been quite a variety but, for the most part, Birmingham was an enormous concentration of small and medium sized businesses. There weren't so many very large businesses.

Fig. 12.1. Steel tube in a drawbench shop. Source: Booklet, Tubes Ltd, 1948.

Tilson: When you say small, do you mean about 50 employees, and medium sized about 200?

Woodward: 200 and up to 500 or so, yes. Amongst the larger companies I could name TI Group, GKN, Lucas, Dunlop, IMI, Rover Group, Hardy Spicer (now GKN Transmissions), Tangyes, on the border of Handsworth and Smethwick, and Belliss & Morcom (both companies engaged in heavy engineering). There were two companies making railway rolling stock, including underground carriage and buses. There was Metropolitan Cammell Carriage and Wagon at Saltley and the company now named Metro-Cammell Weymann at Washwood Heath.

Tilson: Metro-Cammell make the Midland Red buses and suchlike?

Woodward: Yes, but, when a separate company, Midland Red buses were made at Edgbaston. However, they certainly manufacture for other bus companies. They made carriages for railways all over the world. There is also Bromford Tube making hot rolled pipe. They're part of British Steel Corporation, selling heavy steel pipe, mostly to the oil and water industries. There was John Wright & Co. at Aston (later called Radiation) which made the New World gas cookers, which was bought by TI. The plant has since been closed down. Wolseley Motors were at

Drews Lane. Morris Commercial Vehicles (as it was known) was at Adderley Park, Saltley. There was a great variety of small firms. There was (and still is) Geo. H. Hughes making truck and trolley wheels. They had 500 employees counting part-timers, were originally in Aston and later on at Tyburn. Accles & Shelvoke at Aston, a former subsidiary of ours, which was founded by Mr. Accles of Accles & Pollock, does light engineering. Boxmag, one of our subsidiaries at Aston, makes electro-lifting magnets and magnetic separators. That's another typical smallish Birmingham business. Then there is the whole of the jewellery trade with a mass of mainly small companies. Another very interesting Birmingham company is Webster & Horsfall of Hay Mills. They make steel wire and rope. They supplied the German piano manufacturers with piano wire but they lost the business because of the First World War.

Tilson: Was this wire drawing industry one of a number in the Birmingham area?

Woodward: There were others. Wrights Ropes (now British Ropes) owned a subsidiary at Bromford, called Rollason Wire, now closed. Wrights Ropes made steel rope in Birmingham but, as far as Birmingham was concerned, a company that size didn't play an immense part like, say, Austin Motors, or Dunlop, but it was typical of the variety of industry in the Birmingham area.

Tilson: Much of it involved metal working of various kinds. What would you say about the effects of the Second World War on the engineering industries?

Woodward: Well, they took a fair bashing, because Birmingham was heavily bombed and a lot of the smaller factories were severely damaged. They struggled through the war and needed much re-equipment afterwards.

Bidmead: The old Fisher & Ludlow factory in Bradford Street was one of those which was heavily bombed.

Woodward: During the war a very important factory in Birmingham was the Castle Bromwich aeroplane factory, which was built to make Spitfires.

Tilson: Yes, there was a television programme about Castle Bromwich during World War 2 on BBC on 13 November 1988. Evidently, about 11,500 planes (or over half of all those built) were made there.

Woodward: Later on in the war they changed to Lancaster bombers. The aerodrome was over the road where Castle Vale housing estate is now. There was an aerodrome established, I think, about the time of World War 1. The Spitfires and Lancasters used to be rolled across the Chester Road. The factory was operated by Vickers and they were very big employers during the war. It was taken over by Fisher & Ludlow after the war and later went into the British Motor Corporation. It's now owned by Jaguar.

Bidmead: BSA's production, too, was very high in the war. They made rifles and also the guns for the Spitfire, latterly.

Woodward: Weren't BSA heavily damaged in the bombing?

Bidmead: Yes, with heavy casualties. Wolseley Sheep Shearing Machine Company (as it was then called) was also badly bombed at one time. They made the blades for the original Whittle jet engine.

Tilson: Can you say anything about the stimulus to production in the war? Demand for military equipment must have kept some firms buoyant, at least.

Woodward: It kept many of them buoyant, I would have thought. In Birmingham, during the war, even little companies in the Jewellery Quarter - and there were a lot of them - turned over to war work. They could do light machining to make small components for many purposes. And companies got together on various committees, which included representatives of management and unions, to discuss production problems and supply problems, to try to help each other and sort things out. There was a co-operation amongst companies that doesn't happen today in the same way. There are trade associations but the committees which existed during the war were much closer to the sharp end. But then after the Second World War, when competition between firms was restored to normal, these inter-company joint production committees had no role to play.

Tilson: What about the modernising of capital equipment after the war?

Woodward: After the war, in the engineering industry, the emphasis, and a lot of the top management time, was taken up with the acquisition of new plant, new plant layouts, putting up new buildings, expansion. I should think they probably spent more time worrying about that sort of thing than they did worrying about the profit and loss account in the early years after the war.

Tilson: Was there much competition from firms which weren't UK firms, pre-Second World War?

Woodward: I would say not so much. For example, we had the ex-colonial markets to ourselves, to begin with, especially for motor cars. The export business was quite strong and we sold products which we couldn't sell today. We could sell our bicycles anywhere. TI was one company which was obliged to establish factories in Africa and India or lose these markets entirely.

Bidmead: It was during the late '50s, I suppose, that competition came from abroad. The Japanese really knocked the motorcycle industry.

Woodward: Yes, the British motorcycle industry was almost destroyed.

Tilson: There was a great contrast between the Birmingham way of making motorcycles, with a lot of hand labour, producing expensive machines, and the Japanese way, which was to manufacture cheaper machines and produce a lot more of them.

Woodward: That's how they started, with the simplest of machines. Honda started by motorising a bicycle and they developed from there. But they started with modern factories, whereas firms like Norton had multi-storey factories, with machine tools at different levels and components being moved by manual labour.

Tilson: Why did they evolve like that? When there's heavy machinery to move about, having one floor on top of another doesn't sound very practical.

Woodward: No. I suppose that, when those factories were built, labour was cheap and the cost of labouring and moving stuff about on trucks wasn't a major factor.

Bidmead: The heavier machinery in the press shops, as far as we can both recall, was all ground floor. The lighter machinery was above but assembly was generally on the ground floor because the components flowed downwards.

Tilson: What was the thinking behind a 3-tier building?

Woodward: Perhaps economy of land was a factor and perhaps early designs simply followed the designs of flour mills. Another factor was that it facilitated the use of belt drives to machinery on floors above from a steam engine on the ground.

Bidmead: The rating system might have had some effect. It was effective utilisation of space.

Tilson: After the war, the introduction of new technology must also have had its impact on Birmingham engineering firms?

Bidmead: Yes, it did. New machines were installed, new working practices were introduced and BSA were the first people using female labour on the assembly of motorcycles in this country, I think, although it's difficult to substantiate such statements exactly. They made a small motorcycle, the Bantam, after the war, which was completely assembled by women.

Tilson: Why were women brought in?

Woodward: To provide cheaper labour. Rates used to be very different. If a woman did the same job as a man she was paid less.

Tilson: That sort of economics became increasingly more important after the war. But women workers had been employed during the war, anyway.

Fig. 12.2. Dorothy Bailey and colleague at Castle Bromwich in World War 2, sewing Spitfire rudders by hand in the dope room. Source: *Birmingham Evening Mail,* 15 September 1988. Photo courtesy of Birmingham Post & Mail Ltd.

Bidmead: Oh yes, in multitudes.

Woodward: They did all sorts of jobs. They ran lathes and other machines at the Castle Bromwich aeroplane factory (Fig. 12.2), for example.

Bidmead: That really brought women into factories, other than in the weaving industry up North and that sort of thing, where their employment was long-established.

Tilson: I think it was also common for women to be employed in nail-making.

Woodward: That was hand work, likewise chain-making. There was a lot of outwork.

Tilson: Can we talk about design in the engineering industries? What would you say about the influence of design theory?

Woodward: Herbert Read's *Art and Industry* was an outstanding book in its day, which I read with great interest.

Tilson: Do you think his theories about function and appropriate ornament had any influence in any practical way in your industry?

Woodward: I think they were very slow to be recognised and to have any influence.

Tilson: What can you tell me about the work of the designer in the engineering industries in terms of models, tools and so on?

Woodward: In the early post-war years TI was mostly concerned with designing more efficient machines and tools because, at that time, much of the turnover of the TI Group was concerned with basic products like steel tube and aluminium sections. They did, however, own Simplex Electric which made Creda cookers and design was very important there. I would think, however, that TI's bicycles were well designed.

Bidmead: It's a difficult question. The motorcycle industry had designers, of course, as did the agricultural and horticultural industry, but they were engineering designers who (in the motorcycle industry) specialised on the engine and were not so concerned with aesthetic appearance.

Tilson: Well, take Alec Issigonis, the design engineer. Had he any equivalent in the motorcycle industry?

Woodward: The vertical twin engine (the Speed Twin) was introduced by Triumph Motorcycles not long before the war. This was a milestone in motorcycle engine development and was designed by Edward Turner.

Bidmead: There were others, I suppose, but none as well known as Issigonis (Fig. 12.3).

Woodward: Encouraged by early successes with lightweight machines, especially in the US, the Japanese produced sophisticated larger machines with which they had notable success in the Isle of Man. They also introduced attractive improvements such as electric starters. They invested heavily in design and development and in production facilities and thereby reduced costs.

Fig. 12.3. Sir Alec Issigonis' memorial service at St. Philip's Cathedral, Birmingham, with the first Morris Minor, the first Mini and a 1988 Mini in attendance. Source: *Birmingham Evening Mail,* 5 November 1988. Photo courtesy of Birmingham Post & Mail Ltd.

Bidmead: Price came into it as well as good design, but don't forget that the telescopic fork, instead of the girder fork, was an innovation. It gave a much better ride.

Woodward: That was developed before World War 2 by BMW and introduced by AJS and Matchless on army machines.

Bidmead: BSA bought up Sunbeam, which was a high quality machine.

Woodward: I agree, but I think British manufacturers were handicapped by the production facilities as compared with the Japanese. Also, their marketing was much stronger than ours.

Tilson: They have had long term strategies. What would you say about how they went about marketing compared with the British?

Woodward: They were very aggressive and I think our marketing was more haphazard. We sold what we could wherever we could sell it but the Japanese said 'right, we are now going to attack *that* market with *this* product and we are going to be market leaders with this particular product'. They would fix the price low and then drive out the competition. Having established themselves with a foothold in one particular product (whether it was a motorcycle, a radio, or whatever), they would branch out from there, enlarging their range and slowly pushing back the local opposition. It was a different technique. Also, in those days we had an Empire, which enjoyed preferential tariffs on purchases from the UK, and if someone went with a lawnmower, or a cycle, or whatever it was, to such places as (just for argument's sake) South Africa, or Australia, they said 'right, we'll have that, it's made in Britain', and they bought it. We were not faced with such keen competition in those days. Things started to change as countries became independent after the war. It began with India, I suppose, which again was an open market for us.

Tilson: It sounds as though that may have been the root cause for the lack of research and development in industry as it evolved.

Bidmead: Yes, we became too complacent.

Tilson: But also, two World Wars and having to rebuild industry, particularly after the Second World War, can't have helped, can it?

Bidmead: No, and we also lost - certainly in the First World War, which was terrible - the cream of our young people.

Woodward: It poses a big question. Germany was smashed up worse than we were. How is it, therefore, that the Germans have done far better in producing motor cars, since the war, than we have? Extremely heavy reparations were imposed on the Germans after the First World War, including good plant and machinery and their best liners. The view was held after the Second World War that this contributed to the immense German inflation of the post First World War years and the subsequent rise of the Nazis and that the right way forward for world peace was to get Germany and its allies on their feet again by helping them to rebuild their economies. This would ensure the right conditions in which democracy could be established and flourish. And the Germans have worked hard, too.

Tilson: They had, I think, a stronger tradition in design education and in apprenticeships.

Bidmead: We did have reasonable apprenticeships. Incidentally, it was President Truman who introduced the Marshall Plan for economic aid. It made a great contribution to the revival of industry in Europe. But Britain was still left with a lot of old machinery whereas the Germans, being flat on the ground, were able to introduce brand new machinery.

Tilson: I think that's probably a very important point. The oil crisis, too, has been given as a reason for the demand in the transportation industry being affected, from 1973/74.

Woodward: There was a great stimulus to make the internal combustion engine more efficient, to get more miles per gallon. Smaller cars were also introduced.

Tilson: There was a period of change from the end of the '50s, from the old methods to the evolution of a new era.
Bidmead: The engineering industry went through a trying time during that period. In some companies (Austin Rover, for example) there was industrial unrest and certainly (in many) increasing union influence. It was a trying time right up to and including Prime Minister Heath's time. It was industrial unrest from the miners that lost that Government the next election, and we did go through a period when the unions were emerging and getting stronger. Union leaders are much more interested now in companies being successful.
Tilson: Has the government intervened to alter the course of the engineering industries in the area? I understand that some industries were hampered by not being allowed to expand on their own premises.
Woodward: Through regional policy, Wolseley were induced to build a large factory at Knighton. There must be many other cases in general engineering. Government pressure brought about the formation of BMC (British Motor Corporation, Austin + Morris etc.). Expansion was directed to factories in the North, Halewood (Ford) for example. They would have much preferred, and it would have been more economic, to have expanded their established plants.
Tilson: Did that affect the motorcycle industry?
Bidmead: No, it didn't. It certainly affected the motor industry because they were also directed to Scotland. Would you say that the capital injection into modern machinery was not ideal, certainly in the motorcycle industry?
Woodward: Well, for whatever reason, I think it was lacking. I don't know whether it was because the companies weren't profitable enough and they couldn't afford it, or that it wasn't realised how far they were getting behind the opposition until it was too late.
Bidmead: It's just struck me, Roy, reading through out booklet on ***A Short History of Wolseley Webb****, that it's also our centenary in 1989. Didn't Wolseley start in 1889?*
Woodward: That's right.
Bidmead: (reads) Wolseley headed for Great Britain from Australia in 1889 and after some difficulty finally set up a new company, Wolseley Sheep Shearing Machine Company. Two companies - Geo. H. Hughes and Wolseley Engineering (formerly the Wolseley Sheep Shearing Machine Co.) - joined together in 1958. Hughes started in 1869 and Wolseley started in 1889. Other engineering companies joined the group as time went by.
Tilson: When did Wolseley stop making motor cars?
Woodward: Wolseley Sheep Shearing Machine Co. (as it then was) stopped making motor cars in 1901, when the motor car business was sold to Vickers Sons & Maxim Ltd. They established a new company, Wolseley Motors, in Adderley Park. It was sold to Morris Motors which merged with Austin Motor Co. to form the British Motor Corporation. Eventually Wolseley Motors went to Drews Lane and at Adderley Park Morris started to make commercial vehicles.
Tilson: Were they also making components or was it just full scale models?
Woodward: They made full scale models and many of the components, but were making sheep clippers, principally, at the time. The Managing Director, Herbert Austin, was a clever designer and engineer who started to make motor cars (Fig. 12.4), but he didn't make any money at it. They sold the motor car business in 1901 including stocks of components and thereafter concentrated on sheep clippers. Later on, Herbert Austin wanted to make another motor car, but the Wolseley Sheep Shearing Board wouldn't back him, so he bought a vacant small printing factory at Longbridge in Birmingham and established the Austin Motor Company there. He remained as Chairman of Wolseley Sheep Shearing Machine Co. until 1933. He was a brilliant engineer and designer. He got a bee in his

Fig. 12.4. Wolseley car, 1899. Photo courtesy of The British Motor Industry Heritage Trust - The Rover Group.

bonnet about producing a motor car and he went ahead and did it. He probably also wanted to diversify away from sheep clippers.

Bidmead: He was an entrepreneur and an innovative engineer - like Issigonis, who did the Mini.

Tilson: It does seem that the existence of the entrepreneur was very important to get things going.

Woodward: Yes, and it still is.

Tilson: Was it easier in those days?

Woodward: Yes. There were not so many restrictions as there are today. Take Geo. H. Hughes, who had a neighbour making spoke wheels. He found he could sell his neighbour's wheels to pram manufacturers and others and eventually established his own business. His neighbour declined a partnership in the business, preferring to be an employee - a mistaken decision, with hindsight!

Tilson: What range of the market were the Wolseley cars and early Austin cars aimed at?

Bidmead: I suppose the Wolseley was at the middle end of the market and the Austin Seven (Fig. 12.5) was at the bottom end. Wolseley Motors in the early '30s made a successful and famous model called the Wolseley Hornet, a name that was revived for a Mini variant.

Tilson: You haven't mentioned anything about recent years. Is there anything positive to say about the last ten or fifteen years?

Woodward: Well, it's been a period of great change in industry in general and it hasn't been a happy time for many Birmingham companies, nor for our Birmingham subsidiaries. We've sold Hughes and Accles & Shelvoke to their managements, leaving us with Boxmag in Birmingham. I'm glad to say that both Hughes and Accles are now thriving, Boxmag too!

Fig. 12.5. Austin Seven Tourer, 1927. Photo courtesy of the British Motor Industry Heritage Trust - The Rover Group.

Tilson: What is there about Boxmag that has meant it's been retained?
Woodward: We thought it was worthwhile to retain because of its wider contacts with industries with expansion potential. The old Wolseley factory has been closed but we retained the sheep clipping and electric fencing business. We gave up making sheep clippers. We now import and sell them through a different subsidiary.
Bidmead: Our electric fencing is also now imported and is sold under the Wolseley name through a subsidiary in agricultural machinery. We now have companies in distribution and manufacture all over the UK, and large subsidiaries in America, almost entirely in distribution. The Group's main business is in the distribution of central heating and plumbing products here and in the USA.
Tilson: What proportion of your trade is over there compared with over here?
Woodward: Distribution USA accounts for about 40% of turnover, Building Distribution UK, about 40% and UK manufacturing and other activities about 20%.
Tilson: Where are the main Wolseley manufacturing plants?
Bidmead: Only Boxmag is in Birmingham. Antiference (which makes plastic

products, aerials and curtain rails) is at Aylesbury, Mendle (also in plastics) is in the Rhondda Valley, Nu-Way is at Droitwich, Godwin in Gloucestershire, Totton Pumps in Southampton, Boddington at Horsmonden, both Ashley & Rock and Ranton are at Ulverston and Brentford, McConnel at Ludlow, Kidd Farm Machinery at Devizes, Parmiter & Sons at Tisbury, Dihurst Holdings at Exmouth and Astralux at Brightlingsea.

Tilson: Do you think that what has happened to your firm is typical?

Woodward: Unfortunately, yes. Many companies in Birmingham have had the same problems to face as our engineering subsidiaries in recent years. Some have closed, some have contracted, some have developed new businesses. As far as the Group is concerned we have diversified into new activities and products. Our redundancies in relation to our total numbers of employees have not been especially severe, but unfortunately many of them have been in the Birmingham area. Unpleasant decisions have had to be taken and drastic changes made, but rewards are seen today in the new confidence abroad in Birmingham and the resurgence of business here, much of it in new service industries.

REFERENCES

1 Laurie Bidmead retired from the company on 31 August 1989. This interview was conducted in December 1988.

2 Wolseley Motors was bought by Vickers Sons & Maxim in 1901 and was subsequently sold to Morris Motors, one of the antecedents of the Rover Group.

CHAPTER 13

THE CYCLE INDUSTRY IN BIRMINGHAM 1890-1920

Andrew Millward

By the outbreak of World War 1 cycle manufacture, excluding the subsidiary trades, was the third largest local trade behind jewellery and brassfoundry in terms of employment in the West Midlands region and was the major centre of cycle manufacture in Britain.[1] In the thirty year period after 1890 Birmingham overtook Coventry as the centre of the trade both in terms of output[2] and employment (see Fig. 13.1, Table 1) and this short survey will attempt to explain the circumstances surrounding this shift in location and the underlying characteristics of the Birmingham trade which contributed to its emergence as Britain's main cycle manufacturing centre.

The Growth of Birmingham's Cycle Industry after 1890

An indication of growth trends can be gained from entries under "Cycle Manufacturers" and "Cycle Fittings Manufacturers" in Birmingham Trade Directories. (see Fig.13.2, Table 2). It is clear that by 1890 Birmingham already had a number of enterprises engaged in manufacturing cycles and components. During the following decade the boom in demand for cycles attracted new firms into the industry.

Prior to 1900 26% of all new entrants into Birmingham's cycle industry were previously established in some other trade and there is a clear connection between the growth of Birmingham's cycle and cycle component industry and its existing industrial activities. One study notes that 45 engineers, machinists, diesinkers, rivett makers and millwrights, 12 toolmakers and stock and die makers, 33 stampers, brassfounders, metal moulders, casters and metal spinners, 10 wire and metal merchants and ironmongers and 7 blacksmiths, locksmiths, and gasfitters, became cycle and component manufacturers during 1870-1900. Overall, the entrants covered a wider variety of commercial and manufacturing activities such as watch and jewellery making, umbrella making, coach and axletree manufacture, tobacconists, coal and timber merchants, japanners and enamellers, drapers, tailors and milliners, pawnbrokers, button and clasp makers. The drop-out rate in the industry was high, however, and few entrants achieved sustained periods of manufacture. In the period up to 1900 54% of firms entering prior to 1896 expired within 4 years and of the 1028 enterprises which joined before 1900 508 failed to stay the course.[3]

Those firms which originated within the industry itself included Harry James who set up as a cycle manufacturer on his own account after being Works Manager at William Andrews' sewing machine and cycle business.[4] F.J. Osmond began his Osmond Cycle Company in 1894 with a local tube manufacturer, A.C. Hills, after being a manager in the cycle firms of Buckingham & Adams and the Whitworth Cycle Co.[5] P.C. Wilson similarly progressed through the Howe Machine Co., Humber & Co., and Rudge-Whitworth before joining with Henry Woodhouse to

TABLE I

	1891		1901		1911	
	Male	Female	Male	Female	Male	Female
Birmingham & Aston	2315	260	5742	1651	6183	3188
Coventry	3854	205	5372	602	4957	925
England & Wales	10965	559	28537	2929	29063	6328

Source: Census of England & Wales 1891, 1901 & 1911

N.B. The figures are indicative of the shift towards Birmingham as the major centre of the industry although the complete absence of quantitive measures of output for the different manufacturing centres during this period of transition rules out locating the precise timing of the change. Such assertions relating to levels of output are based on estimates from contemporary accounts. (see note 2)
Further difficulties arise due to the inconsistency of Census data. The 1891 Census figures refer to 'Bicycle, Tricycle Makers & Dealers'. The 1901 Census figures also include employment in 'Motor Manufacture' and the 1911 figures are for 'Cycle Makers'.

Fig. 13.1. Table I. Employment in the Cycle Industry 1891-1911.

TABLE II

	Cycle Manufacturers	Cycle Fittings & Accessories Manufacturers		Cycle Manufacturers	Cycle Fittings & Accessories Manufacturers
1890	72	27 *	1906	280	70
1891	–	–	1907	255	60
1892	114	31 *	1908	255	62
1893	–	–	1909	270	61
1894	156	42 *	1910	220	62
1895	152	53 *	1911	204	65
1896	177	63 *	1912	186	63
1897	239	102	1913	174	60
1898	309	145	1914	170	66
1899	328	145	1915	151	64
1900	325	115	1916	139	63
1901	314	95	1917	132	60
1902	286	87	1918	123	59
1903	280	72	1919	122	63
1904	290	76	1920	133	75
1905	265	67			

Source: *Kelly's Directories* for Birmingham

*Only "Fittings Manufacturers" listed.

N.B. The figures are intended only to give an indication of the growth of these activities and are not intended as a precise measure. Agents for *Kelly's Directories* may have overlooked some enterprises for whom cycle work was a minor part of their business. Also, while some firms manufactured fittings and complete bicycles and are listed under both headings, there are some instances where firms engaged in both activities are listed under only one in the directories. Over the period, changes in the final compilation of activities meant that some areas of accessories manufacture were separately listed and are thus excluded from the above count.

Fig. 13.2. Table II. Entries under "Cycle Manufacturers" and "Cycle Fittings & Accessories Manufacturers" in Birmingham Trade Directories 1890-1920.

form the Badminton Cycle Co., in 1895.[6] New enterprises also emerged from within the cycling community: for example, both Osmond and P.C. Wilson were ex-cycle racing champions. Firms which originated from outside the industry included Joseph Appleby, with his five sons, who entered production of his patent chain in 1886 after 30 years working in the pen trade with Perry & Co.[7] Edward Wilson, a foreign traveller for the Birmingham merchant house of Hudson, Edmonds & Co., persuaded the company to enter cycle manufacture and, when financial difficulties ended the firm in 1895, Wilson and George Patterson (a cycle maker since 1891), bought the business in liquidation and established the New Hudson Cycle Co. from the cycle making branch.[8]

The firms diversifying into cycle and component manufacture did so for various reasons. Prior to 1890 sewing machine manufacturers such as William Andrews, Thomas and James Crompton and Buckingham & Adams all entered the cycle industry during periods of recession in the sewing machine industry.[9] J.H. Brookes moved into cycle manufacture soon after the McKinley Tariff in the US affected its bedstead manufacture.[10] The Wolseley Sheep Shearing Machine Co. of Birmingham went into cycle production in May 1897 as a way out of financial misfortunes.[11] The arms trade was prone to fluctuations in demand and a number of firms diversified, such as Bourne & Son who entered the cycle industry in the mid 90s when trade was slack.[12] The Birmingham Small Arms Co. entered the cycle industry for the second time in 1893 after a break of five years, first of all to produce hubs and extending its range of components by 1896.[13] In the same year George Kynock & Co. of Witton diversified its range of activities to include cycles after the installation of a casting shop in 1895.[14]

Not all diversification activity was simply a response to crises of profitability or excess capacity. Perry & Co's pen nib manufacturing business was prospering at the time of entering production of the cycle chain patented by their long-serving employee, Joseph Appleby, in 1885.[15] The inflow of firms entering cycle, component and accessories manufacture during the 'bicycle boom' of the mid-1890s is an indicator of the attraction of the profits to be made at this time. That this growth came about so quickly can be explained by two factors. Firstly, it was possible to minimise capital outlay through renting machinery, drawing on trade credit, buying in components and accessories and sending out work such as nickel plating and enamelling to specialists.

Premises did not need to be particularly specialised in terms of design and, prior to 1900, some 14 Birmingham cycle and component manufacturers established themselves in premises previously occupied by tailors, drapers, outfitters and 6 in grocer's shops.[16] Secondly, the evidence from studies of the industry as a whole in this period suggests that the capital needed for starting up and expanding companies could be found from ploughed-back profits and local business contacts and in some cases through private and public flotations.[17]

The Cycle Components Industry

While, by 1890, Birmingham had fewer manufacturers of complete cycles of the size and stature of the Coventry branch of the trade, Birmingham, as a centre of the metal trades, had been a major supplier of materials, semi-finished goods and accessories for use in manufacture, assembly and finishing from the early days of the trade.[18] Therefore, when Birmingham's cycle manufacturing began to take off, it could rely upon an established group of local firms for its supplies.

These specialist suppliers often sprang from established firms who recognised the cycle industry as a promising area for expansion. Firms ordinarily engaged in stamping and piercing turned to the specialised production of stampings for cycle frames, the main suppliers being Thomas Smith & Sons of Saltley and Thomas Smith of Aston and Coventry. As cycle design progressed, increasing technological demands were made on suppliers of components. By 1890 the diamond frame safety design, utilising seamless steel tubing, with ball bearings extensively employed in wheel hubs, bottom brackets, headsets and pedals and with a chain driven rear wheel had emerged (Fig. 13.3), but it owed much to innovations and refinements in the production of components.[19]

Fig. 13.3. A Humber Safety of diamond-framed design, early 1890s. This machine had cushion tyres, but by 1895 pneumatic tyres were widely in use. Reproduced courtesy of the Science Museum.

Seamless steel tubing production had begun in Birmingham before the cycle industry developed, but the process was costly and difficult and little progress was made towards large scale low cost production until the 1880s when William Charles Stiff established the Credenda Cold Drawn Seamless Steel Tube Co. in conjunction with Herbert B.S. Bennett and Thomas W. Piggott in Ledsam Street,[20] Birmingham. Soon afterwards Max and Reinhard Mannesmann of Dusseldorf took out a UK patent, in January 1885, by which solid steel ingots could be rolled into seamless tubes suitable for subsequent cold-drawing, using a mandrel and conical rolls. The process was modified by British tube manufacturers. Although the Credenda Co. was the main supplier to the industry by 1890, cycle manufacturers turned to other tube makers where necessary and as demand grew more firms turned to specialised production and existing firms expanded. James Hudson publicly floated the business he established in 1883 as Hudson & Co., in 1892, concentrating on seamless steel tubing for frames and wheel rims at Selly Oak and Bournbrook.[21]

The application of chain drive to bicycles and tricycles gave rise to a number of specialist suppliers. Although the cycle industry was served by the Manchester firm of Renold and Co. for supplies of their bush roller chain, patented in 1880,[22] some Birmingham companies (such as the Abingdon Works Co., Perry & Co.Ltd., and F. Brampton & Co.) produced novel designs used by the trade until Renolds' patent expired in 1894. The development of the bicycle had involved widespread use of ball bearings even before 1890 and savings in costs had been achieved by specialist suppliers such as William Bown, but the widespread application of free-wheel systems and variable gears which developed during this time depended on even further reductions in cost. Britain's manufacturing capability in ball bearings was weak and American and German producers, through capital size and wide-spread application of machine tools, began to undercut the British price to the point where Birmingham Small Arms Co. (BSA) ordered 100,000 gross of German bearings for use in its components, given that they were 50% below the price of British supplies. BSA later resumed manufacture of ball bearings with imported Ludwig Loewe machine tools.[23]

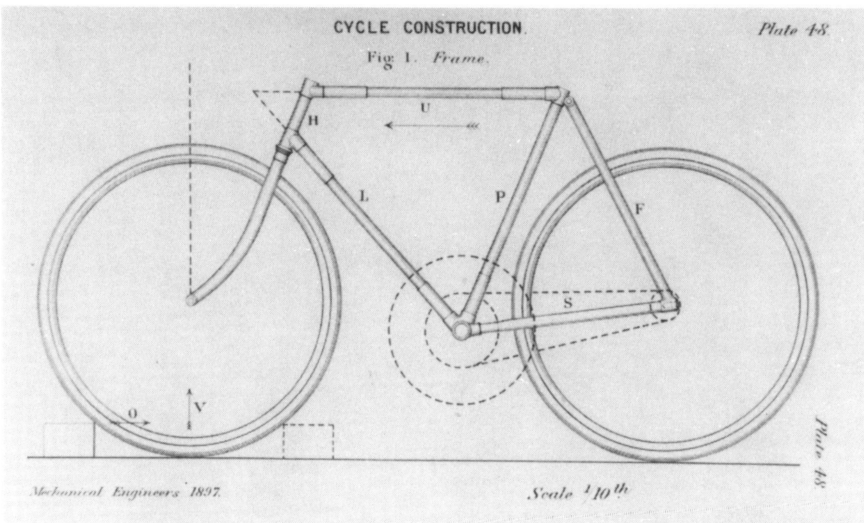

Fig. 13.4. Osmond Cycle construction. An illustration from F.J. Osmond's lecture to the Birmingham Jubilee meeting of the Institution of Mechanical Engineers in 1897. Osmond's cycles incorporated rear chain adjusters and concealed hub fasteners. Source: F.J. Osmond, "Some Points in Cycle Construction", *Proceedings of the Institution of Mechanical Engineers,* 3, 1897.

The Bicycle Boom and the Birmingham Cycle Industry

The need to produce in quantity combined with some degree of standardisation in cycle design after 1890 did not precipitate a speedy progression towards mass production throughout the industry. Although the pace of innovation, particularly in the preceding decade, had produced a diversity of changes in design from the old high-wheeled 'Ordinary' bicycle to the chain driven 'Safety' bicycle, it had implications for the industry in a general resistance to standardising patterns, building up stocks of component parts and investing in specialised machine tools. The existence of a relatively limited market of cycling enthusiasts seeking the latest type of machine and prepared to sell on their old model and buy the latest in the next season encouraged the leading manufacturers to produce high quality machines for high prices, a strategy which mitigated against mass production (Fig. 13.4). The cycling press encouraged this trend and their reactions were lukewarm at the attempt by Lloyds & Son of Birmingham to market low priced cycles in the early 1890s,[24] generally advising buyers to avoid the low priced cycles. Manufacturers had sought to extend their market prior to 1890 through a policy of product diversification into tricycles, quadricycles and through novel innovations in design. This had been at the expense of learning the techniques of quantity production and taking initiatives towards mass production and inter-firm standardisation. Even amongst components manufacturers a similar attitude was in evidence.

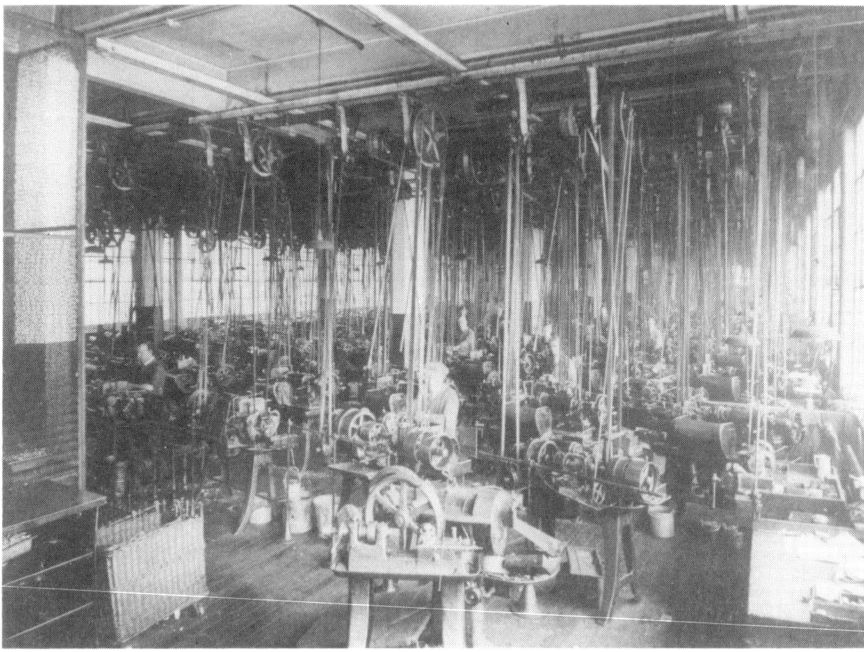

Fig. 13.5. BSA Machine Shop c.1920s showing the range of automatic machinery in use. Photo courtesy of Birmingham Museum of Science and Industry.

The bicycle boom between 1895-97 exposed the limitations of this strategy. The collapse of the boom was to have repercussions for the organisation of the industry and for manufacturing methods. However the massive growth in demand, requiring that firms had to produce both in quantity and to high quality, had already led to some noticeable changes amongst the larger enterprises even before the bicycle boom collapsed. A reduction in outwork and some vertical integration was in evidence. Some firms, such as Thomas Smith, were already mass producing components for the trade. Most manufacturers installed their own plating shops and some installed their own gas plants for brazing. BSA began to manufacture its own castings for cycle parts in November 1896 to ensure sufficient quality and quantity, and the following May embarked on producing its own cotter pins, since outside purchases involved "*insufficient deliveries and inferior quality.*"[25] Most noticeable, however, was the move towards the increased use of machine tools. While machine tools were used long before the boom, the desire to enhance quality and maintain it gave rise to some specialised machine tools, some of which were semi-automatic. While some produced their own tools the majority bought in from specialised suppliers such as Alfred Herbert of Coventry and Ward of Birmingham. [26]

The period of the bicyble boom created pressures of demand on the industry to such an extent that British manufacturers turned increasingly to the US for semi-automatic machine tools to meet demand. In December 1895 Schisclokar & Co. was set up in Birmingham to specialise in the import of machine tools for the cycle trade.[27] However, the need for machines to be modified to suit the cycle makers' individual requirements resulted in added costs and fewer benefits accrued by their not adopting set designs of machine tools and not embracing the American methods of production. Hand & Cake, Accles Ltd., and Components Co. all adapted US machine tools, and Garrard and Osmond Cycle Co. combined US and British machine tools. BSA also combined machine tools from a variety of manufacturers and even designed some of its own, investing £56,000 in 1896/7 alone.[28] Such an unco-ordinated approach to the use of machine tools was possible during the period of the boom when demand was for the high priced machine, but the output losses through failing to optimise the use of the American machine tools prompted one American to comment that "*It's like putting a grand piano into a dwelling of a Hottentot.*"[29] The possibility that the UK cycle industry could be threatened by overseas competition was raised when the US industry witnessed rapid growth during the early 1890s to such a degree that the US seamless steel tube suppliers could not meet the demands of the manufacturers and the resulting 'tube famines' saw orders worth multi-millions of pounds flood over to the British tube manufacturers. Samuel Snell, a cycle fitting manufacturer of Toledo, arrived in Birmingham in 1895, placing such large orders that some domestic cycle firms found their supplies of tubing threatened.[30]

Fig. 13.6. Gent's Safety Bicycle c.1920. Machines of this basic type were the staple product of the industry well into the 1920s. Source: J.T. Lightwood,1928.

Until the end of the century bicycles were largely produced for a leisure market and new machines were beyond the means of the vast majority of the working classes. Demand came from the leisured and middle classes and some of the more prosperous sections of the lower middle classes. Demand also came from overseas and Britain held the position of a quasi-monopolistic supplier to world markets. The boom in the 1890s was largely a result of the popularity of the 'Safety' bicycle, the growth in cycling amongst women and the respectability of cycling amongst fashionable Society, the latter generating considerable demand for high grade bicycles. The manufacturers' production of high grade machines, while more profitable in the short term, proved to be a problem when Society interest petered out by the end of 1897.[31] The surplus demand conditions of the boom allowed cheap foreign imports onto the home market mainly from US manufacturers who were able to gain a foothold in the market for bicycles amongst the price conscious. The collapse of the boom saw a fall in prices and profits and some restructuring of many firms within the industry.[32]

Fig. 13.7. BSA Spring Frame design, c, 1900-6, sold in England and elsewhere e.g. Australia. Source: *BSA Catalogue,* 1906.

The Ascendancy of Birmingham's Cycle Trade and its Development to 1920

As the centre of components production, Birmingham's manufacturers were amongst the first to experience the signs that the boom was over. In July 1897 BSA cancelled its night shift and followed this later with a reduction in the price of its components to assist the small builders.[33] The Birmingham industry was in a stronger position to respond to the collapse. The predominance of small builders in the area producing machines from proprietary parts for the more price conscious consumer was an advantage. Also the components industry had gone further towards mass production and the American methods than any other branch of the trade, and differential import duties on British exports favoured exports of components over complete bicycles.[34] As a result, Birmingham became established as the centre of the trade as some of the Coventry firms either declined or turned to the new motor industry during the post-boom decade. However, depression amongst manufacturers was widespread. Attempts to prevent price-cutting by collusive agreements amongst component and accessories manufacturers failed.[35] Similarly, diversification into the new motor industries prior to 1900 by firms such as Bard Cycle, BSA, Cycle Components and Alldays & Onions was prone to high development costs and was not the panacea for their short-term difficulties.[36] Falling prices led to increased demand levels and created greater competition amongst the remaining firms, cutting profit margins and making sustained profitability difficult. It was soon recognised that the changed market required low priced machines and this would necessitate changed attitudes towards methods of production. New Hudson introduced a low priced machine in December 1898, the result of automatic machinery introduced in its plant in 1898.[37] The price-cutting trends of the immediate post-boom period and subsequent competitiveness resulted in a lower priced, quality bicycle capable of rebuffing foreign competition on the unprotected home market, and in markets abroad, despite the imposition of foreign import duties.[38] Many of the trends in evidence at this time were to continue to affect the industry up to 1939. Seasonality of the industry was more pronounced after the boom, production with modern machinery allowing production to be confined to only a number of months. Studies by contemporaries suggest that Birmingham was particularly affected.[39] From 1900 many firms diversified into cars and motorcycles as these offered an opportunity for sustained output.

The introduction of automatic and semi-automatic machinery alongside remodelling of factories was combined with the reorganisation of the labour process which witnessed a notable transformation in the post-boom years (Fig. 13.5). The demand for skilled labour around 1890 gave way to demands for unskilled labour in the post-boom period. The slump created some unemployment in the industry although some skilled workers probably found employment in the emerging automobile industry.[40] In the changed economic conditions firms found little resistance to the widespread introduction of shift working and the increased use of female and child labour which made the workforce even more pliable.[41]

Once the principle of manufacturing at lower cost was established, attention was given to process innovations within the industry. The introduction of liquid brazing and sheet steel pressings in cycle frames lowered the unit costs of production quite significantly.[42] The Patent Butted Tube Company Ltd., formed in 1898, introduced butted tubing, patented by Alfred Reynolds, in 1897, which removed the need for liners to be inserted for brazing.[43] Interest also foucused on the chemical and physical properties of materials used in order to gain uniformity of size and quality, to optimise the efficiency of machinery and finished product. BSA followed Rudge-Whtiworth's lead in establishing its own research laboratory in 1913[44] and concern about standards within the industry was perhaps reflected in the formation of the Cycle Engineers' Institute in Birmingham in 1898.

The output of the industry predominantly consisted of diamond framed and ladies bicycles with, in many instances, small refinements in detail (Fig. 13.6). Although chainless bicycles and spring frames (Fig. 13.7) were amongst the novelties offered to the cycling public, the developments in freewheels, braking systems Perhaps the most prominent trend was the shift in location of product innovation and refinement from the large to the small makers. The demands for 'specials' from racing and club cyclists were becoming increasingly difficult for larger firms to cope with as they reorganised their production around more rigorously planned schedules. Increasingly, the small enterprising builder would fill this gap in the market. Another feature of these years, which continued between the wars, was the increased willingness to experiment with materials such as aluminium alloys, wood and celluloid in cycle construction.

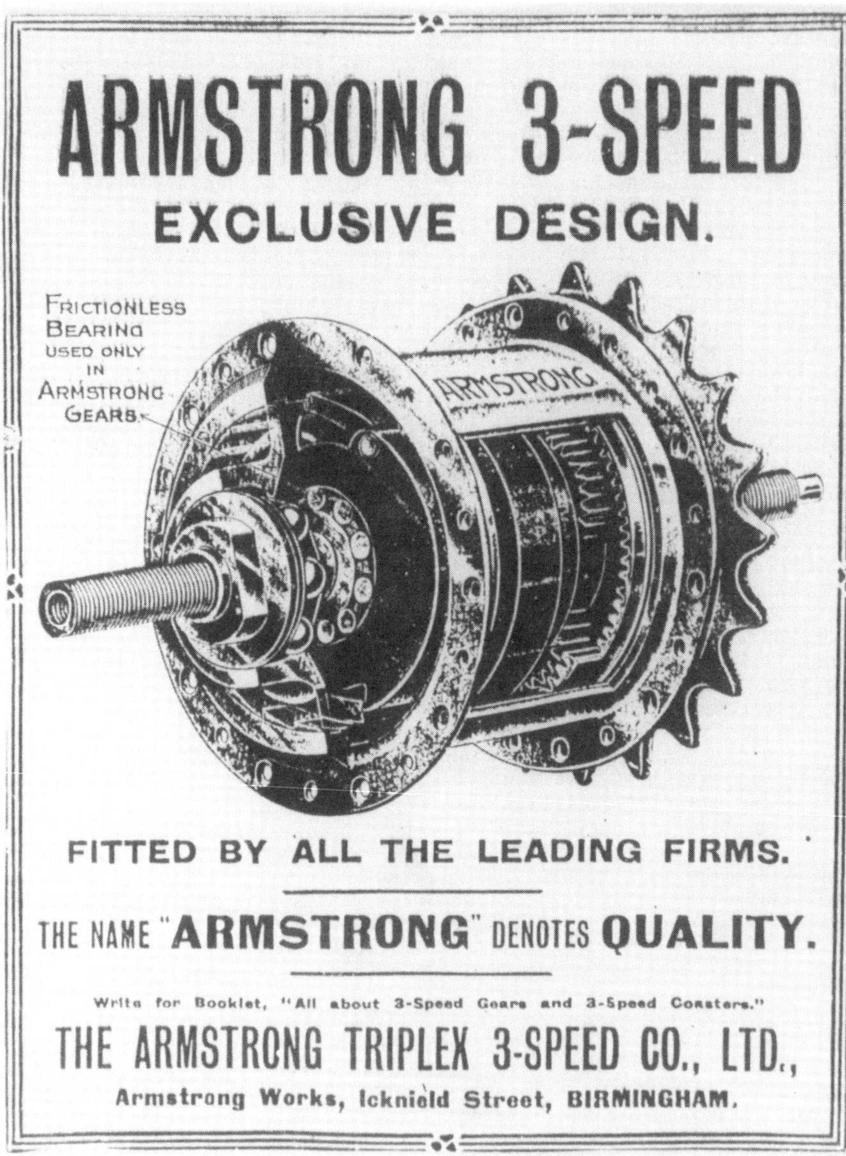

Fig. 13.8. Three-Speed Gears produced by the Armstrong-Triplex Three Speed Gear Co. Ltd., 1906-14, for bicycles and motorcycles.
Source: *Cycling,* February 1910.

There was also some reorganisation of the remaining companies within the industry through amalgamations and mergers. Several large companies merged into Weldless Steel Tubes Ltd. in 1897 (later Tubes Ltd.) in an attempt to fix prices. Cycle Components Co. Ltd. resulted from the amalgamation of five companies in 1894, but proved unsuccessful and was ultimately broken up. Perhaps the most viable merger was in the cycle components industry. BSA and Eadie merged in 1907 to cope with reduced demand from small makers and the following year decided to enter production of complete cycles [45] (Fig. 13.9). However, widespread individualism mitigated against a general merger movement. Although BSA contemplated a merger policy soon after World War 1 they took little action to put it into effect until the 1930s.[46] Similarly, Tube Investments confined their merger activity to tubing manufacture, and settled on just the acquisition of the cycle components manufacturer, J.A. Phillips, in 1919 for the remainder of the inter-war period.

Fig. 13.9. BSA Assembly Room c.1914, still largely labour-intensive despite some automation of components manufacture. Photo courtesy of Birmingham Museum of Science and Industry.

World War 1 accelerated the growth of many of the leading cycle companies, for example, BSA employment rose from 3,500 to 13,000. [47] The War Department bought up all stocks of parts and placed orders for military bicycles and encouraged diversification. [48] Experience in cycle production was easily turned to munitions and aeroplanes. Despite the growth of some large firms the industry was not closed to the emergence of new firms from the ranks of the small makers in the inter-war years, for example Hercules and Phillips who were to become giants in the industry, marketing cheap mass-produced bicycles in the inter-war years.

The industry remained highly competitive. The sale of new bicycles to a mass market was also encouraged by retailing innovations such as more sophisticated advertising, gradual payments schemes and specialised retailing outlets such as

Halford Cycle Co., who began trading in the 1890s in Birmingham as Rushbrooke & Co.[49] Further cost reductions resulted from cheaper accessories, for example, Joseph Lucas & Son (Fig. 13.10) kept up-to-date with manufacturing techniques and diversified lines.[50] The production of tyres, already established in Birmingham by firms such as Palmer Tyre in the 1890s, was centred in Birmingham by 1920, particularly as a result of the expansion of Dunlop's interests in the area and by 1920 most tyres supplied to manufacturers came from Birmingham.[51]

In the inter-war years, Birmingham remained at the fore supplying domestic demand for utilitarian and leisure markets for cycles as well as being a major supplier to export markets. This position owed a great deal to the manufacturing experience gained after 1890, and this experience had wider implications when it was brought to bear on the development of later industries, such as the automobile industry, and in the stimulus it gave to the various branches of light engineering in the area.

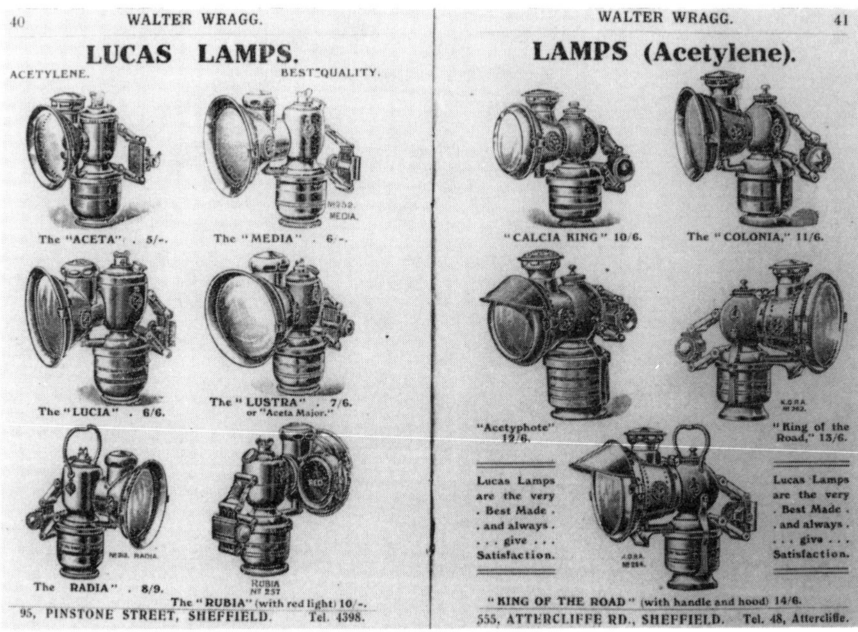

Fig. 13.10. Selection of cycle lamps produced by Joseph Lucas & Son in 1910. By this time the firm had also diversified into automotive components. Source: *Walter Wragg Catalogue,* 1910.

REFERENCES

1 *Census of England and Wales,* 1911.
2 G.C. Allen, p.290ff.
3 A.E. Harrison, 1977, pp.23-4.
4 James Cycle Co., pp.8-13.
5 *Cycling*, 7 February 1891, p.42; 15 August 1891, p.53; 3 November 1894, p.254.
6 Ibid., 31 October 1891, p.266; *Cycle Manufacturer,* 12 December 1892, p.199.
7 *Cycling,* 4 June 1898, p.494.

8 *Birmingham Gazette and Express,* 17 July 1908.
9 A.E. Harrison, 1977, p.29.
10 G.C. Allen, pp.269-70.
11 G.S. Davison, p.19.
12 *Cycle Manufacturer,* 31 August, 1895, p.67.
13 Birmingham Small Arms Co.Ltd., vol.1, pp.22-6, 573-7, 603-4.
14 Imperial Chemical Industries Ltd., pp.29-32.
15 A.E. Harrison, 1977, pp.37-8.
16 Ibid., p.70.
17 A.E. Harrison, 1981; ibid., 1977, pp.352-467.
18 F.W. Grew, pp.27-31.
19 For details of the technologucal development of cycles and components see C.F. Caunter, 1955.
20 *Cycle Manufacturer,* 16 May 1896, p.167; C.R. Marks, 1903.
21 A.E. Harrison, 1977, p.93.
22 B.H. Tripp, 1956.
23 Birmingham Small Arms Co.Ltd., op.cit., vol.2, pp.634, 648.
24 *Cycle Manufacturer,* 10 August 1894, p.35.
25 Birmingham Small Arms Co.Ltd., vol.2, p.699.
26 For details of the development of the machine tool industry in this period see R. Floud, 1976; S.B. Saul, 1968.
27 A.E. Harrison, 1969, p.295.
28 A.E. Harrison, 1977, pp.263-279.
29 F.J. Miller in *American Machinist,* 3 June 1897, pp.18-19.
30 *Cycle Manufacturer,* 7 September 1895, p.74; 12 October 1895, p.128; 1 February 1896, p.11.
31 For details of the social background to the 1890s bicycle boom see D. Rubinstein, pp.47-71.
32 H.M. Perkin, 1980.
33 Birmingham Small Arms Co.Ltd., vol.2, pp.709, 743.
34 N.B. Hudson, pp.116-8.
35 A.E. Harrison, 1969, p.303.
36 A.E. Harrison, 1977, p.316.
37 *Catalogue of the New Hudson Cycle Co.Ltd., for the 1899 Season,* 1 December 1898, p.14.
38 A.E. Harrison, 1969, pp.297-301.
39 A. Fox, 1912.
40 G.R. Carter in S. Webb and A. Freeman, 1912.
41 A. Fox, op.cit., Pt.IV.
42 On the development of sheet steel pressings see A. Muir, 1958.
43 C.F. Caunter, op.cit., p.49.
44 A.E. Harrison, 1977, p.336.
45 H.W. Bartleet, 1931.
46 *The Economist,* 11 October 1919, pp.586-7.
47 N.B. Hudson, op.cit., pp.121-3.
48 F.W. Grew, op.cit., pp.88-9.
49 A.B. Jones, 1981.
50 H. Nockolds, vol.1, 1976.
51 F.W. Grew, op.cit., pp.30-1.

BIBLIOGRAPHY

G.C. Allen, *The Industrial Development of Birmingham and the Black Country,* London, Allen & Unwin, 1929.

H.W. Bartleet (ed. J. Burrow & Co.), *Bartleet's Bicycle Book,* London, 1931.

Birmingham Small Arms Co.Ltd., *History of the Birmingham Small Arms Company 1861-1900,* vols. 1 and 2, BSA, n.d.

G.R. Carter, "The Cycle Industry" in S. Webb and A. Freeman, *Seasonal Trades,* London, Constable, 1912.

C.F. Caunter, *The History and Development of Cycles,* London, HMSO, 1955.

G.S. Davison, *At the Wheel: Impressions of the Leaders of Britain's Greatest Industry,* London Transport Publications, 1931.
A. Fox, *An Investigation into the Cycle Trade in Birmingham,* University of Birmingham thesis, 1912.
F.W. Grew, *The Cycle Industry: Its Origins, History and Latest Developments,* London, Isaac Pitman & Sons, 1921.
A.E. Harrison, "The Competitiveness of the British Cycle Industry 1890-1914", *Economic History Review,* (2nd series), vol.22, 1969, pp.287-303.
A.E. Harrison, *Growth Entrepreneurship and Capital Formation in the United Kingdom's Cycle and Related Industries 1870-1914,* University of York, unpublished Ph.D. thesis, 1977.
A.E. Harrison, "Joint Stock Company Flotation in the Cycle, Motor Vehicle and Related Industries 1882-1914", *Business History,* vol.23, 1981.
A.E. Harrison, "The Origins and Growth of the UK Cycle Industry to 1900", *Journal of Transport History,* vol.6, March 1985, pp.41-70.
N.B. Hudson, *The Growth and Structure of the Bicycle Industry,* University of London, MSc. Econ. thesis, 1960.
Imperial Chemical Industries Ltd., *Under Five Flags: The Story of Kynoch Works, Witton, Birmingham, 1862-1962,* 1962.
James Cycle Co., *Retrospect and Prospect,* Birmingham, 1948.
A.B. Jones, *The Story of Halfords,* Llandudno Junction, Gwynedd, R.E. Jones & Bros. Ltd., 1981.
C.R. Marks, *The Manufacture of Iron and Steel Tubes,* Manchester, John Heywood, 2nd edition, 1903.
H.M. Perkin, *The Bicycle Industry and the Bicycle Boom,* London School of Economics, MSc thesis, 1980.
B.H. Tripp, *Renold Chains: A History of the Company and the Rise of the Precision Chain Industry 1879-1955,* London, Allen & Unwin, 1956.

FURTHER READING

R. Floud, *The British Machine Tool Industry 1850-1914,* London, Cambridge University Press, 1976.
J.T. Lightwood, *The Cyclists' Touring Club Being the Romance of Fifty Years' Cycling,* London, CTC, 1928.
A. Muir, *75 Years of Progress,* Coventry, Smiths Stamping Works Ltd., 1958.
H. Nockolds, *Lucas: The First Hundred Years,* vol.1, London, David & Charles,1976.
D. Rubinstein, "Cycling in the 1890s", *Victorian Studies,* Autumn 1977, pp.47-71.
S.B. Saul, "The Machine Tool Industry in Britain to 1914", *Busines History,* vol.10, 1968.

CHAPTER 14

THE RISE, FALL AND MINIMAL SURVIVAL OF THE BIRMINGHAM MOTORCYCLE INDUSTRY

Barbara M.D. Smith

The rise and fall of the motorcyle industry in Birmingham coincides closely with the city's birth in 1889 and its centenary in 1989. The wider Birmingham area has played a major role in the history of the national industry, with considerable responsibility therefore for both that rise and fall. Central names are Birmingham Small Arms Co. (a famous conglomerate) and the great brand names: BSA, Triumph, Norton, Royal Enfield, Matchless, AJS, Sunbeam, now all but one part of history.

This paper presents a brief post-mortem. The true causes of disaster are difficult to discern amid the nostalgia and "*interpersonal vituperation*"[1] but require examination of both the capabilities of Japanese, and the deficiencies of British, motorcycle companies. The first of these approaches leads to the suggestion of murder by the Japanese; the second to that of "*suicide by neglect or accident before the onslaught was actually completed.*"[2] A third actor with some responsibility for the outcome is the British government. Many of its policies have been considered unhelpful by Dunnett.[3] Judgement may vary as to whether the murder was inevitable. The harder question is whether the Japanese advance could have been halted in the 1950s when effectively there was no motorcycle industry in either war-torn Japan or Germany.

The next step is to indicate the developing competitive circumstances of the industry and then to look at the main companies at least briefly before concluding this study of an important local industry of yesteryear.

The Wider Context: A Statistical Profile

The most economical way to reveal the changing circumstances in which British and Birmingham motorcycle manufacturers have had to operate over the century of the industry's life is to provide a summary statistical profile (Fig. 14.1, Table I). Points from this include:-

(i) *Usage and Demand.* The number of motorcycles in Britain began to climb in the 1900s reaching a peak in 1960 of 1,796,000 licensed machines. But, during the 1960s, licences halved with some recovery in the late 1970s before another fall. Registrations of new machines peaked at 332,000 in 1959 but fell to a quarter of this in 1969. Recovery to 286,000 in 1979 has been followed by a drastic fall back below 1950 levels.[4] These declines had no parallels for cars, meaning that car imports arrived on a basically expanding market.

(ii) *Size of Machine and British Trade.* In the 1950s and 60s, the new demand for small capacity machines, which British producers neglected,[5] created an opportunity for imports (scooters from Italy, mopeds from France, and small motorcycles from Germany and, after 1962, Japan). British producers chose to concentrate on the high value added over 500 cc 'superbikes' mainly for export to the US. This was a high risk strategy.

TABLE I (E=estimate; neg=negligible)

	1909/10	**1920**	**1935**	**1950**	**1960**	**1970**	**1975**	**1979**	**1986** latest
I. British domestic usage and demand									
Current licences (000s)									
Motorcycles	36	288	492	729	1796	1048		1292	1065
incl. under 50/60cc				29	388	444		466	389
incl. over 500cc				40E	67	66		82	98
sidecars				100	145				
Motor cars	53	187	1477	2258	5526	11515		14568	16981
New registrations (000s)									
Number				128	257	105		286	106
% of licences				18%	14%	10%		22%	10%
incl. under 50/60cc				20	75	58		87	38
incl. over 500cc					10	7		24	16
incl. sidecars				7	4				
II. Trade									
Exports (No: 000s)				74	44	56	22	17	1
over 100cc/250-499cc				68/	22	48	neg.		
over 500cc							21		
To Europe				16	5	5	2	9	
To US				9	12	38	14	4	
To Eire & Commonwealth				43	22	16E	4E		
incl. Canada				6	1	5	2		
incl. Aust/NZ				24	3	1	1		
									1982
Imports (No: 000s)				2	135	78	279	281	237
incl. mopeds					70E	32	53		
incl. scooters					57	7	5		
incl. motorcycles					7	39	221		
incl. over 250cc						1	30		
incl. over 500cc							11E		
% motorcycles					6%	50%	79%		
From W. Europe				1	128	34	70	31	13
incl. Italy					36	7	21	19	
From E. Europe					neg.		17		
From Japan					2	41	188	215	215
incl. 0-250cc					2	36	165		
incl. over 500cc							7		
Value per machine (£s)									
Exports from Britain				£94	124	276	716	895	226
Imports to Britain				£47	57	56	186	352	367
III. British production		**1948**	**1954**	**1958**	**1963**	**1968**	**1973/5**	**1979**	**1984/5**
Establishments		21	19	15	12E	6	5E		
Output (No: 000s)		120	188	134	95	91	15	27	
Employment		12	13	9	7E	7	3		
Output per employee p.a.		10	14	15	13	13	5		
IV. Employment in the West Midlands (includes cycles)									
			1959	**1961**	**1966/7**		**1970**		
West Midlands Region			20820	24660	14474		10400	4500	neg.
incl. West Midlands Conurbation				15176	9970		8300		
incl. Birmingham				12866	7480		6120		
Great Britain			36600	41860	23600		20000	13100	9000
V. World production (mainly over 50cc)		**1951**	**1953**	**1958**	**1960**	**1970**	**1975**	**1979**	**1984**
Total (000s)			1959	3129	4618	7810	9536	10653	10308
incl. W. Europe (and UK)			1511	1699	1792	2961	2760	2646	1432
incl. Japan		24	198	504	1494	2948	3803	4476	4026
incl. USSR/E. Europe			250	948	1231	1604	1705	1694	1754
VI. US market	**1920**	**1940**	**1950**	**1960**	**1965**	**1970**	**1975**	**1978**	**1984**
Registrations (000s)	239	136	454	574	1382	2824	4964	5138	5618
Production (000s)						251	361	120	155
Imports (000s)	neg.	neg.	neg.	13	134	307	707	892	
Imports (value, dollars 000s)					152	357	696		
% from UK (in value)					13%	9%	4%		
% from Japan (in value)					72%	82%	87%		
VII. Japanese market (No. 000s)			**1951**	**1956**	**1961**	**1966**	**1971**	**1975**	**1984/5**
In use in Japan			53	1267	4068	8239	8755	8752	
Production			24	333	1804	2447	3401	3803	4026
Exports			½	½	78	976	2279	2691	
% output exported			2%	neg.	4%	40%	67%	71%	
Exports to US						452	1002	761	
Exports to Britain						22	45	201	

Fig. 14.1 Table I. Statistical Profile of the Developing Motorcycle Industry. Source: see B.M.D. Smith, 1981.

(iii) *Production.* The falling away of British production and the low and falling productivity after 1948 or 1954 is evident. Output per employee per year in 1956 is estimated at 19 machines in Britain and 16 in Japan but, by 1971, the comparable figures were still 19 in Britain but 162 in Japan.[6]

(iv) *World Production and Trade.* Outside Britain, the volume and location of motorcycle production has changed dramatically. Production has risen fivefold in the last twenty years. In 1953, threequarters of world production arose in Europe, including Britain. By 1973, Western Europe's share was down to a third with another third in Japan and the rest in Eastern Europe and Asia. Britain and Birmingham were no longer significant in either production or trade though Britain's balance of payments for motorcycles in value turned adverse only in 1973.

Imports into Britain, negligible in 1950, were considerable by 1960, with 95% coming from Western Europe. But 1963/4 saw the start of the Japanese invasion after the signing of the 1962 treaty that ended the break in trade caused by the war. Imports from Japan flagged a little in the late 1960s but recovered from 1972. The Japanese speciality lay in the 50-150 cc machines but their range widened and a few of over 500 cc had reached Britain by the 1970s.

Fig. 14.2. Honda 50 cycle-motor, 1966, an example of a Japanese motorcycle in competition with British machines. Reproduced from C.F. Caunter, 1970, origin: *Motor Cycle*, date unknown.

Imports into Britain from Western Europe dropped in the late 1960s, defeated by falling demand and Japanese competition (Fig. 14.2) in the British market. British producers were thus not alone in losing markets to the Japanese but, like American producers,[7] lacked protection in their home market after the tariffs came down in the 1960s. But France, Italy and (to a lesser extent) Germany kept out the Japanese from their home markets successfully by various means.

The fact is that the Japanese came to operate on a totally different scale to everyone else.[8] A home market of eight million machines, nearly all of small capacity, provided a base from which to export two thirds of production. One million machines were first exported in 1968. But both home and export markets were fought for amongst the Japanese themselves. By 1975, four companies dominated the Japanese industry and the world market.[9]

But BSA, at its peak in the 1960s, produced only 50,000 machines a year; 43,000 at Small Heath (helped by Redditch) and another 7,000 at Triumph at Meriden. This scale, especially when made up of competing marques, could not provide the economies of scale to justify anything approaching mass-production. The demand was there until the early 1960s but (like Land Rover) the management saw a benefit in the premium offered by scarcity despite the (realised) likelihood that others would offer to fill the gap. However, attempts to enter the scooter and the three-wheeler 'shopper' market proved disastrous. On the other hand, BSA continued its well-established policy of buying up companies in non-motorcycle sectors, although it also sold out of others rather than make the necessary investment.[10]

Fig. 14.3. BSA 'Sloper' 500 cc motorcycle, 1930. Source: *Classic Bike*, August 1981.

Were there any factors, apart from lack of imagination and ambition, that prevented BSA in the 1950s and 1960s from pushing into the Japanese and other markets? Indeed, there were. Labour, for one thing, was in short supply, and often also steel and other metals and components, not least because of the dominance of the better-paying car industry. Motorcycle sales were alternately stopped and started as part of Keynesian demand management at times of year that fitted ill with market rhythms.[11] Demand for small machines in Britain was held down by regulations that required moped and scooter drivers to have licenses, driving tests, etc. Moreover, finance for expansion would not have been easy to find, a vicious circle of low productivity[12] and low profits curtailing the funds that could have broken out of that circle. But neither regional policy nor poor industrial relations were factors.[13] Central, though, I am sure, was a weak and divided management, complacent that British motorcycles would sell without undue effort, investment or change and diverted by internecine arguments and difficulties in other product fields.[14]

Problems were not restricted to BSA. Indeed, as the case studies that follow show, the interesting point is that all significant British motorcycle producers clung to the big machines, made serious mistakes and effectively collapsed despite having machines that were in demand (though not necessarily profitable to make). Essentially, British motorcycles remained substantially hand made by craftsmen as the components were not fully interchangeable. They were not engineered for production routinely even in the 1970s.

The Motorcycle Companies

Gradually most of the British motorcycle industry has been absorbed into the two groups, BSA and AMC (Associated Motor Cycles Ltd.) which, in a state of collapse, united to form Norton Villiers Triumph in 1973. Yet those parts that remained outside still managed to fall by the wayside. While the increasing competition from Germany, Italy and, subsequently, Japan provides the backcloth to this defensive consolidation and collapse, it does not explain it - except as providing a deterrent to outside investment, public or private, in this already suspect British industry.

Fig. 14.4. Ariel Motor Tricycle, 1898. Reproduced from C.F. Caunter, 1970, by permission of the Science Museum.

A. Birmingham Small Arms Co.Ltd. (1861-1973), (including Ariel (1893-1961), Triumph (1888-1973), New Hudson (1909-1933 and 1945-1957), Sunbeam (1912-1957) and others.

BSA was started in 1861 as a joint venture by twelve local gun firms in Birmingham to make rifles by machinery at a greenfield site in Small Heath, then on the edge of Birmingham, beside the canal and railway. Gun orders were always irregular and, from the 1880s, BSA applied its machinery to making parts for bicycles (1889s), cars (1908 and after 1921) and motorcycles (1909) (Fig.14.3). The first motorcycles were made at Redditch in the Eadie plant acquired in 1907 and also at Small Heath. In both World Wars, BSA had over 20,000 employees. In 1945, it was producing rifles, bicycles, cars, steel and machine tools as well as motorcycles. [15]

In 1944, BSA acquired Ariel Motors (first motortricycle 1898 (Fig. 14.4); first motorcycle 1905) from Jack Sangster. [16] Ariel employed about 450 employees at its factory in Grange Road, Bournbrook (Figs. 14.5, 14.6). Production was moved to Small Heath in 1961. In 1951, BSA acquired the Triumph Engineering Co. again from Jack Sangster [17] who, along with Edward Turner [18] the Managing Director and designer at Triumph, joined BSA's board. Triumph, founded by Bettmann in 1888 [19] had its works in central Coventry. Sangster had purchased Triumph in 1935 to produce motorcycles (the car side going its separate ways). After Triumph's factory was blitzed in 1940, a new works was built in the green belt at Meriden. This was expanded to employ 1,250 in the 1950s while about 3,500 were employed on the motorcycle side at Small Heath. BSA made 1,250 motorcycles a week at Triumph in Coventry. In the 1960s, 75% were exported, largely to the US, bringing in valuable dollars.

Fig. 14.5. Ariel Machine Shop, c.1936. Photo provided by Jerry Young.

There is no room here to relate the comings and goings of the 20 or so plants in 10 product sectors within the BSA Group or of its directors and executives. But it is relevant to point to the failure to integrate expertise and production across the Group, [20] and the absence from the Board of Directors, after 1960, of men familiar with motorcycles or prepared to appreciate the arguments of those that were.[21] After Sir Bernard Docker departed in a famous night of the long knives in 1956,[22] Sangster became Chairman, to be replaced, in 1961, by Eric Turner,[23] a youngish accountant from the aircraft industry. Eric Turner (no relative or friend of Edward) brought in executives made redundant from the aircraft industry at that time. The new ideas and technology, applied from the new Research and Development unit at Umberslade Hall without enough consultation with existing experienced designers at Small Heath, brought disaster in 1969. New models proved unsaleable, £8m worth being brought back from the US as virtual scrap. An expensive production line for the Ariel 3 tricycle for shoppers was never needed, machines reaching the American market after the season and with parts missing. In 1971, debts, redundancies, industrial disputes and collapse of the joint venture with Alfred Herbert led to a new management under Lord Shawcross.

Fig. 14.6. Connie and Jackie Young on a country outing c.1947 on Ariel motorcycle with Red Hunter sidecar by Swallow. Photo provided by Jerry Young.

Ambitious plans for a new product range caused an approach to the government for financial assistance in 1972.[24] The outcome, however, was the proposal that BSA merge with Norton under the chairmanship of (car) racing driver Dennis Poore, as an investment by the Manganese Bronze Holdings Group of Ipswich.[25] To cut a long, complex story short, Norton Villiers Triumph was born in 1973, with talk of *"a new generation of motorcycles and in due course the concessioning of up-to-date plant"* to manufacture them economically[26] *"to create a healthy British industry."*[27] Only later did it become clear both that Poore lacked any real strategy to accomplish this and that the government were persuaded against BSA's proposals, however practical.[28]

The crunch issue then became which of the three remaining works were to close.[29] Consultants considered each appropriate for closure in turn, followed by protests, worker action and reprieves before final closure.[30]

But, at Meriden, the unions and workers proposed to buy out their factory and, after a change of government brought Wedgwood Benn to the Department of Trade and Industry, did so via the Meriden Co-operative.[31] Benn also commissioned the Boston Consulting Group to report on the *"strategy alternatives for the British motorcycle industry."*[32] The alternatives were meagre. NVT had collapsed further into debt and losses by 1975 towards which further government help (beyond the £24 already provided) was refused on 31 July 1975. Next day, Poore announced the liquidation of the ex-Villiers plant in Wolverhampton.[33] Small Heath had gone into receivershp in 1973 with closure postponed into 1975. The Meriden Co-operative limped along for several years to finally expire in 1983.[34]

Thus the BSA name on new motorcycles disappeared effectively in December 1975.[35] The BSA name persisted longer in other sectors like guns,[36] but the Small Heath factory was demolished.[37]

B. Associated Motor Cycles Ltd., (1937-1966), including AJS (1897-1931), Francis and Barnett Ltd. (1895-1965), James Cycle Co.Ltd. (1880-1965), and Norton Motors Ltd. (1898-)

The first AJS motorcycle places the start of this second major group in 1909 in Wolverhampton. But, in 1931, A.J. Stevens and Co., was acquired by H. Collier & Sons of Plumstead, near Woolwich, London, already the owners of Matchless.[38] The name switch to Associated Motor Cycles (AMC) took place in 1937. In 1948, the Woolwich works, with its 1,000 employees, was described as the largest in the world.[39]

AMC specialised in large capacity machines, 350 and 500 cc. It entered the lighter market by acquisitions in the West Midlands. In 1947, AMC took over Francis Barnett, whose first motorcycle was produced in 1919 and whose factory was in Lower Ford Street, Coventry, with a subsidiary one in Greet, Birmingham and a second in Coventry in the 1950s.

In 1950, AMC took over the James Cycle Co., established 1880 and producing its first motorcycle in 1905. James' factory was in Gough Road, Greet, in Birmingham, not far from both BSA and Francis Barnett. Like Francis Barnett, James made lighter motorcycles, using Villiers engines as well as its own.

Then, in 1953, AMC bought up Norton Motors (established 1898). The Norton factory from 1920 to 1963 was in Bracebridge Street, Aston, in Birmingham. Norton, which had many Grand Prix successes in the interwar years, made heavier motorcycles of 350 and 500 cc, competing with AJS and Matchless, though less profitable than AMC and Francis Barnett.

In characteristically mistaken British style, inter-group competition rather than integration continued after these mergers. Profits peaked in 1954. In 1959, AMC produced about 3,000 machines a year, mainly under 250cc, or 12% of British output.

Thereafter, strategic errors, combined with increasing competition and hire purchase restrictions, brought collapse in 1966. First, a dispute with Villiers led to an unsuccessful attempt to produce an AMC two-stroke engine at Woolwich in 1955-7. The second error was the building of a big extension to the Woolwich works that simply created over-capacity. AMC also became dependent on the US market with 70% of its machines exported there in the 1960s. This reflected the loss of markets for smaller machines to the Japanese. Consequently in 1962, in a rationalisation, Francis Barnett left Coventry to join James in Greet while Norton left Birmingham for Woolwich.[40]

In 1966, after the receiver had been called in, AMC was sold off to Dennis Poore, soon also to become owner of the Enfield name. Poore had already in 1965 acquired the Villiers engine plant in Wolverhampton. He adopted the name Norton Villiers to 'consummate' the 'marriage' of these two groups.[41] 650 and 750cc Nortons continued to be made but James, Francis Barnett, Matchless and (later) AJS machines disappeared.

The Woolwich factory was closed in 1968 and, after some costly delay,[42] a new factory opened for Norton Villiers in Andover, Hampshire, in 1969 where the 750 cc Norton Commando was made.[43] The works closed in the late 1970s.[44]

C. Villiers Engineering Co.Ltd. (1928-1975)

This old and respected cycle, motorcycle and engine concern had its factories around Marston Road in Wolverhampton. At the end of the 1960s, it employed 2,000 people there making 40,000 engines a year.

Essentially Villiers made engines for other motorcycle firms to put in their own machines. In 1957, they took over JAP, their main competitor.

In 1965, Manganese Bronze, of which Poore had recently become Chairman, purchased a 25% interest in Villiers and then took full control, immediately introducing economies.[45] As part of the operation to close the AMC Woolwich plant, engine production was moved from Woolwich to Wolverhampton.[46] In the subsequent Norton Villiers Triumph argument over site choice, Villiers was the third arm, closing finally in mid 1976 after a sit-in and completion of unfinished stock.[47]

D. Enfield Cycle Co.Ltd. (1896-1970)

Enfield was formed in Redditch to purchase the Eadie Manufacturing Co's cycle division and that of Enfield Manufacturing Co. However, BSA took over the Eadie side in 1907, leaving Enfield on its own. The Royal Enfield factory in Hewell Road, Redditch, was completed in 1907 with the Smith family in control until 1962. Motorcycles were produced from 1910. A second factory was added at Westwood, near Bradford-on-Avon, during World War 2 and an associate works in Madras, India, in 1950. Enfields, ranging from 125 cc upwards, were mainly sold on the home market.

In 1962, on the death of F.W. Smith, the company was purchased by E. and H.P. Smith (no relative), the engineering conglomerate based in Birmingham. After Redditch was finally designated as a new town, the Hewell Road site was sold to the Development Corporation in 1966-7.[48] Production of the 750 cc Interceptor, the first 'superbike', was moved to Enfield Precision Engineers at Westwood, though the Enfield name was sold to Norton Villiers. Motorcycle production finally ceased at Westwood in 1970.[49]

The best years for Enfield were 1946-50 but, after 1960, labour shortages, competition and diffusion of Smith family interest combined to weaken the company. Profits, therefore, fell fatally before either the Japanese treaty or the E. and H.P. Smith takeover and asset strip commenced.

E. Veloce Ltd. (1904-1968)

The Veloce company, which made the Velocette range of motorcycles in Spring

Hill and, then, York Road, Hall Green, Birmingham, was owned by the Goodman family.[50] The range included police, racing and trials machines up to 500 cc capacity of "*good and unorthodox design*" [51] (Fig.14.7). Assays into mass-production in 1948, and into the scooter business in 1959, proved unsuccessful. The Goodmans raced their own machines and it was the disabling accident to one of the family that took the heart out of the company. Motorcycle production ceased in 1965 with the loss of 70 jobs.[52]

Fig. 14.7. Velocette L.E. 200 Motorcycle, 1953. Reproduced from C.F. Caunter, 1970, by permission of the Science Museum.

F. Norton Group plc, previously The Norton Villiers Triumph Group plc (1968-), (parent of Norton Motors and Birmingham Small Arms Co. in the 1980s).

Norton Villiers Triumph Group was formed in 1986 to bid for the assets of the old Norton and BSA names and operated a rotary engine and motorcycle business at Lynn Lane, Shenstone, between Sutton Coldfield in Birmingham and Lichfield. The new company has been formed by Philippe Le Roux, a 26 year old former merchant banker.[53]

Back in 1975, as the closure of Small Heath, Wolverhampton and Meriden was planned, four designers and twenty employees had gathered in a small BSA parts warehouse at Shenstone to assemble an Easy Rider moped using Italian components.[54] The operation was a modest success.[55]

The new machine by the new company was the Norton Classic at 600cc of which 100 were made for sale at £5,950 each. The Classic was said to feel "*British*" and "*good*".[56] It joined the police, army and RAC motorcycles produced in the last 5 years by the 80 employees at Shenstone. The Interceptor (1984-8) and the Commander (1988) have seized 20% of the police market in Britain, challenging the BMW monopoly.[57] The latest model is the 588 cc Norton Commander touring motorcycle.[58]

Fig. 14.8. Phillippe Le Roux and his wife Amanda on the Norton 'Classic' motorcycle. Source: *Birmingham Evening Mail,* 10 May 1988. Photo courtesy of Birmingham Post and Mail Ltd.

These machines feature the Wankel rotary engine, which dates back to the 1940s in Germany, a licence for which was bought by BSA back in 1972.[59] Applications for the engine outside motorcycles are being developed.[60] Employment is due to have risen to 120 by the present time.[61] Investments have also been made in a number of engineering companies for motorcycles are only a relatively minor part of the ambitions of this the latest motorcycle producer.

G. Triumph Motor Cycles (Meriden)Ltd., The Meriden Co-operative (1975-1984)

The Co-operative opened in March 1975 under the senior shop stewards' convenor, Dennis Johnson.[62] Two essentials were worker solidarity and financial and moral support from Benn. The latter included £5m in grant and loans. Losses were made but life was prolonged through the efforts of George Robinson, Harold

Lever and Arnold Weinstock (of GEC),[63] with NVT Motorcycles continuing to be responsible for all marketing until 1977. In 1978, with an output of 16,000 a year, [64] its 750 cc Triumph Bonnevilles were largely made by hand by the 650 employees,[65] 80% of production was exported. But, with competition mounting, mass-production infeasible and wage demands increasing,[66]life was uncertain, despite the appointment of a professional management team in 1977. With the departure of the Labour Government in 1979 and the recession of the 1980s, the Co-operative slowly folded amidst bitterness, selling the Meriden plant in 1983.[67] Survival in the new smaller works was not prolonged. [68] Otherwise the sharp downturn in motorcycle registrations after 1983 would surely have been fatal.

Conclusion

So this great Birmingham industry has become virtually extinct in the face of internal failings, an anachronistic product and foreign competition. Can Norton or even the Japanese survive in the western industry in the 1990s? It will be interesting to see. Openings remain for Wankel applications outside motorcycles, for off the road and racing machines and customised accessories - and Watsonian Sidecars, Rickmans and others survive.

REFERENCES

1 B.M.D. Smith, *The History of the British Motorcycle Industry 1945-1975,* 1981, p.3. See also B. Ryerson, 1980; B. Hopwood, 1981; I. Davies, 1980.
2 B.M.D. Smith, 1981, p.7.
3 P.J.S. Dunnett, 1980.
4 In 1980, motorcycle demand seemed to have recovered but, since then, demand has again slipped away.
5 The British disparaged such machines and many of their models tended to be unsuccessful and not pushed to be so. The reasons for this include the separation of the cycle from the motorcycle industry and the need for a licence to ride a moped or scooter here.
6 B.M.D. Smith, 1981, p.29.
7 While the bulk of British production and 75% of exports went to the US in the mid 1960s, the Japanese provided 70% of American imports at this time.
8 P. Carrick, 1976, p.15. At the end of the war, Honda fitted a small engine to a bicycle frame.
9 Honda, Yamaha Motor Co., Suzuki Motor Co., Kawasaki Heavy Industries. B.M.D. Smith, 1981, p.20.
10 See ibid., pp.52-4. Thus BSA failed either to diversify or develop existing lines. Motorcycles were 27% of sales in 1956, 34% in 1958-9, 41% in 1959-60, 24% in 1969-70.
11 Via hire purchase regulations etc., see P.J.S. Dunnett, e.g. pp.87-94, and evidence from companies' accounts etc., see B.M.D. Smith, 1981, pp.40-1.
12 Ibid., pp.29, 42-3.
13 In contrast to the car industry. Ibid., pp.43-4.
14 E.g. Sir Bernard Docker's departure in 1956.
15 B.M.D. Smith, 1981, p.50. BSA produced 1,000 motorcycles weekly, mostly 500 cc, in 1945.
16 B.M.D. Smith, "John Young Sangster",1986, pp.55-9; P. Hartley, 1980.
17 B.M.D. Smith, "John Young Sangster", op.cit., pp.56-7; I Davies, op.cit.
18 B.M.D. Smith, "Edward Turner", 1986, pp.564-70; I. Davies, op.cit.
19 R.F. Currie, 1986.
20 B. Hopwood, p.128.
21 That is after Leek retired as Managing Director in 1957 and Sangster as Chairman in 1961. B. Hopwood, p.118.
22 B.M.D. Smith, "Sir Bernard Dudley Frank Docker", 1986, pp.121-7. Apparently this was the first time the Prudential had used its influence to oust a Chairman. See also W.R. Sandberg, 1980.

23 B.M.D. Smith, "Eric Turner", op.cit., pp.570-5.
24 B. Hopwood, pp.270, 274-87. He helped to design the range.
25 An investment not a subsidiary. See ibid., p.290.
26 J. Bruce-Gardyne, 1978, pp.295-6.
27 Ibid., p.295.
28 B. Hopwood, pp.273, 287.
29 Actually, there were more than 3 operating, e.g. Kitts Green. *Birmingham Post*, 21 November 1975.
30 J. Bruce-Gardyne, pp.7, 24. See also *Sunday Mercury,* 13 July 1974.
31 *Birmingham Post,* 14 April 1975. 300 employees out of 1,750 were to stay and 100 machines were to be made initially.
32 The Boston Consulting Group, 1975.
33 *Birmingham Post,* 17 December 1975. Closure was postponed by a sit-in, Lord Hesketh proposal and completion of stock. For details of Hesketh V1000 cc motorcycle (made at Daventry 1980-2) see *Financial Times,* 6 September 1982.
34 J. Bruce-Gardyne, p.41.
35 *Birmingham Evening Mail,* 16 December 1975. But the BSA name was used in 1978 motorcycles from Garretts Green and probably Shenstone, see *Birmingham Post,* 24 April 1979.
36 BSA (Guns) still had an address in Armoury Road in 1989.
37 Part too refurbished into the Waverley Trading Estate.
38 G. Grant, 1969 and 1976.
39 Possibly justified as much of Small Heath made other products than motorcycles.
40 B. Holliday, *Norton Story,* 1972, p.113.
41 D. Poore in G. Grant, op.cit.
42 During which transfer to Wolverhampton was considered. *Midlands Industry,* July 1969, p.500.
43 *Midlands Industry*, April 1973, p.190.
44 In NVT's 1978 accounts as trading as Andover Norton Ltd.
45 Labour force cut by 25%, Chairman's Statement 1965.
46 *Birmingham Post,* 3 June 1969.
47 *Birmingham Evening Mail,* 7 June 1976. See also *Birmingham Post,* 23 October 1976; 29 March 1979.
48 Its factory buildings had value as avoiding need for an industrial development certificate.
49 Royal Enfields were then made in Madras and imported.
50 J.W.E. Kelly, c.1977.
51 E. Tragastch (ed.), p.290.
52 *Birmingham Evening Mail,* 3 February 1971. The York Road factory later became Lucas' aerospace electronics plant where the first microprocessors in Birmingham were made. See *Birmingham Post,* 11 October 1979.
53 *Sunday Times,* 13 December 1987.
54 *Birmingham Post,* 21 November 1975; *The Times,* 28 January 1976.
55 *Birmingham Post,* 13 June 1977 spoke of 400 employed at Shenstone and Andover combined.
56 *Sunday Times,* 13 December 1987.
57 *Financial Times,* 13 January 1988.
58 *Birmingham Evening Mail,* 10 May 1988.
59 B. Hopwood, pp.263-5.
60 *Financial Times,* 13 January 1988, including 'drones'.
61 *Birmingham Evening Mail,* 10 May 1988.
62 R. Oakeshott, p.111. See also K. Fleet, p.88ff.
63 J. Bruce-Gardyne, p.42; J. Barnett, pp.36-7.
64 R. Oakeshott, p.112.
65 At the 1983 International Motorcycle Show, new 600 cc Daytona and Thunderbirds were shown and the prototype of the 900 cc Phoenix.
66 Workers received about 15% less than the going rate but skilled men were difficult to obtain and needed.
67 *Birmingham Post,* 21 January 1983. 200 were then employed. See also ibid., 2 April 1984.
68 In receivership in August 1983. See *Financial Times,* 22 November 1983. Triumph

Motor Cycles (Coventry) is in the current telephone directory. See also *Financial Times,* 30 November 1983; *Birmingham Post,* 1 November 1983.

BIBLIOGRAPHY

J. Barnett, *Inside the Treasury,* Deutsch, 1982.
The Boston Consulting Group, *Strategy Alternatives for the British Motorcycle Industry,* House of Commons 532, HMSO, 1975.
J. Bruce-Gardyne, *Meriden: Odyssey of a Lame Duck,* Centre for Policy Studies, 1978.
P. Carrick, *The Story of Honda Motorcycles,* Patrick Stephens, 1976.
R.F. Currie, "Siegfried Bettman (1863-1951)" in *Dictionary of Business Biography,* vol.1, Butterworths, 1986.
I. Davies, *It's a Triumph,* Haynes, 1980.
P.J.S. Dunnett, *The Decline of the British Motor Industry,* Croom Helm, 1980.
K. Fleet, "Triumph Meriden" in K. Coates (ed.), *The New Worker Co-operatives,* Institute of Workers' Control, Spokesman, 1976.
G. Grant, *AJS: The History of a Great Motorcycle,* Patrick Stephens, 1969; 1976.
B. Holliday, *Norton Story,* Patrick Stephens, 1972; 1978.
B. Hopwood, *Whatever Happened to the British Motorcycle Industry,* Haynes, 1981.
J.W.E. Kelly, *A History of Veloce Ltd,* unpublished Ph.D thesis, University of Bradford, c.1977.
R. Oakeshott, *The Case for Workers' Co-operatives,* Routledge, 1978.
B. Ryerson, *The Giants of Small Heath,* Haynes, 1980.
W.R. Sandberg, "Norton Villiers Triumph and the Meriden Co-operative" in W.F. Glueck (ed.), *Business Policy and Management,* McGraw Hill, 1980.
B.M.D. Smith, biographical articles on "Edward Turner (1901-1973)"; "John Young Sangster (1896-1977)"; "Sir Bernard Dudley Frank Docker (1896-1978)" in *Dictionary of Business Biography,* vols. 2 and 5, Butterworths, 1986.
B.M.D. Smith, *The History of the British Motorcycle Industry 1945-1975,* University of Birmingham, Centre for Urban and Regional Studies Occasional Papers, 3, 1981.
E. Tragastch (ed.), *The Illustrated Encyclopaedia of Motorcycles,* Hamlyn, 1977.

FURTHER READING

P. Carrick, *The Story of Kawasaki Motorcycles,* Patrick Stephens, 1978.
C.F. Caunter, *Motor Cycles: A Technical History,* Science Museum, 1970.
J. Clew, *Suzuki,* Haynes, 1980.
P. Hartley, *The Ariel Story,* Argus Books, 1980.
B. Holliday, *The Story of BSA Motorcycles,* Patrick Stephens, 1978.
H. Louis and B. Currie, *The Story of Triumph Motor Cycles,* Patrick Stephens, 1975; 1978.

CHAPTER 15

CARS AND CORPORATE CULTURE: THE VIEW FROM LONGBRIDGE 1905-1989

Roy Church & Chris Mullen

Throughout the history of the motor industry design has been a crucial determinant of the success or failure of models and firms in particular and of the industry as a whole. Twice since 1905, Longbridge has been a source of radical innovation in car design, innovative in construction and technical specification and novel in appearance. Praised and imitated by other car making nations, the success in producing popular small cars in large volume ensured Birmingham's position as a major centre of the motor industry.

Yet the history of the design component in the manufacturing process, with its inter-related considerations of engineering, architecture, and aesthetics has been neglected, those essential elements having been examined in isolation from each other. Thus, historians of technology have tended to concentrate upon engineering (for example product development, including the choice of power to weight ratio); motoring historians have been obsessed with architectural structure (for example height, width and length); historians of design have been preoccupied with style (radiator grilles for example), while economists and historians have tended to relegate the importance of design to considerations of prices, costs and production processes.

In concentrating attention on policy aspects of design at Longbridge, our intention is to explore largely uncharted territory on the hinterland between design and industrial history, offering a tentative analytical outline of the history of industrial design of cars made in Birmingham. This we do by focusing upon seven models which we regard either as critical to the success of Longbridge, or as typifying design of a distinctive period, and to ask how design was important to Longbridge, when and why did changes occur and by what process?

Design has passed through clearly identifiable stages in the development of the motor car (Fig. 15.1). They may be characterised partly in terms of the state of engineering and production technology, partly in terms of the structure and organisation of the industry, and partly with reference to factors external to the industry, notably government legislation (affecting, for example, tariffs, taxation, safety and pollution), foreign competition and influences, and also perhaps aesthetic standards *per se*. Until shortly before World War 1 the designing of motor cars was very much the province of the engineer-entrepreneurs, who, like Herbert Austin, copied or created an engine and chassis built to meet the modest requirements of contemporary motorists. A relatively high income group, they sought mechanical reliablility, road travel at modest speeds and a degree of comfort commensurate with an ability to pay. Mechanical performance was the responsibility of the manufacturers; bodies were constructed by specialists whose origins in the horse carriage trade were evident in most cars built before the 1930s.[1]

Austin, a professionally qualified engineer, built his first motorised vehicle in 1895 while employed as manager of the Wolseley Sheep Shearing Machine Company of Birmingham. A three-wheeled, 2 horsepower, open-framed vehicle of tubular construction with tiller steering, it was followed in 1900 by the Wolseley Voiturette which was the first of his four-wheeled vehicles. Built on a channel section steel frame, this single-cylinder 5 horsepower car evolved by Austin, won the first great public trial over a thousand miles in 1900, and established its creator as a major figure in the industry.[2] However, though original in design, the Wolseley Voiturette was soon superseded by the basic concept of the Renault layout. This included an embryo bonnet encasing the engine, a steering column (with handlebars), side-by-side seating for two passengers and, from 1899, was available in a totally enclosed body (Fig. 12.4). This set the pattern for future car design.[3]

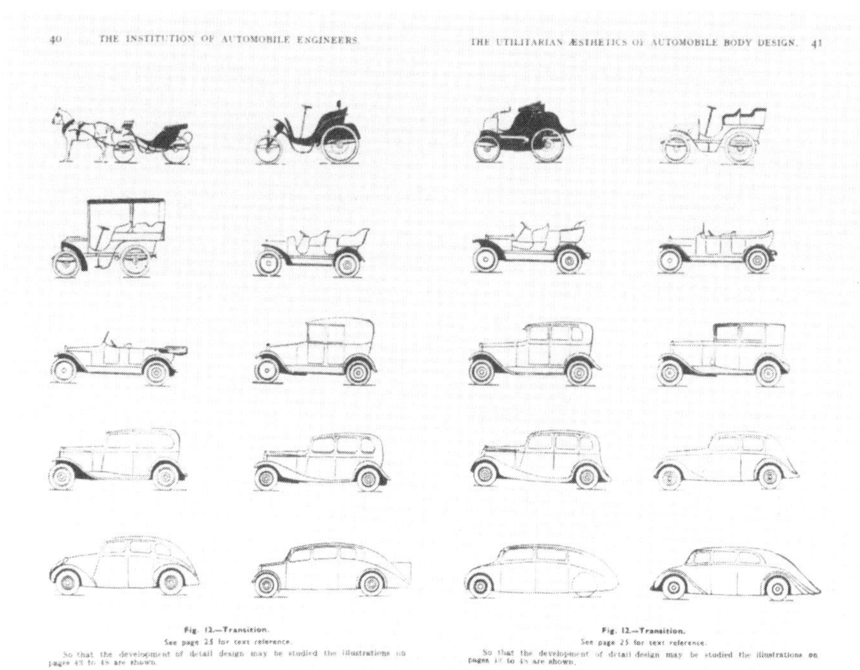

Fig. 15.1. Car body design, Transition, from W.O. Kennington, "The Utilitarian Aesthetics of Automobile Body Designs", *Proceedings of the Institute of Automobile Engineers,* 1934-5. Photo courtesy of Rover Group plc.

The year 1905 saw the formation of the Austin Motor Company, the Longbridge factory bringing together (unusually in a single location) the construction of chassis and a variety of car bodies for fitting to the first Austin 18/24 chassis. The carriage body of the 'Longbridge' limousine (Fig. 15.2) for the 25/30 hp chassis is representative of Austin's satisfaction with the survival of coachbuilding principles: ash frame with metal panels attached with square and stately contours, the carriage lamp deployment of the lights and the emphasis on sumptuous upholstery. However, Austin was shortly to criticise the carriage builders for a lack of accuracy in measurement and construction of bodies supplied to car makers.[4]

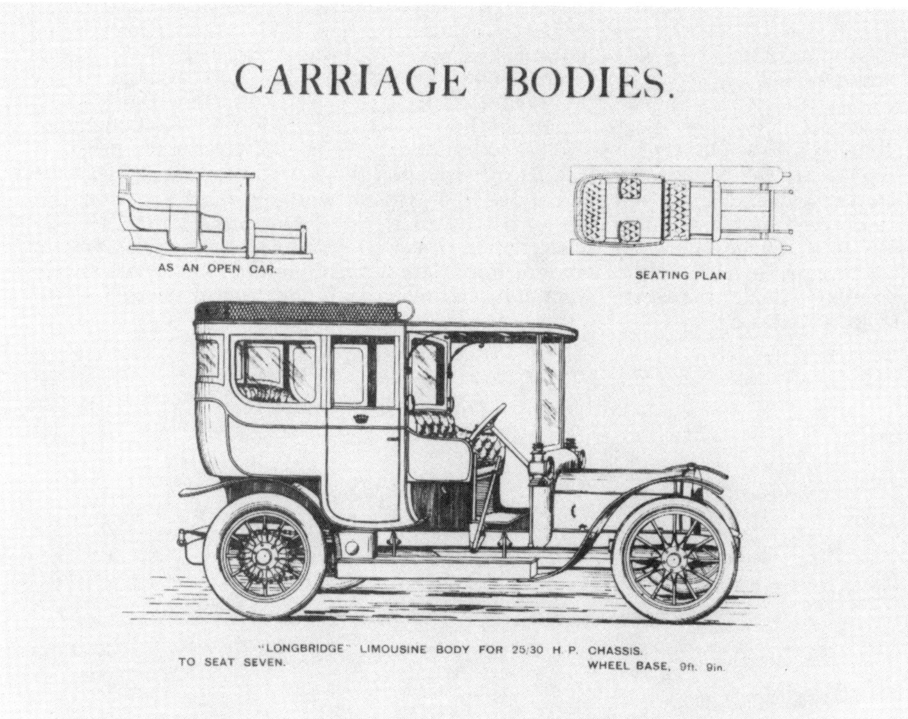

Fig. 15.2. Longbridge Limousine Body for 25/30 H.P. Chassis, Austin Motor Company, catalogue, 1907, "*We believe this catalogue marks the first occasion where a firm openly illustrated the details of its cars by direct copies of the working drawings. . . .*". Photo courtesy of Rover Group plc.

Unlike William Morris, the other major volume car producer, Austin may be described as a designer. He was an engineer who, in addition to expressing a strong social purpose in extending car ownership, possessed an acute visual sense, and regarded the act of drawing and intuitive problem solving as more significant than the act of mathematical calculation or written description. Speaking of the period he spent as a youth in Australia where, incidentally, he attended art school, he later reflected, "*it seems that I was then - as I am now, best able to express myself by means of the pencil.*"[5] It was characteristic of his attitude to problem solving that, from an early date, provision had to be made for his rough sketches, executed in transit on napkin, blotter or sketchpad, to be delivered to the Drawing Office by courier.

After the war, increased standardisation of sub-units, such as frame, engine, transmission and body, was a consequence of a transformation of production methods which enabled the light cars of the 1920s to become affordable by other than a minority of the professional and business classes, and directly to rival the cheapest forms of motorised travel such as the motorcycle combination. In order to break out of the financial difficulties which had resulted in 1921 in his removal from sole managerial responsibility by a committee of shareholders and the Midland

Bank, he used his private resources to develop (independently of Longbridge's design procedures and management structures) a new light car, inexpensive and economical, that was to be launched at the motor show in 1922 as the Austin Seven.[6] The initial design concept was roughed out at Austin's home at Lickey Grange, sometimes in full scale drawings. He then engaged a trusted draughtsman from his personally selected team in the car drawing section of the Longbridge drawing office, Stanley Edge, who became designer draughtsman for the project.[7] Experience in an aeroplane drawing office during the war and familiarity with the motorcycle industry, equipped Edge to prepare working drawings from his employer's rough sketches and verbal instructions. The project then secretly moved to Longbridge where construction began on an *ad hoc* basis, and, flying in the face of financial realities and much opposition, the diminutive yet square sturdy box-like vehicle, the Seven, went into full quantity production in the mid 1920s (Figs. 15.3, 12.5).

Fig. 15.3. The Austin Seven, promotional brochure, 1924 "*Cheaper than Taxis, Shopping a Pleasure*".. Photo courtesy of Rover Group plc.

Austin set out his belief in the functional car in 1929: "*The fancy day is brief and spasmodic. The utility day is with us always. So with cars. We have innumerable fads and fancies in matters of shape, size, colour and trimmings, but when we get down to our bedrock need, when the importance of motor vehicle rivals that of our daily bread, then we find that what we are looking for is transport. . . .*"[8]. The Seven provided that transport, and, as John Heskett has observed,[9] it set the pattern for European small car development towards motoring low in initial and running costs, well in advance of the Fiat Topolino (1935) and the Volkswagen (1936-7).

During the 1920s a tolerable level of mechanical reliability, an accepted basic body shell shape (of steel pressings rather than the metal clad ash frame of the coachbuilders) and the stability of model design which resulted, saw Longbridge concentrate on the production of increasingly standardised, relatively low priced cars. Their design characteristic was that of mechanical efficiency and utility: a degree of comfort and value for money rather than aesthetic appeal. The momentum generated by the success of the Seven was not, however, followed up by the company. Austin himself seemed generally content to consolidate upon a dominant design and a successful engineering solution. Stanley Edge, who had returned to the Longbridge drawing office, soon left for Standard Motors of Coventry: "*I had grown to expect new designs would be steadily flowing from drawing offices, but this was rarely the case.*"[10]

In part this reflected a change in market conditions. The intense price competition that characterised the industry after the war reduced the number of car manufacturers from nearly 100 to 41.[11] In the following decade, when Austin emerged briefly as the largest British car manufacturer, the characteristic dynamic was that of price stability in the short run, allied with model price competition (designing to a price rather than pricing a design) over the longer period. Hence, during these years, the number of models and variants offered by the major producers proliferated as they sought to increase or protect market shares. Chassis and engines were standardized as basic components, while slight modifications and cosmetic styling changes were added to attract dealers and purchasers, for whom the annual motor shows in London became a major event.[12] Those developments tended to reinforce Austin's deep suspicion (expressed by his own sales department or the motoring press) of consumer-led design.[13]

In effect these new trends presented car manufacturers with a dilemma, for whereas the increasing standardization of product and advanced production techniques in the 1920s had enabled them to reduce costs and prices, the styling which was adopted in the 1930s in order to stimulate consumer demand ran counter to the search for continued cost reductions.

In the context of the debate on the introduction of elements of streamlining into the company's products, Austin cannot be dismissed as a xenophobic reactionary. He travelled widely in the United States and in Europe, and was often the only British exhibitor in foreign car shows. In 1929, at the suggestion of Vicenzo Lancia, he engaged the Italian, Ricardo Burzi, as stylist at Longbridge, having admired his work at the Paris Motor Show.[14] Perhaps as a result, Austin's philosophy of utilitarian design came under the greatest pressure in 1934. In that year, the Austin Seven saloon, the Ruby (Fig. 15.4), was introduced, with more fluid body lines, a radical integration of radiator within the body, a lengthened bonnet and absence of projecting fittings-changes that Austin publicly regretted as a capitulation to the vagaries of public taste. He saw one particularly unwelcome intervention: "*Thirty years ago, when I started to build cars, I took some little interest in the shape of the body in comparison with the chassis, and from that time up to some ten years ago, the design of a car was governed by practical considerations, such as its ability to turn corners quickly. In the last ten years, however, the big concerns with their enormous outputs have had an important influence, and have tried to evolve designs offering new advantages, and here, I think, the woman's influence has come in.*"[15]

Austin's regret at the design changes introduced with the Ruby, a confession of failure to influence events, is indicative of the way that decision making in design at Longbridge was coming to be dominated by executive committees. The procedure is neatly described by Nikolaus Pevsner who researched industrial design in Britain in 1935. "*Almost everywhere the ideas for new models originate with the director*

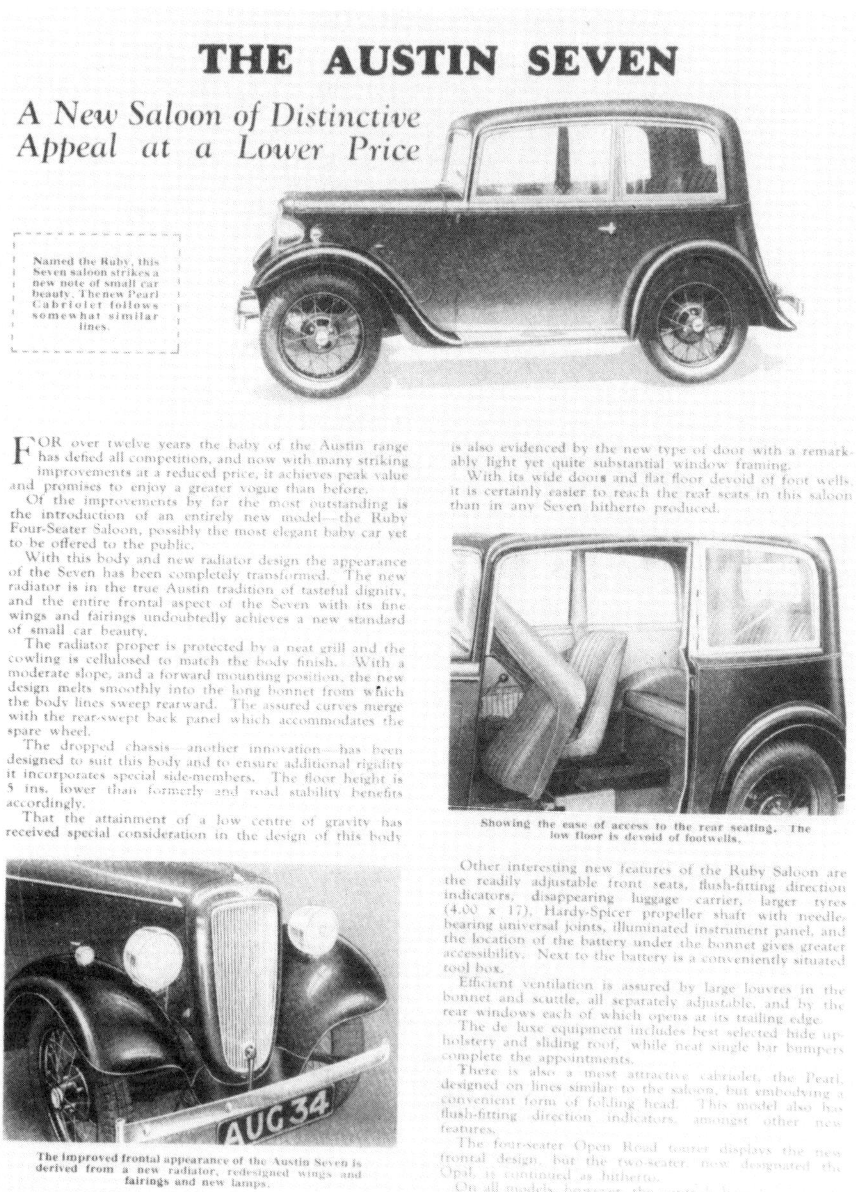

THE AUSTIN SEVEN

A New Saloon of Distinctive Appeal at a Lower Price

Named the Ruby, this Seven saloon strikes a new note of small car beauty. The new Pearl Cabriolet follows somewhat similar lines.

FOR over twelve years the baby of the Austin range has defied all competition, and now with many striking improvements at a reduced price, it achieves peak value and promises to enjoy a greater vogue than before.

Of the improvements by far the most outstanding is the introduction of an entirely new model—the Ruby Four-Seater Saloon, possibly the most elegant baby car yet to be offered to the public.

With this body and new radiator design the appearance of the Seven has been completely transformed. The new radiator is in the true Austin tradition of tasteful dignity, and the entire frontal aspect of the Seven with its fine wings and fairings undoubtedly achieves a new standard of small car beauty.

The radiator proper is protected by a neat grill and the cowling is cellulosed to match the body finish. With a moderate slope, and a forward mounting position, the new design melts smoothly into the long bonnet from which the body lines sweep rearward. The assured curves merge with the rear-swept back panel which accommodates the spare wheel.

The dropped chassis—another innovation—has been designed to suit this body and to ensure additional rigidity it incorporates special side-members. The floor height is 5 ins. lower than formerly and road stability benefits accordingly.

That the attainment of a low centre of gravity has received special consideration in the design of this body is also evidenced by the new type of door with a remarkably light yet quite substantial window framing.

With its wide doors and flat floor devoid of foot wells, it is certainly easier to reach the rear seats in this saloon than in any Seven hitherto produced.

Showing the ease of access to the rear seating. The low floor is devoid of footwells.

Other interesting new features of the Ruby Saloon are the readily adjustable front seats, flush-fitting direction indicators, disappearing luggage carrier, larger tyres (4.00 x 17), Hardy-Spicer propeller shaft with needle-bearing universal joints, illuminated instrument panel, and the location of the battery under the bonnet gives greater accessibility. Next to the battery is a conveniently situated tool box.

Efficient ventilation is assured by large louvres in the bonnet and scuttle, all separately adjustable, and by the rear windows each of which opens at its trailing edge.

The de luxe equipment includes best selected hide upholstery and sliding roof, while neat single bar bumpers complete the appointments.

There is also a most attractive cabriolet, the Pearl, designed on lines similar to the saloon, but embodying a convenient form of folding head. This model also has flush-fitting direction indicators, amongst other new features.

The four-seater Open Road tourer displays the new frontal design, but the two-seater, now designated the Opal, is continued as hitherto.

On all models, however, the controls have been greatly

The improved frontal appearance of the Austin Seven is derived from a new radiator, redesigned wings and fairings and new lamps.

Fig. 15.4. "The Austin Seven, A New Saloon of Distinctive Appeal at a Lower Price", *The Austin Magazine,* September 1934, "*Named the Ruby, this Seven saloon strikes a new note of small car beauty*". Photo courtesy of Rover Group plc.

or manager, and incidentally, within eighteen months before the car is put on the market. He may make some rough sketches or more careful drawings according to his ability, or else describe to the body engineer or the coachwork manager what he means. Only after this are more detailed drawings made by the designer and submitted to a board of experts (in one factory called the Elegance Committee) in which the sales manager has a particularly important voice." Compared with the stylistic excesses in European and American cars, Pevsner regarded the British as "*one of the best industries in the world as far as design is concerned.*" His conclusion must have delighted Austin: "*One sees only a few superfluous frills, no 'arty' decoration either floral or cubistical. . . .not much fuss, a clear and precise expression of function.*" [16] However it is clear that the debate on design and styling, was nevertheless unresolved at crucial periods. The 10 hp Sherborne (Fig. 15.5), launched in January 1936, is typical of uneasy compromise, the traditional upright front evoking the past, and the sloping tail in one shapely, unbroken curve, a tentative gesture towards streamlining.

The model price competition inaugurated in the 1930s, of which the tendency to styling was such a notable feature, was resumed after the immediate post-war years, when the re-entry of European car manufacturers into the international market ended British producers' short-lived dominance. Longbridge, since 1952 part of the British Motor Corporation under Leonard Lord's direction, spearheaded an attempt both to recapture overseas markets and to supply an expanding home demand, where aggressive marketing of the Volkswagen 'Beetle' heralded a revival in the popularity of low cost utility vehicles. [17]

Fig. 15.5. The Sherborne Saloon, Austin Motor Company, catalogue, 1936, "*The mud wings are wide and deep, those in the rear being swept in a regular cuve toward the tail without being flared. . . .*". Photo courtesy of Rover Group plc.

It is revealing of post-war attitudes at Longbridge that in a promotional brochure for the Austin Cambridge of 1954, for the first time product development is seen almost exclusively in terms of emerging refinements of styling (Fig.15.6), the initiation of the project on the stylist's drawingboard and the development of artists' impressions emerging even before the contribution of the engineer. This new emphasis on styling within the organisation and the commissioning of freelance stylists was a conscious attempt to aspire to accepted international design standards in domestic and export production. Only after the basic design concept was evolved did intensive inter-departmental consultation take place.[18] By inviting Alec Issigonis to Longbridge in 1956, BMC's chief executive, the motor engineer Leonard Lord, sought to capitalise upon the experience of Issigonis in developing the redesigned and extremely successful 1948 Morris Minor at Cowley. With Lord's personal backing Issigonis was put at the head of a small experimental design team that circumvented the usual systems of decision making to explore possibilities in the small car market. Lord's brief was simply to develop a small economic car to carry four people in relative comfort and offering the same standards of serviceability of normal cars.[19]

Fig. 15.6. *GS5 into Cambridge,* promotional brochure for the Austin Cambridge, 1954, "*The shapes and contours of the now approved and doubly checked model are next transferred to a giant drawing board and proportionately increased to life size. From this large drawing templates will be made and used in the building of the full-scale model.*" Photo courtesy of Rover Group plc.

The design premises of the Mini (Fig. 15.7) share several similarities with those of the Austin Seven. Both cars were initiated by farsighted individuals working on an intuitive basis who deliberately avoided the existing committee structure at Longbridge. Both cars sought to provide the minimal means for conveying travellers economically and in tolerable comfort. Neither market research nor contemporary styling conventions influenced the Mini concept. The design, which was to remain substantially unaltered for 25 years, incorporated rubber suspension, front-wheel drive and an engine mounted transversely to save space. Like Austin, Issigonis associated styling with 'fashion', which he regarded as an unwholesome influence, exerted in the showroom by the woman of the household. In exploring the flux in the relationship of the constituent elements of design, it is important to demonstrate both men's reliance on clear and vivid presentation of their ideas through the act of drawing. Indeed their freehand sketches are often difficult to tell apart. Issigonis clearly saw himself out of his own time. "*I am the last of the Bugattis, a man who designed whole cars. Now committees do the work.*" [20]

The 1970s witnessed rapid decline in British industry's international position. The chronic weaknesses were exposed in a series of reports, commissioned by the government in 1975, which pointed to inadequate rationalisation of production and reduction in models, overmanning and restrictive practices, and ageing plant and lack of new models. [21]

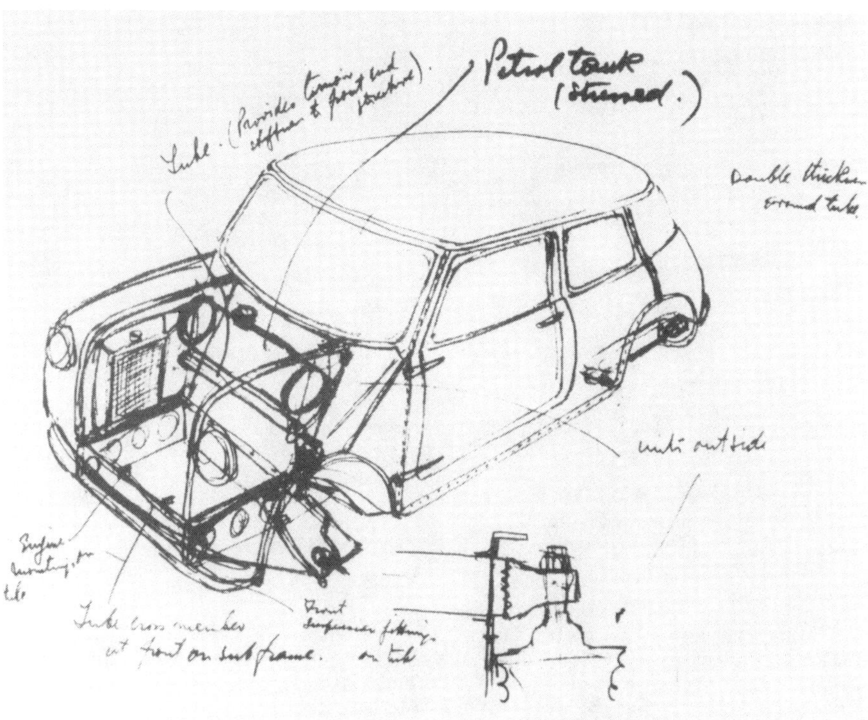

Fig. 15.7. Alec Issigonis, preparatory drawing for the Mini, c.1958, "*A designer, yes I am; an engineer most certainly; but not, definitely not, a stylist.*" Photo courtesy of Rover Group plc.

In the late 1970s, when the government's rescue plan for the industry was put into operation under Michael Edwardes, the Austin Morris Group relied on three ageing models for volume sales, - the Allegro (introduced in 1973), the Marina (1971) as well as the twenty year old Austin Mini, in production since 1959. The product-led strategy for the company was seen to depend on the development of new models to remedy the product gap.[22] Rather than develop a Mini equivalent, Longbridge decided on a 'supermini', a family hatchback car offering a more comfortable, quieter ride and more attractive, conventional styling. Launched as the Metro in 1980, this model was to be developed while the gap in the mid-car sector of the market was being tackled with the Maestro project.

Fig. 15.8. The Austin Metro, "*. . .it is not the result of some whim of a designer or stylist, but is a response to carefully-tested public opinion.*" Photo courtesy Rover Group plc.

Unlike the Mini, the Metro (Fig. 15.8) was designed for a clearly identified market. Unusually a series of body clays was shown to the public at clinics where preferences in styling and detail were recorded and included in the decision making process. A Metro was even sent to Europe "*to have the car brought up to their level of fits and finishes by external design consultants.*"[23] The introduction of computer-aided design contributed significantly to Longbridge achieving its launch day in October 1980, not least by saving time on working drawings. Widely regarded as successfully combining sound aerodynamic principles with visual appeal, nonetheless technical performance disappointed expectations. While Metro sales killed off the Mini, the Metro failed to expand the total of small car sales. To address perceived weaknesses in Longbridge products, a central design facility was set up under Royden Axe, previously overall director of automotive design at Chrysler Corporation in the United States, in which the designer was expected "*to take a positive role in leading product design, and in producing a cohesive range of quality products.*" [24]

In his recent valuable survey of design and society since 1950, Adrian Forty identified similarities between the process of design prior to manufacture in the textile industry of the 1830s with the Metro project. He emphasised that the act of selecting preliminary designs to be produced is one made, not by the designer, but by the entrepreneur, who carries responsibility for manufacture and commercial risk.[25] This timely correction to what Forty perceived as the conventional version offered by designers in describing their role, however, overlooked the possibility of historical development. In the motor industry, at least, some of the leading entrepreneurs were also engineers who, especially before the streamlined decade of the 1930s, with varying success produced cars possessing engineering and architectural features which were their own in conception and creation. Moreover, the decline of the design role of the engineer-entrepreneur was a protracted process which depended on the speed and effectiveness of corporate reconstruction and strategy.

The history of car design at Longbridge reveals a tension between the trend towards bureaucratic management structures and the distinctive corporate culture created by the assumptions, attitudes and aspirations of its strong-minded founder. For 35 years Austin dominated car design, dedicated principally to dependability and value for money, showing minimal concessions to consumers' preferences for differentiation based on non-functional quality and style. This almost puritanical approach to the market, combined with a vision of wider car ownership achievable by radical innovative design, was a formula repeated in the mid 1950s, when Issigonis was asked to operate outside the company's formal committee structure. Adequate to ensure technical adaptation of Austin cars and to introduce occasional 'face lifts', the committee structures failed either to develop a continuing process of differentiation which translated into greater market penetration or to create a design capacity which, when required, might transform the company's product range. In part this reflected the incompleteness of reorganisations following the mergers of the 1950s and the drastic restructuring of the late 1970s. Until that time car design at Longbridge continued to be affected by its creator. For Herbert Austin's enduring influence on the Longbridge ethos, within the corporate culture which he established, was perpetuated under Leonard Lord whose deployment of Issigonis in a personal capacity as a creative designer was to continue the tradition of Longbridge car design and production until, in 1982, for the first time since its launch in August 1959, the Mini was no longer among the top six best selling motor cars in the UK, and the design of its successor, the Metro, and of subsequent generations of cars for mass consumption, lay with corporate committees responsible for product development. For in the 1980s, in order to improve adaptive capacity in competition, the separate concepts of production, design and styling were superseded by an integrated process of product development, which henceforward would be as critical to corporate success as was the idiosyncratic engineering and designing genius of the founder of Birmingham's volume car manufacture when the industry was in its infancy.

The year 1989 not only marked the City of Birmingham's centenary, it also registered the ultimate phase in the erosion of the historic Austin tradition. For in that year the Austin marque finally came to an end as a result of an industrial restructuring which saw the British volume car industry taken over by British Aerospace plc from which emerged a car division called 'Rover'.

REFERENCES

1 R. Church, "Markets and Marketing in the British Motor Industry before 1914", *Journal of Transport History,* Spring 1982, pp.1-12.
2 Z.E. Lambert and R.J. Wyatt, pp.35-9.
3 C.F. Caunter, pp.21-5, 50-1.
4 R. Church, 1979, pp.24-5.
5 "Sir Herbert Austin, His Life Story", *The Autocar,* 23 August 1929, p.370.
6 R. Church, 1979, pp.57-72.
7 S. Edge, "The Birth of a Small Car", unidentified magazine, Rover Technical Library, p.22.
8 Sir H. Austin, "The Importance of Purpose", *Pall Mall Magazine,* August 1929, p.15.
9 J. Heskett, p.124.
10 J. Wood, "The Birth of the Austin Seven", *Thoroughbred and Classic Cars,* August 1977, p.16.
11 R.J. Overy, table 8, p.136.
12 G. Maxcy and A. Silberston, pp.99-111; R. Church and M. Miller, "The Big Three: Competition, Managing and Marketing in the British Motor Industry, 1922-1939" in B. Supple (ed.), pp.180-1.
13 R. Church, 1979, pp.89-90.
14 P. Turner, "The Paradox of Herbert Austin", *Motor*, 10 January 1981, p.9.
15 W. Kennington, "The Utilitarian Aesthetics of Automobile Body Design", *Proceedings of the Institute of Automobile Engineers,* 1934-5, p.67.
16 N. Pevsner, pp.130, 137.
17 G. Maxcy and A. Silberston, p.187.
18 *G.S.5 Into Cambridge,* promotional brochure, 1954, Rover Technical Library.
19 E. Eves, "How it Happened", *Autocar*, 3 April 1982, p.v.
20 A. Hope, "The Genius Today", *Autocar,* 25 August 1979, p.34.
21 K. Bhaskar, pp.3-54.
22 K. Williams, J. Williams, C. Haslam, table 4.12, p.95.
23 M. Edwardes, p.196.
24 B. McAlhone (ed.), p.24.
25 A. Forty, p.241.

BIBLIOGRAPHY

K. Bhaskar, *The Future of the UK Motor Industry,* London, Kogan Page, 1979.
C.F. Caunter, *The Light Car: A Technical History,* London, HMSO, 1970.
R. Church, *Herbert Austin: The British Motor Car Industry to 1941,* London, Europa, 1979.
M. Edwardes, *Back From the Brink*, London, Pan, 1984.
A. Forty, *Objects of Desire,* London, Thames & Hudson, 1987.
J. Heskett, *Industrial Design,* London, Thames & Hudson, 1980.
Z.E. Lambert and R.J. Wyatt, *Lord Austin: The Man,* London, Sidgwick & Jackson, 1968.
G. Maxcy and A. Silberston, *The British Motor Car Industry,* London, Allen & Unwin, 1959.
B. McAlhone, *Directors on Design: The Car Industry,* London, SIAD, 1985.
R.J. Overy, *William Morris, Viscount Nuffield,* London, Europa, 1976.
N. Pevsner, *An Enquiry into Industrial Art in England,* London, Cambridge University Press, 1937.
B. Supple (ed.), *Essays in British Business History,* Oxford University Press, 1977.
K. Williams, J. Williams, C. Haslam, *The Breakdown of Austin Rover,* Leamington Spa, Berg, 1987.

FURTHER READING

R. Barker *et al, Automobile Design,* Newton Abbot, David & Charles, 1970.
J. Ensor, *The Motor Industry,* London, Longman, 1971.
A. Nahum, *Alec Issigonis,* London, Design Council, 1988.
L.J.K. Setright, *The Designers,* London, Weidenfeld & Nicholson, 1976.
R.J. Wyatt, *The Austin Seven 1905-52,* Newton Abbott, David & Charles, 1977.

CHAPTER 16

LUCAS INDUSTRIES PLC: AN OUTLINE

Barbara Tilson

Lucas Industries described itself in its publicity literature of the late 1980s as "*a leading international manufacturer of aerospace, automotive and industrial systems and components.*"[1] Although the strength of the Lucas group of companies was built on the automotive industry and traditional engineering skills, the group's business has increasingly been directed towards high-tech applications. In recent years the upheaval experienced by manufacturing industry, specifically the automotive and allied components producers, has led to a mood of diversification and change. Symbolic of this, perhaps, for Luxas, is the current run-down of its core headquarters (the old Great King Street works founded by Joseph Lucas) (Fig.16.1) and the move to Solihull. Here, on the outskirts of Birmingham, is sited the headquarters of Lucas Aerospace, which heads its manufacture of "*high technology systems and equipment for all military and commercial aerospace and defence applications.*"[2]

By 1988 Lucas Aerospace (one of three Lucas sections) also had manufacturing and product support operations in Australia, Canada, France, West Germany and the US. Lucas Automotive is engaged in the manufacture of automotive components, such as braking systems, diesel fuel injection systems, petrol injection systems and body systems. The activities of Lucas Industrial are directed towards the electronic and hydraulic components business.

The move to Solihull is also expressive of the de-centralisation of Birmingham's industrial base. Rapid transportation and digitial communications have combined with other factors such as spiralling costs to make location within the city's industrial core a requisite no longer. Old-fashioned factories, too, are inappropriate to modern business methods. Furthermore, the effective shrinking of world boundaries and the need to develop new markets has resulted in a growing internationalism. It is probably now rare to find a major producer without foreign subsidiaries. While UK firms, including Lucas, develop trading links elsewhere, foreign companies, too, are operating similarly here. In 1988, Lucas could state in its "Company Profile" that over 70% of its sales were overseas. The firm was making components, not just for UK firms, but for "*almost every vehicle manufacturer in the world*" and it expected to export in that year, "*systems and components worth over £600 million*". The fact, however, that over half all cars produced in Japan at this time were equipped with brakes made under licence to Lucas, perhaps illustrates its significance in world automotive technology and is just one example of its cross-national co-operation.[3]

While manufacturing industry, and specifically (here) the Lucas company, undergoes a metamorphosis to meet the challenges of a modern high-technology era, the memory of the Lucas tradition evokes recollections of a now-bygone age. Although, with the death of Oliver Lucas in 1948,[4] the company's direct links with its founder, Joseph Lucas, were broken,[5] the origin of the firm is recalled through the company name. The former Joseph Lucas (Industries) Ltd was renamed Lucas Industries in 1974, when Pentagram Design Partnership was consulted. The firm's subsidiaries were prefixed with the Lucas name and their corporate identity was given the now familiar green diagonal. Demonstrated thereby is the company's appreciation of the importance of a cohesive marketing strategy.[6] This appreciation flourished on the arrival of Bernard Scott as Chairman in 1974, when he initiated a series of business reviews.[7]

Fig. 16.1. Lucas Industries plc. works at Great King Street, 1989.

The company grew out of the oil dealing and wholesalers business which Joseph Lucas started in 1860 as a one-man business. Lucas senior started making lanterns and lamps in his workshop, the Tom Bowling Lamp Works,[8] at Little King Street in 1875.[9] In 1883 his elder son was taken into partnership to form Joseph Lucas & Son and the company became a public company, Joseph Lucas Ltd in 1897, with Joseph Lucas as its first Chairman.[10] An exhaustive two-volume study was produced by Harold Nockolds in 1978,[11] which traced the evolution of the company.

Nockolds subtitled his first volume on Lucas the *King of the Road*, which was a reference to Lucas' cycle lamp, patented in 1880[12] (see Fig. 13.10). From the outset, therefore, the links between Lucas and vehicle accessories were formed. The company flourished, firstly with the cycling boom, subsequently with the rise of the automobile, and diversified later into aeronautics. As Lucas Electrical, the automotive electrical products section of the group was to become one of the largest employers in the Birmingham area in the motor industry. In his table of

"*Examples of Larger Firms in the Motor Industry by Employment, Birmingham MDC, 1986*", Walker showed that Lucas Electrical (and its subsidiaries) employed 11,000 people in 10 West Midlands plants, second only to Austin Rover (Longbridge) which, with 13,328 employees, was the biggest employer.[13] Walker further noted the "*sharp fall in employment in the motor and related industries over the last 15 years in the Birmingham area, the effects being particularly severe since 1978.*"[14]

It is not appropriate to digress here into a detailed analysis of reasons for the difficulties of the UK vehicle and components industries, although certain factors, such as the period of general economic recession and the effects of the oil crisis are easily appreciated. A study by the Economic Planning Group of the Motor Industry Local Authority Network (MILAN) stated that the European car industry had operated at a loss each year since 1979. There was a partial recovery from that of 1979-80.[15] Increased competition from Japan was given as a factor, here, which is doubly interesting, as it relates directly to the similar decline of the UK motorcycle industry which, again, was to hit particularly hard in the West Midlands area.[16]

Walker noted that components production at Lucas had declined in line with the shrinking of the UK motor industry and the expansion of plants abroad. He stressed the relationship of Lucas to motor manufacturers, particularly Austin Rover. The MILAN study noted that the UK motor industry had undergone "*a painful period of restructuring*" in the last decade.[17] The group's leanest year was in 1980-1. In 1983 its automotive activities were in a loss position and the healthiest figures were achieved in aerospace. [18] However, although Lucas Electrical had shed some 13,000 jobs in the West Midlands area from the 1970s to 1986, the company remained the leading components manufacturer in the region.[19] In roughly the same period, i.e. 1977 to 1985, there was a reverse swing in the total number of employees in Lucas Industries during a period when industry in general was undergoing a period of readjustment. By May 1987 the employment trend in Birmingham and the West Midlands was still downward. By October 1988, however, the press reflected on "*the healthier situation in both motor and other engineering*", when Lucas, too, looked "*in good health*" with increased profits. [20]

Part of Lucas Industries' own restructuring, which can be seen in the light of UK industry's determination to achieve international competitivity, has involved the acquisition of foreign subsidiaries. For example, in May 1987 it was reported that Lucas "*had recently made a number of overseas acquisitions in the aerospace industry, which have brought immediate business benefits from firms like Boeing and General Electric*". [21] It was the opinion of a company spokesman here that aerospace was "*the single most important long-term strategic growth area that we have identified*". Recent developments in the group can be seen in the light of this view. For example, Lucas has shed a considerable number of its older companies, such as the largest Birmingham factory of Lucas Electrical in Shaftmoor Lane, Hall Green (sold to the Italian Magneti Marelli, in which Fiat owned a large stake),[22] and its plastics components subsidiary in Formans Road, Sparkhill,[23] which is also now part of an Italian-led group. A *Financial Times* survey noted that the company strategy of "*breaking away from dependence on the UK and seeking international markets (had) been obvious for nearly three decades*", since Lucas Girling (the brakes division) moved into West Germany in the late 1950s, followed by Lucas CAV to France and Spain.[24] The investment in overseas aerospace was evidently aimed largely at the US, France and Germany.[25] The present phase of restructuring can be seen also as resulting from "*an investment programme involving dramatic changes in manufacturing, work practices and products*"[26] which entailed a £15 million Government-backed investment programme embarked upon in 1984.

Lucas' expansion to become a group company arguably commenced in the 1920s, during the post-war boom in motorcycles and cars (Fig. 16.2). Its Formans Road factory was opened as its first branch factory in 1923 for the production of batteries and in 1926 the company acquired two main competitors, CAV and Rotax. The latter evolved as the focus for the company's main interests in aviation and was the forerunner of Lucas Aerospace. The aviation equipment licence was acquired in 1932 on the purchase of a two-thirds share in British Bendix. During World War 2 the company was a leading producer of aircraft parts undertaking, for example, wing sub-assembly of the Spitfire. Large important aviation acquisitions were made in the period 1968-70 as part of the Government's rationalisation of the aircraft industry. By 1975 there were 80 models of aircraft fitted with Lucas Aerospace parts and the company could describe itslef as the "*largest company of its kind in Europe.*" [27] Although profit from aerospace activities more than doubled in the period 1983 to 1987, the largest contributor to group sales and profits in 1989 remained Lucas Automotive.[28] Nevertheless, the company continued to move away from its base in automotive components towards high-tech activities, announcing in June 1989 its intention to purchase by August 1989 the US aeronautics subsidiary of Smiths Industries, Avitron International, which then had annual sales of £25 million. [29]

Fig. 16.2. Austin Seven Saloon, 1927, in which Lucas components were used. (See also Fig. 12.5). Photo courtesy of the British Motor Industry Heritage Trust - The Rover Group.

From the earliest days of lamp manufacture, through to the present day, innovative product engineering has formed the cornerstone of the company. This, said Nockolds, "*was indeed the heart of Lucas thinking, for without the right products the best organisation and the highest efficiency and marketing would not suffice to make the company successful.*" [30] J.M. Benoy noted, too, the highly-rated position of design and development, the attention given to appearance design and the close working liaison between technical engineers and designers in the company. [31] He illustrated how the engineering considerations of 1890s cycle lamps had evolved in the first half of the twentieth century towards solutions which were both functional and aesthetic and, incidentally, more streamlined, as oil and acetylene gas fuelled car lamps gave way to electrical power amidst calls for greater standardisation. [32]

Numerous patents were registered over the years and a good number of awards for excellence in, for example, technical innovation and design engineering, were received.[33] Design Centre Awards included the Girling 'Twinstop' brakes of 1976, Vehicle High Contrast Signal Lamps of 1981, Homofocal Car Headlamps of 1981 and 1984, Anti-Lock Braking System of 1987 (see Appendix for details). A climate of innovative progress has been maintained through technical education in product engineering, through research and development and through the continuing emphasis on strong design engineering teams operating in-house. With the imminent closure of the Great King Street premises, an era is ending at Lucas, but the company's flexibility and creativity ensure its maintenance of a competitive edge in modern engineering.

REFERENCES

1 "In-Brief", *Lucas Press Guide,* undated publicity leaflet (c.1987).
2 *A Quick Look at Lucas,* publicity leaflet, 1988.
3 Ibid.
4 Recorded in "The Lucas Story", undated typescript sheet.
5 He was the founder's grandson. See Bernard Scott's foreword in H. Nockolds, vol.1, p.8.
6 H. Nockolds, vol.2, p.402.
7 Ibid., pp.383, 393ff.
8 The Tom Bowling lamp was a ship's lamp, named after a popular sea shanty. See J.M. Benoy, p.7.
9 H. Nockolds, vol.1, p.31.
10 "The Lucas Story".
11 H. Nockolds, vol.2, 1978.
12 H. Nockolds, vol.1, pp.37-8.
13 B. Walker, p.35. Its total workforce in 1989 was 56,000. See "Economic oily patch will test Lucas driving skills", *Guardian*, 24 October 1989.
14 Ibid., p.36.
16 See Tilson/Woodward/Bidmead interview and B. Smith article on the motorcycle industry.
17 Op.cit., p.5.
18 *A Quick Look at Lucas.*
19 B. Walker, op.cit.
20 *Guardian*, 24 October 1988.
21 "Lucas to profit in Airbus deal", *Birmingham Post,* 15 May 1987.
22 "MP protests over Lucas cuts", *Birmingham Evening Mail,* 10 October 1987.
23 See B. Tilson article on the plastics industry, Chapter 18.
24 24 June 1987.
25 "Lucas aims for defence deals", *Birmingham Evening Mail,* 12 June 1987; "Lucas buys in US and Germany", *Birminghm Evening Mail,* 10 February 1988.
26 *Financial Times,* op.cit.
27 "The Lucas Story".
28 *Guardian,* 24 October 1989.

29 "Lucas in £8m US Deal", *Birmingham Evening Mail,* 15 June 1989.
30 H. Nockolds, vol.2, p.392.
31 J.M. Benoy, p.6ff.
32 Ibid., pp.8-9.
33 Queen's Awards to Industry of 1966 to 1974 are listed in H. Nockolds, vol.2, p.416.

BIBLIOGRAPHY

J.M. Benoy, "Joseph Lucas Limited", *Design,* January 1953, pp.6-11.

Economic Planning Group Development Department, *Visit to Austin Rover,* MILAN, Economic Policy and Research Papers, 1, 1986.

H. Nockolds, *Lucas: The First Hundred Years, vol.1: The King of the Road; vol.2: The Successors,* Newton Abbot; London, 1978.

B. Walker, *Changes in the UK Motor Industry: An Analysis of Some Local Economic Impacts,* Motor Industry Local Authority Network (MILAN) and Institute of Local Government Studies, University of Birmingham, October 1987.

CHAPTER 17

DUNLOP IN BIRMINGHAM: THE MAKING OF AN INDUSTRIAL EMPIRE

Joan Skinner

The development over a few decades of the Dunlop company from a small workshop in Belfast to a huge, international organisation is owed chiefly to the entrepreneurial flair of its founders and the meeting of two Irish families on the playing fields of Birmingham. The history of that development began in 1888.*

In the later 1880s, the introduction of the 'Safety' bicycle brought a new population into bicycling. The machine was faster and, by its very name, safer than the 'Ordinary' (Penny-farthing), but suffered badly from vibration. The fault was partially mitigated by saddle springs and a variety of engineering devices but the problem was not fully solved until John Boyd Dunlop designed a pneumatic tyre in 1888.

Dunlop was a veterinary surgeon of Scottish origin then practising in Belfast. His pneumatic tyre consisted of an inner tube of ductile rubber inflated through a non-return valve in the wheel rim. Expansion was restricted by a layer of fabric (Gents' Yacht Sail Cloth in the first instance) which was protected from road attrition by an outer cover of rubber, thicker on the tread and thinning on the sides. The parts were held together with rubber solution, the whole being attached to the wheel by flap extensions of the fabric lapped over and glued to the wheel between the spokes (Fig. 17.1).[1]

To accommodate the tyre, a new kind of bicycle was required, with wider forks and other modifications, and was first made by Edlin & Co. cycle manufacturers of Garfield Street, Belfast. Trials showed that propulsion was easier and faster, and that noise and vibration were abated. Fifty pneumatically-tyred cycles were sold locally but problems arose that were beyond the resources of Dunlop, Edlin and his partner, Sinclair, to overcome.[2] Prospects for commercial exploitation were improved when Dunlop approached a cycle agent and a newspaper manager in Dublin with a view to syndication. The two men, Bowden and Gillies, brought in William Harvey du Cros, a paper bag manufacturer, who agreed to co-operate in floating the enterprise so long as he assumed complete control, appointed the directors, wrote the prospectus and issued shares to the public.[3]

William Harvey du Cros was a successful business man who, although knowing nothing of bicycle or tyre manufacture, knew a great deal about cycling, bicycle performance and the cycling world. He was a noted athlete and President of the Irish Cyclists' Association. He also had six sons; they, too, were cycling enthusiasts and knew about the world of business. This family became the founders of the Dunlop empire. A company, THE PNEUMATIC TYRE AND BOOTH'S CYCLE AGENCY CO LTD., was floated. Du Cros senior was the Chairman, J.B. Dunlop and Richard Booth were two of the four directors and Finlay Sinclair (erstwhile partner of Edlin) was the Works Manager. The Edlin company of Belfast was taken over.[4]

* The sequence of firms from 1888 to 1989 is indicated by firms' names in upper case.

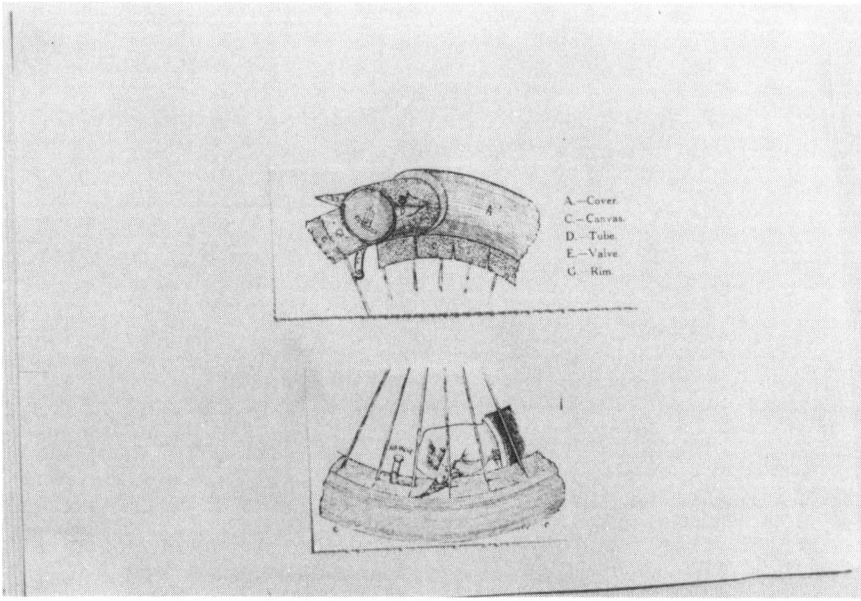

Fig. 17.1. Original Pneumatic Tyre designed by John Boyd Dunlop in 1888. Sketch. Source: *The Dunlop Gazette,* vol.1., no.2, 1919.

In a small workshop at Upper Stephen Street, Dublin, ten employees made tyres by hand from materials imported from the Silvertown Rubber Company. Some improvements were made. The airtube was contained in a canvas tube and a second layer of canvas cover extended into the hold-down flaps. The cross-thread of the square-woven canvas tended to chafe the rubber but it was not until some five years later that the problem was overcome with a fabric, made and patented by David Moseley of Manchester, in which the threads ran all in one direction.[5]

At cycling trials and at the 1890 *Stanley Cycle Show* in London the new pneumatic tyres were laughed to scorn, with calls of "*pudding wheels*".[6] But the proof of the pudding was vindicated when the du Cros cycling team won every race they entered in England and captured British and World records.[7]

Great consternation and visions of disaster had arisen in 1889 with the discovery that Dunlop's patent was void; a prior (but never exploited) patent had been granted to Robert William Thomson in 1846. And, despite major advantages, the pneumatic tyre had obvious defects: it was expensive, ugly, non-detachable and, when punctured, had to be completely stripped down and rebuilt. But these difficulties were not insurmountable and were resolved by plucking the very best of other people's inventions. Charles Welch's patent for a wired edge that made the tyre detachable was acquired by one of the du Cros sons waiting on Welch's doorstep until he agreed to sell. Shortly afterwards, with fierce negotiation and aggressive determination, W.E. Bartlett's 'Clincher' beaded edge, detachable tyre patent was bought for £200,000. Bartlett was permitted, under licence from the company, to manufacture his own tyre on payment of a royalty of 2/6d (12½p) per tyre, which helped to offset the price paid for the patent. An improved valve, patented by Charles Wood,[8] brother of one of the directors, was purchased with equal rapidity. As cycling experts, the du Cros family were able to identify which patents were most appropriate for improving the pneumatic tyre. Other patents were purchased from time to time and not used but, for a number of years, the company was involved in expensive litigation to protect its most important patents.

Expansion: Coventry and Birmingham

Thus, within a few years, the founding company was in possession of what were virtual world rights of the first practical pneumatic tyre. A manufacturing base was set up at Coventry, the centre of the cycle industry. Three du Cros brothers crossed the Atlantic to found a tyre industry in Canada and the US. The Dublin factory moved to new premises but complaints in the locality about noxious smells led to the company's departure from Dublin. In 1893, with Booth's Cycle Agency omitted from the title, the PNEUMATIC TYRE CO.LTD. settled in Coventry.

Local manufacture of suitable cycle frames was encouraged by William du Cros founding the CYCLE COMPONENTS MANUFACTURING CO. LTD. in 1894, from a merger of R.W. Hall Manufacturing Co. Ltd. (engineers), Thomas Warwick & Sons Ltd. (cycle tyre makers), Hudson & Co.Ltd. (manufacturers of welded steel tubes), and the Westwood Wheel Co.Ltd. (wheel manufacturers and from whom the patent for the indented wheel, tubular edged rim was purchased).[9] Harvey du Cros junior and the prinicpals of the defunct companies formed the Board of Directors. Thereby, the new company acquired local standing, reduced competition, found new outlets for its products and those of the Pneumatic Tyre Company and brought together a very useful body of knowledge, experience and expertise.

But, in the ambitious drive towards a dominant place in the market for the pneumatic tyre, by way of self-sufficiency and containment, the du Cros family still lacked one major factor. They knew nothing about rubber or rubber manufacture. Tyres were still hand-made from bought-in components[10] and the company had no control over the supply or quality of its most important raw material.

To reconcile the tyre company's Irish staff to exile and to encourage integration with the English, another son, Arthur du Cros then General Manager of the Pneumatic Tyre Company, created an Anglo-Irish Social Club in Coventry and recruited as employees several Irish international rugby footballers, including Ben Tuke, who then played as part of the Coventry Rugby Football team. On the rugby field, as Coventry met Moseley in 1893, the du Cros family met Moseley players, Frank and Fred Byrne.[11] Their father, Thomas Byrne, also had six sons, four of whom had achieved international and county honours at rugby, cricket and hockey in the Birmingham and Warwickshire area. That the du Cros family were Irish Protestants of Hugenot descent and that the Byrne family were Catholics and of minor Irish nobility, was of little consequence since a happy coincidence of this sporting link was the fact that the Byrne family had been 'in rubber' since 1855.

Thomas Byrne senior was first General Manager of J. Kirby & Son, gutta percha manufacturer of New Street, Birmingham and then, circa 1871, on his own account as proprietor of the Birmingham India Rubber Company at the same address, with works at Charles Henry Street and, later, at the City Rubber Mills, Lichfield Road, Aston.[12] On the death of Thomas Byrne in 1889, the two eldest sons, William and Robert, took over the family business. A family feud ensued. In 1898, the Birmingham India Rubber Co. joined with the Leyland Rubber Co. to become the Leyland & Birmingham Rubber Co.Ltd. the founding firm of BTR plc which, ironically, took over the Dunlop Co. in 1985.[13] Meanwhile, in Lichfield Road, three of the younger Byrne brothers, Thomas Charles, Edward Joseph and James Frederick had, in 1892, established themselves as BYRNE BROS INDIA RUBBER CO.

manufacturing tyres and other rubber goods, sharing the premises with the company for whom they had previously worked, the Birmingham India Rubber Company, but calling the works Manor Mills. It was there that, through their association with the Byrnes in sporting circles, the du Cros family "*served its apprenticeship as rubber makers*" and acquired a ready-made base in rubber manufacture.[14]

Fig. 17.2. Part of Fort Dunlop viewed from the Base Stores, with the administration building at top right. Source: *Fort Dunlop: The Story of a Factory,* 1967.

A new enterprise, THE RUBBER TYRE MANUFACTURING CO. LTD. was floated in 1896,[15] which purchased such part of the Byrne brothers' company as related to the manufacture of india rubber tyres, together with machinery, goodwill, debts, patents and rights, for a cash payment and shares in the new company. Edward Joseph Byrne was appointed Managing Director. The Rubber Tyre Company also purchased 31 Lichfield Road from the executors of William Tranter, extended the premises and called them Para Mills. The Byrne Brothers' Company precluded by agreement from making tyres, moved to a new factory at Salford Street to manufacture general rubber goods, taking with them the old name of Manor Mills. The arrangement, whereby the du Cros family and their chosen business associates came into possession of an already-operating works with an experienced workforce and Managing Director, also included the British rights to use the Doughty press, a machine invented by the American H.J. Doughty, which reduced tyre moulding and vulcanizing time from two hours to three minutes. By that process, as Arthur du Cros observed, "*tyres could be turned out like shelling peas*", the cost of manufacture was reduced and uniformity and durability were increased.[16] All tyre manufacturing was then moved to and centred upon Para Mills. The space there recently vacated by the Birmingham India Rubber Company was allotted to another newly-formed company, the CLIPPER PNEUMATIC TYRE CO. LTD.[17] which was licensed to make tyres under the Bartlett 'Clincher' patent and another patent acquired from the Bagot Pneumatic Tyre Company. In 1899, the Clipper Company produced its first motor vehicle tyre.

While the future of the product was being settled, attention had been directed to securing an unassailable company structure. In 1895, the original Pneumatic Tyre Co. Ltd. was sold to Ernest Terah Hooley.[18] John Boyd Dunlop's holdings were bought out and his connection with the company was severed, not without acrimony. In 1896, Ernest Hooley floated the DUNLOP PNEUMATIC TYRE CO. LTD. Four years later, a subsidiary of that company, the DUNLOP RUBBER CO. LTD. with Arthur du Cros as Managing Director, took over the Rubber Tyre Manufacturing Co. (in 1900) *and* Byrne Bros. India Rubber Company at Salford Street (in 1901). The latter, now precluded from manufacturing any kind of rubber goods, set up a business producing and marketing chemical and other materials used in rubber compound. By an agreement of 16 July 1901, Edward Joseph Byrne was retained by the Dunlop Rubber Company as Advisory Rubber Expert for four years and to give advice and assistance in connection with the working of the Doughty patent for two years, but was otherwise not permitted to engage in any activity or company concerned with rubber tyres or other rubber goods. The Clipper Company was wound up in 1903 and the Cycle Components Company at Coventry in 1904.

Fig. 17.3. 'Core'-built tyres, 1932.

Thus, by the first years of the twentieth century - coinciding with the expiry of the Welch patent - all had been safely gathered in. With a well-protected company structure and an integrated manufacturing base located centrally to markets and the burgeoning motor vehicle industry, a platform was now established for expansion, diversification and extension of control over the supply and production of materials. To keep in touch with developments in the motor industry, directorships were obtained at the Austin Motor Co. and at Napier & Son. Solid tyres for motor vehicles were produced at Manor Mills until after World War 1, overlapping the production of motor vehicle pneumatic tyres. In 1906, the Rim & Wheel Co. was established at Coventry and, in 1909, company-owned rubber plantations were opened in Malaya and a factory in Japan for rickshaw and bicycle tyres. Golf balls, produced in 1908, represented the first diversification and, in 1909, the production of aeroplane tyres and components provided the foundation of a later Aviation Division. Then, in 1912, the DUNLOP RUBBER CO.LTD. became wholly independent, taking over both parent and founder companies.[19]

Fig. 17.4. Machine for tyre-building by the 'drum' method. Source: Publicity leaflet for company film, *Men of Inchinnan,* 1950.

Fort Dunlop

In 1914 a huge textile mill was built at Rochdale and others were purchased at Bacup and Hollinwood[20] but, by that time, despite large extensions of Para Mills into Rocky Lane and Catherine Street and of Manor Mills at Salford Street and Jamieson Road, the available floor space was insufficient for the company's widening activities. A 260 acre site at Castle Bromwich was purchased from the Birmingham Corporation. The 'first sod' of that 'stronghold of the tyre industry', Fort Dunlop, was turned in May 1915.[21] During World War 1, as more and more buildings were erected at the Fort, production was largely for military purposes. In the subsequent economic depression of 1921, a disastrous loss of £8 million, through incompetent rubber dealing resulted in a total replacement of top management and the end of du Cros hegemony. The company, however, continued to expand.

Fig. 17.5. Tyre-building machine for giant tyres.
Source: *India of Inchinnan,* 1965.

Between 1923-5, Charles Macintosh & Co. of Manchester was bought for the production of waterproof materials and clothing and the Liverpool Rubber Co. for footwear. The first tennis balls were manufactured in 1934 and a Sports Company established in 1928 that eventually acquired Slazenger (tennis racquets), John Letters (golf clubs) and Carlton Plastics (badminton racquets). W. & A. Bates Ltd. of Leicester, manufacturers of latex thread (later to be manufactured at Hirwaun, Wales) became part of the Dunlop organisation in 1925. Dunlop invented 'Dunlopillo' in 1929 and 'Semtex' flooring in 1937, for which the architecturally-famous factory at Brynmawr became the production unit. Belting was produced at Cardiff. In 1932, a Scottish tyre base was added with the takeover of the India

Tyre Company at Inchinnan. After World War 2, during which Dunlop made barrage balloons, inflatable decoy tanks and other military ware, the acquisition of Tyresoles Ltd. formed the basis of a Remould Section. Acquired in 1958, the John Bull Tyre Group and Metalastik were to become the Dunlop Polymer Engineering Division. Hoses, fire armour and oil seals were manufactured in Northumberland after the takeover of F. Reddaway & Company of Manchester and George Angus Ltd. In 1957, a new synthetic rubber manufacturing plant was established at Fort Dunlop. By that time, Dunlop owned ninety-four factories and had a work-force of 100,000, and the numbers continued to increase thereafter. As well as earlier overseas expansion, there were factories in the US, Ireland, India, New Zealand, France, Brazil, Trinidad and Zambia. Plantations and factories were owned in Malaysia and Nigeria. [22]

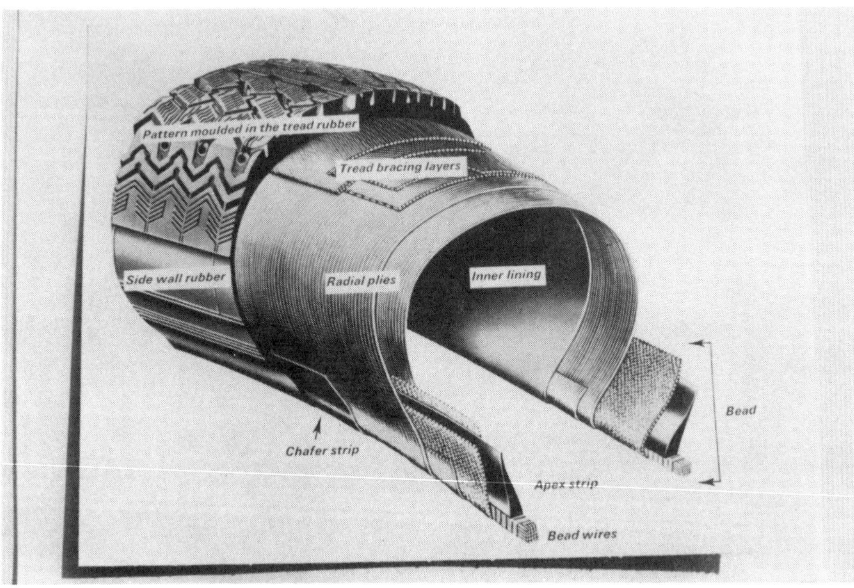

Fig. 17.6. Components of a motor vehicle radial tyre.
Source: *Building a Tyre,* 1970.

The wide range of operations, with over two thousand different products, was recognized by the removal in 1967 of the word 'Rubber' from the company's title, to become simply DUNLOP LTD. However, for most of its existence, tyres represented at least half of the company's output. An investigation in 1953-55 by the Monopolies Commission had revealed that the company was responsible for more than one third of the supply and production of pneumatic tryes in the UK. [23] Penalties were imposed, however, only in respect of distribution practices and price fixing.

To the passing public, Fort Dunlop is the massive and familiar landmark beside the M6 motorway, but that was only the Base Stores building. Beyond it was constructed the vast manufacturing area that is the real Fort Dunlop and, beyond that, were the company's playing fields and apprentice training schools (Fig. 17.2). By analogy, a brief rehearsal of the company's entrepreneurial activities and historic rise should not obscure the contributions Dunlop has made to science and technology, training and education, worker amenities and facilities or, indeed, to the progress made in pneumatic tyre-making over a very short period. Secrecy is endemic in the rubber industry and every firm has to protect its own advances; examples and illustration given here are, of necessity, out of date. From the hand made, glued-on version (shown in Fig. 17.1) the industry developed 'core-built' tyres, layered on in the shape of the final form (Fig. 17.3). Then came 'drum-built' tyres and the evolution of huge machines from which the components were drawn down for assembly (Figs.17.4, 17.5, 17.6, 17.7). Compound ingredients and mixing machines, fabric treatment, moulding and vulcanizing machines and methods have kept pace. Not until after World War 1 was a cord fabric developed for motor vehicle tyres. Short-staple cotton was replaced by continuous filament rayon, latex-dipped nylon or terylene; steel thread was incorporated into very large tyres. The introduction of 'carbon black' (an essential ingredient by 1912) vastly improved strength and durability, and gave tyres their black colour.[24]

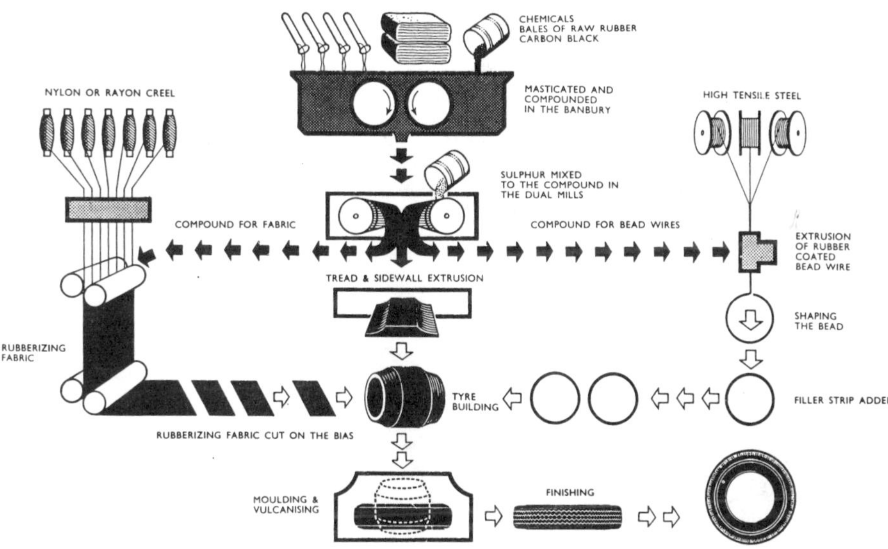

Fig. 17.7. Summary of stages in making a Dunlop car tyre.
Source: *Fort Dunlop: The Story of a Factory,* 1967.

In the design and fabrication of tyres, once the Dunlop company was securely established, improvements were made in-house. Research and development and testing departments were established in 1906, increasing to very much larger proportions at Fort Dunlop, where the company had its own testing fleet and proving ground. As evident at the outset, when the first pneumatic tyre could not be fitted to existing bicycle models, tyre making was recognized as a responsive and reciprocal industry. As motor vehicle technology advanced, with higher-performance engines, faster speeds, lighter bodies, lighter steering and lower-built chassis, tyre designs had to be modified accordingly. Better road holding, resistance to heat generation, improvements in flexibility, strength and durability, tread patterns to resist skidding, water and dirt retention and to avoid excessive noise, were all developmental issues. Standardization of wheel and tyre sizes reduced the number of models and thereby improved output but also increased competition. Nevertheless, from the humble bicycle to giant earthmovers (with tyres each weighing one ton), from rickshaws to racing cars, tractors and aircraft, each vehicle has demanded its own specific tyre with specific properties. Conversely, advances in tyre design have influenced vehicle design, particularly with regard to suspension, steering and braking. A minor, very early, example occurred when the textile component was changed to weftless cord to produce a better-performing and longer-lasting tyre. The loss of internal friction previously generated by the cross-thread in canvas deprived the Austin 7 of some shock absorption; the onus was then on the manufacturer to improve the car's suspension. Reciprocal discussions and experiments have also influenced road-building and surfacing.

Over the years, the market for tyres has been for original equipment to newly-manufactured vehicles, mileage contracts with haulage and passenger transport fleets, for new kinds of vehicles and, in large proportion, for replacement of worn, existing tyres. Research, development, experimentation and rigorous testing were fundamental to keeping (at least) one step ahead of competitors and required the same kind of determination and flair that had assembled and expanded the Dunlop empire. In recent years, however, Dunlop and the market failed each other. The ailing giant was taken over by BTR plc in 1985, tyre manufacturing having already been sold to the Japanese firm Sumitomo. The name 'Dunlop' was too valuable and too well-known to be allowed to disappear and remains extant. Its original owner, John Boyd Dunlop, with whom it all began but who benefitted so marginally, does, therefore, have some kind of memorial. The Byrne family, although seminal to the existence of the company, remains unsung. A history of the many thousands of Birmingham workers, whose labours contributed so much to the making of the Dunlop empire, has yet to be written.[25]

Acknowledgement and grateful thanks are due to the many people and sources, too numerous to mention individually, who contributed so willingly and helpfully to the Dunlop Archive Project; to Dunlop Limited who financed the Project; and to Derek Green, its manager until its uncompleted work was terminated in 1982.

REFERENCES

1 A.J. Wilson, "The First Pneumatic Tyre: How We Repaired it", *Dunlop Gazette,* vol.1, No. 2, 1919, pp.12-13.
2 F. Sinclair, "Conception of the Pneumatic Tyre", *Dunlop Gazette,* vol.5, No. 3, 27 March 1924, p.9.
3 A.P. du Cros, 1938, p.80.
4 Ibid., pp.82-3.
5 *Rubber and Pneumatic Tyre,* p.22.
6 Ibid., p.20.
7 A.P. du Cros, 1954, p.4.
8 Patent for Wood's valve is given in A.P. du Cros, 1938, as No. 4175, March 1891.
9 Public Record Office (PRO), company files BT31/5764/40383.
10 "*Mrs Madeleine Pinches gives particulars of tyre-making nearly forty years ago," Dunlop Gazette,* vol.7, No. 2, 25 February 1926, p.7. Mrs Pinches was employed in the Pneumatic Tyre Co. as a tyre maker in Dublin and Coventry and was later Forewoman of the Tube Department at Manor Mills and Fort Dunlop.

11 All information on the Byrne family is drawn from a file of primary material collected under the auspices of the Dunlop Archive Project.
12 The premises at Aston Cross, 31 Lichfield Road, had been built in 1866 by William Tranter, gun maker and inventor.
13 Personal communication from D.F.P. Sharrock, Secretary, BTR plc, 1 April 1985: "*The present BTR plc was originally the Leyland & Birmingham Rubbert Co.Ltd. which changed its name to BTR Leyland Industries Ltd. in 1969*."
14 A.P. du Cros, 1938,p.210.
15 PRO company file BT31/6863/48276.
16 A.P. du Cros, 1938, p.210.
17 PRO company file BT31/7286/51567.
18 Ernest Terah Hooley also arranged the purchase of Trafford Park, Manchester, in 1896 and became Chairman of Trafford Park Trading Estate.
19 Information from A.P. du Cros, 1938; "Dunlop, A Commonwealth of Industry", supplement to *The Times*, 16 September, 1954; *A Brief Outline of the Development of the Dunlop Rubber Company Limited*, 1957; *Dunlop: A Brief History*, n.d.
21 "For Dunlop's Tenth Birthday", *Dunlop Gazette*, vol.7, No.9, 28 October 1926, p.3.
22 As ref.19 (excluding A.P. du Cros).
23 The Monopolies and Restrictive Practices Committee, 1955.
24 *Rubber and Pneumatic Tyre*, op.cit.
25 The Dunlop Archive Project collected oral history, archive material and artefacts, whereabouts now unknown to the writer.

BIBLIOGRAPHY

A Brief Outline of the Development of the Dunlop Rubber Company Limited, Dunlop Rubber Co. 1957.
A.P. du Cros, *Recollections*, typed ms., Dunlop Rubber Co, 1954.
A.P. du Cros, Wheels of Fortune: A Salute to Pioneers, Chapman & Hall, 1938.
Dunlop: A Brief History, The Dunlop Group, n.d. (c.mid 1970s).
The Monopolies and Restrictive Practices Committee, *Report of the Supply and Export of Pneumatic Tyres*, HMSO, 1955.
Rubber and Pneumatic Tyre, Dunlop Education Section, 1970.
The Development of a Great Industry, Dunlop Rubber Co. illustrated booklet for shareholders, 1920.

FURTHER READING

A Donnithorne, *British Rubber Manufacturing: An Economic Survey of Innovations*, Duckworth, 1958.
H.O. Duncan, *The World on Wheels*, privately published by the author in Paris, 1927.
Fort Dunlop: The Story of a Factory, Dunlop Education Section, 1967.
India of Inchinnan, Dunlop Rubber Co, Marketing Division, 1965.
India Rubber Journal.
G. Rae, "The Statistics of the Rubber Industry", *Journal of the Royal Statistical Society*, February 1938.
E. Tompkins, *History of the Pneumatic Tyre*, Dunlop Archive Project, 1981.
Dunlop papers in the Central Reference Library, Birmingham, Local History Department.
Interested scholars may also consult the writer's archives.

CHAPTER 18

THE PLASTICS INDUSTRY IN BIRMINGHAM AND DESIGN IN BAKELITE, BEETLE AND MELAMINE

Barbara Tilson

Over this century the plastics industry has expanded enormously in variety and complexity and it is no exaggeration to say that plastics have revolutionised our lives from clothing to communications. Within this industry, the principal firms producing and manufacturing in thermosetting plastics warrant particular attention, not least because their history spans much of the twentieth century, but also because they present considerable scope in the study of product and interior design history during the period.

Simply, plastics can be said to be either thermoplastic or thermosetting. The former can be softened again and remoulded, whereas the latter, once chemically set, cannot. Principal materials in the thermosetting group are the formaldehydes - phenolic, urea and melamine. Melamine is known by its chemical name; the type of phenolic which is most well known is bakelite and urea formaldehyde is better known by one of its trade names - beetle. All three materials have distinguished connections with the Birmingham area. The use of the word 'area' here is deliberate, for it is in some ways arbitrary to confine such a study to the city alone. The West Midlands region remains an important location for the manufacture of plastics materials and products. Within this region, it might be realistic to see Birmingham (formerly at least) as the nucleus of plastics manufacture.

Manufacturing in Plastics: Birmingham in its regional and wider context. Bakelite and the Phenolics Industry

The pioneering nature of Birmingham's role in the development and commercial application of plastics is undeniable, for the city's connection with plastics is a long and eminent one which goes back to the earliest days of plastics manufacture. In particular, it was here that Alexander Parkes conducted his experiments towards the cellulose nitrate thermoplastic he named parkesine (subsequently known as celluloid) which was first displayed publicly at the 1862 Exhibition.[1]

Parkesine was chiefly seen as an 'ersatz' (or cheap replacement) for fancy goods in natural materials such as ivory and tortoiseshell.[2] In much the same way, the earliest phenolics were, in their turn, seen as a superior replacement for celluloid in the fancy goods trade, hence the emotive name 'Fireproof Celluloid'[3] for one early producer. Parkesine was also envisaged for more industrial applications in the developing communications industry, specifically for the insulation of under-sea telegraph cables.[4] Similarly, when Sir James Swinburne founded the Fireproof Celluloid Company (a forerunner, through the Damard Lacquer Co, of Bakelite Ltd) in London in 1904, the problem of insulation of electrical cables was one to which he addressed his chemical experiments in phenolics.[5]

Another major field of investigation was the perfection of a substitute for natural shellac. This natural resin, used in the production of varnishes and lacquers, was both expensive and difficult to obtain. Perhaps its most significant use was in the lacquering of brass bedsteads and, as Birmingham still excelled in this trade at the turn of the century, it was this which compelled Swinburne to set up a manufacturing plant in Birmingham. Consequently, the Damard Lacquer Co was established in 1910/11 at 98 Bradford Street within the heart of the industrial city.[6]

Successful production of commercially applicable phenolics was achieved in the United States and England before World War 1. Certainly, it was the patents of Dr. Leo Baekeland from 1907/8/9 which were of the greatest significance in laying the foundation stone of the phenolics industry.[7] Most of the other major innovators, including the Damard Lacquer Co, were forced either to limit their own production to areas or processes not covered by the Baekeland patents or had to negotiate their own production under licence from Baekeland. But, more than this, his formation of the General Bakelite Co in 1909/10 at Perth Amboy, N.J.[8] and (with his manager, Rossi) his entrepreneurial accumulation of a power base in phenolics production, were to lead ultimately to a beneficial unity of cross-national industrial co-operation for, with the merger between the concerns of Baekeland, Aylesworth (Condensite Corp) and Karpen/Redman (Redmanol Chemical Products Co) the Bakelite Corporation was formed in 1922. More importantly for the UK industry, a number of UK firms were brought into the organisation between 1926 and 1927 when Baekeland acquired a majority shareholding. Of these the most important were the Damard Lacquer Co of Birmingham and London, and its competitor, Mouldensite Ltd, of Darley Dale.

This merger produced the firm of Bakelite Ltd which had its manufacturing centre in Birmingham, first at 98 Bradford Street, then shortly in purpose built factories at Greet (from 1921) and subsequently (from 1931) at Tyseley. Its first Chairman was Swinburne. Chemist Howard Potter led experiments with phenolic resins and varnishes at the former Damard Lacquer Co after they had been initiated by Sir James Swinburne. Bakelite Ltd became perhaps the foremost producer of phenolic materials and industrial laminates for the electro-telecommunications market in Britain and it had only one real competitor for its laminate product in the rival formica. Yet it acutely illustrates the changing nature of the plastics industry that the seemingly mighty, too, can fall victim of industrial evolution, corporate 'smash and grab' and unfortunate government policies, for Bakelite (UK) Ltd. was closed in 1985.

Beetle Wares and Production of Urea Formaldehyde

The fortunes of that other giant in the Birmingham area, British Industrial Plastics (now BIP Chemicals Ltd), at Oldbury, have followed a less drastic path. Once a wide-ranging group of companies which included tool-making, engineering and moulding operations in addition to materials manufacture, the firm is now solely a producer of plastics materials. It has, however, considerably expanded its range in the newer thermoplastics to tap a growing market. BIP, too, has fallen victim to a larger predator in the shape of the asbestos firm, Turner and Newall, in a takeover which occurred in 1961.

BIP grew out of an earlier company, British Cyanides Co Ltd, which was established in 1894 to serve the metals trades, specifically to produce cyanide for use in gold extraction.[9] The virtual cessation of its US market in 1922 forced the firm to search for other ventures. This resulted in the experiments with thiourea obtained from sulphocyanide which was envisaged for use in the textiles or vulcanited rubber processes. It was their research chemist, Edmund Rossiter's, tests with thiourea and formaldehyde which led to the realisation of the first colourless synthetic resin or 'organic glass' (1923-5) in the thermosetting group.

The radical possibilities this invention brought for the production of thiourea and, shortly, urea mouldings in beetle and scarab in the whole spectrum of colours (Fig. 18.1) and (more importantly) white consumables, is perhaps difficult for us to appreciate now, accustomed as we are to colourful plastics for every conceivable purpose.

Fig. 18.1. Moulders at Streetly Manufacturing Co. c.1948 using beetle urea. *Growth of a Group,* c. 1949. Reproduced by permission of BIP Chemicals Ltd.

Applications for beetle (or 'beatl', as it was named initially) were shortly found in the market for domestic wares. The first public showing of tablewares moulded from beetle is now legendary. Of the three firms which moulded experimentally for an exhibition at Harrods in 1926, one (Brookes & Adams Ltd.) was a Birmingham firm, located at Barr Street, Hockley, another (Streetly Manufacturing Co. Ltd.) was sited at Sutton Coldfield, Birmingham, and the other (Thomas De La Rue Ltd.) was situated at Walthamstow. Brookes & Adams branched out into plastics moulding from its base in brass and bronze die pressing. Streetly Manufacturing Co. started plastics moulding during World War 1 when it commenced the production of railway fog signals in phenolic.[10] From 1926 to 1928, when it was taken oven by British Cyanides Co. Streetly sold its beetle wares under the trade name beaconware.[11] As a trade moulding subsidiary of British Cyanides, almost any kind of work was undertaken, from cigarette boxes to electrical fitments.

Another important early moulder was C. Hughes & Co.Ltd. of Tenby Street North, Birmingham, using the trade name linga longa. Hughes' range of domestic wares and fancy goods was displayed, for example, along with Brookes & Adams' comparable wares in bandalasta (Fig. 18.2), at the Beatl Shop in London's Regent Street.[12] Although linga longa wares were virtually identical with bandalasta wares in the late 1920s and early 1930s, the more dominant of the two firms was almost certainly Brookes & Adams.[13]

Fig. 18.2. Tableware moulded in beetle urea in the late 1920s. Top: Teapot in bandalasta by Brookes & Adams. Below: Matching teacup and plate in linga longa by C. Hughes & Co. Photo by permission of BIP.

Trade Moulding in the Birmingham area.

Trade moulding specialists arose in the years following World War 1 to provide industrial components, initially for the tele-communications trade, and technical equipment for industry and the home. The plastics industry in the growth decades of the 1930s and 40s was largely stimulated by the expanding electrical and tele-communications fields. One of the most important local trade moulders was evidently Moulded Products Ltd. (Fig. 18.3), for whom Siemens, the electrical company, was a particularly important client in its production of telephones. However, the firm made anything from flower pots to gear knobs and electric plugs. It even experimented with phenolic coffins which (perhaps not surprisingly) did not catch on.[14]

The years 1937 to 1946 were a peak period for the early plastics industry due to the stimulus provided by the wartime demand for military equipment. Thereafter, post-war trading difficulties occurred with shortages of plastics raw materials and worn-out equipment. New products had to be developed for a peacetime market. One solution to the trading difficulties experienced in this new era of competition was in strength through amalgamation.

The Birmingham area has evolved as a major centre for industries connected with transport manufacture. Much production of smaller specialist parts has been subcontracted out and a complex network of components firms serving the large automotive industries has evolved. Much of this work has been 'metal-bashing', formerly in zinc alloy but perhaps more usually, now, in aluminium or plastics. In more recent decades, thermoplastics have largely superseded bakelite phenolic for automotive products. Of specialist components manufacturers, the largest is Lucas Industries plc, the aerospace, automotive and industrial systems and components group. It is symptomatic of the industrial upheaval in both the automotive and plastics industries, and of the growing 'Europeanization' of industry, that in August 1988 its former plastics subsidiary (now European Plastic Moulders Ltd), was acquired by a Dutch firm, Schuttersveld Holdings B.V., which was itself part of the Fiat group. In January 1989 the plant still produced components such as battery boxes for Lucas, but it was evolving as a trade moulder serving industry at large.[15]

Fig. 18.3. Television moulded in bakelite by Moulded Products Ltd for Sobell Industries Ltd. *Bakelite Progress,* Spring 1952.

Design in the Plastics Industry for Domestic Products and Interiors. Decorative Laminates

Warerite laminates, produced by Bakelite Ltd, were materially comparable with formica, having a core of bakelite-impregnated paper and a melamine (or formerly a urea) outer skin. The firm's manufacture of decorative grades evolved from its production of industrial laminates for the electrical and telephone industries. This had commenced, initially at the Darley Dale works and from 1931 at Tyseley, Birmingham, following the formation of the firm by merger in 1926/7. It was reliant on the expertise of Baekeland's Canadian laminates plant. Bakelite Ltd was experimenting with decorative laminates from 1936.[16] Its artmur laminates were produced with veined and marbled effects in pastel colours or with simple stylised pictorial motifs such as a yacht or a leaping deer.[17] Its decoratives laminates business, however, was to expand following the acquisition of a flourishing laminates concern at Ware, Herts., in 1940. Although the firm's decorative laminates business expanded considerably during the 1950s and 60s bakelite industrial laminates were always its dominant line.

In 1951 Martyn Rowlands was brought in as a creative designer.[18] The date is significant, for it was the year of the *Festival of Britain* and an era which was noteworthy for the enthusiastic promotion of better design in industry. Warerite decorative laminates, reproducing water colours by Phyllis Bray, were displayed at the 1946 *Britain Can Make It* exhibition (Fig. 18.4) and, for the 1951 *Festival,* the Festival Design Group initiated designs for the Regatta Restaurant and elsewhere.[19] Rowlands was employed by Bakelite Ltd at its London office to provide a free design service for the plastics industry. Something of this kind was evidently envisaged in the late 1940s when the firm's Industrial Design Unit was offering its services in design from "*the interior treatment of railway buffet cars to pen holders, and from filing cabinets to paint boxes*".[20] The intention was evidently to stimulate manufacturing in plastics, by which the firm would (naturally) benefit. There was little opportunity for Rowlands in product design at Bakelite Ltd, for his expertise was directed more towards exhibition and laminates pattern design. Freelance designers, including his wife, calligrapher Pat Rowlands, were also brought in.

Fig. 18.4. Table tops in warerite after a watercolour by Phyllis Bray, displayed in the 1946 *Britain Can Make It* exhibition. *Bakelite Progress,* May 1947.

Around 1953/4 a branch design studio was established at the Tyseley laminates works, initiated by Works Manager, Reg Hulse. It was first led by Jack Lambley and, from 1957, by Jack Crumpton. The London studio, under John Benmore (Fig. 18.5), continued for some time until all design work was transferred to Birmingham. When the two studios were in operation, the London studio was responsible for the more elaborate artistic designs.[21] In the 1950s, some particularly flamboyant designs by freelance commercial artists and designers were

Fig. 18.5. John Benmore, graphic artist, Bakelite Ltd, preparing a warerite design in the London studio. *Bakelite Progress,* Autumn 1956.

produced in warerite, such as the vivid foliate designs by West Indian textiles designer Althea McNeish for the SS Oriana.[22] Utilitarian signs and textures for domestic ranges were initiated from Birmingham and certain pictorial laminates were taken from prints of local scenes. An example was the mural for Forward Trust's Birmingham headquarters (Fig.18.6).

Warerite seems to have maintained its supremacy over formica during the 1950s, but a determined publicyt campaign was evidently being waged by its rival. The success over the years of the advertising campaigns for formica laminates is indicated by its incorporation into popular generics.

Fig. 18.6. Warerite mural after a print by H.W. Brewer of central Birmingham, 1885, displayed in the headquarters of Forward Trust, Birmingham. *Bakelite Plastics Review,* 1964/5.

Design in Beetle and Melamine Focusing on the Product Design Unit at BIP.

A number of firms in the Birmingham area evolved as important UK moulders of products for the domestic consumer, notably Brookes & Adams and Streetly Manufacturing Co, which were both concerned also with design. Brookes & Adams had made a reputation for itself in the 1920s and 30s as a producer of beetle urea products of Art Deco flavour, sometimes moulded in exuberant mottled effects in imitation of hand blown glass. Streetly took on its first staff designer in 1931 in the person of A.H. 'Woody' Woodfull.[23] Until then, design was undertaken chiefly by the engineer and eminent tool designer, Jim Butler.

In 1951, again in response to the mood of design reform symbolised by the *Festival of Britain*, BIP applied itself (as did Brookes & Adams at this time) to raising design standards. Woodfull was brought from Streetly in 1951 to set up a Product Design Unit for BIP, based at Tat Bank House, Oldbury. He gathered around him a talented group of assistant designers which included John Vale, Barrie Eccleston and David Harman Powell.

Woodfull's PDU gained an enviable reputation in the plastics trade and brought distinctions to the firm through awards from the Design Centre and the Worshipful Company of Horners.[24] A noteworthy example was the Midwinter Modern tableware of 1957 (Fig. 18.7), designed by A.H. Woodfull and John Vale. Roy Midwinter collaborated with the PDU on this design, with its quartic flatware, which was produced for W.R. Midwinter by the Streetly Manufacturing Co.[25] The Midwinter ware was a stimulus towards the first Gaydon range of 1961 (Fig. 18.8), which was designed by A.H. Woodfull and the PDU's Barrie Eccleston. It was moulded by Streetly and sold through another subsidiary, BIP Gaydon Ltd. Visually, its combining of elliptical and circular forms evoked a cubo-constructivist geometry. The Design Centre Award winning Fiesta melamine range of 1960[26] by Ronald Brookes for Brookes & Adams was, again, not too dissimilar from these PDU/Midwinter designs, but was produced in stronger colours including a voguish black.

Fig. 18.7. Tableware designed by A.H. Woodfull and John Vale for W.R. Midwinter, 1957, moulded in melamine by Streetly Manufacturing Co. Photo courtesy of John Vale.

These tableware examples were chosen to illustrate the links between firms and between industries, but they were also representative of a revolution in the home (particularly in the kitchen and dining room) in the use of economical plastic equipment. It is noteworthy, too, that Woolworth was an important client for some years. However, it would be wrong to assume that the PDU was wholly concerned with tableware. On the contrary, many areas were addressed such as

Fig. 18.8. Gaydon tableware designed by A.H.Woodfull and Barrie Eccleston, 1961, moulded by Streetly Manufacturing Co. in melamine. Source: Advertisement, *Ideal Home*, October 1961. Reproduced by permission of BIP Chemicals Ltd.

exhibition design, toys and nursery equipment, electrical fitments and radios (Fig. 18.9), gardening goods and handles. The road safety device, designed by A.H. Woodfull and winner of a Horners' Award for 1961, was a more technical example.[27] Nor was work undertaken solely for production in thermosetting materials. Many new thermoplastics had appeared since 1951, the PDU's work was now often in consultancy rather than creative activities, and design tasks were undertaken for any material.

When the PDU was formed, staff design departments were, perhaps, rare but by the latter 1950s these were more usual. By the 1970s there was increased competition from freelance design practices, combined with the effects on the plastics industry of difficulties over the shortages and rising price of oil for raw materials. The decision was taken to close the PDU. Its closure and the cessation of BIP's moulding activities at Streetly were perhaps only part of a period of decline in the region's thermosetting industry which, arguably, culminated in the termination of the Bakelite plant at Tyseley. There appeared to be no in-house equivalent of the PDU in the plastics industry in the Birmingham area in 1989.

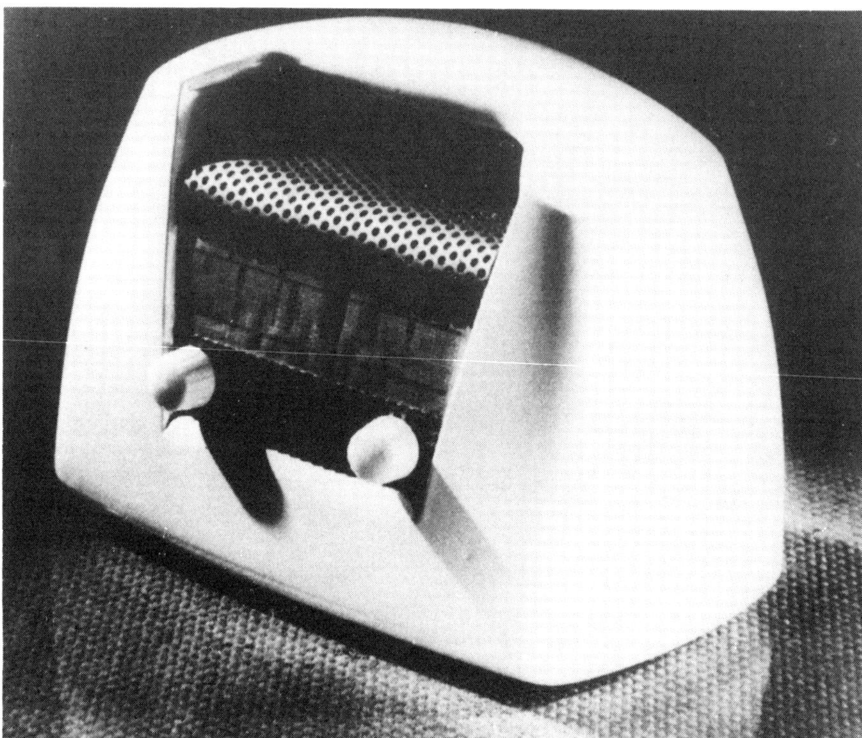

Fig. 18.9. Radio for Ultra moulded in beetle urea and possibly the first set to sell ¼ million. Designed by A.H. Woodfull, late 1930s. Prototype in wood. Photo courtesy of A.H. Woodfull.

Factors towards Decline and Change in the Plastics Industry in the Birmingham area.

The complexity of reasons for change in the local plastics industry cannot be tackled here at length. One factor, however, concerned the action of unions to prevent capacity production on new high-output machinery in the 1960s at a time when industrial welfare was reliant on the ability to compete. Another was the intervention of central government to assist Northern areas of relative deprivation by preventing the expansion of firms on their home territories in the Birmingham area. This may have assisted the North, but it was devastating to industry here, both in and out of the plastics industry. For example, it meant that BIP was prevented from expanding at Oldbury. Instead, BIP Whiston was established c.1965 in Liverpool.[28] Again, Bakelite Ltd's new PVC plant was built not at Tyseley, where they wanted it, but at Aycliffe in County Durham.[29] This business was later sold to BIP Chemicals Ltd by Bakelite Ltd's (then) owner, Union Carbide Corporation.[30] It was to here that production of warerite decorative laminates was transferred in 1968, while only the phenolics and industrial laminates businesses were retained in Birmingham. Furthermore, the survival of local firms has been decided by managment based elsewhere in a climate of 'merger mania' and asset stripping.

Although one era of plastics production may have ended, it might be more realistic to see the industry as proceeding through a period of transition. Indeed, plastics continue to be produced and moulded, although the high-tech era has brought clients in digital technology. Entrepreneurial vision and dynamics remain crucial to the future of industry. Future success may lie, however, not in the ever-speedier, price-reducing manner of competition, but through quality in design, in quality control, and through greater awareness of the importance of design and the designer in industry.

REFERENCES

1 J.M. Goldsmith, 1934, (originally written in 1922), is a reliable and detailed account of Parkes' achievements.

2 See A Parkes' paper read to the Society of Arts entitled "On the Properties of Parkesine and its Application to the Arts and Manufactures", *Journal of the Society of Arts,* December 15 1865, p.83.

3 In particular, W.H. Story, one of James Swinburne's assistants at the laboratories of the Fireproof Celluloid Company (or Fireproof Celluloid Syndicate, as it was also referred to) in London, patented a phenolic substitute for celluloid, jet, ivory, horn and bone. Patent Specification no. 8875, 27.4.05.

4 See A. Parkes, op.cit. and B.L. Davies, p.9. The first submarine cable was laid in 1850.

5 As described in T.J. Fielding, p.4.

6 James Swinburne, pp.4-5, described how brass bedsteads, which were in fashion, were made "*in quantities*" in Birmingham and that this was the reason the works was moved from London.

7 It appears that his patent no. 21,566 of 12.10.08 for "A Condensation Product and Method of Making Same" was a master patent. This patent was first registered in the US on 15.10.07.

8 See J.H. Dubois, p.86ff.

9 The history of BIP is told in Cyril Dingley, (c.1962), and *Growth of a Group,* (c.1949).

10 See *The Beetle Magazine,* Christmas 1939, p.19. Here, in the biography of assistant supervisor Mrs W. Berry was described her original task of packing fog signals at Streetly in c.1922.

11 See *The Beetle Magazine,* Summer 1938, p.12.

12 See *The Beetle Magazine,* February 1948, p.196.

13 Hughes' daughter, Mrs Cafferata, recalled, for example, that C. Hughes would be sub-contracted by Brookes & Adams for moulding purposes when demand exceeded Brookes & Adams' production capacity. Information from interview of November 1986.
14 Information from an interview of December 1985 with Ron Ireland, son of one of the original owners of Moulded Products Ltd.
15 Information provided by Mr Bates, European Plastic Moulders Ltd, 21.12.88.
16 T. Fielding, pp.35, 61.
17 As pictured in *The Beetle Magazine,* Christmas 1938, p.17.
18 Information from Martyn Rowlands, intereview November 1988.
19 Warerite-topped tables in a pattern derived by Martyn Rowlands from crystal structures were shown in *Bakelite Progress,* Winter 1951-52, p.5.
20 *Bakelite Progress,* February 1949, p.4.
21 Information from interviews with Reg Hulse, April 1987; Jack Crumpton, June 1987; John Benmore, August 1986.
22 As featured in *Bakelite Plastics Review,* n.d. (c.1961).
23 Information from A.H. Woodfull, with whom I conducted a series of interviews during 1986.
24 Awards from the Worshipful Company of Horners were for the Baby's Hi-Gene Chair (Woodfull, 1951), 'Build-a-Plant' Flower Construction Toy (Woodfull, 1952), Shoe Horn (1953), All-Plastics Greenhouse (Powell, 1954), Demountable Shower Cabinet (Eccleston 1960), Road Safety Device (nylon wheel disc) (Woodfull, 1961). A Design Centre Award was obtained for the Midwinter Modern Tableware (Woodfull/Vale, 1957). A joint Co.Id/ City of Birmingham Award was received for outdoor seating for F. Lewis & Sons (Vale, 1953).
25 A.H. Woodfull (in interview op.cit.) recalled the collaboration with Roy Midwinter while Roger Dingley, former Managing Director of BIP Gaydon Ltd, (in interview of November 1987) who knew the family personally, also recalled the involvement of Mrs Midwinter herself in the design of shapes.
26 The Fiesta plates won the award in 1960. The tea cup and saucer was of customary type, while the stacking cup was given an unusual treatment which required a different method of holding the cup. The finger could not grip the loop of the handle as this was joined to the cup only at the top.
27 As illustrated in *Beetle Bulletin,* 26, 1961, p.17.
28 See *Beetle Bulletin,* 46, n.d. (c.1975), p.10.
29 "A New Vinyl Resin Plant", *Bakelite Progress,* Spring 1954, p.3.
30 Information from A. Lloyd. Interview of March 1986.

BIBLIOGRAPHY

B.L. Davies, *Technology of Plastics,* London, 1949.
C. Dingley, *The Story of BIP, 1894-1962,* Birmingham, n.d., (c.1962).
J.H. Dubois, *Plastics History USA,* Boston, 1972.
T.J. Fielding, *History of Bakelite Ltd,* London, n.d. (c.1948).
J.M. Goldsmith, *Alexander Parkes, Parkesine, Xylonite and Celluloid,* unpublished manuscript, 1934 (written in 1922). In Central Library, Birmingham.
Growth of a Group: A History of the BIP Group, 1895-1949, London, n.d. (c.1949).
J. Swinburne, *Early History of the Damard Lacquer Co.* typescript, n.d. In Science Museum Library.

FURTHER READING

J. Butler, *Compression and Transfer Moulding of Plastics,* London; New York, 1959.
M. Kaufman, *The First Century of Plastics: Celluloid and its Sequel,* London, n.d. (c.1964).
Turner and Newall: The First Fifty Years, 1920-1970, (?Manchester), 1970.

CHAPTER 19

CADBURY LTD AT BOURNVILLE: DESIGN & PACKAGING
An Outline

Graham Parker, Design Manager, Cadbury Ltd (retired 1988); revised and extended by Barbara Tilson.

Aside from being one of the largest and most distinguished companies in Birmingham, and the trade name of a major British chocolate producer, the name of 'Cadbury' is also synonymous with the Quaker founders of Bournville village (see chapter 13) which lies adjacent to the factory (Figs. 19.1, 19.2, 19.3). So long-established is Cadbury's that a study of its designs for packaging and advertising embraces virtually the entire history of printed wrappings and publicity for mass-produced goods.[1] Pack styles have ranged over the decades from the utilitarian to the exorbitantly exclusive, from the plain wrappings of World War 2 packs to the fancy novelties in silk and velvet of the late nineteenth century.

Fig. 19.1. The Bournville Factory, pen drawing, 1879.
Photo courtesy of Cadbury Ltd.

Fig. 19.2. The Bournville Factory in the late 1980s, extended and rebuilt. Bournville Lane is running left to right across the lower end of the complex. Photo courtesy of Cadbury Ltd.

A Brief Resumé of the Firm and its Manufacture.

The company's links with Birmingham go back to 1824, when John Cadbury opened a grocery business in Bull Street, moving to warehouse premises in Crooked Lane in 1831 and to a larger factory in Bridge Street (off Broad Street) in 1847. Cadbury had started preparing cocoa and drinking chocolate for sale himself at Bull Street, and by 1842 16 varieties were in production. On the move to Bridge Street, Cadbury Brothers was formed, when John Cadbury took his brother Benjamin into partnership. From 1861, John Cadbury's sons, Richard and George, continued the business.[2] The company's move to Bournville in 1879 is well known, not least for that ideological paternalism which resulted in the creation of the Bournville workers' village.

In the early years of production at Cadbury's, chocolate drinks alone were produced. Eating chocolates appeared on the company's listings in the 1840s and the variety of their manufacture of these novelties (which included chocolate assortments) expanded from the mid 1860s, when Richard and George Cadbury introduced the cocoa press. Interestingly, with the current concern for additive-free foods, Cadbury's reputation in the later nineteenth century was built on the purity of its products, which were unadulterated with flour - a practice of the day. The catalyst for the firm's publicity of its quality products was the Purity of Foods Act of 1873-5.

It was perhaps not coincidental that all three founders of chocolate manufacture - Cadbury, Fry and Rowntree - should have been Quakers, given the wholesome, natural, health-giving character of their product, for these features have traditionally been associated with Quakerism. One of these early competitors - Fry - was absorbed by the Cadbury company in 1918. Cadbury's has itself been subject to a more recent merger with a well-known soft drinks firm in 1969, and Cadbury Ltd is now the confectionery activity of Cadbury Schweppes.

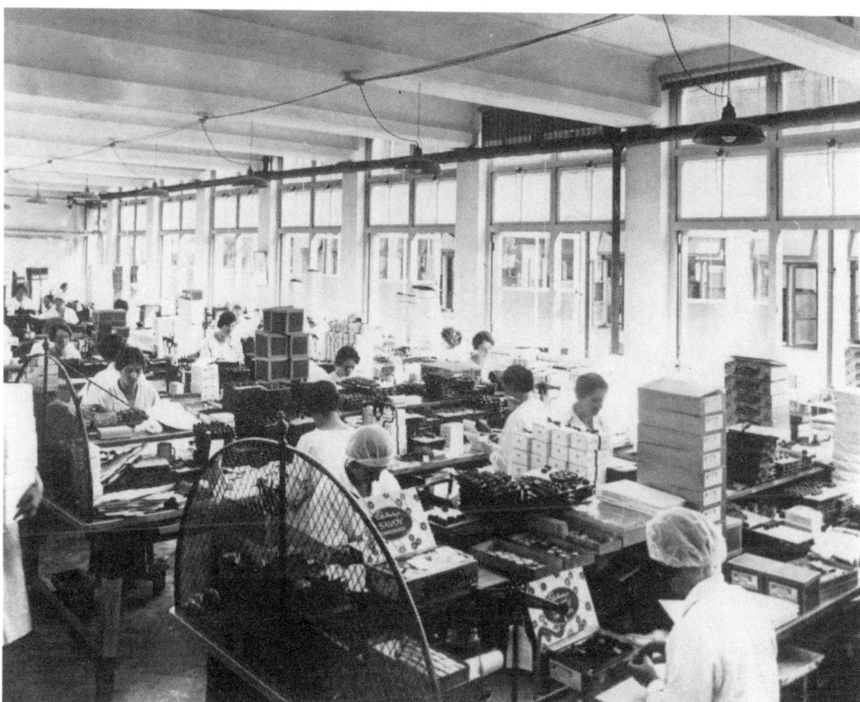

Fig. 19.3. Packaging Chocolates at Cadbury's, c.1925.
Photo courtesy of Cadbury Ltd.

Cadbury's and Design

It is possible to trace, in the earliest decades of chocolate packaging at Cadbury's, the supersedence of an essentially eighteenth century technology of typographical letterpress and decorative engraved label and pack designs by the chromolithographed examples of commercial Victoriana in the latter half of the nineteenth century. Purely typographical labels which had their origins in book types were generally monochrome, examples of these being the plain but tasteful labels for 'Genuine Cocoa Paste', 'Fine Crown' (Fig. 19.4) and 'Sir Hans Sloane's Milk Chocolate' drinks.[3]

Fig. 19.4. 'Fine Crown' chocolate wrapping, pre-1847.
Photo courtesy of Cadbury Ltd.

Decorative packaging was introduced in the 1840s with the production of eating chocolate. Fancy packs were considered suitable for such novelties from the outset. Two of the earliest labels were based on engravings of Victoria and Albert and of the Birmingham Town Hall, which was opened in 1834. Both had the Cadbury Brothers designation and therefore dated from post-1847.

The importance which Cadbury's attached to the role of design in promoting their products was reflected in the early establishment of a design department at the company at the end of the nineteenth century. Sophia Pumphrey was the first artist to join Cadbury's in 1896. However, prior to the formation of the design department, Richard Cadbury was influential in this way. An artist by inclination rather than by training, he was responsible for creating the first designs for illustrative chocolate assortments of 1868-70, following the introduction of boxed packs. These were decorated with portraits of his own children and with holiday scenes in a manner characteristic of mid-Victorian sentimental charm. The 1880s and 1890s saw a peak of late Victorian virtuosity in packs which were intended to be collectors' items as much as exclusive confectionery. Designs ranged from the floral, pastoral and romantic to opulent silk-lined caskets and rich velvet jewel boxes (Fig.19.5). Novelty packs were a feature of Cadbury packaging until World War 2. One-off commemoratives have been produced periodically over the years, for example for royal souvenir packs. The most recent example here was to commemorate the wedding of Prince Andrew and Miss Sarah Ferguson in 1986.

Fig. 19.5. Velvet and silk-lined caskets from c.1890s.
Photo courtesy of Cadbury Ltd.

Despite developing its own in-house design department, freelance artists and designers were also used. Perhaps the first of these was a local artist, Cecil Aldin, who undertook a series of posters and advertisements for Cadbury's, some of them with a humorous theme, at the turn of the century (Fig. 19.6). The company's designers also responded to the mood of design reform in the early 1930s, arising in particular from the findings of the 1931 Gorell Committee, which was concerned with promoting better standards of design in manufacture through the Society of Industrial Artists and Designers, for example. Cadbury's answer was to commission chocolate box illustrations from established artists such as Laura Knight (Fig. 19.7), Arthur Rackham and Mark Gertler. None of these designs proved successful, because they were not in the popular mode of the day. Whether this arose due to the brief they were given, or whether it was due to an unfortunate

Fig. 19.6. Cadbury's Cocoa advertising designed by Cecil Aldin, c.1900. Photo courtesy of Cadbury Ltd.

choice on the company's behalf is difficult to ascertain. Nevertheless, Rackham's moody and disturbing fantasy, Knight's unappealing portrait, and Gertler's humdrum still life (among others) were decidedly ill-conceived.

Product designers were also commissioned for packaging ideas and arguably one of the most successful designs was the novel anthropomorphic 'Bournvita' plastic beaker designed by A.H. Woodfull (Fig. 19.8). Its unusual design is emphasised by comparison with a more customary beaker shape (Fig. 19.9). Subsequently, the Product Design Unit at BIP, Oldbury, on the fringes of Birmingham (see chapter 18) was commissioned for further packaging designs.[4] The PDU comprised a team of industrial designers led by A.H. Woodfull. It was established in 1951 (again, triggered by a mood of design reform) to provide a design service for industry at large.

Fig. 19.7. Design for chocolate box packaging by Laura Knight, c.1931.
Photo courtesy of Cadbury Ltd.

Fig. 19.8. Cadbury's 'Bournvita' mug in beetle urea, designed by A.H. Woodfull. Advertisement by BIP Tools Ltd. Source: *The Beetle Magazine*, vol.3, no.30, Summer 1952. Reproduced by permission of BIP Chemicals Ltd.

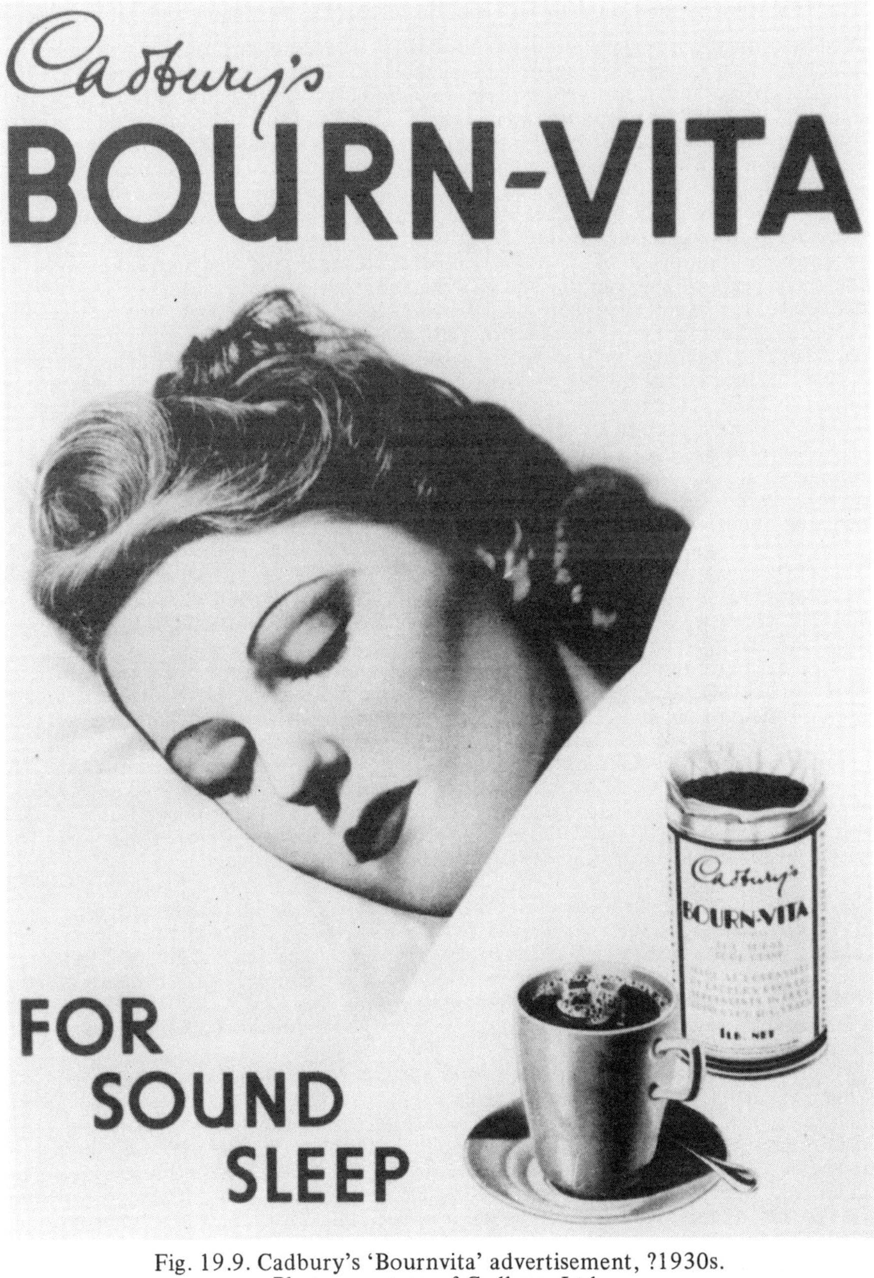

Fig. 19.9. Cadbury's 'Bournvita' advertisement, ?1930s.
Photo courtesy of Cadbury Ltd.

The Evolution of the Company's Corporate Identity in Packaging and Advertising.

A variety of devices have been introduced by the company over the decades by which it has become instantly recognizable. These have comprised pictorial themes, logos, and distinctive colours to emphasize the quality, consistency and memorability of their products. The role of design in the marketing of its products has long been appreciated by the firm. As has become customary in the modern corporation, the two aspects have been drawn closer together. Design at Cadbury's is often initiated by the Marketing Department in response to perceived consumer needs, which are given visual form in the Creative Design Department and are tested with the products through market research.

Cadbury's adoption of corporate colours, (a regal gold and purple) evolved in the early years of this century and have become synonymous with their Dairy Milk chocolate, for which they were used from 1920. Dairy Milk was first introduced in 1905, following Fry's precedent in 1902 as the first British manufacturer of milk chocolate to emulate its Dutch originator, as did the major Swiss manufacturer, Nestle. Bournville chocolate, with its distinctive dark red wrapping, was introduced in 1908 and Milk Tray, with purple packaging, in 1915. The foil and band wrapping commenced in 1932.

In advertising, the 'Glass and a Half' (Fig. 19.10) theme has been the longest runner, from its introduction in 1928 for poster and press advertising to the present, where it is often incorporated into wrapping designs. Initially this pictorial theme was reserved solely for Dairy Milk but in the early sixties it was taken up for wider advertising. An earlier pictorial trademark was the stylised cocoa tree interwoven with the Cadbury name (Fig. 19.11). This was registered in 1911 and was used consistently until 1939 and for a short time following World War 2. It was used on various items such as presentation boxes, catalogues, tableware and promotional items and was imprinted into wrapping foil.

It is, perhaps, the Cadbury logo itself with which the firm has become identified. This cursive script, resembling the comparable but earlier Art Nouveau logo of Boots, was itself created in 1921 for use on the transport fleet and was based on the signature of William A. Cadbury. However, its decidedly Art Nouveau character became more marked subsequently and has undergone subtle modifications to reach its present style with its flowing, curvilinear lines. The script logo was, until 1952, used only on sales catalogues and seal designs on special boxes and stationery. At this time, when the graphic designer, Norbett Dutton, re-designed the company's whole moulded range, the logo was adopted for major brand names.

As with the adoption of specific colours for individual brands, so certain motifs have been identified with particular products. For example, the view of Milk Tray as an affordable product was reinforced by its relative plainness and, by the mid thirties, it was a market leader. In 1971, doubtless in response to the Pop era, when there was a revival of interest in complex organic designs, a William Morris style pack for Milk Tray was brought out. This was superseded in 1978 by the white orchid, suggestive of class, sophistication and tradition, which has continued to the present time.

Floral themes have remained a staple subject for Cadbury's packaging almost from the outset. A floral name was even given to one brand - Roses' chocolates. Packaging for this leading twist-wrap chocolate assortment, originating in 1938, has undergone subtle changes over the years without losing the essential character of the design. Early designs incorporated a rose in sampler embroidery effect, which was later replaced by a more realistic example. In 1958 a Roses poster won the Poster of the year award, while in 1966 the Roses Easter Carton won a Packaging Star Award.

While, currently, the company is conscious of tradition and custom in its consumer appeal, it is maintaining its record of innovation and response to socio-

Fig. 19.10. 'Glass and a Half' advertisement, ?1970s.
Photo courtesy of Cadbury Ltd.

cultural changes. Certain packs, for example, are geared to an image-conscious youth market, for which traditional floral or landscape designs would be inappropriate. Its modernity is expressed in the sophisticated combinations of newer materials as they have become available since the 1960s, such as PVC, vacuum formed plastics and metallised film. High-speed packaging production lines have been introduced over the last decade for blocks, boxes and foil wrapped novelties, which are manufactured on reels with photocell mechanisms determining cut-off points. With the lifting of EEC trading barriers in 1992, future international competition may result in present national differences merging to form a European design style. This situation will place even more emphasis on the effectiveness of companies' point of sale and marketing strategies as they compete for market leadership.

REFERENCES

1 In 1989 a Visitor's Centre was under construction on the Cadbury's factory complex, to house the history of chocolate production and examples of packaging and advertising etc.

2 The early history of the company is taken from *The Story of Cadbury Limited,* 1987, an information leaflet produced by Cadbury Ltd. Further details were provided by Helen Davies, Library Information Officer, during my visits to the company in November 1988 and February 1989. Packaging and product information is drawn from a fact sheet draft of Cadbury's design, prepared by Graham Parker and kindly made available to me by Patricia Dunbar, External Services Manager. A longer typescript on Cadbury's design is "The Cadbury Contribution to the Art of the Chocolate Box", Design Studio, Cadbury Ltd, 1975, housed in the company's library. Further detail is supplied by the editor.

3 Sir Hans Sloane (1660-1753) was an English botanist and physician-in-ordinary to the King, as described in T.B. Rogers, pp.20-1.

4 Two known designs which did not enter production were the 'Captain Choc Bloc' toy plastics boat packaging designed by A.H. Woodfull in the 1950s and the beaker in polypropylene with a urea holder of c.1958-9, designed by Barrie Eccleston. Information from the designers.

FURTHER READING

Cadbury Brothers Ltd, *Industrial Record 1919-1939,* Bournville, 1947.

Several books were issued by the firm under this or a similiar title, e.g.:-

Cadbury Brothers Ltd, *Industrial Challenge,* London, 1964.

G. Jones, "The chocolate multinationals: Cadbury, Fry and Rowntree, 1918-1939", in G. Jones (ed.), *British Multinationals: Origins, Management and Performance,* London, 1986, pp.96-118.

B. Murray, "George Cadbury", in D.J. Jeremy and C. Shaw (eds.), *Dictionary of Business Biography,* vol.1, London, 1984.

T.B. Rogers, *A Century of Progress 1831-1931,* Bournville, 1931.

See also P. Atkins' bibliography for further listings.

Fig. 19.11. Cadbury's wrapping showing the cocoa tree interwoven with the Cadbury name, 1909. Photo courtesy of Cadbury Ltd.

CHAPTER 20

CONTEMPORARY DESIGN IN BIRMINGHAM AND THE MIDLANDS REGION

Barbara Tilson interviews David Beard part-time lecturer at Birmingham Polytechnic, also of David Beard Associates and formerly Designer Selection Service director at the Design Council and Tim Davis, a partner in the Harborne (Birmingham) design consultancy, Ryland Davis Associates.

Tilson: David, when were you a student at Birmingham Polytechnic?

Beard: From about 1959 to 1962. When I was a student here there was a very strong regional interest, but now a lot of that has broken down. There were people like Ron Brookes of Brookes & Adams, which had a small showroom in Edmund Street (on the site which is now the library) that became a centre for SIAD meetings and so forth. It was a shop window filled with the Fiesta range that he did. There was quite a strong group of designers in the days of 'Woody' Woodfull, John Vale and David Harman Powell (see chapter 18). They all studied here at different times. John Vale later set up his own freelance design business in Harborne (Figs.20.1, 20.2) and David Harman Powell moved away. Design activity, however, was very local in those days. For example, BBC set designs, television accessories and graphics, were local to the Midlands. Things started to change noticeably in the 1960s with companies being absorbed into bigger conglomerates and their headquarters and the decision-making moved away. There are many designers in this area, but most are employed full-time in industry as staff designers. Consultancies are often smaller in size and number here but, over the last ten years, there's been a very rapid increase in the number of consultancies everywhere and, for that reason, designers have been selling their services more aggressively. Much of the design work available is being done by London-based companies and the bigger and more glamourous ones tend to be London-based. PEL is one of the great Midlands firms, who have used Fitch in London, mostly (I believe) Peter Crutch, their chief designer. When companies, such as Hostess Furniture and PEL, require freelance designers, they look to London, as do many other Midlands companies. Midlands-based designers tend to look outside the area as well.

Tilson: Does this mean that there's not much freelance design business in the Midlands, or in Birmingham itself?

Beard: I used to run the Design Council's Designer Selection Service, which was essentially a 'marriage broker' business. Designers would bring their portfolios to try and find work, because my job was doling out work as it became available. When I ran the Designer Selection Service, there were many enquiries from Midlands-based designers who were looking for work, but there were remarkably few enquiries from firms in the Midlands. Now, that's not to say that the demand wasn't there. It could quite simply have been the result of local designers doing their public relations bit very well, servicing local industry so that it didn't need to come looking. John Barnes, for example, used to do a lot of design work for Avery Scales of Birmingham (Fig.20.3). If you extend out to Leicester, there's Roger Jones of Jones Garrard, but most of their work comes from well outside the Midlands. Again, take the case of DCA Design Consultants of Warwick (Fig. 20.4; see also Fig. 1.13). They have quite a reputation for designing railway rolling stock and suchlike, so they've just opened an office in Australia because they're doing a rapid transport system for N.S. Wales. Even consultancies based in the Midlands tend to do a very substantial proportion of their work outside the area.

Fig. 20.1. John Vale. Switchplate for J.A. Crabtree & Co Ltd, Walsall, winner of a Design Centre Award, 1980 (See appendix). Photo courtesy of J. Vale.

Tilson: Do you think that this is general, outside London, or do you think it's specific to this region?

Beard: In a survey published a couple of years ago now, most of the industrial design practices in London, of any repute, claimed that 60% of their work was from abroad.

Tilson: Abroad where? America?

Beard: America, Japan. An enormous amount of work for Japanese firms is done by British designers. The new Minolta camera range, for example, has been designed by BIB in London. Kenneth Grange has been working with Japanese sewing machine manufacturers and the like for probably 15 years. He seems to have a higher reputation abroad, in many ways, than he does here. It reflects manufacturers' attitudes towards the importance of the role that design plays within the company business. The Management Development Unit, which I have been involved with at Birmingham Polytechnic, found a case where a manufacturer, who wanted to produce silver picture frames, was reluctant even to invest £700 for a set of tools. There have always been some excellent patrons of design in the Midlands. BIP, for example, always had a good commitment to it, while PEL Furniture and Best & Lloyd, the lighting firm, continue to do so.

Fig. 20.2. John Vale. 'Petite' children's typewriter for Britains Petite Ltd, Nottingham, 1989. Photo courtesy of J. Vale.

Tilson: Do you think local firms are more reluctant to see design as important?
Beard: It arises from the nature of manufacturing industry here. For example, I used to think that, in the jewellery industry, you would find firms who made jewellery. In fact, when you examine the jewellery trade more closely, you find that an enormous percentage of firms don't actually make a finished product. There's one chap I came across recently who simply makes fastenings for bracelets and someone else just makes endless chains. Another company simply does assembly work and sells the product to the wholesaler.
Tilson: It's one aspect of the components business, which, I suppose, is the major aspect of manufacturing in the West Midlands.
Beard: Yes. They are sub-contractors, serving other firms. Let's say you're a plastics moulding supplier to the automotive industry and you're asked to quote for a component for Rover Group. You will receive a specification and the

drawings, so your input is design, in the sense that it's doing the tooling and suchlike, but done simply to comply with that specification. Because a lot of the work is subcontracted, it means that there isn't any real design as such. There are some wonderful companies of that type near here, one of whom - Tubular Bends - just manipulates tubular steel, which is a highly specialised business. They make components for Hostess Furniture, for example. Within the design business everybody who's done any furniture, or suchlike, knows Tubular Bends, but the firm doesn't have a design input of its own. It just makes to order.

Tilson: Did the situation change about 10 years ago through company ownership, or management, moving out of the area?

Beard: When we were going through that 'leaner, fitter Britain' campaign in the early Thatcherite era, there were a lot of takeovers and amalgamations. I think that much of the investment decision was taken away from local companies, because, although they were autonomous manufacturing plants, they were also part of much larger operations. That's probably true of most areas. Take a company like TI, for which Crisp and Wilson designed. They did a good job for one division of TI and, at their request, it was publicised throughout the vast and varied TI organisation. Now, many companies are bought either for an asset-stripping exercise or for diversification, and so a lot of the real decision-making moves away, perhaps even abroad. The Sony plant in Wales is an interesting example, because many decisions which concern it are made abroad, although a very high percentage (perhaps 85%) of its componentry and other products is made here. Take another example - the Tatung company in Telford, making TVs and suchlike, for whom John Law (also a Birmingham Polytechnic lecturer) used to be chief designer. (*asks John*) Where are the decisions made for Tatung, relating to the products that the company finally runs with?

Law: About half the management group are Taiwanese and the Taiwanese managing director here makes the decisions. Any profits made in the UK are reinvested here.

Tilson: What kinds of projects do you think designers who are living and working in this area would get involved with, generally speaking? Indeed, is it possible to generalise?

Beard: That's difficult to say, because each practice tends to have a specialisation, which may develop through chance. Take the DCA operation as an example. When I was at the Design Council, London Transport came looking for somebody to do a new range of rolling stock for the Underground and I included David Carter's DCA Design Consultants on a list. Until that point I don't think they'd done any rolling stock, but they were appointed to do the job. They received a lot of publicity, became experts in transportation design and are doing the N.S. Wales Rapid Transport System in Australia. Alan Birch, who teaches here at Birmingham Polytechnic part-time, is typical of the freelance designer anywhere in the UK. There's also John Yair, who operates from the stable block at Hagley Hall, and has about 8 people in his consultancy. He's done a lot of work, for example, for Anglepoise. A typical commission was the knuckle joint on the stem of an existing desk lamp (Fig. 20.5). The problem was to design a hinge joint which could carry a cable through the middle of it. He has undertaken further work for Anglepoise since then (Fig. 20.6).

Tilson: What date was the knuckle joint commission?

Beard: It came through the Design Council so it was probably about 1981. That was the first one he did for them. It developed into the sort of relationship, which small practices can offer, which is far better than some of the bigger ones. They phone up and say 'We've got a problem here, John, can you sort it out?' You become almost one of their staff designers except that you're used just as and where necessary.

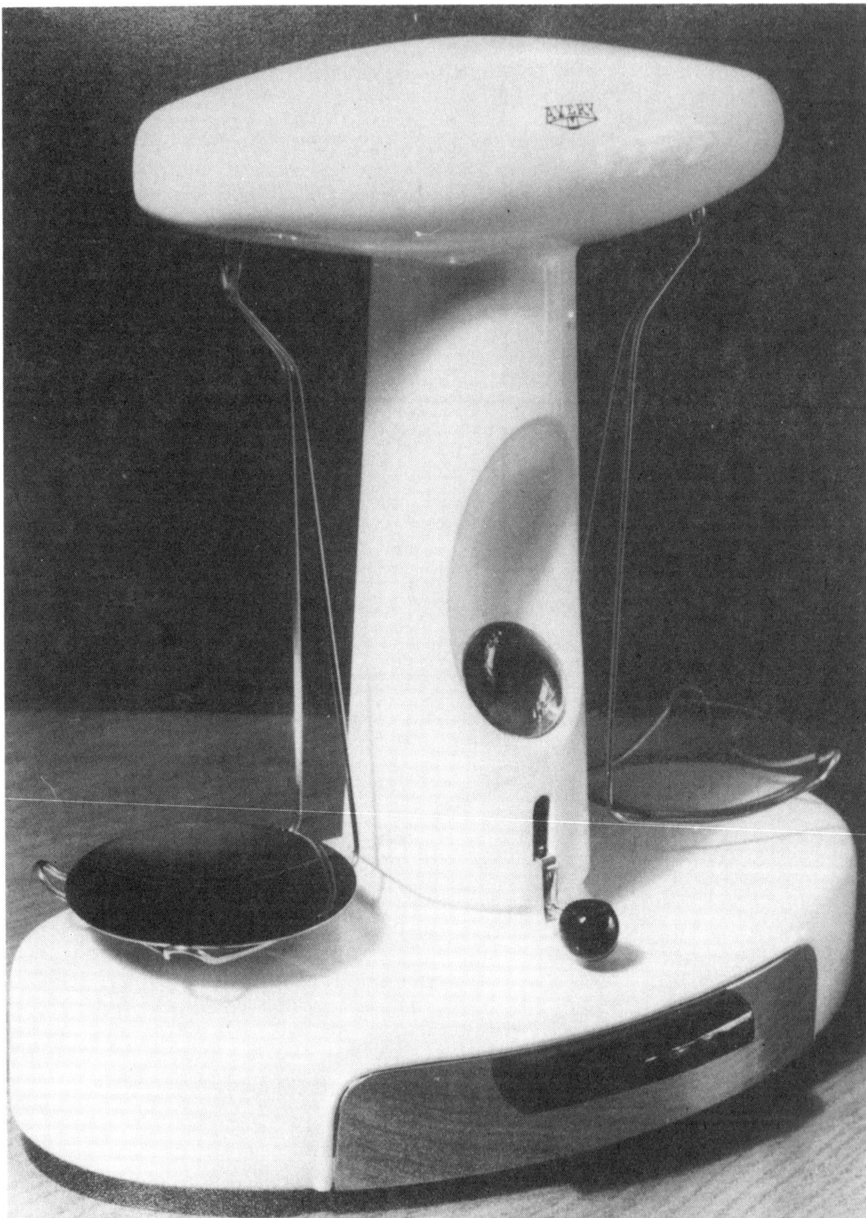

Fig. 20.3. John Barnes. Scales for W. & T. Avery, Smethwick, Warley (later taken over by GEC), 1947. Photo provided by the designer 1987.

Fig. 20.4. David Carter. 'Orbit' castor for Joseph Gillott & Sons, Victoria Works, Birmingham, winner of a Co ID Award, 1961 (see Appendix).
Photo courtey of DCA Design Consultants.

Tilson: Where are Anglepoise based?

Beard: Redditch. (*Asks Maurice Juggins, a fellow lecturer*) Maurice, are Anglepoise part of Terry's? I thought there was historically some link between Anglepoise and Terry's Spring Company, which was connected with the sprung steel business.

Juggins: Terry's shut down and Anglepoise branched off, run by one of the Terry's stepsons.

Beard: John Yair came through the typical route. He went from Birmingham Polytechnic's Industrial Design course, here, to BSR, who used to make record changes and domestic equipment. He designed domestic applicances for them - vacuum cleaners in Germany etc., but he's been freelance for probably 15 years now. He knows local industry very well, and has done a lot of work for a door furniture manufacturer - another traditional local industry, and has recently designed for J. Hudson & Co. (Figs.20.7 - 9).

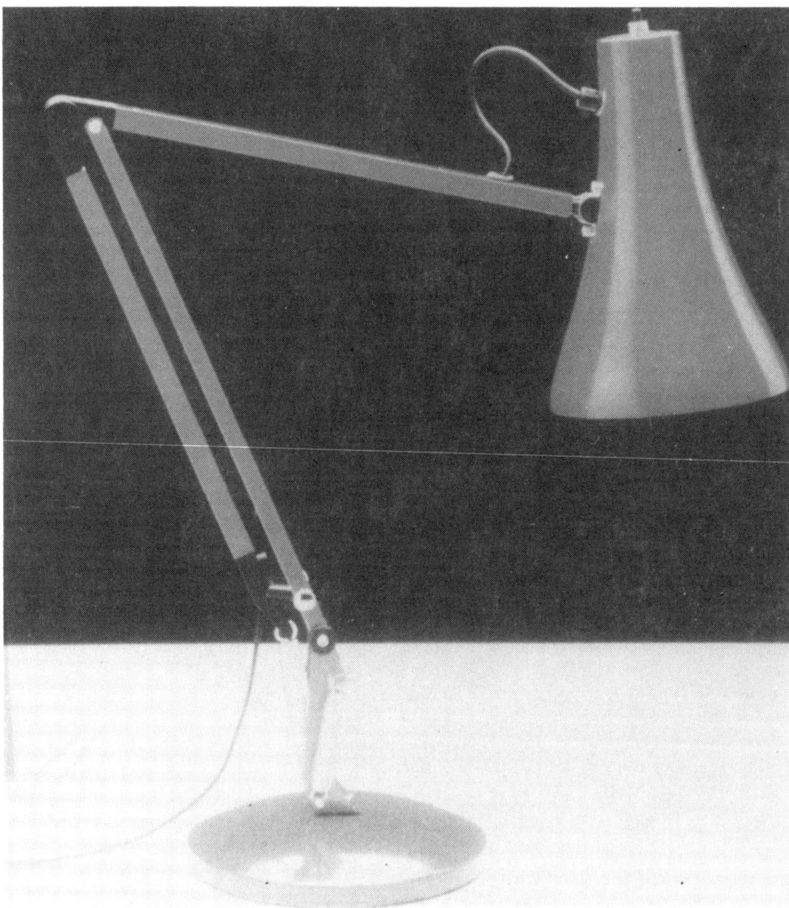

Fig. 20.5. Anglepoise lamp model 90, showing re-design by John Yair, c.1981. Photo courtesy of Anglepoise Lighting Ltd, Redditch.

Fig. 20.6. John Yair. 'Quad' uplighter designed for Anglepoise Lighting Ltd, in production 1989. Photo courtesy of Anglepoise Lighting.

Fig. 20.7. John Yair. Injection moulded pea-less whistle designed for J. Hudson & Co, prototype, 1989. Photo courtesy of J. Hudson & Co.

Fig. 20.8. J. Hudson & Co. Acme 'Thunderer' brass whistles. Above: 1885. Below: 1890-1900s. Photo by permission of J. Hudson & Co.

Tilson: How significant do you think the Design Council is now as a focus and a stimulus for the practice of design?

Beard: It's difficult to say because the Design Council has undergone such a change in the last six months that many of its traditional functions have ceased. One example is the triangular swing ticket which used to be applied to products which had been selected by the Design Council as good for whatever reason. Their product selection service has also gone. Until fairly recently, too, it was possible to go into the design index in the basement and choose your product area - ceramics, tableware, cutlery, furnishing fabrics or whatever. You would simply go through all the products which had been submitted to the Design Council and which their various selection panels had thought was a reasonable product. Four criteria were considered - quality of manufacture, aesthetics, value for money and material selection, combined with suitability for purpose. Quality of manufacture was related to the suitability of materials. The value for money element was very subjective. How can you say something is good value? In some instances it's obvious but in others it's a very difficult judgement to make. As a shop window for serious manufacturers, it's quite a serious blow that it has gone.

Tilson: Why do you think there's never been a Design Centre and shop in Birmingham? Is it because the practice of freelance design here is less extensive?

Beard: Until the mid 1950s going to London was a real adventure, but I think that travel has been condensed so much by British Rail and the independence of most young people with cars that the need for locally-based operations has diminished. Fax machines and other advanced communications have had a profound effect. Birmingham is also near to London, too near in a sense, and yet too far. Places like Liverpool and Newcastle can sustain an independence simply because, physically, they are a great distance from London, whereas Birmingham (although I probably shouldn't say this) has become almost a part of Greater London. As it's only an hour and half to Euston on the train, any differential has disappeared.

(*These issues were also examined by Tim Davis from the perspective of a practising designer currently based in Harborne, Birmingham*).

Tilson: Would you say that the design business is London-centred and that there isn't much work of this kind in Birmingham?

Davis: The number of design consultancies in the London area far outweighs the total in the rest of the country put together, and all but one or two of the largest consultancies are in that part of the country. The big London names include Pentagram, Conran, Fitch, David Davies. What tends to happen is that most of the high profile users of design services employ design consultants who are London-based because they are well known and, inevitably, they have the sort of experience which is relevant. What is somewhat ironic is that the Midlands (and further northwards) contains the vast bulk of manufacturing industry. I'm speaking of product design, not graphic design, because there is an enormous distinction. Looking at the proportion of spending by companies on different types of design - the largest proportion is spent on publicity and graphics, which is tied up with the advertising field. From that point of view, it does not matter whether you're an insurance company or whether you are producing iron castings. Many insurance companies, banks etc. have their head offices in London and use London consultancies for that kind of work. From a product design point of view, manufacturing is not necessarily in the south east, although a lot of companies have their head office down there. As that is where design work is initiated, inevitably they tend to find their consultants there.

Tilson: Is it a different kind of work that is available in the Midlands?

Davis: It's exactly the same kind of work. Company personnel who employ designers are either in marketing or may be engineers. It is the marketing side of any company which spearheads product developments.

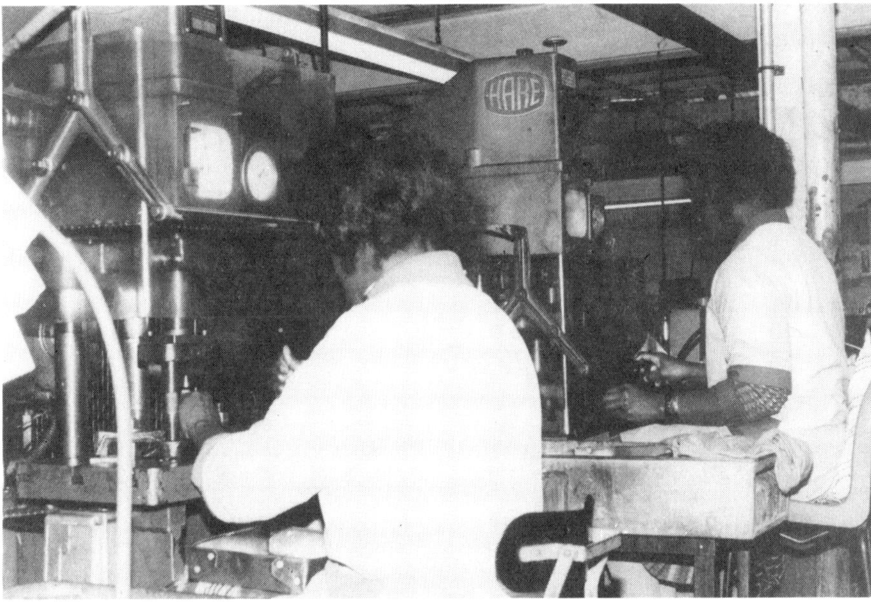

Fig. 20.9. J. Hudson & Co, Birmingham. Women workers operating whistle template cutting presses, 1989. Photo by permission of the company.

Tilson: Therefore they are concerned with economics and public relations?

Davis: They look at things, essentially, from the viewpoint of what the market place requires.

Tilson: Can you tell me about companies which have a tradition of employing freelance designers, because many companies have their own design teams, don't they, such as Lucas and the Rover Group?

Davis: Large companies of that sort inevitably do because they are, essentially, engineering-based companies and most of their designers are engineering designers. From time to time they employ freelance consultants to help with their work. One example is Hostess Furniture at Bilston (Figs. 20.10, 20.11) for whom Richard Snell is design director.[1] *He and I were students together at Birmingham Polytechnic. They commenced as producers of steel-framed furniture for schools and the National Health Service. Following the education cuts of several years ago they decided to diversify and Richard joined them about that time, since when the whole emphasis of the company has changed dramatically. They also employ Fitch, from time to time, to assist with their design work and they have also been courted by Minale Tattersfield. Here is an example of a relatively small Midlands company, part of the Bristol Street Motors group, who have gone straight down to a London consultancy because that's where they believe they will find the expertise, for there are few furniture design companies in Birmingham.*

Tilson: What do West Midlands designers specialise in?

Davis: There are quite a number of product design companies, mostly 1/2/3-man bands. There is one large consultancy, DCA Design Consultants, but they are very much the odd one out in that respect. There is another largish company, Bell & Wickham, towards Leicester. There is a large rapidly growing interior design consultancy, Tibbatts, in St. Paul's Square, Birmingham, on the edge of the Jewellery Quarter. There are a handful of large consultancies with over a hundred people and no more than 20 or 30 consultancies of over 50 people. Many of the largest ones are teamed up with firms of architects, because much of the push recently has been in the retail business in High Street developments. The main bonanza in the design business has been in interiors/retail/publicity cum corporate identity. Product design is, in that respect, the poor relation and has had far less money pumped into it, possibly because the returns are less immediate. More money is invested where it will generate a rapid return.

Tilson: Are consultancies here responding to the needs of the components or engineering industries?

Davis: The connection between where a manufacturing company is and where the designers are is not necessarily a straight geographical relationship. It is not standard for a company in Birmingham - say GKN, Lucas, or Cadbury - to employ Birmingham designers, because it is no more expensive, in geographical terms, to employ somebody who lives the far side of the country or, indeed, overseas. Many English designers work for overseas companies. The design business is so geared to getting the right person to produce the right sort of image for you, be it in terms of the product, interior or whatever, that companies which want to use designers go and find the people with the experience which they consider to be appropriate, rather than looking for somebody on their doorstep.

Tilson: Then, why *would* a consultancy be based here? Is it just an accident of fate?

Davis: In many cases it is. The reason why I'm based here, for example, is because I went to college and got a job here. It was no conscious decision on my part to say 'Birmingham is the place to be', and people at that time said 'what on earth do you want to be in Birmingham for? It's all happening in London'. There is a slightly perverse argument which says that if everybody's in London there must be some scope for consultancies who are nearer their clients and who need more regular servicing. In fact, just that has happened only very recently. A company, who were employing a very large firm of London consultants, rang me recently and said 'you're just round the corner, come and see us. We think it would be a lot more convenient for us to employ someone rather nearer home'.

Tilson: Does the Design Council still play a very significant role in bringing manufacturer and designer together?

Davis: It is very significant in that it is the only organisation that does that on any scale. How well it does that is another matter.

Tilson: The local branch at Wolverhampton provides an advisory service for local manufacturers.

Davis: Essentially what happens is that local manufacturers will contact them and say 'we've got a problem on the design side. How can you help us?' The difficulty is that a lot of manufacturers are not too sure what designers are. Design's become something of a buzz word so people think they'd better get some from somewhere, but they're not sure where to get it from or indeed what it's going to do for them. All they are certain of is that it's the icing on the cake. They're not entirely sure that they really want it and it sounds expensive. Having got it, the tendency is to say 'we could have done that ourselves'.

Tilson: How do you deal with that attitude?

Davis: Very gently. There's always been a degree of antagonism between designer and engineer. Many engineers would see a designer such as myself as some artist who doesn't know one end of a milling machine, or whatever, from another. In fact there is an element of truth there in that part of the problem with designers is that they inevitably do not *know as much as the guy who works for that company. It's necessary to find the right blend between somebody who is not*

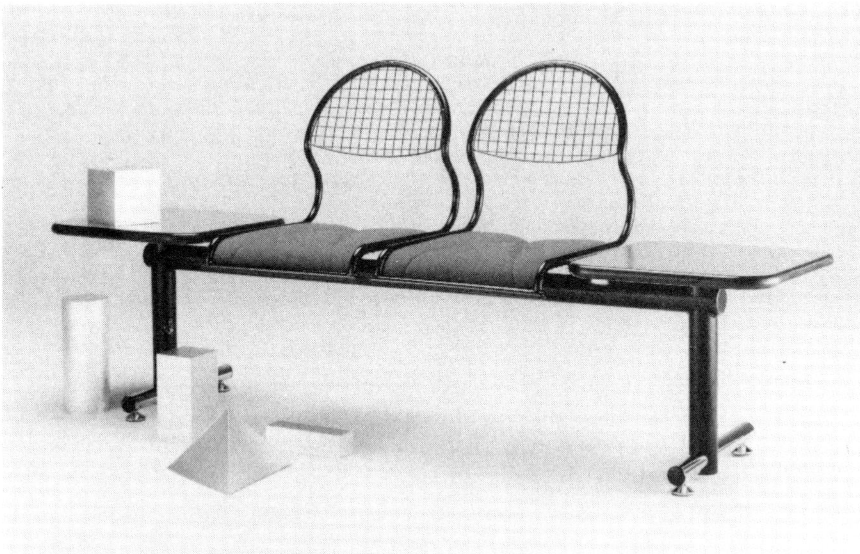

Fig. 20.10. Richard Snell. Concourse units, Modular collection, for Hostess Furniture Ltd, 1981. Photo courtesy of Hostess Furniture Ltd.

Fig. 20.11. Steve Reynolds. Combined table and chair unit, for Hostess Furniture Ltd, 1987. Photo courtesy of Hostess Furniture Ltd.

involved in the day to day problems and does not have to cope with the politics of a particular company, who can view things from a distance and bring to it some experience from all sorts of other places, and to try and blend that with the inside view. So it requires a degree of vision, both from the designer outside and from the company.

Tilson: Do you know why the Design Council regional office is at Wolverhampton?

Davis: I don't, and it seems a curious, extremely low profile location. A regional office should be at the centre of where the business is likely to come from, and the obvious location would seem to be in the centre of Birmingham.

Tilson: I don't know why we have no showcase for contemporary design either. It seems to me to be a dreadful omission.

Davis: Again, I would agree with you entirely and Richard Snell, who heads the West Midlands branch of the Chartered Society of Designers, also has strong views on the matter. However, there are various moves, for example by the Chartered Society of Designers regional group, to put that to rights, within the context of the new Convention Centre.

Fig. 20.12. Bond Warehouse, as in 1988, site of conversion by the Bond Company (Tony Collier, Tim Davis, Peter Southgate). Photo courtesy of Tim Davis.

Tilson: Is the building of the Convention Centre a big stimulus to design, by way of design and art work to go inside?

Davis: The Convention Centre is only one of many stimuli here towards design. For example, Vivien Lovell, who runs the Public Art Commissions Agency, has been championing the concept of one per cent art and has been instrumental in achieving that commitment from the City Council for the Convention Centre. There is also Tony Collier, Professor of Architecture in the Faculty of the Built Environment at Birmingham Polytechnic, who is responsible for the Good Design Initiative in Birmingham (see chapter 1; 2). The Good Design Initiative has generated much action here, from the International Architectural Competition to conferences. He has been the pioneer behind that in collaboration with the head of the Economic Development Unit at the Council. There are a number of people who feel that it is about time something started to happen north of Watford. The great danger is to try and recreate what is happening in London or the south east.

Tilson: Is it *possible* to do that?

Davis: No, it's totally impossible. Trying to put one over the south east is a totally bankrupt notion. It's much more important to create one's own identity. Birmingham, through its location and history, seems to live under this cloud of being dwarfed by the south east. It has an atrocious name for itself because it's received some pretty bad press over the years. The recent royal publications didn't help it too much either.

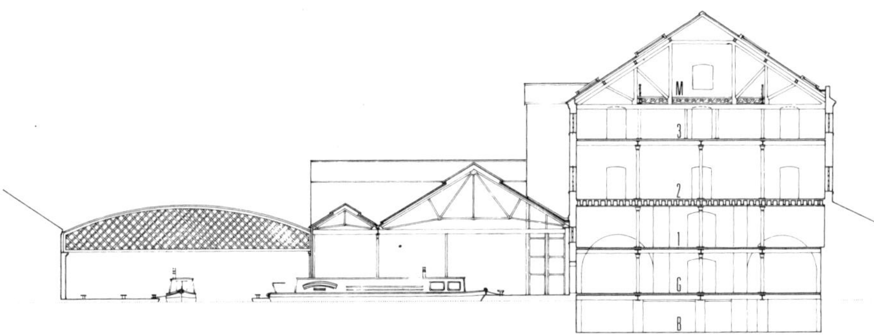

Fig. 20.13. The Bond Company. Elevation of Bond Warehouse conversion, Fazeley Street. Illustration courtesy of Tim Davis.

Tilson: Could you tell me about the interesting warehouse conversion you are undertaking in central Birmingham?

Davis: In 1987, Tony Collier and I teamed up with Peter Southgate to undertake the Bond Warehouse project and formed the Bond Company. The project is quite substantial and is funded partly by private investment, partly by a large grant from the Department of the Environment, and the total development is around £1.2 million. We are converting a large warehouse in Fazeley Street (Figs. 20.12-14) to create space for designers (see also map Fig. 1.9), artists and architects, with galleries, a cafe, bar and other facilities, to provide a focus for design activity in the West Midlands. It's an enormous historic Victorian warehouse on the Grand Union Canal (along with a wharf which comes in off the canal into the site and a collection of houses on the street front) which was originally used as an ice house in the late nineteenth century. At that time, or perhaps just after that, it was owned by Fellows, Clayton and Morton who had a big building just up the road from there and were one of the main canal companies in the Midlands in the last century and the early part of this one. More recently it's been used as a bonded warehouse for storing liquor before the duty has been paid on it. You have to put wine and spirits in a warehouse under lock and key approved of by

Fig. 20.14. Grand Union Canal crossing over the river Rea with the Bond Warehouse behind.

Fig. 20.15. Grand Union Canal, behind Fazeley Street, showing rear of Fellows, Morton and Clayton Warehouse (centre right building) and Bond Warehouse (in distance). Canal bank restored. Photo February 1989.

HM Customs and nothing can go out until the duty has been paid. The area is sandwiched between the intended development in and around the Bull Ring and Digbeth, and the Birmingham Heartlands Development, coming down through Aston and the Science Park. This patch on the Grand Union Canal (Fig. 20.15) has been turned into a conservation area, and it's probably the last of the inner city areas to come up for development, because it is a very unexplored and unexploited part of the inner city. It's essentially a manufacturing area, with a scrap-yard, cement works, an engineering works and other light to medium industrial uses. This particular warehouse and the area around it is about half a mile from the city centre. If you compare it with what's happened in the Jewellery Quarter or down Broad Street, you'll find development occurring there, but little has happened to develop this area for many years.

Tilson: Is it intended to retain the character of the shell of the old Bond Warehouse?

Davis: Most certainly, because it's a conservation area, so it is not permitted to knock things down. The main warehouse is a stunning structure in traditional brick and cast iron, with most extraordinary timber work, particularly in the roof, where there are giant timber trusses.

Tilson: Are there plans to set up a similar centre as a multi-functional media centre?

Davis: That's intended for the Digbeth area. There's a big move in that direction with the rise of independent television, independent film units and programme-making companies. These redevelopment schemes are intended to provide Birmingham with a higher profile in design and the cultural industries.

REFERENCES

1 Richard Snell was subsequently appointed to Birmingham Polytechnic's Faculty of Industrial Design as head of Furniture in September 1989.

CHAPTER 21

APRICOT COMPUTERS: A CASE STUDY FOR INFORMATION TECHNOLOGY IN BIRMINGHAM

Jes Dorrell

Over the last ten years, the world's high technology industries (and the micro computer sector in particular) have shown one of the most spectacular growth patterns in economic history. However, as the high-tech boom has largely been a regional phenomenon, it has had limited effect on the problems created by the recession which ravaged so many of the UK's traditional industries. The boom was concentrated around two UK centres: England's own Silicon Valley (the M4 corridor) and Scotland's Silicon Glen. Apart from a few isolated success stories, Britain's traditional industrial areas have largely been on the outside looking in.

Centres like Birmingham, Sheffield and Manchester have been ill-equipped to exploit the opportunities offered by the new industries. With local workforces dominated by engineering, textiles, steel and other heavy industries, there have been very few local skills or suppliers to tempt potential high-tech investors.

Despite the engineering recession in Birmingham, employment has remained concentrated in traditional areas. The most recent figures available show more than 70% of the city's manufacturing workforce still engaged in metal goods and automotive industries.[1] At the height of the high-tech boom in 1987, the West Midlands had become one of only two regions in the country where employment in electronics was actually falling.[2]

Against this background, it may seem a curious anomaly that Britain's most successful micro systems manufacturer should have emerged not from one of the new high-tech breeding grounds, but from Birmingham and that products conceived and built in Birmingham were able to hold back the might of world leader International Business Machines (IBM) in the UK market for almost two years, between 1983 and 1985.

Yet Birmingham-based Apricot Computers have a bigger base of installed machines than any other UK-based PC manufacturer, with more than 200,000 units worldwide. Today, Apricot stands as one of Europe's premier computer systems integrators, with expertise in hardware, software and services.

However, while the majority of the company's interests have continued to be based in Birmingham (Fig. 21.1) and the surrounding areas of the West Midlands, the experience of Apricot is a significant illustration of the prospects for high-tech business in areas still dominated by traditional industries.

Ironically, it is often manufacturing, typically the *raison d'etre* of the traditional industries, that forces high-tech companies to look outside these areas. While manufacturing is rarely the dominant activity in high-tech business, it does have quite specific requirements in terms of local labour, services and suppliers.

Accordingly, Apricot's plans for a range of machines of its own design and manufacture in 1983, led the company to Glenrothes in Scotland, an area almost 400 miles north of their headquarters, but an area where the necessary infrastructure for the start-up of a £10 million computer plant was already in place.

At the same time, however, Apricot also invested in the West Midlands, creating a research and development facility from scratch, and substantially expanding its sales, marketing and distribution operations in the area.

Two years later, the company built a £1 million research and development complex on the Birmingham University site at Edgbaston, designed by local architects Mason Richards Partnership. Its 100 hardware and software design engineers are today one of the most highly respected microprocessor technology groups in the world.

Fig. 21.1. Apricot Computers' headquarters on Hagley Road, Edgbaston, Birmingham, architects: unknown. Logo designed by Colman RSGG, A London advertising agency, 1985. Photo courtesy of Apricot Computers plc.

Company background

Apricot Computers started life in 1965 as Applied Computer Techniques, a Birmingham based mainframe computer bureau established by Roger Foster, who still heads the group today as Chairman.

Applied Computer Techniques (ACT) offered computerised accounting services to the small-medium sized businesses for whom a dedicated computer facility was not a viable option in the late 1960s and early 1970s. Roger Foster came from an accounting, rather than a computer background. With so many potential users in a thriving and highly concentrated local economy, Birmingham was a natural location for a service of this type.

Although the bureau business is no longer a part of the Group, this 'big systems' background has had a major influence on the subsequent development of the company. Throughout its history, Apricot has remained committed to a total systems integration approach, as distinct from hardware vending.

This background has been reflected in Apricot's emphasis on innovation and added value, together with a continuing inevestment in software. Today, the Group devotes over 40% of its Research & Development budget to software development.

By the late 1970s, the company had diversified into minicomputer software distribution, computer maintenance and distribution of the first generation of microcomputers. ACT sold around 500 8-bit Series 800 machines running its own 'Nebula' accounting software, and even the bureau operation subsequently offered its clients a microcomputer-based solution.

In 1979, the economy floated on the London Stock Exchange to become only the second listed UK computer company after ICL, in the most successful flotation of the decade.

However, in 1981, when the bureau still represented over 50% of group sales,[3] a decision was taken which was to change the shape of ACT, and the British computer industry, dramatically.

Early that year, ACT directors visited California to study the latest product designs of Chuck Peddle. Peddle was the leading figure in the developing micro industry, having already developed the Commodore Pet, the first business microcomputer to become widely available.

Having examined plans for what was to become known as the ACT Sirius 1, which was one of the world's first 16-bit microcomputers, Roger Foster secured the UK distribution rights before the product even left the drawing board.

The company's prior experience with the Series 800 systems enabled ACT to offer its rapidly expanding dealer base a relatively high level of technical support, while the established maintenance operation was able to grow in parallel with the installed base of machines.

Throughout this period, ACT retained a commitment to software. The company made a significant investment in Pulsar - a 16-bit accounting software suite which made good use of its bureau accounting experience.

In fact, right up until 1983, Apricot was able to grow and diversify rapidly within the West Midlands area from its Birmingham base. The city's central position and strong road and rail links gave the company a natural base for its administrative, marketing and distribution operations, while its maintenance and warehousing operations were housed in new, purpose-built units at Oldbury, only minutes from Juction 2 of the M5.

From distributor to manufacturer

The decision to manufacture microcomputers of ACT's own design was determined by a number of factors. Firstly, it offered ACT much more control over the future of its microcomputer business. Quite apart from the inherent vulnerability of being the distributor of another company's products, distribution rights gave little, if any, influence over the manufacturer's product development plans.

Secondly, the development of its own product range enabled ACT to address international markets, which was a key requirement for the fast growing company.

Perhaps most important of all, ACT were convinced that innovation and advanced design would be essential features for products that would ultimately be competing in the marketplace with IBM.

Fig. 21.2. Apricot Computers' factory in Glenrothes, Scotland, designed by the Edinburgh office of Gerrard & Mead, opened 1983. Photo courtesy of Apricot Computers plc.

In the UK, the early availability of the Sirius machine had given ACT an invaluable head start. With the Sirius "dominating the UK market",[4] it quickly attracted a large base of applications software. In less than a year, ACT's catalogue of third party software available for the Sirius had exceeded 1,000 products.

The IBM-PC software base, in contrast, could largely offer only American products at that time, giving the Sirius a clear lead, particularly in the most important field of accounting software.

It was this software base that shaped the proprietary design of the first ACT-designed machine. The original Apricot PC was designed for software compatibility with the Sirius, not with the IBM-PC.

In an industry dominated by the large, functional boxes and low price/performance of the IBM-PC, the Apricot PC was little short of a revolution in personal computer design. It immediately positioned ACT as a British version of Apple, being innovative and non-IBM compatible.

The Apricot PC was powerful, compact, ergonomically designed and transportable. Innovative features included the Microscreen - a small LCD panel in the keyboard which provided a programmable function key template to support different applications. This enabled users to identify and select key functions without learning complex commands.

Incidentally, the original Apricot was also the first major commercial PC to use the 3.5" disk format, predating IBM's eventual move to this format by four years.

Research and Development

The Apricot PC was conceived and developed in-house, with help from a specialist design consultancy to create the Apricot's distinctive styling.

The project was handled by ACT Advanced Technology, a 40-strong Research & Development operation set up specifically to develop the new machine.[5] This division was based in Birmingham, allowing ACT to build on its existing distri bution, software development and support skills. Its early success in assembling a world-class development facility demonstrated that the attractions of a south-eastern location were less important than enterprising and innovative management.

Establishing a manufacturing operation in the West Midlands, however, was clearly a different proposition. The company began its search for a suitable site by examining the alternatives in the West Midlands e.g. Dudley Enterprise Zone. With very few local electronics component suppliers and little experienced high-tech assembly labour, the area was unable to offer the close support that ACT's new manufacturing operation would need.

With the Birmingham area ruled out of the equation, ACT identified three options for manufacturing the Apricot - locating outside the UK, subcontracting the whole operation, or finding a different UK site.

Neither of the first two options offered the level of control that the company needed. With ACT's strong emphasis on design innovation, a subcontractual operation would have given third parties too much control over production schedules and quality. Similarly, the company felt that an overseas manufacturing base might have adversely restricted the level of liaison needed between its Research & Development, support and manufacturing staff.

By locating in the UK, the company could overcome these shortcomings while underlining its role as a British company and exploiting the wide availability of financial support.

In January 1983, the company began to examine possible development areas throughout the UK, eventually settling on Scotland's Silicon Glen. A presentation by the Scottish Development Agency (SDA), and the Glenrothes Development Corporation, convinced ACT that Glenrothes offered the best start-up opportunity for the new manufacturing plant.

The deciding factor was the strong network of electronics subcontractors and skills in the Glenrothes area. Scotland's commitment to the electronics industry has undoubtedly been important to the success of the Silicon Glen concept. By 1984, a Locate in Scotland office had been opened at Los Angeles (the centre of the US high-tech industry) and the SDA had put together an impressive package of incentives and facilities for potential high-tech investors.[6]

It is an approach that has generated a whole series of computer industry success stories for the region. Alongside Apricot, major 1980s investors have included DEC, Ferranti and Compaq, and a recent announcement by Sun Microsystems indicates that the success is continuing.[7] Together, thirty high-tech manufacturers, including 13 American companies, now account for a third of all employment in Glenrothes itself.[8]

It would be misleading, however, to attach too much importance to marketing initiatives and government funding in Scotland's success (or failings elsewhere) in the electronics field. The long history of the electronics industry in Scotland had created a strong infrastructure of skilled labour and suppliers, well before the creation of the Silicon Glen concept. In Glenrothes itself, for example, the first electronics manufacturing operation, Beckman Instruments of California, had been established as early as 1958.

High labour mobility was another important consideration for ACT. Although Glenrothes has a population of just 50,000 in 1989, its effective catchment area takes in well over 200,000. As the fastest-growing region in Fife, it is located at the heart of the most concentrated centre of electronics manufacture in Europe.[9]

The Apricot project represented an investment of £10 million, covering development, land, plant and initial working capital. Glenrothes Development Corporation were able to support this investment with 20% of all capital costs, plus an additional discretionary grant.

The new plant (Figs. 21.2, 21.3) was in production by the end of August 1983 and, inside 12 months, production of the Apricot machine was running at 3500 units per month. By the end of 1984, the Apricot (Fig. 21.4) accounted for well over 50% of Group turnover, and the company had grown to become the UK's biggest personal computer manufacturer.

The first two years of Apricot production proved to be the highpoint of the company's success as a volume PC manufacturer. In 1985, the group adopted the name of Apricot Computers, to mark the business's new orientation.

As the IBM-compatibility standard became established throughout Europe, the Apricot's proprietary architecture left it increasingly exposed. When the computer systems market collapsed worldwide in 1985/6, Apricot announced losses for the first time, after 13 years of substantial growth.

Fig. 21.3. Glenrothes factory interior showing main Apricot assembly area. Photo courtesy of Apricot Computers plc.

This situation led to two major developments at Apricot. Firstly, the company made a commitment to industry standards, which meant a move to full IBM compatibility. Secondly, Apricot abandoned its emphasis on high volume, single user microcomputers like the original Apricot PC, in favour of more powerful personal computers, multi-user and networking systems.

The strategy that was put in place over three years ago is essentially that which still underpins the group today.

Fig. 21.4. Apricot PC Xi, developed at Apricot Research & Development in Birmingham, launched April 1984. It achieved sales in 30 countries. Platics design, 1983, by Cata, Gwent, and Cross Almond & Partners (dissolved). Photo courtesy of Apricot Computers plc.

Apricot Computers Today

Apricot Computers plc is committed to the design of systems which comply with industry standards worldwide. This approach gives Apricot and its customers significant price advantages over proprietary systems, while enabling the company to add value in the application of its specialist connectivity skills to other vendors' products.

Key markets include the financial sector, central government and defence.

The group addresses these areas through three major divisions.

Birmingham based Apricot Financial Systems, which evolved out of the original minicomputer software company, is now established as the UK market leader in investment management systems, with its DEC minicomputer-based QUASAR software. Following the acquisition of Kendal-based Adatco in 1988, the company is also building a major presence in the insurance sector.

Apricot Computer Services now employs over 700 people from its headquarters at Oldbury, where it is ideally positioned to provide maintenance and installation services to customers throughout the UK.

Fig. 21.5. Computer model of a jug kettle as designed on screen using Deltacam's integrated 3D design and manufacture software, CUT. Machining data will automatically be generated from the product geometry to enable a cavity mould for a plastics moulding to be cut on a CNC machine tool with simultaneous control of up to five axes. Photo courtesy of Deltacam Systems Ltd.

Furthermore, with two significant acquisitions in the last two years, Apricot Systems Division is now established as a broad-based operation in its own right. The 1987 acquisition of former Wokingham-based network specialists Digital Micro Systems, catapulted Apricot to the forefront of the local area network market. The acquisition of Sigmex International, in 1988, took the group into the specialist computer graphics and image display market for the first time.

Sigmex, which has offices in Sussex, France and Germany, develops sophisticated command, control, communication and information systems, used by government, defence, scientific and public utility establishments throughout Europe. Using Apricot technology developed in Birmingham. Sigmex has recently been able to extend its product range with a series of 'graphics work-station' products that take it into markets where its earlier systems would not have been a viable proposition.

Meanwhile, Apricot's microcomputer systems range is now centred on high added-value systems based around industry standard 32-bit processors. The division's skills as a systems integrator - its ability to specify, install, support and maintain a complete solution - have enabled it to win major contracts from nation-wide organisations such as the DHSS, MoD and the Post Office. All of these Apricot skills still reside in Birmingham.

One of the most important factors in the success of the move upmarket has been the strength of Apricot's Research & Development base at Birmingham University. The decision to move to full IBM-compatibility did not end the company's commitment to innovative product design, although one commentator feared the decision could be "*the death knell for innovation in British-designed PCs*",[10] underlining Apricot's importance as a design force in the UK micro industry.

In fact, the changeover to industry standards has helped Apricot to develop its design strengths still further. Instead of re-inventing the wheel, Research & Development personnel have been able to concentrate on creating enhanced value and performance within recognised world standards.

The decision to locate its Research & Development in Birmingham demonstrated Apricot's confidence in its ability to attract the right skills to the new facility. The University link was also a significant factor, in that it provided opportunities for exchanging staff, knowledge and resources between the university and industry. Apricot has worked on a number of joint projects with University staff, including a major collaboration with the University's linguistics department on voice input technology.

Apricot Research & Development also provides direct assistance to other computer industry leaders. In 1987, for example, the company was appointed by Microsoft to develop complex elements of the new OS/2 LAN Manager system. Research and Development now accounts for more than one in six of Apricot's 1500-strong workforce, with the vast majority based in Birmingham.

Birmingham and the future

It is significant that both of the city's universities have strengths in technology, and they are now providing a positive environment for the development of high technology industries. Together, Aston Science Park and Birmingham Research Park now house more than fifty high-tech companies, and both locations have recently opened major new development phases.[11]

Outside the specialist research operations that have grown up around these campus locations, however, Birmingham's IT industry has been very slow to develop. It is still largely confined to the computer service companies that have grown up to serve the local economy - just as ACT themselves began in 1965.

There are, of course, a handful of notable exceptions. Ironically, one of the leading computer-based success stories to emerge from Aston Science Park, Deltacam Systems, has developed from the city's traditional engineering base, supplying CADCAM systems and CNC machining services for industrial users (Fig. 21.5).

Another of the city's leading computer companies, Kalamazoo, has also emerged from a traditional business base, expanding into computer solutions from its original strengths in manual book-keeping systems.

Apart from sales and support offices set up by major manufacturers like IBM and ICL, Birmingham has so far been unable to attract significant inward manufacturing investment in the computing or electronics field.

In computer services, software and Research & Development, however, Birmingham is now beginning to build a sound base for future development. In nearby Redditch, Istel has become one of Europe's leading systems, software and communications groups. Once again, Birmingham's traditional engineering base has been a key influence, for Istel has evolved from BL Systems, the computing arm of Rover Group, and it is a UK market leader in computer-integrated manufacturing systems for industry.

One recent exception to this rule is London-based Hoskyns Group plc, one of the top five systems houses in the UK. Hoskyns has invested £3 million in a new Birmingham research and development centre, the Hoskyns Technology Park in Aston. Coupled with a £3 million investment in training, the company hopes to employ more than 300 in the area by the early 1990s.

Alongside Apricot's Birmingham-based technical operations in support, maintenance, software and research and development, these companies are creating a vital skill base for the city. A recent study of Silicon Valley in California has highlighted the importance of a few major manufacturers in sparking off the success of the whole area. Their presence, it is argued, has been crucial in attracting high-calibre personnel into the region.

Here at least, the Apricot example may provide a positive pointer to the future for Birmingham. As Apricot Computers grows in stature as a systems company, it may yet have a catalytic effect on the development of the second city's IT industry.

REFERENCES

1 *UK Census of Production,* 1984.
1 Ibid. SIC Group 4 (metal goods, vehicle industries): 106,535
SIC Group 5 (other manufacturing): 41,734
2 *Computer Weekly,* 27 October 1988.
3 *ACT Report and Accounts,* 1982.
4 *Financial Times,* 3 March 1983.
5 *ACT Report and Accounts,* 1983.
6 *Computer Weekly,* 27 October 1988.
7 Ibid., 10 November 1988.
8 Source: Glenrothes Development Corporation.
9 Source: Scottish Development Agency.
10 *The Times,* 1 July 1986.
11 *Birmingham Business Today*, Autumn/Winter, 1988-9.

CHAPTER 22

CONCLUSION: 'GOOD DESIGN' IN BIRMINGHAM

Barbara Tilson

Design has become something of a 'buzzword' in Birmingham, such a high profile it now has. In part this prominence has been fostered through the Good Design Initiative and other ventures, but arises also from current major developments. To a large degree, 'design' is presently synonymous with 'architecture' and 'urban planning', though there is no reason why this same focus of attention could not also be applied to manufactured goods.

Good Design and Other Initiatives

Set in motion in 1987, with the competition results and conference taking place in 1989, the Good Design Initiative itself was due to run for two further years. At the half-way stage it was difficult to predict the achievements and spin-offs of the Initiative. It might be more realistic, too, to regard the Initiative as only one reflection (albeit an important one) of a growing concern for design, heritage and culture, and their commercial and economic potential. 'Action' and 'Initiative', as in Jewellery Quarter Action, Highbury Initiative and Good Design Initiative, symbolise current dynamic endeavours.

– *The International Design Competition 1987-89*

An exhibition at Gas Hall (26 June to 1 July 1989) provided a chance to see all 310 entries and the winning designs.[1] Entries were received from the UK and many foreign countries, in Eastern Europe, Asia, Australia and the American continent. There were three first prize winners - for a Jewellery Quarter Gateway (Lousie Cotter, David Naessons), a High-tech Building at Aston Science Park (Thiam Hwa Eng, Stephen Gage, Gee Seng Heng) and a Primary School in Small Heath (John Pardey, Ronald Yee) (Fig. 22.1).

Although the competition provided a commendable opportunity for younger architects, a niggling regret remained that the centenary year could not have seen a competition of truly international stature involving leading architects, perhaps with a section for younger entrants. However, the City Council itself partly redressed this omission by setting up a further competition for established architects in Summer 1989.

– *The International Design Conference, Birmingham, July 6-7 1989*

This was the most important public event of 1989 to address the question of the future of urban Birmingham and is therefore worth reviewing here. It was a conference about power - of developers, of the City Council, of architects and

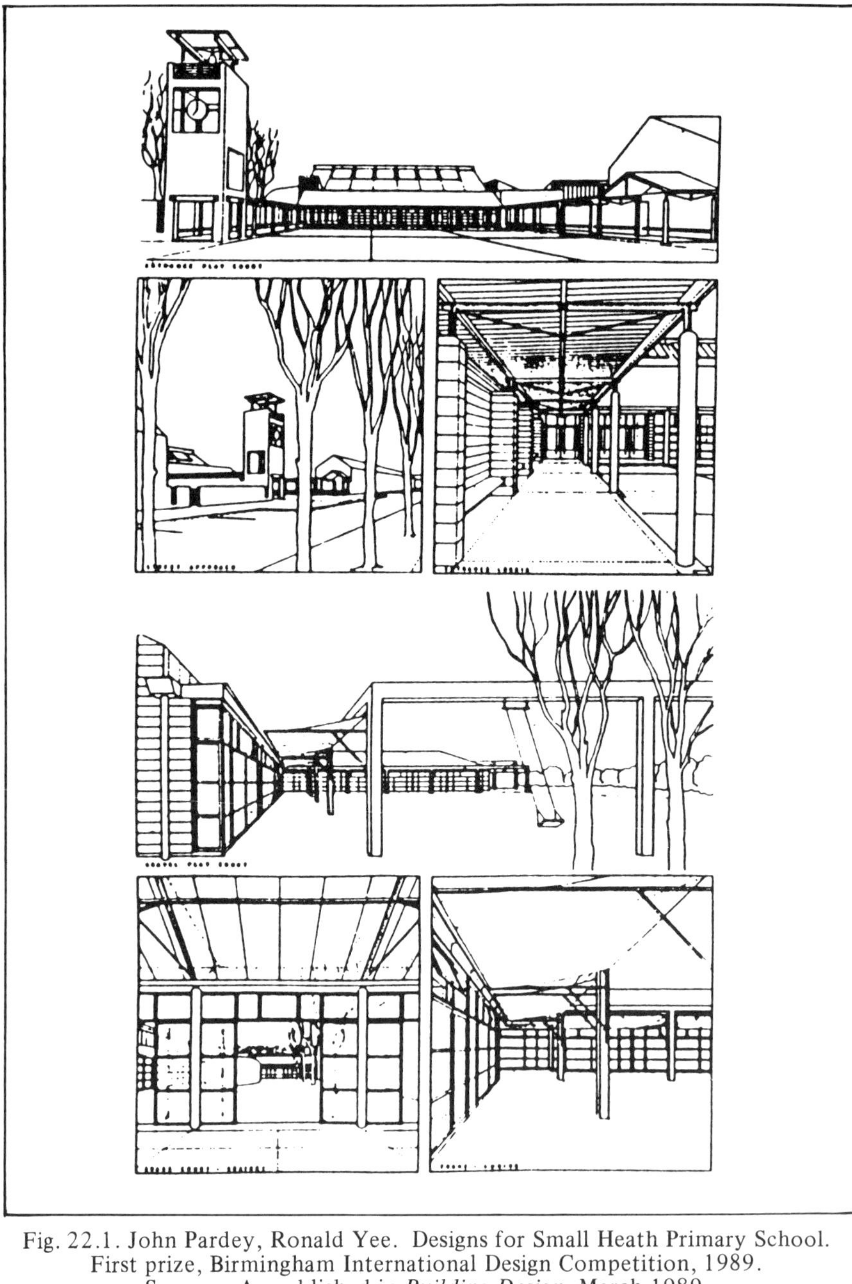

Fig. 22.1. John Pardey, Ronald Yee. Designs for Small Heath Primary School. First prize, Birmingham International Design Competition, 1989. Source: As published in *Building Design*, March 1989.

planners - to shape our city. Vital issues were aired about Birmingham's architecture and urban environment, many of which were also discussed at the Highbury Symposiums.[2] A distinguished body of speakers included Lord Asa Briggs, Maxwell Hutchinson (Chairman, RIBA), Peter Palumbo (Chairman, Arts Council), Michael Graves, Don Hilderbrandt, Prof. Alice Coleman and eminent local figures.

Numerous speakers praised the city's C18 and C19 buildings but deplored its modern architecture, including Michael Graves, who told delegates that he also found Birmingham's older buildings "*wonderful*" and its older ones "*awful*". Joe Holyoak (Birmingham for People) criticised much recent commercial building as "*exclusive*" and "*fortress-like*". Maxwell Hutchinson regretted that only three RIBA awards had been given to Birmingham in 17 years, although there were two more in 1989.[3] Conference agreed that International Style methods of clearing a site and imposing buildings on the urban landscape disadvantaged the population and altered the urban character and sense of place.

There was much discussion about planning consent for developers' proposals and concern was expressed that developers may pay little heed to the needs of the population, but act for commercial reasons. Conference toyed with the idea that an independent body should be set up to formulate and to oversee the implementation of a set of planning and design principles for Birmingham.

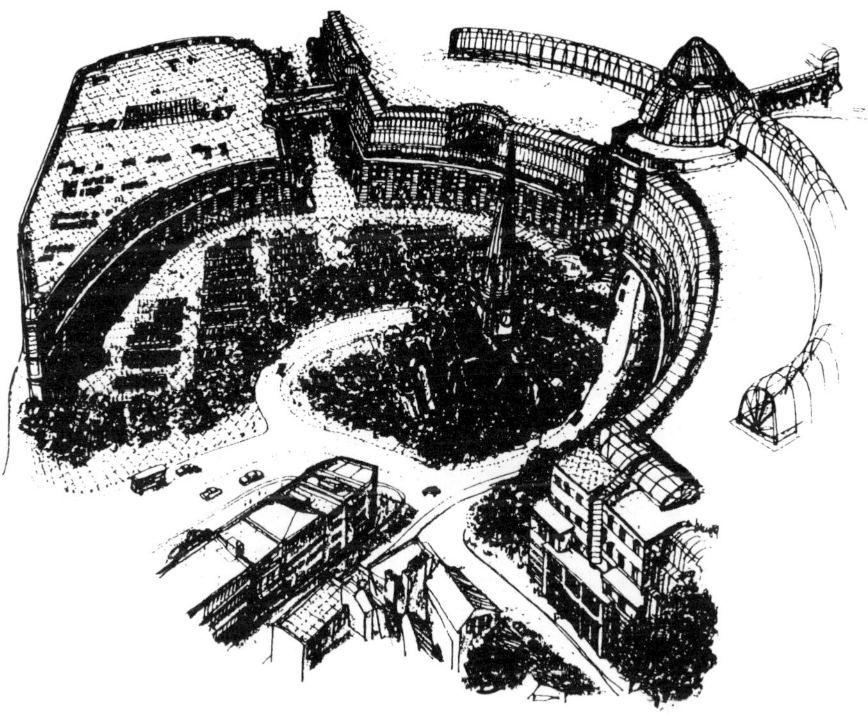

Fig. 22.2. Chapman Taylor Partners. The Galleries redevelopment of the Bull Ring. Perspective, 1989. Source: *The Galleries at the Bull Ring,* 1989.

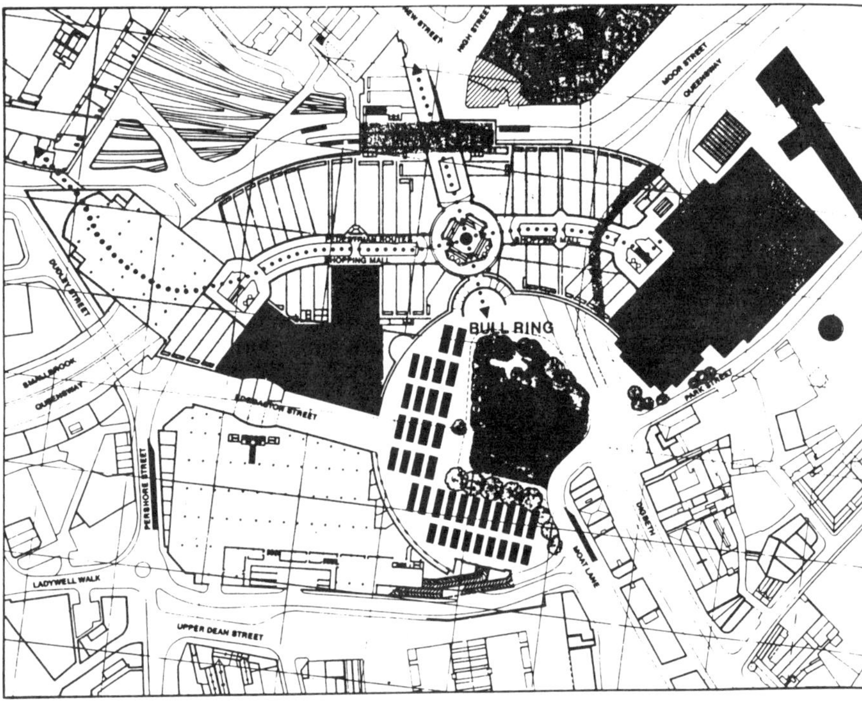

Fig. 22.3. Chapman Taylor Partners. The Galleries redevelopment of the Bull Ring. Plan. Source: *The Galleries at the Bull ring*, 1989.

Speakers noted the lack of public spaces which were *enjoyed* by people. Vivien Lovell (Public Arts Commissions Agency) stressed the unity of art/sculpture with architecture to enhance and humanise public spaces. The London and Edinburgh Trust-backed Galleries design (Figs. 22.2, 22.3) for Bull Ring redevelopment by Chapman Taylor Partners was questioned,[4] especially by Joe Holyoak, Birmingham for People having put forward its own alternative proposals (Figs. 22.4, 22.5).[5] It was recommended that the Bull Ring should be re-established as the primary public space it was before 1950s/60s development.

There was virtual unanimity that the primacy of the Ring Road should be diminished, though it was also argued that this fast traffic route is an asset to business access. Don Hilderbrandt (consultant to Birmingham City Council)[6] examined ways in which parts of the city, such as New Street, could be pedestrianised. He noted that Birmingham's Ring Road bisects all three main sectors of the city centre - the commercial, industrial and civic-suggesting measures which could be taken to restore them, such as the rejoining of Newhall Street.

The needs of the people were a prevailing theme. One speaker commented that one third of the populace are either in receipt of social services benefit or are their dependants. Such facts further stressed the divide between developers and citizens. Many lower income families are housed in high-rise blocks, but work is under way to relocate people to low-rise development. Prof. Alice Coleman, whose study of housing estates includes four Birmingham examples, stressed the role of the architect in helping to lessen anti-social behaviour through housing and landscape design.[7]

Chairman, Prof. Tony Collier, emphasized how vital sponsorship from industry and commerce is to support ventures like the Good Design Initiative, while Peter Palumbo saw industry replacing royalty as primary sponsors of architecture and the arts. Personally, I would like to see the Good Design Initiative involving more than just architecture and planning. It seems particularly relevant, in a manufacturing city like Birmingham, to include the products of its manufacture and crafts and visual communication, too.

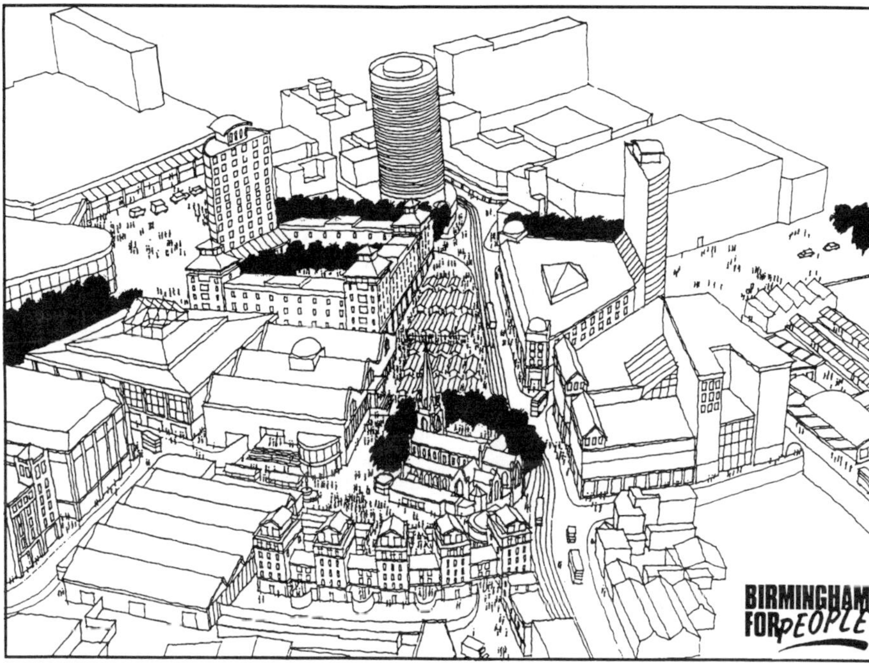

Fig. 22.4. Birmingham for People. The People's Plan. Perspective of Bull Ring proposals drawn by Joe Holyoak.
Source: *Towards a Better Bull Ring,* 1989.

Where do we go from here?

While the Bull Ring is superseding the Convention Centre as the *bête noir* of redevelopment, what is at stake is the future of the whole city centre as an urban heart which is emotionally and visually inviting and liveable. However, as Prof. Tony Collier observed,[8] the danger of this fixation with putting things right in central Birmingham, is in ignoring that there *are* attractive parts of Birmingham outside it - the Botanical Gardens, Sutton Park, Bournville Village and St. Agnes

(Moseley) conservation area among them. Other regenerative work, too, is taking place which is equally significant to the city's business and domestic revival. The remodelling of Nechells local community (largely council housing) in one of three urban development areas is a case in point, but there are other examples which receive little or no public attention, such as the Tyseley industrial estate.

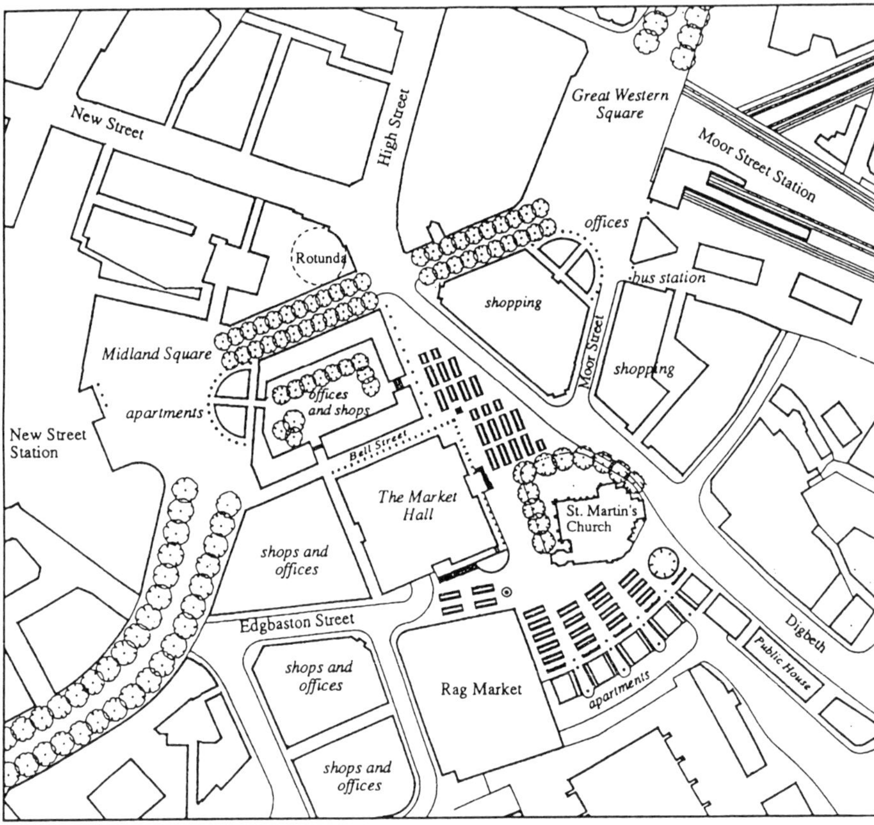

Fig. 22.5. Birmingham for People. The People's Plan. Plan of Bull Ring proposals drawn by Joe Holyoak.
Source: *Towards a Better Bull Ring, 1989.*

Undeniably, Birmingham is undergoing a radical transformation of a fundamental nature. The city is in transition, set to take international status in the twenty first century, though it is presently difficult to estimate what effects this will have on its citizens. While this sense of renewal and forward-thinking is laudable, Birmingham should not lose sight of its past industrial history nor its present manufacturing base. Undoubtedly, with hindsight it will be realised that the present renewal too often obliterates the past without adequate record, without sufficient appreciation of its historical interest, and without enlightened consideration of ways in which the past can be integrated with the present, or more areas conserved wholesale, rather than razed to the ground under the bulldozer of modern development.

REFERENCES

1 See *Birmingham International Design Competition: Assessors' Report,* February 1989. Press coverage includes *Building Design,* March 1989.
2 Two symposiums have been held, to which British and foreign experts were invited to discuss Birmingham's urban planning issues. Highbury Initiative phase one took place in March 1988 and phase two in September 1989. A report of the 1988 proceedings was published as *The Highbury Initiative: Proceedings of the Birmingham City Centre Challenge Symposium,* Birmingham, 1988. Phase two reviewed by Terry Grimley, *Birmingham Post,* 21 September 1989. See also Judy Hillman, *Birmingham City Centre: A Personal View of Progress,* published to accompany Highbury Initiative phase 2, Birmingham, September 1989.
3 1972: Repertory Theatre (Graham Winteringham, S.T. Walker & Partners). 1977: Neville House, Edgbaston (John Madin Design Group). 1987: Belgrave Middleway, housing (City Architect William Howland). 1989: Lee Bank Health Centre (Associated Architects); and (in addition to those City Architect's Dept. awards described in Chapter One) Nelson Mandela School (City Architect William Howland).
4 For CTP proposals see *The Galleries at the Bull Ring: Believing in Birmingham,* LET promotional, 1989. Also, *Birmingham Post,* 24 August 1989.
5 Two documents are published by Birmingham for People. See bibliography. See also Joe Holyoak, "Second Chance", *The Architects' Journal,* August 1989, pp.20-25; *Birmingham Post,* 24 August 1989; B. Tilson, "Birmingham's Second Chance", *RIBA Journal,* November 1989, pp.44-50.
6 Hilderbrandt is an American planning consultant, president of LDR International, with offices in Maryland and Cardiff. His findings arose from a pedestrianisation study commissioned by Birmingham City Council after Highbury phase one. See *Birmingham Post,* 6 July 1989.
7 See interview in *Birmingham Evening Mail,* 6 July 1989; Also, A. Coleman, 1985, based on research with the Design Disadvantagement Team, King's College, London.
8 *Birmingham Post,* 15 September 1989.

BIBLIOGRAPHY

Birmingham for People, *What Kind of Birmingham? Issues in the Redevelopment of the City Centre,* Birmingham, January 1989.
Birmingham for People, *Towards a Better Bull Ring - A People's Plan,* Birmingham, 1989.

FURTHER READING

Alice Coleman, *Utopia on Trial,* London, 1985.

STOP PRESS:– AT A PRIVATE MEETING OF COUNCIL POLICY MAKERS (as recorded in the *Birmingham Evening Mail,* 20 November 1989) THE GALLERIES SCHEME FOR THE BULL RING WAS REJECTED AS UNSUITABLE.

APPENDIX

BIRMINGHAM AND WEST MIDLANDS RECIPIENTS OF BRITISH AWARDS 1957-1989

Since 1957 the name of the award has undergone the following changes:-

DOTY	**Designs of the Year**	**First awarded 1957**
COID	**Council of Industrial Design Awards**	**1959**
DCA	**Design Council Awards**	**1973**
BDA	**British Design Awards**	**1987**

1957	Thomas Webb & Sons, Dennis Glass Works, Stourbridge. Table glass set. Designer: S. Fogelberg.
1957	**W.R. Midwinter Ltd, Aldridge Road, Streetly, Sutton Coldfield, (works of manufacturer). Melmex plastics tableware. Designers: A.H. Woodfull, J. Vale.**
1957	Walker & Hall Ltd, Elkington Sales Ltd, Goscote Works, Walsall. Cutlery and flatware - Pride. Designer: David Mellor.
1958	J. & J. Wiggin Ltd, Old Hall Works, Bloxwich, Walsall. Stainless steel toast rack, Old Hall. Designer: Robert Welch.
1959	Walker & Hall Ltd, Elkington Sales Ltd, Goscote Works, Walsall. EPNS teaset - Pride. Designer: David Mellor.
1960	**Brookes & Adams Ltd, Birmingham. Fiesta melamine plates. Designer: Ronald Brookes.**
1960	Izons & Co Ltd, Albion Works, West Bromwich. Anniversary Ware casserole etc. Designers: John Reid, Sylvia Reid.
1961	**Joseph Gillott & Sons Ltd, Victoria Works, Birmingham. Orbit furniture castors. Designers: Company's design staff + R. David Carter.**
1962	J. & J. Wiggins Ltd, Old Hall Works, Bloxwich, Walsall. Range of dishes - Old Hall. Designer: Robert Welch.
1962	Walker & Hall, Elkington Sales Ltd, Goscote Works, Walsall. Cutlery and flatware - Symbols. Designer: David Mellor.
1965	Old Hall Tableware Ltd, Old Hall Works, Bloxwich, Walsall. Alverston cutlery. Designer: Robert Welch.
1965	GEC (Installation Equipment)Ltd, Church Lane, West Bromwich. S782/3 Ceiling roses, DS6708/9 C Switches. Designers: Noel London (London & Upjohn) (shape); GEC (engineers).
1966	**Best & Lloyd Ltd, Cambray Works, Wattville Road, Handsworth, Birmingham. Cantilever 41555 Mark 2 desk lamp. Designer: Gerald Abramovitz.**
1967	**Reynolds Tube Co Ltd, Tyseley, Birmingham.**

Aluminium gas cylinder.
Designer: (unspecified).

1969 **Deavine Irvine Products Ltd, Crown Works, Baltimore Road, Birmingham.**
Ease-e-Load range of trolleys.
Designer: H. Martin.

1969 Yale Locks & Hardware, Willenhall, Staffs.
Yale automatic deadlatch, Mercury 33.
Designers: R. David Carter + Company's design team.

1970 **IMI Developments Ltd, Birmingham.**
Opella 500 series of plastic taps.
Designers: Company's design team + Martyn Rowlands.

1973 Archibald Kenrick & Sons Ltd, West Bromwich, Staffs.
OlympiCastor.
Designers: Archibald Kenrick & Son.

1974 W. & T. Avery Ltd, Smethwick, Warley, Worcs.
Digital price computing scale.
Designer: (unspecified).

1975 **British Leyland UK Ltd, Austin Morris Division, Longbridge, Birmingham.**
Air temperature control device.

1976 **Girling Ltd, Kings Road, Tyseley, Birmingham.**
Girling 'Twinstop' brake.
Designers: C. Newstead, M.J. England, N.S. Moss, N. Crabtree, B.A. Clay.

1976 Massey Ferguson Engineering Centre, Maudsley Road, Coventry.
M F 30 Drill.
Designers: A.J. Bailey, F. Ward, R.S. Sargent, G. Holmes, M. Dean, H.B. Rogers.

1977 Press Components Co Ltd, Green Lane, Walsall.
'Presco' and 'Presswick' stairways.
Designers: D.G. James, H.R. Davies.

1977 **Dunlop Ltd, Tyre Technical Division, Fort Dunlop, Birmingham.**
Delugrip road surfacing materials.
Designers: G. Lees (Univ. of Birmingham), A.R. Williams, R. Bond.

1978 **Triplex Safety Glass Co Ltd, Eckershall Road, Kings Norton, Birmingham.**
Triplex Ten Twenty windscreen.
Designers: S.E. Kay, J. Pickard, V.J. Osola, D.C. Wright, H.R.S. Jack.

1978 Dunlop Ltd, Energy Equipment Division, Holbrook Lane, Coventry.
Thermimax gas burner combustion system.
Designers: P.G. Ware, G.K. Mercer, G.L. Finney, E. Shuttleworth, A.R. Baker.

1979 Motor Panels (Coventry)Ltd, Holbrook Lane, Coventry.
Standard panel concept for commercial vehicles.
Designers: G.R. Allen, T. Karen (Ogle Design), T. Strong, A. Scott.

1980 J.A. Crabtree & Co Ltd, Court Parade, Aldridge, Walsall.
'Corinthian' lighting switches.
Designers: G.J. Spencer, J.D. Vale (design consultant) (see Fig.20.1).

1981 **Austin Motors Ltd, Bickenhill Lane, Birmingham.**
Austin Mini Metro.
Designers: Product Engineering Division, led by R.J. Bates; Engineering Dept., led by R. Brocklehurst, F.A. Coultes, D.E. Bache.

1981 **Lucas Electrical Ltd, Great King Street, Birmingham.**
Vehicle high-contrast auto signal lamps.
Designer: S. Green.

1981 **Lucas Electrical Ltd, Great King Street, Birmingham.**

	Homofocal headlamps. **Designers: G.R. Draper, R.F. Tolley, D.A. Birt, H. James.**
1982	Land Rover Ltd, Meteor Works, Lode Lane, Solihull. Range Rover 4-door. Designers: Company's Product Engineering Division; Carbodies Ltd (detail draughting).
1983	Rota Bolt Ltd, Peartree Lane, Dudley. RotaBolt. Designers: S. Caney, N. Vale, J. Hirst, J. Thorp.
1983	Wonderclip Ltd (became Tridon Surflex), Loxdale Street, Bilston. Dandy clip. Designer: P.J. Huxtable.
1983	H. & G. Tankers Ltd, Hayes Lane, Lye, Stourbridge. Road tanker. Designers: P.R. Holdstock, R. Small, L. Roe, M.P. Fullwood.
1984	British Castors Ltd, Bagnall Street, Hill Top, West Bromwich. Travelaid range of light duty furniture castors. Designers: S.T. Screen, R.J. Spencer, A. Gray, J.R. Heathcock.
1984	**Rabone Chesterman Ltd, Whitmore Street, Birmingham.** **Multiview spirit level.** **Designers: J.S. Willetts, D.F. Poole, E.P. Arch.**
1984	**Lucas Electrical Ltd, Great King Street, Birmingham.** **Homofocal auto headlamp - model 35FR.** **Designers: G.R. Draper, D.A. Birt, H. James, A. Smith, R.F. Tolley.**
1987	Austin Rover Group Ltd, Canley Plant, Coventry. M16 Austin Rover. Designers: R. Bertodo, S. Hiljemark.
1987	**Lucas Girling Ltd, Kings Road, Tyseley, Birmingham.** **Lucas Girling/Ford anti-lock auto braking system.** **Designers: G.P.R. Farr, J. Cart, B.J. Holby, C.R. Ennos.**
1987	Simon Engineering Dudley Ltd, Dudley. Simon Super Snorkel firefighting equipment. Designers: D.H. Ashworth, D.L. Johns, Marchant Filer Dixon (consultants), Michael Neale & Associates (consultants).
1989	Crabtree Electrical Industries Ltd, Lincoln Works, Walsall. Pendant safety lampholder. Designers: P.J. Doherty, I.J. Pickering, P.R.K. Glover.

Source: Design Council File on Award Winning Products.

For Bibliographies see individual chapters

INDEX

Note:- Companies commencing with initials are indexed under the first initial e.g. J. Hudson & Co. is under J. Designers and other individuals are indexed in the usual way, surname first.
Organisations well known by their abbreviations are indexed under the abbreviation.
Products, models and designs are in italics, ditto exhibition titles.
Illustration are shown as in the caption i.e. 20.4 Ax = Appendix.

The Design History Society has played a leading role in the development of the study of design in its historical context. It has drawn together individuals from different disciplines and different countries, all of whom share an interest in the design process. Founded in 1977, the Society is still a young organisation enthusiastic to hear from individuals and organisations interested in its activities and willing to support its efforts to promote the study of design past and present.

The Society's *Newsletter* (published quarterly) regularly circulates information about events such as specialist study days, the annual Banham Memorial Lecture and the Society's Annual Conference to the membership and affiliated organisations. It provides members with a mouthpiece to air their views, maintain a dialogue about current issues, and publishes news and reviews.

The *Journal* of Design History is published quarterly. Over the last decade design history studies have expanded rapidly. The widespread recognition of the cultural significance and economic importance of design provides a broad base on which to build and the *Journal* seeks to promote links with other disciplines exploring material culture, such as anthropology, architectural history, business history, cultural studies, design management studies, economic and social history, history of science and technology, and sociology. The *Journal* also aims to play an active role in the further development of forum for dialogue and debate and by addressing current matters of interest. In addition to full-length articles, the *Journal* publishes shorter case studies of objects, design typologies, and design practice. It carries book reviews and notes on collections and archives.